THE SOURCES OF HISTORY:
STUDIES IN THE USES OF HISTORICAL EVIDENCE

GENERAL EDITOR: G. R. ELTON

THE SOURCES OF HISTORY:
STUDIES IN THE USES OF HISTORICAL EVIDENCE

GENERAL EDITOR: G. R. ELTON

The Sources of History:
Studies in the Uses of Historical Evidence

Historical Demography

by

T. H. HOLLINGSWORTH

THE SOURCES OF HISTORY LIMITED
in association with
HODDER AND STOUGHTON LIMITED

Printed in Great Britain for Sources of History Limited,
47 Dean Street, London, W.1. by The Camelot Press Ltd.,
London and Southampton

Contents

Figures

General Editor's Introduction

By what right do historians claim that their reconstructions of the past are true, or at least on the road to truth? How much of the past can they hope to recover: are there areas that will remain for ever dark, questions that will never receive an answer? These are problems which should and do engage not only the scholar and student but every serious reader of history. In the debates on the nature of history, however, attention commonly concentrates on philosophic doubts about the nature of historical knowledge and explanation, or on the progress that might be made by adopting supposedly new methods of analysis. The disputants hardly ever turn to consider the materials with which historians work and which must always lie at the foundation of their structures. Yet, whatever theories or methods the scholar may embrace, unless he knows his sources and rests upon them he will not deserve the name of historian. The bulk of historical evidence is much larger and more complex than most laymen and some professionals seem to know, and a proper acquaintance with it tends to prove both exhilarating and sobering—exhilarating because it opens the road to unending enquiry, and sobering because it reduces the inspiring theory and the new method to their proper subordinate place in the scheme of things. It is the purpose of this series to bring this fact to notice by showing what we have and how it may be used.

G. R. ELTON

CHAPTER 1

Demography

INTRODUCTION

Demography, as Göran Ohlin once remarked, has the same ingredients as all the most popular stories: sex and death. Add to these man's fascination for numbers and his antiquarian love of the past, and historical demography ought to be very absorbing indeed. The reason why it is not the favourite subject of research students, however, must be stated bluntly: historical demography is very difficult to do well, because it draws upon such a wide variety of disciplines. Far from being at the fringes of learning, it stands at the centre.

The ideal historical demographer will need to have a keen historical sense and a command of all the knowledge and resources of modern demography, requiring a thorough acquaintance with the methods and findings of every national system of census and vital registration in the world. He will be deeply versed in economics, sociology, religious observance, archaeology, anthropology, climatology, epidemiology, and gynaecology; and he will understand the mathematical techniques of the statistician so well that he can advance improvements on them of his own. He will be a good palaeographer, an expert on taxation law and practice, on town planning and agricultural methods, at all times and places; he will know how to collect quantitative information, to code and punch it on cards or tapes, and to produce an analysis of it by computer. He will be a voracious reader, with a command of at least a dozen languages, reading a hundred issues of learned periodicals and as many books, emanating from every part of the world, from cover to cover every year.

The ideal historical demographer, of course, does not exist; and anyone with any part of his qualifications can have some hope of being able to make a useful contribution to the subject. Yet we hope to show, in the course of this book, that all the qualifications of the ideal historical demographer are desirable, in a group of men working together if not in a single individual. For comparison of different estimates relating to population is always illuminating, whether of mere total numbers within an area or of such a complexity as (say) the mean interval between third and fourth births in five-child families when birth control was not suspected, breast feeding normally continued for one year, and the third child had not died within a month of being born. Corroboration from independent sources by independent methods is the very kernel of historical demography, for two fairly weak but quite different arguments that reach the same conclusion are very much better than one.

And all historical arguments are more or less weak, for no one can ever be totally certain or totally uncertain of anything. The degrees of certainty run from 'sure' to 'very likely' to 'probable' to 'possible', and on through 'unproved' and 'rather unlikely' and 'improbable' to 'presumably wrong' and 'wrong'. Statistical information about the past has to be classified, provisionally, somewhere along this scale, and from time to time some of it has to be moved to another position, of greater or less confidence. The scale has no ends, so that we never reach absolute, but only practical, certainties.

This book, therefore, faces one major and one minor problem before it can begin. The major problem is that the author is nowhere near the ideal historical demographer and is sure to do injustice to great parts of his subject. No solution can be found except the indulgence of his readers, but any who feel their own work unfairly criticized are at least offered a few hostages to fortune in the form of original suggestions of the author's invention, which their irritation may spur them to improve.

The minor problem is to indicate, as far as possible, the degrees of belief which the various figures deserve, and suitable qualifying phrases are scattered throughout the pages. The reader is merely warned here to be careful not to treat all the numbers he is given as equally reliable.

Ideal historical demographers being non-existent, the work of historical demography has always been done, and will continue to be done, by specialists in only some of its skills. It takes so long to edit an old list of taxation returns, to read the relevant literature on a given country, or to reconstitute the families of a single parish from its register, that the worker in the field scarcely has time to watch others reap their harvest as well; yet co-ordination is required from the different specialists unless much of the value of their hours of toil is to be wasted.

This volume, may, at least, help to acquaint some of the specialists with each other. It has, therefore, four main purposes: to explain the techniques of demography, to describe the historical sources of information on population, to discuss the more important work that has already been done in historical demography, and to suggest what improvements and further work are possible. Although writing in English, there is perhaps undue emphasis on the English sources of data and the peculiar problems they raise, for historical demography is really a science not unlike archaeology. At the same time, the reader who is ignorant of any but English material will find that many of the questions raised in English work have arisen elsewhere and will gain some idea of how they have been tackled.

After describing the nature of demography in general and of historical demography in particular, the main part of the text deals with the various sources of data in turn, beginning with the best and most obvious and descending gradually to the oddest and least valuable. In the final chapter, the fruits of such research are discussed in relation to demography and history. The three appendices deal with special points that could not be considered in detail in the main text.

METHODS AND PURPOSE OF DEMOGRAPHY

Demography is the statistical study of population, and as such embraces all aspects of population movement that are capable of numerical measurement. In the first instance, the total population is the essential idea; the others follow from it as the requirements of study become more and more complex. Even the total population, however, is not a simple idea, for there are four 'populations' that are used by demographers in modern population studies: *total* population, *civil* population, *resident* population, and *de jure* population. All these differ slightly: the total population is simply the number of people in an area at a given moment; the others are refinements upon the idea of the total population, invented because of the administrative needs of government. The civil population is the number of civilians who are normally resident; the resident population is the same as the civil, but with the members of the armed forces included; and the *de jure* population is the population of a particular nationality, wherever they reside. Although for a large country there is very little difference between these four populations, there may be important differences in historical populations, particularly of small communities. A population figure for the past, given in a report or other document without qualification, may refer to the total population as defined above or to some other population, of different size, that the clerks of the period did not think it worth while to distinguish from the total population as properly conceived. This difficulty seems to be most acute in certain medieval populations, where figures sometimes differ very sharply between one era and the next, so that over a period of fifty years, perhaps, the population may appear to have changed by a very large amount. The inclusion or exclusion of certain groups may explain these apparent changes, and one need not be surprised if the documents do not always make it entirely clear exactly who was to be counted and who was not.

Because demographers wish to measure population at more

than one moment, the idea of change of population is naturally the next that arises. The simple population change is divided first into natural changes and mechanical changes. Natural changes subdivide into births and deaths, each being expressed commonly as an annual rate per head of the population. The difference between births and deaths is known as the natural increase (or decrease) of the population. Similarly, the mechanical changes consist of immigrants and emigrants, and annual rates can be calculated for each. Four rates thus determine the change in the population size as a whole; the first two are commonly known as vital rates, whereas the latter two are called migration rates.

Thus far, demography is at the level of an ordinary person's understanding; birth-rates and death-rates, in particular, have been well enough understood by the common man for a century or more. However, in order to understand population phenomena more fully, demographers have tried to study each component of population change in further detail. The procedure is similar for each of the four rates, although the migration rates have, in fact, been much less studied than the vital rates. The main basis for analysis of the vital rates is age, since it is obvious that human fertility and mortality vary greatly with age, and consequently the behaviour of a population must be expected to depend to a large extent upon its age structure. At the same time, there are some circumstances in which the sex structure of the population also plays an important role, and since sex is a very easily determined characteristic of an individual it is common to analyse a population by age and sex simultaneously, and to study the vital rates also by age and sex. The next concept is therefore the age and sex structure of a population, the ages being usually grouped by five-year or ten-year periods. Population pyramids are sometimes drawn to illustrate the age and sex structure of the population, showing graphically whether the structure is 'top-heavy' (few people at the younger ages) or 'gashed' (an age-group much below its neighbours) or 'bottom-heavy' (very many children), for example. (See Figures 1–4.)

Figure I   POPULATION PYRAMID (I)

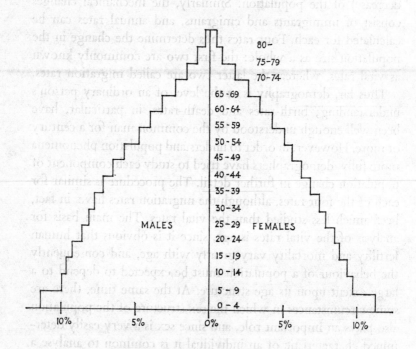

	80–	
	75–79	
	70–74	
65–69		
60–64		
55–59		
50–54		
45–49		
40–44		
35–39		
30–34		
MALES 25–29	FEMALES	
20–24		
15–19		
10–14		
5–9		
0–4		

10%   5%   0%   5%   10%

Stationary structure
(Princeton model table West Level 6)

Figure 2   POPULATION PYRAMID (2)

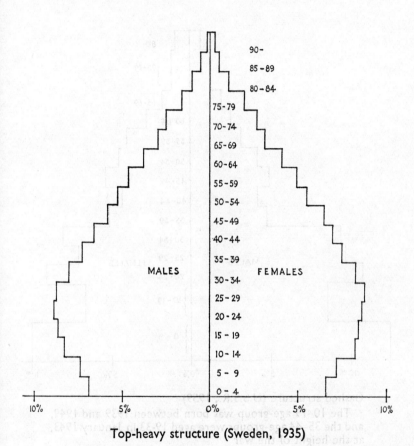

Top-heavy structure (Sweden, 1935)

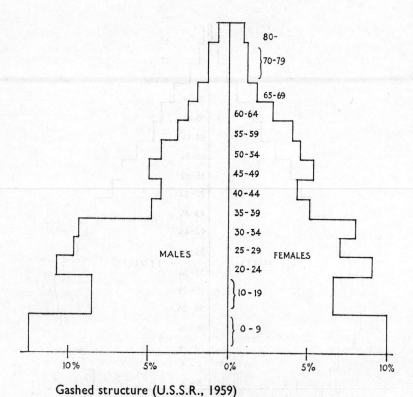

Gashed structure (U.S.S.R., 1959)
    The 10–19 age-group was born between 1939 and 1949, and the 35–44 age-groups were aged 19-33 in January 1943, at the height of the war

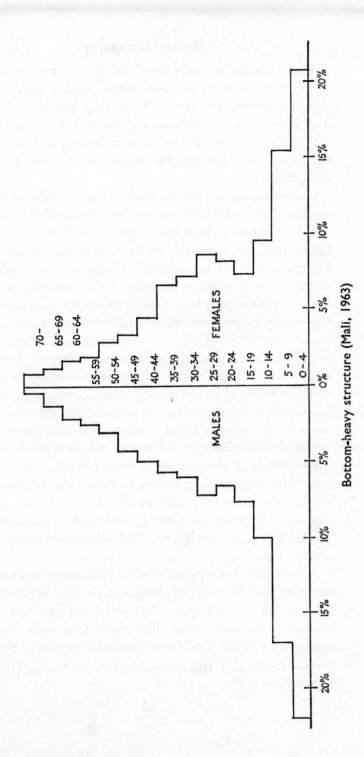

Figure 4

POPULATION PYRAMID (4)

	70-
	65-69
	60-64
	55-59
	50-54
	45-49
	40-44
	35-39
	30-34
MALES	25-29	FEMALES
	20-24
	15-19
	10-14
	5-9
	0-4

20% 15% 10% 5% 0% 5% 10% 15% 20%

Bottom-heavy structure (Mali, 1963)

Vital rates are normally calculated specific for age and sex, which means there are as many rates to calculate and consider as there are age and sex groups. There may well be twenty such vital rates for a population at a given period of time, in fact. The analysis is inevitably much more complicated, and it is at this stage that demography begins to become a separate discipline.

Certain conclusions can be reached from a study of the age-specific birth- and death-rates that limit the possible figures that could be obtained about past populations. A study that gives figures that seem impossible on the basis of present knowledge, for example, must be regarded as suspect. This might arise through a study of infant mortality. Infant mortality rates have been determined for a large number of modern populations, and it generally happens that the rate falls with age during the first months and years of life in a regular manner. From certain populations in the past, this regularity is not observed, but instead an odd pattern occurs in which the apparent mortality of the very youngest babies of all is extremely light compared with the later mortality.[1] It seems much more probable that there was heavy under-enumeration of infant deaths at ages under a month or so than that the modern overall pattern did not apply. The fundamental causes of the patterns at present found depend chiefly upon facts about human resistance to disease, and thus little effect of the different social conditions of today would be expected. The only difference is in the general level of mortality; the relationships of the rates by age to each other ought to be the same now as then.

A further level of sophistication has been created in an attempt to understand the causes of changes in the vital rates, allowing for age and sex differences. Any social criterion that can be measured may have some effect upon these rates, and thus demography at this level draws largely on sociology. The most

[1] On this point, see L. Henry, *Manuel de démographie historique*, Geneva and Paris, 1967, pp. 134-7.

obvious influence upon fertility is marriage (apart from age and sex, of course), and governments have been measuring the rates of marriage in a rough way for a very long time. In England, as well as in most Continental countries, marriages were recorded in the parish registers, as well as baptisms and burials, from the very beginning of the registration system. Indeed, when the early nineteenth-century demographers were attempting to trace population trends in England during the eighteenth century, it was to the marriage levels, rather than the levels of baptisms or burials, that many of them turned. Although clandestine marriages were very common at one time, particularly before 1695,[1] there was every reason to suppose that marriages would have been recorded much more completely than baptisms or burials in the parish registers after Lord Hardwicke's Marriage Act of 1753. Although it was not known what fractions of the population were marrying each year, it was not unreasonable to suppose that marriages increased with the population in a fairly simple way.

The series of age-specific fertility rates must now be duplicated into a legitimate and an illegitimate series, and it is not surprising that the rates are greatly different. Legitimate fertility is further divided nowadays into groupings by the age of the mother at marriage and the duration of the marriage. In fact, these two, together with the mother's actual age, make up a group of which only two members are independent; the usual thing today is to regard the present age of a mother as being less important than her age when she was married and how long she has been married. The reason for this is that there is a sharp falling off in

---

[1] D. J. Steel, 'Sources of Births, Marriages and Deaths before 1837 (I)', *National Index of Parish Registers*, I (1968), pp. 292–318 in particular. The Report of the Commission into Marriage Law estimated, in 1868, that over one-third of all the marriages performed in the United Kingdom during the first half of the eighteenth century had been clandestine, that is, not regular Anglican marriages in a parish church. The 1695 Marriage Act, moreover, had penalized clergy for marrying people without banns or licence, which in places increased the numbers of marriages performed in parish churches considerably.

fertility after a certain number of years of marriage in modern societies. It is therefore less important how old a woman is than how long she has been married, provided she married moderately young.

Within a series of marriage data, it has become quite common to study the intervals between births; tabulations are, accordingly, required of births according to parity. The historical populations that are being studied today are also often analysed in this way. The reason for making such detailed analysis of historical populations is that the birth-intervals between successive births in the same family have often been found to change very little, given the size of the family, until the last pair of births. That final birth-interval, however, is almost always much larger than the earlier intervals. The pattern is remarkably regular and can be regarded as evidence for some kind of family limitation whenever it is found. In the eighteenth century, for example, it is of great interest to be able to decide whether family patterns were of that type or of the alternative type, with the birth-intervals showing no particular tendency except perhaps increasing slightly as the mother grows older. The latter type suggests that there was no conscious limitation of the family at all.

This type of fertility analysis has also led to the use of the concept of a marriage cohort, defined as a group of people who marry at the same time. Cohort fertility cannot readily be converted into current fertility, since it takes place over a considerable period and not a single year.

Mortality may be studied actuarily or medically, and to the demographer the actuarial approach naturally comes to mind first. A series of age-specific death-rates for each sex forms the basis of what life insurance statisticians call a life table. There are practical difficulties to overcome before the curve of mortality against age is satisfactorily smooth (owing chiefly to wrong ages in the data), and the first year or two of life are difficult to handle because mortality falls rapidly then, but the main point of a life table is that it gives probabilities of dying within a particular age-interval. These are not quite the same as the age-specific death-rates. For example, the rate at which persons aged 20 to 25 died in a year would be an age-specific death-rate; the corresponding mortality rate is the probability that someone aged 20 would not live to be 25 if he were liable to the death conditions of the year in question. A table of survivors from a group of births can be calculated, age by age, from the mortality rates, and the average length of life of all these survivors is called the expectation of life at birth. Although figures of expectation of life are widely quoted today, one should remember that it is a devious and rather artificial notion.

Mortality has been studied from the medical point of view for a very long time. In the old Bills of Mortality,[1] for example, some figures on the causes of death were given; the plague was always a threat, and the London Bills, indeed, were almost certainly begun because of the plague. In modern times there has been a division of diseases into infectious and degenerative: the former affect all people in much the same way, but very young children are particularly liable to them since they have not obtained any immunity to infection; degenerative diseases are those to which liability increases with age. Formerly, most deaths were caused by infectious diseases, and the literature in the medical periodicals used to be taken up with discussions of ways of prevention or cure of infection. In the twentieth century, however, infectious disease has been largely eliminated in the more advanced countries, so that degenerative diseases now account for the great majority of deaths. Among the most important degenerative diseases are heart diseases, cancer, and vascular lesions. Two categories of cause of death are not covered by these two: endogenous infant mortality, which are deaths very soon after birth of babies that scarcely managed to live at

[1] The Foot and Mouth outbreak of 1967/8 in England and Wales provided a modern counterpart to the Bills in so far as daily interest was expressed in the number of new cases. The weekly Bills were discussed, during an epidemic, in much the same way.

all; and deaths by violence, which affect all ages to a rather similar extent, and might be thought of as a kind of infection, although they are uncommon compared with deaths from infectious diseases.

Just as fertility can be measured by marriage cohorts, mortality can be studied by generations. The life-time experience of mortality is then studied as a whole, which is often the easiest approach in historical work.[1] The more advanced demographic techniques that have been evolved to deal with occupational changes, migration, or household sizes, are both complex and, as yet, of unproved value. In historical work, it would be highly desirable to study these things, of course, as well as the simpler causes of population change. However, we are as yet hardly in a position to state with much confidence how the population at present is affected by changes in the social structure. The chief reason, in fact, is that we scarcely know how to measure the social structure itself adequately. In historical populations there is some ground for making more attempt at social analysis, because the difference between two epochs may be so great, in the social sense, that some rough measurement of changes is possible. Any contemporary social changes must be taking place relatively slowly, and the proper tools to study them may not exist. We may, therefore, attempt to study such a gross social variable as the change in household size over the centuries (and we will need to do so if much of the data is of household numbers and not of population itself). The migration of peoples is also likely to be very important in some circumstances, and, although we hardly know how to study its causes, there are a few instances (as in Ireland in the seventeenth century where 44,210 people were transplanted in 1653–4 from the rest of Ireland to Connaught, thereby more than doubling the population of that

[1] See R. A. M. Case, Christine Coghill, Joyce L. Harley and Joan T. Pearson, *Chester Beatty Research Institute Abridged Life Tables, England and Wales 1841–1960 Part 1*. London, 1962.

province)[1] where migration was deliberately planned and some estimate of its extent can be made. Here, however, we are really studying the migration itself, rather than its causes; the causes are known and need not be studied.

The techniques of demography have been developed to meet the growing interests of demographers. They are still not fully adequate to predict population trends in the future or to understand all the population changes that are now taking place. It is possible that new techniques will have to be evolved to study historical populations, even though the data are usually much less reliable and complete for the past then they are for the present. The ultimate goal is to understand the past with a view to understanding the present and predicting the future; it is likely that a good knowledge of the past will yield new insights into the underlying causes of population change that themselves will stimulate further research on the current population trends.

THE DATA OF MODERN DEMOGRAPHY

(1) *Advanced Countries*

All the more advanced countries collect demographic data in two main ways. The first is the census, which is held at regular intervals; the whole population is enumerated and certain information about each individual is recorded. The second way of collecting data is the vital registration system, which operates continually; every vital event taking place in the country has to be registered, again with certain information about it. The

[1] W. H. Hardinge, 'On Circumstances attending the outbreak of the Civil War in Ireland on 23rd October, 1641, and its continuance to the 12th May, 1652; the numerical extent and manner of the Transplantation of Irish into Connaught and Clare; the extent, value, and distribution of the Forfeited Lands; their insufficiency to satisfy the Debts and Arrears due to Adventurers and Soldiers; the solution of that difficulty under the Acts of Settlement and Explanation; and the results of these operations', *Transactions of the Royal Irish Academy*, 24 (Part 3) (Antiquities) (1874), pp. 379–420.

details of both census and registration vary from country to country and often also from time to time.

Age, sex, nationality, and usual residence are almost always required at a census, and further information that is often obtained concerns occupation, place of birth, marital status, and children previously born. There is, obviously, no real limit to the information that might be obtained except the costs of getting it. Here, not merely the census officials' time and the cost of processing the data should be taken into account. The final limiting factor is more likely to be the patience of the members of the population themselves, who will have to answer questions readily and honestly if the results are to have any value. Should they be discouraged by too long a census schedule, they are liable to answer questions at random or facetiously. If more than a minute fraction of the population behaves in this way, the whole census operation is in jeopardy, because its results will be in doubt. Moreover, since it is very expensive to correct a large number of wrong schedules, the only recourse will be to do an entirely new census. For this reason, questions such as religion, race, or income are often avoided by governments in a census, notwithstanding their obvious interest and value.

The second main source of demographic data in the advanced countries of the world today is the vital registration system. This usually includes marriages as well as births and deaths, although only the two latter, of course, affect the size of the population directly. The sex of each child born, the date of its birth, and some information about its parents are usually recorded, the father's occupation and the mother's age being obviously worth collecting. The cause of death, as well as the age and sex of the dead person, are almost always on the death certificate, together with other information, such as the nationality, marital status, or place of birth, according to the local regulations. Marriage registers record, naturally, the ages of the couple, and probably some indication of their parents' occupations. Previous marital status is usually also required. In addition to these three registers, some countries maintain a system of registration of changes of address, recording some of the usual demographic data about each mover. The address register then serves to provide data on migration.

The completeness of the registration of vital events is generally worse than that of the census; but if both are fairly well done, as is true in all the advanced countries, the only poor data are for very young children, who tend to be forgotten at a census or given wrong ages, but whose births are usually registered. The birth, marriage, and death statistics are normally good for any country where literacy is high and the population lives in a modern way, with consequent need to produce birth, marriage, and death certificates to prove legal rights on certain occasions. The legal penalties for non-registration are scarcely daunting and merely act as a goad to the lazy; the registration officials would not be able to coerce most of the stragglers into registration unless they were very few. Every national system has provisions that are designed to make evasion difficult, but in practice it seems clear that the high degree of completeness normally obtained in an advanced country can be credited chiefly to the population's own desire to be registered and only secondarily to the efficiency of the officials.

The registration of migration, where it is done, bears out the same point. No country claims more than about 95 per cent completeness for its internal migration measurements, for the census results generally show that at least 5 per cent of moves had been missed for one reason or another. A continuous register of population has been in operation in the Netherlands for over 100 years, yet it has not been possible to dispense with the regular Dutch censuses. If the population register were correct, or almost correct, the census would be a waste of effort. The discrepancies are caused by people who do not let the authorities know whether they have moved; they may have good reasons of their own for being so obtuse, or else care little about the penalties.

All advanced countries publish the main results of their censuses in many volumes, and usually also retain unpublished information that can be obtained on request. Further tabulations are sometimes made for outside bodies on payment of a fee, for the potentialities of a census of population are immense, even though only a few questions are asked of each person. It is the task of the Census Office in each country to determine what to publish and in how much detail.

There are also, naturally enough, official publications of the data collected by the vital registration system. As well as the area totals of births, marriages, and deaths, broken down into groups by age and sex, there is the possibility of combining census data with registration data to produce estimates of the vital rates. Since this would only be strictly possible at the time of a census, the inter-censal population is normally estimated by age and sex for each year, and appropriate vital rates calculated. There can be some inaccuracy here, owing to errors in the measurement of migration, and occasionally it is found worth while even to recalculate a series of vital rates for the period preceding a census when the errors caused by wrong allowance for migration prove unduly large.

(2) *Less developed countries*

The quality of the population data for many of the less developed countries of the world today is very similar to that for the whole world 200 years ago or more. That is to say, there are few places from which no data whatever emerge, but there are equally few places from which there are first-rate data, and more than 30 per cent of the world's population did not get counted at all during the decade 1955–64.[1] Since a census every decade is regarded as the minimum for a modern country, we must assume that all demographic data from these countries are extremely fragmentary. Most of the shortcomings are found in Asia or in Africa, and of course China is the main contributor to the total of people, estimated at 988 million, who have not been counted for a decade or more.

[1] *United Nations Demographic Yearbook, 1964,* p. 2.

At the same time, there are many demographic indicators that are still unknown for countries that have had a recent census. In particular the numbers and average size of households, which are of particular interest in medieval historical demography, are only known for about 9 per cent of the population of Africa, 13 per cent of the population of Asia and about 15 to 25 per cent of the population of South America.[1]

As well as these shortcomings in the census collection, there are many shortcomings in the quality of the data that have been collected. For most of the countries where illiteracy is common, the age data are subject to extreme variations in the ages actually reported. This phenomenon has been studied extensively and a theory of graduation of ages has been built up to correct for it.[2] It bulks very large, for instance, in every census of India. The ages ending in an even number, or that are a multiple of 5, are always more popular than those ending in the digits 1, 3, 7 or 9, and the round tens are the most popular of all. It is by no means unknown for as many people to give their age as 60 exactly as for the eight ages 56–59 and 61–64 combined.

The main difficulties in population analysis tend to be: (i) that there may not have been an enumeration of any kind for many years, or indeed, ever at all; (ii) that the data that do exist are tabulated only for a relatively small number of demographic indicators, and indeed, may not have been collected at all on some of the most interesting characteristics of the population; and (iii) that what does exist may be erroneous owing to faults in the census itself. Many attempts have been made by the United Nations and the governments concerned to improve the quality of population data in those parts of the world that do not have at present a high standard. The difficulties fall under four heads: social, political, religious, and economic.

More social difficulties have to be overcome than is often

[1] *Ibid.*, p. 3.
[2] George King, 'Report on Graduation of Ages', *Census of England and Wales, 1911*, Vol. VII, pp. xxxix–xlviii.

realized. For example, illiteracy amongst the population will mean that the census enumerators have to make all the enquiries about the family relationships, the wife's fertility, and their places of birth, as well as the simple questions about the number of inhabitants in the house and their ages; if the enumerator is lacking in tact in any way, there is no means of recovering the information that should have been collected. Moreover, the questions framed in a government office in the capital city and well understood by the educated census enumerator may seem incomprehensible or meaningless when put to the humble peasant, so that with the best will in the world absurd answers may be given, and (even worse) wrong answers that seem plausible enough may frequently be returned. Courses of training are run for the enumerators, and pilot censuses taken in advance to test the methods (as, for example, in Hong Kong in 1961), but even then errors do occur.

The two chief political reason why census material is sometimes worthless arise because the census is frequently used either as a basis for determining the apportionment of power in the democratic legislature of the country or else as a basis for making taxation assessments. The classic example of a census that went awry for the former reason is the Nigerian census of 1963. Although it was carried out with United Nations experts' help and under their personal supervision, the temptation to inflate the returns was too great for the integrity of the local headmen who realized that their own and their kinsmen's power would be enhanced by returning a high figure for the local population. It is at this level that reality conflicts forcibly with theory, for although the census was repeated a similar result was obtained. There was no alternative to using the information supplied by the local headmen over most of the country as at least the basis for taking the census at all, if not the actual census count itself; since the distances to be covered, over difficult territory and with a limited number of regular staff, were so great that an actual enumeration of the people by permanent officials would have been impossible. The suspicion that a taxation will follow a census is more ancient and by no means unjustified. In later Ming China (sixteenth and early-seventeenth centuries), for instance, the census probably counted scarcely half the population.[1] Bearing these two points in mind, one must not be surprised at the suggestion that ancient 'counts' of population may sometimes have missed half the population concerned, and others may have returned a figure twice as high as the number of people really there.

Religious objections to the obtaining of demographic data are less frequent, but it was never the normal practice in the Ottoman Empire to take a census, for instance, although taxation lists were frequently compiled. Actually counting the people was held to be irreligious, a feeling that seems to go back to the Israelites, probably to King David's census.[2] There is nowadays less resistance to a counting in itself, but there are still those who object on religious grounds to revealing any information, for example, about the women in their household. This might extend in an extreme case to a refusal to allow the enumerator to know how many women there were. Although the law of a country may oblige the population to return prescribed information at a census, it is therefore by no means easy to ensure that information wrung out of the people by the law will be accurate. If the inhabitants actively resent the questions that their government asks, it is not impossible for them to give false information.

The economic difficulties are obvious. The cost of taking a census of a population must always be considerable, and the further cost of recruiting and training the staff to make the enumeration adds to the cost very greatly if there is no means of employing that staff at any other time. It might be thought

---

[1] Ho Ping-ti, *Studies on the Population of China, 1368–1953*, Cambridge, Mass., 1959, pp. 3–23.
[2] Described in 2 Samuel XXIV.

that a registration system of births and deaths would have the effect of improving the population data, since at the very least the registration officials could take the census. This is true in the more advanced countries, once the system has begun to work fairly well, but it is notorious that registration of birth data in India, for example, is deficient by a factor of perhaps 40–50 per cent. It is apparently impossible to extend the coverage of the registration system to the entire population of India, even if enough educated officials could be recruited. The main snag is that in certain areas there is no one who knows the population well enough to undertake the post of enumerator in the first instance, and it would be prohibitively expensive to pay a man to live amongst the people for a year or two before beginning registration at all. In fact, the registration depends not on the mere acquiescence of the population (as the census does) but upon the active co-operation of the people. They must come to be registered, whereas the census enumerators come to count them.

The quality of some contemporary demographic data may be improved by sampling. If we have a western population where a good census already exists, and the main function of the sample is to reduce the cost to the lowest level compatible with obtaining the information wanted to a high enough degree of accuracy, then an elaborate statistical theory has already been developed of how best to draw this sample from the population. This theory, however, has little application in most of Africa, Asia or Latin America. In many countries there is no good basis to take for a sample frame in the way that a European or North American can take the most recent census of an area. Where the sample has to be its own census, there is a serious risk that the sample fractions will not be maintained rigorously. It was only realized in 1967, for example, that the population in the 1966 sample census of Great Britain was undercounted by 2 or 3 per cent owing to mistakes in the sample frame. (The figure was estimated by making a second enumeration in certain selected areas very shortly after the sample census itself.) Since Great Britain had a full census only five years earlier, has high standards of census-taking and literacy, and a well-mapped territory, one would have expected the figure to have been much lower than 2 per cent. The possible error in a sample census in a less developed country is often placed as high as 20 per cent, and it is easy to see that such a high degree of inaccuracy often renders further analysis nugatory. However, it is not always necessary to know the population size accurately as long as the vital rates can be calculated with confidence. If the sample that is drawn is random, it is still possible to calculate correct fertility ratios from it that will give us the information that is needed about fertility levels. In India, there is now a 'continuous sample round' that is the main basis of assertions made about the Indian birth-rate. The birth-rate computed from the registration and census data alone is, as we have noticed, quite misleading.

The many shortcomings in the population data of the world today throw some light on the errors to look for in historical data. The chief weakness of many counts is that people are missed out; it is always much easier to miss out a person than to include someone twice, if only for the reason that it requires less effort. A census might, for example, count 2 per cent twice and miss 10 per cent completely. It is therefore wise to assume that a population count is normally a net understatement rather than a net overstatement. The chief exception to this rule will be where being counted offers a great advantage to the population itself. The political example of Nigeria has been given above; one might also cite the figures produced for the insertion of I.U.D.s in certain countries where a small bonus is given to each woman fitted. A considerable number of women reappear time and again simply for the bonus, making the effectiveness of the I.U.D.s for birth control seem very odd. Another example where one must suspect overstatement is in any enumeration connected with famine relief, flood relief, war compensation, or the like. The normal expectation of an inhabitant of any country in the past (and most countries in the present) is that the census officials intend to tax the area or raise soldiers from it, and therefore they will tend to try to avoid being counted. Only if the possibility of a benefit arises will the population rise up to, or indeed surpass, its true value.

CHAPTER 2

History and Demography

The study of population in the past embraces two fields that are really better kept apart, historical demography and demographic history. The former is the study of the ebb and flow of the numbers of mankind in time and space by a combination of geography and history using statistics, and the main concern is to achieve accurate estimates of human numbers. For example, how many people lived in the Ottoman Empire or in ancient Rome? What was the population of China under the Western Han or of England in the fourteenth century? Such questions are by now familiar to historians, although the demographer is in a position to weigh the estimates with more discernment than the general historian is likely to be able to muster.

But estimates of total numbers is demography at its crudest level. They are the first sketch, it is true, but the full picture is much more elaborate. Even though the estimates of total numbers may never become entirely accurate, estimates may still be made of the distribution of the population by sex and by age group, and of its rates of change. All the demographic analysis that is possible will be wanted, in order to throw light on what social trends were occurring and to try to explain such phenomena as price changes or military weakness, political unrest or the supply of labour. It is often possible to estimate some of the more complex demographic rates to a fair degree of accuracy without knowing the actual size of the population itself especially well. Of course, where there is plenty of information (as for example for Europe in the second half of the nineteenth century), very detailed study is possible. Nevertheless, it is fair to say that no society has been analysed in such full detail as yet. Where the information exists in principle, it is very easy to invent more analyses than human resources can possibly undertake within reasonable limits. Even using a computer, one could generate piles of figures that no demographer would ever be able to digest.

This is not the usual contingency, however, in historical demography. Tolerably complete vital data do not exist for many parts of the world at any time in their history, and even for the more favoured parts of the world there is only a century or two of fairly comprehensive information. This is not perhaps entirely unsatisfactory to the historian; but it is exasperating to the demographer, because demographic changes are like waves passing through an ocean: not sudden flurries, but a deep swell. For example, suppose the legitimate fertility of women over 35 falls fairly abruptly to almost zero. The effect is to reduce the birth-rate, and at the same time to shorten the mean interval between successive generations. The lowered birth-rate affects the age-structure, which in twenty years' time will affect the birth-rate anew. It will be at least a century—if no other demographic changes occur—before a new stable pattern will emerge. For this fundamental reason—that a century or more is required to produce actual stability when the demographic rates are in fact stable—the demographer prefers to deal with a period of 150 years at least, although it is always difficult to get such a long series of data. Moreover, since *changes* in the stable pattern are particularly interesting, the perspective ought ideally to be longer still, since 150 years is about the minimum period in which any change could be isolated and studied.

When a fact of historical demography is once established, however, it serves as a corner-stone for history. An obvious example is the Black Death, which affected Europe in the fourteenth century. The details are still far from clear, but it is plain enough that the significance of a loss of a half or a quarter of the population within a short time must have been enormous, for almost every aspect of life would be affected. Similarly, it is valuable to use the practical results of modern demography to review and revise past estimates of total populations or of numbers of men of military age. The relative strengths of two nations may have been very well known at the time, yet nowhere recorded by a contemporary. Conflicting estimates may exist, and again the demographer may be able to supply a guide to their credibility.

All this, then, is historical demography proper. What is its cousin, demographic history? Although it must be admitted at once that there is no accepted distinction between the two, it is always interesting and often helpful to make nice distinctions, since it serves to show us different facets of the complex that is the whole subject.

DEMOGRAPHIC HISTORY

Demographic history must clearly be history, a sister of political history and constitutional history. It must seek to describe past events in a coherent way, using population as its yardstick, and population changes as the events of main interest that other factors must explain. We may illustrate the distinction by the periods that one naturally chooses in English history. A natural period in historical demography is 1538–1837, the age when parish registers are a prime source of data.[1] In demographic history, however, the natural period might be 1348–1666, the years when the plague dominated population change. We shall return to the question of demographic history, or history seen from the demographic point of view, in the final chapter.

DEVELOPMENT OF HISTORICAL DEMOGRAPHY

The main purpose of this book, however, is to describe the methods of research that are used nowadays to elucidate the levels and trends of population in the past. They vary greatly, some

[1] This is pointed out by E. A. Wrigley in *An Introduction to English Historical Demography from the Sixteenth to the Nineteenth Century*, London, 1966, p. xi.

being highly ingenious, others crude. Their value also varies, and the crudest methods are not always the least useful.

If we think that the population in ancient Rome, for instance, is most unlikely to have been packed more closely than in Paris in 1806, and we can measure the area contained within the walls of ancient Rome, then we have an upper limit for the population of ancient Rome. This is historical demography, not demographic history; and we might go on to discuss the probability that Rome could have had about half the density of Paris in 1806 and produce our estimate of Rome's population. We might further argue that the mortality of ancient Rome was higher than that of rural parts of the Roman Empire because of the higher density of population, just as is found at almost all times and in almost all places between urban and rural parts of the same community, and support this with evidence of ages at death taken from tombstone inscriptions. Net in-migration would then be required to maintain the city's population. The birth-rate and net in-migration rate might be guessed, and so on. All this would be historical demography.

Historical demography has its own history, of course. In 1662, Graunt[1] deduced (among other things) that London was both growing in numbers and moving slowly westwards.[2] He was the first to study historical records of population critically, with a view to deducing entirely new facts from them, and not merely adjusting the figures to correct for over- or under-enumeration.[3]

---

[1] J. Graunt, *Natural and political observations mentioned in a following index, and made upon the bills of mortality. With references to the government, religion, trade, growth, ayre, diseases, and the several changes of the said city* [London]. The third edition, of 1665, as reprinted in *The Journal of the Institute of Actuaries*, **90**, 384 (1964), pp. 4–61.

[2] See also p. 47.

[3] See also B. Benjamin's foreword to the 1964 reprint of Graunt's pamphlet; I. Sutherland, 'John Graunt: a tercentenary tribute', *Journal of the Royal Statistical Society* (Series A), **126**, 4 (1963), pp. 537–56; D. V. Glass, 'John Graunt and his Natural and political observations', *Proceedings of the Royal Society* (Series B), **159**, 974 (17 March 1964), pp. 1–32.

For a long time, interest was only in the immediate past and then only for the purpose of finding the current trend so as to make a guess at the immediate future. A much more ambitious idea fired Rickman, the organizer of the first five censuses of Great Britain from 1801 to 1841, although he died in 1840. Rickman began by using his official position to have data on baptisms, burials, and marriages collected for the eighteenth century, and he later extended these series back to 1570. There are some serious shortcomings in his work and, unfortunately, all the actual returns before 1700 are lost. However, Rickman understood the importance of long periods in demography, and did remarkably well in the circumstances. Glass[1] has recently traced the history of historical demography. He emphasizes that demographic methods have improved greatly since about 1940.

Such work is not, of course, confined to England, and several other countries probably have better data. China has immense collections of census data going back for 3,000 years, but the problem of their interpretation is still only toyed with. France, Italy and Germany also have a great deal of data that have scarcely been analysed in depth, but the Dutch and Hungarian sources have been fairly comprehensively discussed. Faber and others,[2] in particular, have shown how very diverse and voluminous the material is, even for a small country. The general reason for lack of interest in population history until lately is, no doubt, the historical lack of interest that the authorities have normally shown in the common people. Indeed, at the time of the Domesday Book (1086), the English Crown seems to have been as much interested in acreages and head of cattle as in men and women. Moreover, if no great changes in numbers were expected in the future or supposed in the past, there would be little point in

[1] Glass, 'Introduction to *Population in History*' (edited by Glass and D. E. C. Eversley), London, 1965, pp. 1–22.

[2] J. A. Faber, H. K. Roessingh, B. H. Slicher van Bath, A. M. van der Woude, and H. J. van Xanten, 'Population changes and economic development in the Netherlands: a historical survey', *Afdeling Agrarische Geschiedenis Bijdragen*, 12, (1965), pp. 47–113.

making a count. The only frequent reason for counting people, in fact, was for raising taxation. Evasion, however, must have been fairly common, and sometimes might be widespread. It was with the rise of the merchant (as opposed to military or clerical) towns of Europe in the sixteenth century that we find a genuine interest in actual numbers.[1] Venice, after taking (in 1440) the first census in Europe since Roman times that is worth calling a census at all, counted the population six times[2] between 1540 and the end of the century, a frequency of almost once a decade. The separation of counting itself from fiscal, military, or ecclesiastical surveys of the population was no doubt made possible by the new habits of mind of the rising bourgeoisie, which in another context we should call the Renaissance. Tokugawa Japan and Ch'ing China counted the whole taxable population (although the non-taxable may have been fairly numerous), but the early development of censuses really came in Canada, Iceland, Sweden, Austria, Norway, Germany, Spain, and the United States of America. It was part of the pattern of thought of the Enlightenment that numbers should be measured regularly, as a matter of public importance, and it was also linked with the growing idea of democracy. But the overriding fact was that numbers were increasing, making frequent counts imperative. Research into the demography of the more distant past scarcely developed until the nineteenth century, when censuses had become fairly common.

SOURCES OF DATA

One of the best general summaries of the sources of historical demography has been given by Génicot.[3] It only deals with

[1] R. Mols, *Introduction à la démographie historique des villes d'Europe du XIVe au XVIIIe siècle*, Louvain, 1954–6, Vol. 1, p. XXIII.

[2] *Ibid.*, pp. 19–20.

[3] L. Génicot, 'A propos des preuves d'une augmentation de la population en Europe occidentale du XIe au XIIIe siècles', *Cahiers d'Histoire Mondiale*, **1, 2** (October 1953) pp. 446–62; reprinted in translation in *Change in Medieval Society: Europe north of the Alps, 1050–1500* (edited by S. L. Thrupp), New York, 1964.

medieval Europe, but it does discuss most of the categories of evidence that are available. Génicot lists the following eight sources in order of decreasing precision, by which he means the degree to which they can be expressed in statistical series:

(1) military and fiscal documents;
(2) inventories of seigneurial property and rights;
(3) genealogies, derived from descriptions of families in charters, or else already compiled;
(4) prices, especially agricultural prices, over the long term;
(5) number and extent of towns;
(6) changes in technology and the fragmentation of traditional land holdings;
(7) changes in ecclesiastical geography and the construction or alteration of public buildings;
(8) colonization of new territory seized from the Moslems.

To these eight, we can add the census, the civil registration system, Bills of Mortality and ecclesiastical records, which would all rank above (1); wills, marriage settlements and eye-witness estimates, ranking next after (3); and we can extend (5) to include all evidence derived from archaeological remains, and (8) to include all types of colonization of new land. Graveyards can also provide us with one further source of demographic statistics, if a sufficient number of corpses can be found and assigned an age at death. They are most unreliable sources for making any demographic estimate, however, so we should rank them below (8).

With some revision of the description, we now have the following sources, in approximate order of usefulness:

(1) censuses, especially if given by name and age
(2) vital registration data
(3) Bills of Mortality
(4) ecclesiastical records, such as parish registers and communicants' lists
(5) fiscal documents
(6) military records

(7) inventories of property

(8) genealogies

(9) wills

(10) marriage settlements

(11) eye-witness estimates

(12) prices, over the long term

(13) number and extent of towns

(14) archaeological remains

(15) methods of agricultural economy

(16) ecclesiastical and administrative geography

(17) new buildings

(18) colonization of new land

(19) cemetery data, both from skeletons and tombstone inscriptions

It must be emphasized, however, that not all of these are equally available. In particular, we rarely have inventories of property for any large extent of land. (The Domesday Book, of course, is a great exception.) A small-scale inventory is less valuable, naturally.

QUALITY OF DATA

When we begin to consider numerical data drawn from the past, one first question is often overlooked, namely what a figure is in itself. It is all too easily supposed that a figure is the exact result of a clearly defined count and therefore has a definite meaning. Statistical techniques, however, accustom us to the idea that a figure is in fact merely the result of the counter's judgment, in the sense that he counted and recounted and adjusted his total until he felt that there was no point in elaborating it further, and this final total is the figure that he will have given us. When there are only a small number of people to be counted, say ten or twenty, we naturally expect the count to be entirely accurate.

But even in this instance, there will be occasions when time or the purpose of the count were such that an accurate total was unnecessary. Even when the total number to be counted is small, therefore, there is a possibility that the count will be wrong. Figures for larger populations than this, even though the population be clearly defined, are almost always inaccurate, because of the difficulty of organizing a count on such a large scale as a national census. Lack of time and normal human failings are the chief reasons, and they can result in substantial differences between the truth and the published result.

Any historical figure of population, in particular, needs to be very carefully considered before it is used for demographic research. We need to define the area in which the population lived, the date at which they were alleged to have been counted, and any portions of the population that might have been excluded from the count. This last consideration is less important today than it was in the past, because figures based upon tax returns (as opposed to figures based upon national censuses) are very dependent upon the system of collecting the tax. Having decided what a figure of population from some past record was intended to mean at the time it was compiled, we then have to decide what it means for us. We are not immediately interested in the collection of tax or in the number of houses that there were, but in the population. A corresponding interest in population for its own sake was remarkably uncommon amongst governments before the second half of the eighteenth century, although there are some cities in Europe that published Bills of Mortality from an early date; for instance, the annual series for Augsburg goes back to 1500.

Having determined what our information really is, the next step in the philosophy of historical demography is to consider how we came to obtain it. The main problem is selectivity; there is reason to suppose that the records that have been lost tend to be those in which there was little of interest, and the records that have been preserved were the ones that were in some way remarkable. There was also, of course, some accidental preservation of whole sets of records, but after many centuries the natural tendency is to throw away anything that seems to have nothing of interest about it. If this tendency is found in the chroniclers who record deaths in a battle, for example, we shall have the figure when it seemed remarkably high or low more often than when the mortality was normal.

The usual historical technique when dealing with information of this kind is to discard a certain amount of it as incredible or fanciful and to analyse the rest. We may do a little better than this if we care to examine in detail the reasons why a figure might be accurate or inaccurate. These may be classified in three ways:

First, whether the original writer, or source, is likely or unlikely to have known the true figure that he pretends to give us. Our opinion here will depend upon his access to official records, proximity to the events described, the likelihood that anyone should have known the truth, and so on.

Second, the honesty or dishonesty of the source. If he could have known the truth, the division is into whether he told it or whether he lied; and if he could not have known, the division is into whether he admitted his ignorance or made a guess. The motives for such lying are various, and it does not necessarily follow that a false report should be totally disregarded. Provided it would get credence, the false figure would have been published; and it will give us some idea of what level of figure was regarded as credible at the time. Thus when Boccaccio tells us that 100,000 people died in the Black Death at Florence in 1348,[1] although the figure seems high and was no doubt deliberately inflated for narrative effect by the famous story-teller, it was not so high that his readers would regard it as a fantastic lie, and so gives us some notion (albeit little) of the population and mortality in Florence at that time.

Third, high or low bias. Each of the four categories already

[1] *Decameron*, first day; before the first story.

found can be further divided in this way, except those who both knew the truth and told it. The difference in attitude to the past that arises here is as old as Montesquieu and Hume. Montesquieu argued in 1721[1] that the population of the world in ancient times was at least ten times as high as in his own day, while Hume claimed a generation later[2] that the population of the past had never reached a figure as high as that of the eighteenth century. Since that date, a controversy has raged around this point and general opinion greatly favours Hume.

If the source both could have known the truth and told it, it is still possible, however, for the information that he gives to be silly as opposed to wise. This is not strictly a division into high and low estimates, but it separates the useful facts for today from such oddities as the number of persons, 120,000, in Nineveh who did not know their right hand from their left,[3] which is the only numerical source we have on which to estimate the population of the city—about a million, perhaps. If lies were deliberate, there may in fact have been high or low misrepresenting, and if not, there is still the possibility of lying by accident. Copying errors fall into this last category. They bulk large in most critiques of historical sources, but, although they are probably quite common, they do not necessarily result in gross misconceptions. If the last digit of a figure is copied wrong, it does not matter; if the first digit is wrong, we may be able to detect it. Reasons for exaggerating population figures include boasting of one's own strength, exultation over the size of a defeated enemy army, asking for relief from famine, and revelling in the extremes of an epidemic mortality that had recently been survived. Depreciation of known population data is rather less common, but when tax returns were made from local areas or when the officials were too lazy to do their job properly, it may often have seemed

[1] *Lettres Persanes*, letter CXII.
[2] 'Of the Populousness of Antient Nations', *Political Discourses*, Edinburgh, 1752, pp. 155–261.
[3] Jonah IV, 11.

expedient to return a low figure of population, below the level that was known to obtain.

In the other half of the possibilities, when the source did not in fact know what the true figures were, those who admit their shortcomings divide into those who confine themselves to vague adjectives and those who give us crumbs of information. Being told that mortality was 'severe' is of almost no practical use to a historical demographer, since anything from twice to twenty times the normal level might have been so described, but when we read of the corn supplies for Constantinople in the eighteenth century,[1] it is clear that a reasonable estimate of population and mortality at the time of the plague can be made, and moreover we are given the basis of the estimate.

The last set of possibilities occurs when the source did not know the truth and made a guess without telling us so. This is the worst situation of all, and has to be detected as best we can. When he over-estimated he will sometimes have given an absurdly large figure that we can now see to have been false, and when he under-estimated we can sometimes see that his figures cannot possibly relate to the whole population in question. However, there must be many instances when estimates of this kind are not so wild that we can dismiss them out of hand, yet were guesses nevertheless on the part of the original author.

METHODS OF ANALYSIS

Most of this book describes actual examples of pieces of historical demography. As an introduction to the quantitative approach to sources, we give here two concrete examples, one very simple and the other complex, although the data are very few in both examples.

The techniques of demographic research were originally very simple, if we may describe them as techniques at all. A king who

[1] Sir James Porter, 'Answer to some queries respecting Constantinople', *Philosophical Transactions of the Royal Society*, **49**, Part I (1755), pp. 96–109.

had taxed his people might have had a count made of the number of households in the country that paid the tax. It would then be a matter of demography to calculate how many recruits the king might hope to get for his army, knowing the number of households. A typical calculation might have been as follows:

> 2 million households taxed
> means 10 million people in all—because 5 is the average household size
> so 5 million will be males—because ½ is the usual sex-ratio,
> and 3 million of them will be adult males—because 40 per cent are children
> deduct 2 million, who are householders—and needed by their families,
> and there are 1 million adult males available for military service.

The calculation depends upon four assumptions that really require checking. Was five the average size of a household? Were males half the total population? Were 40 per cent of the males children? Were all the householders males?

The political point in the calculation, whether all adult males who are not householders can safely be regarded as enlistable men, is the only part that does not concern us. On the other hand, it is very much the demographer's province to assess the relationship between the number of households returned as taxed and the real number of households in the country. The king, on the other hand, might regard any households that escaped his tax-collectors as households that would also probably provide no soldiers, and therefore write them off.

The above is an example of primitive demography. A more elaborate example can be provided from Cornwall's data for Hambleton in Rutland in the sixteenth century.[1] Records exist

---

[1] J. E. Cornwall, 'The people of Rutland in 1522', *Transactions of the Leicestershire Historical Society*, **37** (1961–2), pp. 7–28.

for the years 1522, 1524, and 1525 for this village. Cornwall quotes two sets of figures: persons assessed at £2 and over and those assessed at £1 or nil. In the first class, 19 names appear three times, 6 appear twice, and 8 appear once. In the second class, the corresponding figures are 4, 4, and 7, suggesting worse coverage for the poorer people. Cornwall remarks that the coverage seems to be better than 80 per cent for this village, but that the death-rates may have been running high. In fact, we can estimate both the coverage and the rate of migration for each class.

Let us assume that the same proportion of the population is counted in each year, and that deaths and migration between counts were independent of liability to be counted or missed by the tax-collectors. It is then possible to estimate the total size of Hambleton's population in each class (supposed constant, although the numbers assessed in the three years were in fact 37, 34 and 34 respectively). An algebraic method is extremely complicated, and we here merely show the results, obtained by iteration.

For the first class (£2 and over), the mathematically best fit to the data is by a coverage of 101·42 per cent (i.e. over-coverage); an annual death-cum-emigration rate of 10·56 per cent; and a population of 25·46 people. The second class yields a coverage of 103·88 per cent; an annual death-cum-emigration rate of 25·58 per cent; and a population of 8·66. We may illustrate what could well have happened by reference to the second class, as follows.

In 1522, nine men lived in Hambleton assessable at £1 or nil. Call them *A, B, C, D, E, F, G, H,* and *I.* All nine were assessed. By 1523, two (*H* and *I,* say) had left through death or emigration, and their places were taken by another two men, whom we shall call *J* and *K. J* and *K* will have been either heirs or immigrants to Hambleton. In 1523, there was no assessment. By 1524, a further two men had left—probably from amongst the old seven of *A* to *G.* Suppose, therefore, that *F* and *G* left in 1523/4 and two new men, *L* and *M,* must be added. Then in 1524, the assessed popula-

tion in this class was *A, B, C, D, E, J, K, L,* and *M*. More death
and migration follows in 1524/5, and this time we should allot the
quota of two changes between the two groups *A* to *E* and *J* to *M*;
suppose therefore that *E* and *M* disappear and their places are
taken by two new men, *N* and *O*. In 1525, everyone is assessed
as usual, the population being *A, B, C, D, J, K, L, N,* and *O*.
We thus have 4 people (*A, B, C,* and *D*) assessed three times;
4 people (*E, J, K,* and *L*) assessed twice; 7 people (*F, G, H, I, M,
N,* and *O*) assessed once; and no one missed altogether. These
figures agree with what Cornwall published, although one might
go deeper still, and consider the possibility of return migration.

For the richer class, there is no essential difference. Two or
three people leave each year, and the enumeration is well-nigh
correct. After 3 years, there have been 33 different people assessed,
although the resident population is only 25 or 26.

The calculations on the Hambleton data are quite tedious,
although the numbers are very small. The assumptions made,
however, are only that both assessment and death-cum-migration
are constant in each class and act independently. The results are
not intended to be accurate to the places of decimals given, but
only to estimate to what extent the variations in the lists could
be caused either by poor enumeration or by migration and
death. The evidence here is that the assessors were very exact,
and if anything overzealous; death and migration were responsible for almost all the differences between the three lists. A different pattern of figures would appear if missed assessments were
causing the different names in the lists. The higher rate for the
poorer people evidently reflects not only higher death-rates but
higher gross migration as well; spatial mobility might well be
high for the propertyless. Supposing annual death-rates of 4 per
cent and 6 per cent for the two classes (pure guesses, of course,
but the right order of magnitude), annual gross migration would
be about 7 per cent for the majority, but about 20 per cent for
the really poor.

We have assumed, of course, that we know nothing of the

rate of return movement to Hambleton that would be indicated by absence in 1524 and presence in 1522 and 1525. Cornwall published no details, but we must be wrong to assume that return migration never occurred. If, on the contrary, it was quite common, we should get noticeably different results. However, Cornwall implicitly assumed that all the effects were caused by under-registration and none by migration, which is even less likely.[1]

PUBLISHED WORK OF NOTE

There is no lack of works relating to historical demography, especially in the last fifteen years or so. Only a little of the vast literature is described here, although much more of it will be mentioned in later chapters.

The Société de Démographie Historique was founded in Paris in 1962, and it has published its *Annales* each year since 1964 (in the first year, they were called *Études de Chronique*). Each annual volume of the *Annales de Démographie Historique* contains an extensive bibliography as well as several original articles. It is a rapidly expanding publication (1964, 285 pages; 1965, 333; 1966, 440; 1967, 558), bearing witness to the fast-growing interest in historical demography in France, although it covers work in all parts of the world. The beginner is warned that the bibliography section of the *Annales* is expanding faster than the whole, and has filled 482 pages already, making about 4,000 items.

Louis Henry's *Manual of Historical Demography*[2] combines a high level of demographic expertise with illustrations of its application drawn very largely from French parish register

[1] His calculations on the population of Buckinghamshire in 1524–5 depended on this assumption; see Cornwall, 'An Elizabethan Census', *The Records of Buckinghamshire*, **16**, 4 (1959), pp. 258–73. The results are therefore too high, although he rightly remarks that Russell's figure for the county in the sixteenth century was also too high; Cornwall should only have lowered it further. See J. C. Russell, *British Mediaeval Population*, Albuquerque, 1948, p. 279.

[2] Henry, *Manuel de démographie historique*, Geneva and Paris, 1967.

studies of the age of Louis XIV and Louis XV. It is thus excellent in its treatment, although limited in its scope. No one working seriously on the demography of any parish register should ignore it, since most of what Henry says is also applicable outside France.

The chief work of historical demography itself that has appeared so far, in the sense of detailed scholarship and careful weighing of the different methods of approach, is that of Mols[1] on the towns of Europe. As he explains at the outset, his work is limited: it is not a general work on historical demography, but on Europe; it is chiefly on Western Europe, since language difficulties prevented him from studying Scandinavian, Slavonic, Hungarian, or Turkish sources; it is on towns only, since as well as having better data, one town is comparable with another, which shortens the work; it deals only with the fourteenth to eighteenth centuries; and finally, it is only an introduction to Mols' narrowed field, not a full survey of it. However, this narrow introduction fills 1,246 pages and includes nearly 1,000 different references, at least a quarter of which are, moreover, to books rather than to articles.

The literature of historical demography is so wide and so little summarized as yet that it is scarcely possible to grasp it whole. At a national level, however, some progress can be made; and, considering its size, Hungary seems to be among the leaders of the field. Kovacsics has edited two whole volumes of historical demographic research, *Sources of Historical Statistics*,[2] which in practice is largely a collection of demographic sources; and *The Population of Hungary from the Conquest until 1949*,[3] which amounts to a critical population history of the Magyars.[4] These are solid

[1] *Op. cit.* above on p. 42 (footnote 1).

[2] *A Történeti Statisztika Forrásai*, Budapest, 1957.

[3] *Magyarország történeti demografiája: Magyarország népessége a honfoglalástól 1949-ig*, Budapest, 1963.

[4] See also A. Armengaud, 'L'histoire de la population hongroise', *Études et chronique de démographie historique*, (1964), pp. 151–4.

volumes, redeemed for the ignorant foreigner by summaries in a dozen pages or so at the end in Russian and in English, while the Hungarian Central Office of Statistics publishes a *Historical Statistical Yearbook*,[1] each number containing several important papers. Shorter articles often appear in the Hungarian quarterly journal, *Demográfia*.

The French have made a systematic attack upon their demographic history, directed from the Institut National d'Études Démographiques, under the genius of Louis Henry and with powerful support from the leading French demographers and many of the French historians. The parish registers and, where they exist, the nominative lists of inhabitants, are the prime sources that are used, and the Fleury–Henry manual[2] explains just how they are exploited. Two things are being attempted: first, to collect aggregative data on the general movement of population from year to year; and second, to reconstitute families in parishes where the quality of the registers permits it and so to achieve the more detailed demographic analysis that will show the mortality by age, the age at marriage, and above all the fertility levels. Since 1958, when Gautier and Henry published their study of Crulai, a village in Normandy,[3] it has been realized that family reconstitution, or tracing a complete family's vital history from the parish register, is often possible. Although family reconstitution can be done for only a small proportion of the parish's population, the results may be close to the average for the whole, at least if the register is well kept and there is not too much migration. A sample of parishes from the whole of France for the ancien régime has been selected, and many workers are now devoting several years to collecting and analysing the material

[1] *Történeti statisztikai évkönyv*, 1960, 1961–2, 1963–4.

[2] M. Fleury and L. Henry, *Nouveau manuel de dépouillement et d'exploitation de l'état civil ancien*, Paris, 1965. This is a revised version of a manual by the same authors published in 1956.

[3] E. Gautier and L. Henry, *La population de Crulai, paroisse normande. Étude historique*, Paris, 1958.

from these sample parishes. Reports from separate parishes appear frequently, and are usually described briefly in the French demographic periodical, *Population*. The American quarterly, *Population Index*, also lists most of such published studies as they appear.

It must be admitted that the recent stimulus towards historical demography in England has come directly from the French work mentioned above. A Group for the History of Population and Social Structure has been set up at Cambridge and has organized a similar sample survey of the English parishes. The first reconstituted parish has been in Colyton, in Devon, which was studied by Wrigley.[1] The publications of the Cambridge group[2] so far are chiefly intended to foster interest in the question rather than to be definitive works, and they have succeeded admirably. Family reconstitution by computer is an important goal of the group and, with the help of N. S. M. Cox of Newcastle University, it seems within their grasp.

The *Annales de Démographie Historique* describe the latest advances in most countries, but in particular Kula[3] has also given an exposition of the state of Polish historical demography and Pascu[4] has described the prospects for Rumania. Almost all European countries are now producing studies at an increasing rate, and the Czechoslovak Academy of Sciences has organized a Commission for Historical Demography that

[1] E. A. Wrigley, 'Family Limitation in Pre-Industrial England', *Economic History Review*, Second Series, **19**, 1 (April 1966), pp. 82–109, and 'Mortality in Pre-Industrial England: The Example of Colyton, Devon, Over Three Centuries', *Daedalus* (Spring 1968), pp. 546–80.

[2] *An Introduction to English Historical Demography from the Sixteenth to the Nineteenth Century* (edited by E. A. Wrigley), London, 1966; P. Laslett, *The World we have Lost*, London, 1965.

[3] W. Kula, 'Stan i potrzeby badán nad demografją historyczną dawnej Polski (do początków XIX wieku)', *Roczniki dziejów społecznych i gospodarczych*, **13** (1951), pp. 23–106, and summary in French.

[4] S. Pascu, 'Les sources et les recherches démographiques en Roumanie (Période prestatistique)', *Actes du Colloque international de démographie historique*, Liège (April 1963), pp. 283–303.

has begun to produce a periodical, *Historická Demografie*. The actual sources of Italian historical demography were listed voluminously thirty years ago, covering (including an index and a bibliography) more than 4,000 pages of print.[1] Although such things as the dates covered by each parish register are given, little use has been made of this formidable basis for research. Slicher van Bath[2] has edited a list of 1,095 Dutch sources more recently.

There have been numerous attempts to state the sources, methods, and problems of historical demography. Génicot's work has already been mentioned; Bourdon[3] had earlier emphasized that the data are usually incomplete, and that we require a knowledge of the background in order to interpret the demographic data, and Simiand[4] had suggested what work could be done in the 1930's; but in the last century Daszynska[5] merely described the sources and how the simpler calculations were made. Howells, however, has recently written a useful article on archaeological methods,[6] and Cicotti's long critique of our knowledge

[1] Comitato italiano per lo studio dei problemi della popolazione, commissione di demografia storica, *Fonti archivistiche per lo studio dei problemi della popolazione fino al 1848. Presentate al Congresso Internazionale per gli Studi sulla Popolazione, Roma 7–10 settembre 1931–ix*, Rome, 1933; also *ibid.*, serie II, 1935–41.

[2] B. H. Slicher van Bath, *Voorlopige systematische bibliografie van de Nederlandse demografische geschiedenis*, Wageningen, 1962.

[3] J. Bourdon, 'Les méthodes de la démographie historique', *Bulletin of the VIIth International Congress of Historical Sciences*, 5, 3, Warsaw (July 1933), pp. 588–95.

[4] F. Simiand, 'Des possibilités des recherches statistiques historiques', *Bulletin de l'Institut International de Statistique* (Tokyo), 25, 3 (1930), pp. 818–34; 'Recherches statistiques historiques', *ibid.* (Madrid), 26, 2 (1931), pp. 673–94; and 'Tâches envisagées et tâches à envisager par la commission des recherches statistiques historiques', *ibid.* (London), 28, 2 (1934), pp. 490–5.

[5] Z. Daszynska, 'Stoff und Methode der historischen Bevölkerungsstatistik', *Jahrbücher fur Nationalökonomie und Statistik*, 66 (1896), pp. 481–506.

[6] W. W. Howells, 'Estimating Population Numbers through Archaeological and Skeletal Remains', in *The Application of Quantitative Methods in Archaeology* (edited by R. F. Heizer and S. F. Cook) (Viking Fund Publications in Anthropology: No. 28), 1960, pp. 158–76.

of the demography of the ancient world[1] seems still largely just. However, most works are accounts for the general reader of what happened in the past, with little attempt to explain why we believe particular results. They are romances, and not detective stories, as it were. Perhaps the best summary of population history is that of Kirsten, Buchholz, and Köllmann.[2] They give all the chief findings together with 185 maps, and are an invaluable source to the general historian. The references are, however, only given as a bibliography, so that it is not possible to tell what authority any particular statement has. They presumably drew on the German tradition of Behm and Wagner, and later Supan, who published several accounts of 'Die Bevölkerung der Erde' in *Petermanns Mitteilungen* before 1914. This essentially geographical and political approach to population trends contrasts with the more mathematical and theoretical French approach and the rather sporadic English empiricism. The same detailed factual care can be found in Dieterici,[3] even earlier than Behm and Wagner.

Ohlin has written a good short account of world population growth,[4] but between the well-presented facts of the Germans and the dry epitome of the Swede must be placed Reinhard, Armengaud, and Dupâquier's *General History of World Population*,[5] which attempts, like the present work, to cover several

---

[1] E. Cicotti, 'Indivizzi e metodi negli studi di demografia antica', in *Bibliotheca di storica economica* (edited by V. Pareto), Milan (1909), IV, pp. vii–ciii; *idem*, 'Motivi demografici e biologici nella rovina della civiltà antica', *Nuova Rivista Storica*, 14, 1–2 (January–April 1930), pp. 29–62.

[2] E. Kirsten, E. W. Buchholz, and W. Köllmann, *Raum und Bevölkerung in der Weltgeschichte*, Würzburg, 1955–6 and later editions.

[3] See, for example, K. F. W. Dieterici, Über die Vermehrung der Bevölkerung in Europa seit dem Ende oder der Mitte des siebenzehnten Jahrhunderts, *Abhandlungen der Königlichen Akademie der Wissenschaften zu Berlin* (1850), Philologische und historische Abhandlungen, pp. 73–115.

[4] G. Ohlin, 'Historical Outline of World Population Growth', *World Population Conference*, Belgrade, 1965; Background paper, general, No. 486.

[5] M. Reinhard, A. Armengaud, and J. Dupâquier, *Histoire Générale de la population mondiale*, Paris, 1968. This replaces the earlier work (Paris, 1961) of the same title by the two first authors.

interests at the same time. It does not give all the detailed figures, but concentrates on the main problems in the different epochs and how far we have solved them. It is therefore very useful to a demographer who wants to begin a piece of historical research, but not to a historian who wants a ready reference book of facts.

Some mention must be made here also of the remarkable endeavours of Russell.[1] As indefatigable as Mols in collecting material (for example, he has even used the size of families that were murdered in thirteenth-century England[2] as a basis for a demographic argument), he is more reckless than the Jesuit in his attempts to squeeze as much as possible out of what he has found. Russell is, in fact, a pioneer more than anyone previously mentioned, except Graunt, and must be expected to make mistakes. The controversy surrounding his figure of 3·5 persons per hearth in a typical medieval household has left him in a small minority that does not generally prefer a larger figure; his insistence that $1\frac{1}{2}$ per cent of an ancient or medieval economic unit's population would normally live in the local metropolis will, in time, cause him more trouble. On the matter of the relationship between area and population in an old city, Russell has also put forward a definite view while others have sat quiet: 110 persons per hectare, he claims,[3] would be the average, and any evidence leading to a much higher result can be rejected as false. This, too, will cause more controversy yet. Russell's chief virtue, in fact, is that he gives others something to refute. All his figures may be altered eventually, but the debt to him will remain.

A few special studies of recent years should be mentioned in

[1] J. C. Russell, *op. cit.* on p. 52 above (footnote 1), and *Late Ancient and Medieval Population*, comprising *Transactions of the American Philosophical Society*, New Series, **48**, 3 (1958), are his two major works; he has also published many articles on points of historical demography.

[2] *Late Ancient and Medieval Population*, pp. 15–16.

[3] *Ibid.*, p. 63.

this brief survey because of their varied approach. Goubert has written the best account of the whole life of a community (Beauvais) that is based upon demographic research.[1] His linking of parish register and nominative list data with data on taxes, accounts, prices, laws, charters, and so on can be taken as a model for other studies. The linking together of varied sources over a wide area to produce a conclusion on a single point requires a similar degree of attention, and Franz[2] has succeeded in writing the definitive book on the population aspects of the Thirty Years War in Germany. A large number of local dissertations and other studies enabled him, at last, to draw a map of the population decline over the whole Holy Roman Empire between 1618 and 1648. A similar synthesis has not been achieved elsewhere as yet for any epoch or country.

Beloch's work on ancient population[3] is still often cited, but really needs to be brought up to date. Frank,[4] Lot,[5] Cicotti,[6] Russell,[7] and others have queried or amended parts of Beloch's work, and no doubt a new edition will appear eventually.

Ho Ping-ti, although scarcely a demographer, had the immense advantage of being able to read rapidly the relevant parts of the many Chinese provincial histories that are in print. More than 3,000 of them are available, even outside China, and Ho[8] was able to make the first major advance in Western understanding of Chinese population history since the time of Biot, 120 years

[1] P. Goubert, *Beauvais et le Beauvaisis de 1600 à 1730, contribution à l'histoire sociale de la France du XVIIe siècle*, Paris, 1960.

[2] G. Franz, *Der dreissigjährige Krieg und das deutsche Volk: Untersuchungen zur Bevölkerungs- und Agrargeschichte*, Stuttgart, 1961.

[3] K. J. Beloch, *Die Bevölkerung der griechisch-römischen Welt*, Leipzig, 1886.

[4] T. Frank, 'Roman Census Statistics from 225 to 28 B.C., *Classical Philology* **19**, (1924), pp. 329–41.

[5] F. Lot, *La fin du monde antique et le début du moyen âge*, Paris 1927.

[6] *Loc. cit.*, above on p. 57 (footnote 1).

[7] *Loc. cit.*, opposite (1958).

[8] Ho Ping-ti, *Studies on the Population of China, 1368–1953*, Cambridge, Mass., 1959.

before.[1] There is still much that is speculative, but at least we need no longer wonder what, for example, the Chinese term 'ting' really means.[2]

Genealogy-based demographic studies have their special interest, since the data are usually relatively complete. The Genevan bourgeoisie[3] were a very tightly-knit unit, so that neither marriage outside nor emigration was common. The British aristocracy[4] intermarried less, with corresponding difficulties of tracing people. However, in the British study, it proved possible to make an assessment of the under-enumeration of children dying in infancy, which showed that large numbers of them were not mentioned before about 1770, and the true infant mortality was much higher than it seemed; fertility, too, was of course higher. Henripin[5] has made a study of French Canada in the early eighteenth century from a genealogy, but he did not cover nearly as long a time-span as his sources would have permitted.

[1] E. Biot, 'Sur la population de la Chine et ses variations, depuis l'an 2400 avant J. C. jusqu' au XIIIe siècle de notre ère', *Journal Asiatique*, Serie 3, Vol. I, (April 1836), pp. 369–94 and (May 1836), pp. 448–74; 'Addition au Mémoire sur la population de la Chine et ses variations'), *ibid.*, Vol. II (July 1836), pp. 74–8; and 'Mémoire sur les recensements des termes consignés dans l'histoire chinoise et l'usage qu'on en peut faire pour évaluer la population totale de la Chine', *ibid.*, Vol. V (April 1838), pp. 305–31.

[2] See also Ch'ü T'ung-tsu, *Local Government in China under the Ch'ing*, Cambridge, Mass., 1962, assessment of the efficiency of Chinese census-taking is: I. B. Taeuber and Nai-Chi Wang, 'Population reports in the Ch'ing dynasty', *Journal of Asian Studies*, **19**, 4 (August 1960), pp. 403–17.

[3] L. Henry, *Anciennes familles genevoises—Etude démographique: XVIe–XXe siecle*, Paris, 1956.

[4] T. H. Hollingsworth, 'A Demographic Study of the British Ducal Families', *Population Studies*, XI, 1 (July 1957), pp. 4–26, and reprinted with revision in *Population in History* (edited by D. V. Glass and D. E. C. Eversley), London, 1965; *The Demography of the British Peerage*, London, 1965. (Supplement to *Population Studies*, XVIII, 2, November 1964); 'The Demographic Background of the Peerage, 1603–1938', *The Eugenics Review*, **57**, 2 (June 1965), pp. 56–66.

[5] J. Henripin, *La population canadienne au début du XVIIIe siècle. Nuptialité-fecondité-mortalité infantile*, Paris, 1954.

Finally, Glass and Eversley have published[1] a set of twenty-seven assorted articles on historical demography. It is a book that saves a few old pieces of work from undeserved neglect and gives a general impression of where the present activity in historical demography lies. There is a distinct eighteenth-century bias: only two of the twenty-seven articles have nothing to say about that century. At the same time, only one has anything to say about population before 1500, and only one is not wholly about Northern or Western Europe. These limitations, of course, reflect both the current interests of scholars and the difficulties of doing very much with the data from other places and times.

In the following chapters, we shall be considering the literature in more detail. Our approach is primarily via the sources, discussing the various analyses that can be made from each, and occasionally suggesting criticisms or improvements.

[1] *Op. cit.* opposite (footnote 4).

CHAPTER 3

Population Counts

Written information is naturally the chief source for demographic analysis, and in this and the next four chapters we describe and discuss the various written sources, classified by type rather than by country or historical period. In this chapter we consider actual counts of population, including both official censuses and other counts that approximated to a census. It might be thought that there is little to say beyond listing what counts are available, to what places they refer, and at what periods. That would be a formidable task in itself, but the credibility of these censuses needs to be decided first. There are alleged censuses of population in the past that are now regarded as nothing of the kind, and how we determine a count's credibility needs some consideration. The main concern is with what can be done with the less credible data, and with the general question of what demographic analysis is possible from a census.

The earliest census counts are those of China, which go back to the second millennium B.C.[1] It is difficult to attach much weight to these early figures; Durand[2] and most other students of Chinese

[1] See E. Biot, 'Sur la population de la Chine et ses variations, depuis l'an 2400 avant J. C. jusqu'au XIIIe siècle de nôtre ère', *Journal Asiatique*, Série 3, Vol. I (April 1836), pp. 369–94 and (May 1836), pp. 448–74; 'Addition au Mémoire sur la population de la Chine et ses Variations', *ibid.*, Vol. II (July 1836), pp. 74–8; and 'Mémoire sur les recensements des termes consignés dans l'histoire chinoise et l'usage qu'on en peut faire pour évaluer la population totale de la Chine', *ibid.*, Vol. V (April 1838), pp. 305–31. The poor state of the records is also pointed out in H. Bielenstein, 'The Census of China during the Period 2–742 A.D.' *Bulletin of the Museum of Far Eastern Antiquities*, 19 (1947), pp. 125–63.

[2] J. D. Durand, 'The Population Statistics of China, A.D. 2–1953', *Population Studies*, XIII, 3 (March 1960), pp. 209–56.

historical demography make the first tolerably accurate census of the Chinese empire the one that was taken in the year A.D. 2, under the Han dynasty. Those under two years of age were normally omitted by the Chinese census-takers, which would amount to 6 or 8 per cent of the total population if the age were calculated in the Western fashion. However, ages in China are traditionally calculated by counting 'one' as soon as the child is born, and 'two' the next New Year's Day, so the fraction omitted would be much smaller than at first it might appear. The old Chinese population figures, which presumably were copied and re-copied by scribes many times, occasionally seem to be mere fabrications, annual figures in Ming times sometimes only differing in a single digit. Such frauds, however, are easily noticed.

The question of who was counted is more serious. It seemed to Ma Tuan-lin (Biot's source) that slaves were normally few in ancient China and were never counted at a census. This was true, for example, at the census of 755, although 15 per cent of the population were free but untaxable. Slaves might be numerous, however, in the aftermath of civil strife, when many sections of the people would have to undergo a period of servitude as a punishment for their revolt. Some years after a foreign (or factional) conquest, the apparent population would shoot up owing to the inclusion of freed slaves. The period A.D. 270–80 provides an example of this process.

The writ of the emperor of China never ran throughout his ostensible dominions. There were often refugees in the mountains, perhaps carrying on a guerrilla war against the government, and they might be joined by a variable number of dissidents according to the economic and political conditions of the time. In the years A.D. 170–200, for instance, the Yellow Bonnets (as they called themselves) devastated much of China. On the frontiers of the Empire and beyond, there might also be Chinese living outside the ken of the officials who took the (*de jure*) censuses.

Households were an imprecise term in ancient China, it seems, because the retainers of powerful families might not be counted as separate families. About A.D. 600, under the Sui dynasty, many of these retainers founded separate family units, disturbing the nation-wide population figures markedly.

This is still not the whole story. As well as slaves, the ruling classes in China were exempt from the census in the ordinary way—reminiscent of the modern English law that denies the franchise to peers and lunatics. Furthermore, it might have been possible to suborn an official of the Celestial Kingdom so that he would omit one's family from his list. Under the Sui, 2 million people were needed every month for public works; if these each did two months' service per year, 12 million males aged between 22 and 60 must have been available, giving a population of at least 50 million—or substantially more than the census (46 million in A.D. 606).

There was little pretence of scholarly interest in the numbers of the sons of Han; the emperor was interested in revenue, and there was no change of attitude until the Ch'ing dynasty. The Chinese census gives us, through the double series for 'doors' and 'mouths', an estimate of the average size of a Chinese household at each period when a census was taken. The figure is incredible at certain epochs, since the average household size for the whole of China can hardly have really fallen below two persons at any time, which casts grave doubt on the credibility of the Chinese census altogether. However, a fragment of a Chinese census, taken in the spring of A.D. 416 and found by Giles,[1] throws some direct light on Chinese census practice. It appears that, in normal conditions, a complete count really was expected to be made; thirty-eight people are listed in Giles' fragment by age and sex, and the pity is that we do not have a full census of a province or two to analyse by modern methods.[2]

[1] L. Giles, 'A Census of Tun-huang', *T'oung Pao*, **16** (1915), pp. 468–88.

[2] Research on Chinese population that might have been done but for the Chinese Revolution of 1949 is given in Ta Chen, 'The Need of Population

Historical Demography

Various early Israelite counts are mentioned in the Bible.[1]
These seem to have been chiefly counts of men of fighting age,
but the totals are startlingly large: in the time of Joshua (about
1491 B.C.) the population would have to have been about $2\frac{1}{2}$
million; in the time of David (1017 B.C.) 5 million; while in the
time of Jehoshophat (say, 885 B.C.) the population of Judah alone
would be at least 5 million. The last figure, moreover, is based
on the size of the army, which tends to be smaller than the number of men of fighting age.

We should give some consideration to how reasonable these
figures are. We may be inclined to think that the population
must always have been less than it is now, but a 'land flowing with
milk and honey' might have existed in the Near East before
soil erosion turned most of it to scrub and desert. To assume that
the only figures we have are exaggerated because they make out
the past to have been more populous than the present prevents
research from ever bearing fruit.[2]

A fragment has been found from a census of the seventh

Research in China', *Population Studies*, I, 4 (March 1948), pp. 342–52. Further
comments on the historical censuses of China are given in: *idem, Population
in Modern China*, supplement to *American Journal of Sociology*, LII, 1 (July 1946);
A. J. Jaffe, 'A review of the censuses and demographic statistics of China',
Population Studies, I, 3 (1947), pp. 308–37; and Ho Ping-ti, *Studies on the Population of China, 1368–1953*, Cambridge, Mass., 1959.

[1] Exodus XXXVIII, 26; Numbers XXVI; 2 Samuel XXIV; 1 Chronicles
XXI and XXVI.
[2] R. Zimmermann, 'Bevölkerungsdichte und Heereszahlen in Alt-Palästina',
Klio, **21**, 3–4 (1927), pp. 340–3, believed that the population must have been
small, and cites Judges V, 8, as evidence that the army of Israel was only 40,000.
This might, however, be merely the number of men who fought with shields
and spears, not the whole adult male population. Moreover, Judges V, 30,
hints that there were more women than men.
See also C. C. McCown, 'The Density of Population in ancient Palestine',
Journal of Biblical Literature, **66** (1947), pp. 425–36, who deflates Josephus' figures
of 10 or 12 million to less than 1 million for the early Roman period on the
grounds of the nineteenth- and twentieth-century economic geography of
the area.

century B.C. in a district of the kingdom of Nineveh.[1] It covers only 269 people, but seems fairly complete (there are 60 children per 100 adults, for instance, which suggests a birth-rate of about 40 per thousand per annum). The social structure of the community, however, is very strange: (1) 8 men have no wife, 34 have 1 wife each, 15 have 2 wives each, and 7 have 3 or more wives each; (2) there are 75 boys and only 26 girls in the entire population. A possible explanation would be that the girls married very young in Assyro-Babylonian society, at about 10 years of age, perhaps; but the boys stayed at home until they married, at the age of 30 or more. It is more likely that this locality was not typical, or that the census was incomplete.

The Romans have given demography the very word 'census'. The Roman census was instituted in the sixth century B.C. and continued up to the time of Vespasian.[2] There are several riddles about the Roman census; incredible as it may seem, there is still uncertainty whether women were included or not. If women were included, there is also debate whether they were included from the beginning or only at some later date. The most plausible theory is that they were added to the census about the time of Sulla (shortly before 69 B.C.), but there is no evidence for it except a sudden jump in the census figures.

There are figures at six-year intervals for most of the last 200 years of the Roman republic, but they became spasmodic about the time of Caesar and stop altogether in the time of Nero, which is exasperating because that is precisely the time when Rome became extremely important. However, the explanation of the absence of further data is probably not unrelated, for it is

[1] M. Cappieri, 'Uno dei più antichi censimenti', *Rivista italiana di economia demografia e statistica*, **16**, 3–4 (July–December 1962), pp. 163–78.

[2] T. Frank, 'Roman Census Statistics from 225 to 28 B.C.', *Classical Philology*, **19** (1924), pp. 329–41, discusses the interpretation of the Roman census. For a history of censuses before the first census of the United States of America, which particularly discusses the Roman census, see A. B. Wolfe, 'Population Censuses Before 1790', *Journal of the American Statistical Association*, **27**, 180 (December 1932), pp. 357-70.

much more difficult to take a census of a whole empire than of just one city and its surroundings. On the basis of the Roman figures and his background of classical knowledge, Beloch gave the population of Italy in A.D. 14 as 6 million;[1] Frank, doing the same, made it 14 million.[2]

Several pieces of papyrus have been found that refer to Roman censuses in Egypt,[3] comprising mainly the period A.D. 34–A.D. 258. Mean household size appears to have been large (5·9), partly because 11 per cent of the population were slaves and partly because there was apparently a high birth-rate and a high mortality rate in the teen-ages. Wallace[4] has argued that there was a regular series of Egyptian censuses every fourteen years going back to 219 B.C. The Romans, in fact, apparently took over the Ptolemaean system.

Although the Incas in Peru are said to have taken censuses, there are no records in Europe between antiquity and the Renaissance that one can properly call a census. The practice then began in certain European cities of having an occasional enumeration. Amongst the best known are Venice, Florence, Rome, Augsburg and London.[5] Pisa had a complete listing of its inhabitants by age in 1428–9.[6] If net migration could be disregarded the birth-rate of Pisa could be estimated from the age-distribution, and a cursory study suggests that the birth-rate was very high. (See Appendix 1.)

The counts were irregular and rather infrequent; moreover,

[1] K. J. Beloch. *Die Bevölkerung der griechisch-römischen Welt*, Leipzig, 1886.

[2] *Loc. cit.*, above on p. 69 (footnote 2).

[3] M. Hombert and C. Préaux, *Recherches sur le recensement dans l'Egypte romaine*, Leyden (Papyrologica Lugduno-Batava, V), 1952.

[4] S. L. Wallace, 'Census and Poll-Tax under the Ptolemies', *American Journal of Philology*, **59**, 236 (1938), pp. 418–42.

[5] W. McMurray, 'London: its Population in 1631', *Notes and Queries*, 11th Series, **1** (28 May 1910), p. 246, notes a special London census of 1631, giving 71,029 mouths within the walls and 59,239 in the Liberties; Dale lists the very householders seven years later by name. See T. C. Dale, *The Inhabitants of London in 1638*, London, 1931.

[6] B. Casini, *Il Catasto di Pisa del 1428–29*, Pisa, 1964.

they were often wrong. Biraben[1] mentions two censuses of Rheims in 1482 and 1500, where about 15 per cent of the population were classed as 'poor' and left out. As we have seen, regular counts at intervals of not more than ten years require a trained staff of census-takers, which in turn means that the census will be fairly accurate. Doing it in the occasional manner of Renaissance Europe is much more hazardous, and there must be many errors in the figures as compiled. There was great reluctance to publish the results in some towns, since it was held to be a political advantage to your potential enemies if they knew your population. There are also so-called 'censuses' of Castile[2] in the sixteenth century, but their true value is uncertain.

Sicily[3] had a census in 1653 that yielded a population of 873,742, divided among 285 towns. This figure agrees so closely with later information that we cannot improve upon it, but that is only because no further count was made for a long time afterwards.

The 1659 census of Ireland[4] seems, on the surface, very exact. Every hamlet is mentioned, except in a few counties where all the returns, if any, are now lost. On the basis of this count the total population of Ireland in 1659 was put by Hardinge in 1865[5] at 500,091; but two months later, he[6] was saying how well

---

[1] J. N. Biraben, 'La population de Reims et de son arrondissement, et la vérification statistique des recensement numériques anciens', *Population*, **16**, 4 (1961), pp. 722–30.

[2] See J. Nadal, *La población española: siglos XVI a XX*, Barcelona, 1966.

[3] J. Goodwin, 'Progress of the Two Sicilies under the Spanish Bourbons, from the year 1734–35 to 1840', *Journal of the Statistical Society*, **5**, 1 (April 1842), pp. 47–73.

[4] S. Pender, *A Census of Ireland circa 1659, with supplementary material from the Poll Money ordinances 1660–1661*, Dublin, 1939.

[5] W. H. Hardinge, 'Observations on the earliest known Manuscript Census Returns of the People of Ireland', *Transactions of the Royal Irish Academy*, **24**, Part 3 (Antiquities) (1874), pp. 317–28.

[6] *Idem.*, 'On an Unpublished Essay on Ireland, by Sir W. Petty, A.D. 1687', *Transactions of the Royal Irish Academy*, **24**, Part 3 (Antiquities) (1874), pp. 371–7. This paper was actually read on 8 May 1865; the previous one was read on 16 March.

Petty's 1687 estimate of 1,300,000 agreed with the figure of 900,000 [*sic*] for 1659. In fact, Connell[1] puts the 1687 population at 2,167,000, so that we are reduced to the hypothesis that the 1659 figure may have been hearths or adults or males, and not the actual population. Once we begin to shift our ground in such a way, we are in grave danger of altering the data to suit our prejudices. It seems best to regard the 1659 census as worthless. Perhaps that is why it received little notice for 200 years.

Quebec had a proper census as early as 1665, and several more in the years following,[2] and so can claim to be the first country in modern times to institute a regular census system; but Europe's beginning was sporadic. Norway had a census of sorts of the male population in 1664–6[3] and in 1701, while Iceland[4] had a good census in 1703. What amounted to a census was carried out in Bohemia in 1702,[5] when the Government made a survey of all consumers of salt in preparation for a salt-tax. This reminds one of the preliminary survey for the English Marriage Duty that was apparently made in 1694–5, but in Bohemia the total figures are extant. There was, apparently, no particular intention to count the population, and for fifty years afterwards there was no repetition of a census.

Sweden was the first country in Europe in modern times to institute a regular system of census-taking. Indeed, in 1749 the Swedes not only began their censuses, but began vital registration as well. It is interesting that it coincides with the time that the

[1] K. H. Connell, *The Population of Ireland, 1750–1845*, Oxford, 1950.

[2] H. Charbonneau, 'Tricentenaire du premier recensement canadien', *Population*, **21**, 6 (November–December 1966), pp. 1211–15; Charbonneau and J. Légaré, 'La population du Canada aux recensements de 1666 et 1667', *Population*, **22**, 6 (November–December 1967), pp. 1031–54.

[3] K. Ofstad, 'Population Statistics and Population Registration in Norway. Part 3. Population Censuses', *Population Studies*, III, 1 (1949), pp. 66–75.

[4] L. Henry, 'La population de l'Islande en 1703', *Population*, **16**, 1 (1961), pp. 122–3.

[5] F. Gabriel, 'Lidnatost čech na počátky 18. století', *Demografie*, **9**, 3 (1967), pp. 241–9, and 4, pp. 343–9.

emperor Ch'ien-lung asked for the true population of China to be returned in the records. Prior to that, it would seem that out of fear (justifiably) of higher taxes, all districts of China understated their population. A jump of 20 per cent in a single year occurred in the apparent figures—leading Willcox into thinking that the earlier data were right and the later wrong.[1] Supan,[2] too, reduced the population for the later-eighteenth century and Ta Chen has approved of his adjustments.[3]

Following the Swedish lead, in 1754 Austria,[4] and in 1769 Norway[5] and Denmark took censuses, but the Austrian census was not kept going regularly. Finland, under the same régime as Sweden, had early censuses, but in Great Britain the Bill laid before Parliament in 1753 to take a census was defeated, Mr Thornton (M.P. for the city of York) saying of it in the House of Commons: 'I hold this project to be totally subversive of the last remains of English liberty', and much more in the same vein.[6] Hungary had a 'List of Souls'[7] in 1777, but seven counties were missing and the first complete population census was in 1784–7.[8] There was no regularity about the early Hungarian censuses, and Spain's three late-eighteenth-century censuses, too, were followed

[1] W. F. Willcox, 'A westerner's effort to estimate the population of China and its increase since 1650', *Bulletin de l'Institut International de Statistique*, **25**, 1 (Tokyo) (1930), pp. 156–70.

[2] A. Supan, 'Die Bevölkerung der Erde' No. XI, especially pp. 41–51, in *Petermanns Mitteilungen*, **29**, 135 (1901).

[3] Ta Chen, *Population in Modern China*, supplement to *American Journal o, Sociology*, LII, 1. (July 1946).

[4] S. Peller, 'Zur Kenntnis der städtischen Mortalität im 18. Jahrhundert mit besonderer Berücksichtigung der Säuglings- und Tuberkulosesterblichkeit', *Zeitschrift für Hygiene und Infektionskrankheiten*, **90**, (1920) pp. 227–62.

[5] Ofstad, *loc. cit.* above on p. 72 (footnote 3).

[6] Census of 1881, *General Report*, Vol. iv, p. 1.

[7] D. Danyi, 'Az 1777, Évi Lelkek Összeirása', *Történeti Statisztikai Évkönyv* (1960), pp. 167–77.

[8] J. Tamásy, 'Az 1784–1787, évi elsö magyarországi népszámlálás család- es háztartásstatisztikai vonatkozásai', *Demográfia*, **6**, 4 (1963), pp. 526–37, and summary in English.

by a sixty-year hiatus.[1] The first British census was actually taken in 1801, and the system of civil registration began in 1837 (England and Wales; 1855, Scotland). By that time the United States of America, moved by the political consideration of allocating representation in Congress to the different states, had begun its system of censuses (1790). France and Prussia were early on the European scene and some German states had a proper census and registration system before 1800.[2] As the nineteenth century drew on, practically all of Europe, but only a few other parts of the world, began the regular practice of census-taking. Coverage improved and the variety of questions increased. Russia[3] had a census of a kind in 1719 and another in 1857. The first real Russian census, however, was in 1897.

For practically the whole of Africa there are no actual counts of population earlier than 1900. Indian censuses began formally in 1872, but the Indian census figures for total population became reliable only in 1921. As we shall see, most of the mid-nineteenth-century estimates of Indian population were well below the truth.

Australia, Canada and New Zealand, as one might expect, are very well recorded, but these countries' histories begin late in time and they are not very populous. The population of Guadeloupe was counted in 1671, 1730, 1767, 1790 and 1848,[4] but Latin America had little by way of a census before 1900, although Brazil's population in the past may be studied through contemporary accounts. Alden[5] surveys the sources between 1753

[1] See M. Livi Bacci, 'Fertility and Nuptiality Changes in Spain from the late-18th to the early 20th Century' (Part I), *Population Studies*, XXII, 1 (March 1968), pp. 83–102.

[2] K. Kisskalt, 'Die Sterblichkeit im 18. Jahrhundert', *Zeitschrift für Hygiene und Infektionskrankheiten*, **93** (1921), pp. 438–511.

[3] M. Reinhard, 'La population de la Russie au XVIIIe siècle et dans la première moitié du XIXe', *Études et chronique de démographie historique* (1964), pp. 178–83. (A review of the work of V. M. Kabuzan.)

[4] G. Lasserre, *La Guadeloupe, étude géographique*, Bordeaux, 1961.

[5] D. Alden, 'The population of Brazil in the late eighteenth century: a preliminary study', *Hispanic American Historical Review*, **43**, 2 (May 1963), pp. 173–205.

and 1818; Higgins[1] gave 3·2 million as the population in 1806; Heywood[2] estimated the whole population of Brazil in 1860 at $7\frac{1}{2}$ million, including aborigines, with slaves as 3 million of the total.

The Dutch records of Java from 1803 onwards make a fascinating story. An island the size of Ireland and about as populous then as present-day Ireland was found to have a high birth-rate (about 40 per thousand) and a remarkably low death-rate (about 17 per thousand),[3] but no one could have dreamt that Java would ever contain over 60 million people, as it actually does today. One can imagine that Malthus, who was writing at the time, would have used Java as an example of what would happen if human numbers were unchecked had he known of the Javanese demographic potential. Nevertheless, one must agree with Malthus in the long run. The check to population in Java cannot now be far off.

Java's extraordinary population growth since 1800 has also excited many modern studies.[4] Breman[5] pointed out that the data are in fact bad, however, and argued that the 4 million usually allowed for Java and Madura in 1800 ought to be replaced by a more probable 6 million, with smaller increases later in the

[1] W. M. Higgins, 'General Descriptive Atlas of the Earth, etc.', London, 1835.

[2] J. Heywood 'Resources of Brazil', *Journal of the Statistical Society*, **27**, 2 (June 1864), pp. 245–57. M. Haushofer, in *Lehr- und Handbuch der Statistik in ihrer neuesten wissenschaftlichen Entwickelung* (Vienna, 1872), gave 11·28 million, however, as the population of Brazil.

[3] J. Crawfurd, 'Vital Statistics of a District in Java; with preliminary remarks upon the Dutch Possessions in the East, by Colonel Sykes', *Journal of the Statistical Society*, **12** (1849), pp. 60–71.

[4] See E. de Vries, 'Historical evidence concerning the effect of population pressure and growth of technical progress in agriculture', *World Population Conference*, Belgrade, 1965, session A.7, No. 269.

[5] J. C. Breman, 'Java: bevolkingsgroei en demografische structuur', *Tijdschrift van het Koninklijk Nederlandsch Aardrijskiedig Genootschap*, 2 Ser. **80** (July 1963). pp. 252–308.

nineteenth century. Van der Kroef,[1] representing the earlier opinions, believed that the period of most rapid growth was 1815–90, during which years the population multiplied 5·2 times.

Japan, as always, is an exception. From 1721 onwards, there are very exact figures of the taxable classes. About 10 per cent—so it is thought[2]—must be added to the figures of these Tokugawa censuses between 1721 and 1861 to allow for the classes not taxed. The picture here is of a stable population, one of the very few pre-industrial stable populations that is well documented, but even this stability evidently masks great changes in the geographical distribution of population within Japan.[3]

It will be seen from this brief survey that until fairly recent times there are few censuses and these are rather unreliable. Nevertheless, the student of history who is interested in population, no less than the historical demographer, should turn first to the census data, for they are the goal towards which all else aims. Even now, modern censuses are inaccurate; attempts are sometimes made to estimate underenumeration, but it is rarely better than 0·1 per cent and often closer to 1 per cent of the total figures. This, however, is only done at all in the countries where the completeness is high. For a number of countries even today it must be admitted that an accuracy of 10 per cent is about all that can be expected, while a few countries (Afghanistan, Ethiopia, and Outer Mongolia, for example) have still never taken a census in their history. Longstaff[4] has given

[1] J. M. van der Kroef, 'Population pressure and economic development in Indonesia', *American Journal of Economics and Sociology,* **12** (July 1953), pp. 335–71: reprinted in *Demographic Analysis: Selected Readings* (edited by J. J. Spengler and O. D. Duncan), Glencoe, Ill., 1956, pp. 739–54.

[2] R. Ishii, *Population Pressure and Economic Life in Japan,* London, 1937, p. 7. See also I. B. Taeuber, *The Population of Japan,* Princeton, 1958.

[3] See S. B. Hanley, 'Population Trends and Economic Development in Tokugawa Japan: The Case of Bizen Province in Okayama', *Daedalus* (Spring 1968). pp. 622–35.

[4] G. B. Longstaff, 'Suggestions for the census of 1891', *Journal of the Royal Statistical Society,* **52**, 3 (September 1889), pp. 436–57.

a concise summary of the early practice of census-taking.

The quality of a census is, of course, an essential consideration to anyone who tries to use its results, and the above facts about today are worth remembering when we are trying to assess the completeness of an earlier count. With the best will in the world, could they have got it right? It is rarely a copying error and not often a deliberate lie that we have to watch out for. The real enemy is human error. We should not expect a skilled job like counting people, especially if it was only done intermittently, to be very accurately done before the eighteenth century. What little expertise had been gained on one occasion would have been lost by the time it was to be done again.

Benjamin[1] has laid down the rule that the quality of a census depends on how aware the public are of its social purpose, and, while this is true enough, it works in two ways. In countries where the government is, broadly speaking trusted, a better informed public means a better census; but if the government is detested, the more the people know why they are to be counted the worse the results will be.

A major difficulty in interpreting old census data is to decide whether there was a full count—a real census, in fact—or a mere count of men liable for tax or military service, or a count of households. For example, Thomas Denton, the Recorder of Carlisle, made a survey of Cumberland in 1688, and his total of 67,185 might be thought fairly accurate. Yet every parish was given a population that was a multiple of 5, and Jones[2] suspected that Denton had really counted families and multiplied by 5. Preferring a multiplier of $4\frac{1}{2}$ to one of 5, Jones therefore adjusted the 1688 population downwards to a total of 60,466.

Sometimes it seems that wealth rather than people was the

[1] B. Benjamin, 'Quality of Response in Census Taking', *Population Studies*, VIII, 3 (March 1955), pp. 288–93.

[2] G. P. Jones, 'Some population problems relating to Cumberland and Westmorland in the eighteenth century', *Transactions of the Cumberland and Westmorland Antiquarian and Archaeological Society*, **58** (1959), pp. 123–39.

true basis of the count; sometimes only free citizens were counted and foreigners and slaves were omitted; sometimes children or women or both were apparently omitted; sometimes only the area under the direct control of the Government was included. These cases, in the absence of a specific statement on the basis of the count, are impossible to distinguish with confidence. Ancient Rome has been referred to already; at about the time of the second triumvirate, the population apparently multiplied by eight within twenty years. We can be sure that the basis of the count must have changed, but it is not certain for what precise reason the increase occurred. Possibly it was an extension of the city limits; possibly an extension of the count to women and children; possibly an extension to all citizens whether resident in Rome or not; possibly it included the slaves and foreigners resident in Rome; but all these factors acting together would increase the population much more than eight times, so that we have no real way of choosing which extensions to accept. To complicate matters further, the population was certainly increasing rapidly at that time, owing to the great increase in the power of the city as the Empire grew.

Similar difficulties over definitions of the population may have confronted the census-takers themselves. For example, a committee appointed in 1780 to enquire into the high price of grain at Bombay incidentally had a count made of the total population.[1] The results were classified according to socio-religious communities, and the total population of 47,170 was verisimilitudinous. However, it seemed short of the actual number of inhabitants, so the Vereadores were asked their opinion and they said that the district had at least 100,000 people. It is interesting that Edwardes, himself a census official, was inclined to accept the estimate and to reject the count. The total population of the island at that time, he therefore supposed, was nearly 114,000 and not 47,170. The higher figure agrees very well with counts

[1] S. M. Edwardes, *Census of India, 1901*, Vol. 10 (Bombay Town and Island), Part 4 (History), p. 7.

and estimates made at other times, and so in this instance a precise count of the city appears to have omitted two-thirds of the population, although no explanation of how it happened has been given. Apparently accurate counts evidently may simply omit all persons who are in any way difficult to find.

Even in the twentieth century[1] relatively few countries have fully complete census data; before about 1900, most of the world's population was uncounted and evidence about it is very uncertain. Before 1750, we only have a local census here and there, each taken in a different way, and for different areas and at widely separated dates. Such details as do emerge, however, whet the appetite to hunt for more. A village or small town[2] may give us a momentary picture of the ages, sexes, and family relationships of the community, which are quite as interesting as its mere size in total numbers.

There are not many rural censuses in Europe before the eighteenth century, except for very small areas such as parishes. There is thus little basis for generalization about social structure. Occasionally we may be lucky, as in the occupational census of Gloucestershire in 1608[3] where there were 21,758 men aged between 20 and 60, of whom 0·5 per cent were disabled and 10·3 per cent had no occupation. Of the rest, 46·2 per cent were in agriculture, 15·5 per cent in textiles, and so on. Since Bristol was excluded, the relatively industrial character of the county at such an early date is most striking.[4]

ENGLISH ECCLESIASTICAL CENSUSES

The earliest population counts that were more or less complete were often those taken by the clergy, and most of them that were

---

[1] Durand, 'Adequacy of Existing Census Statistics for Basic Demographic Research', *Population Studies*, IV, 2 (September 1950), pp. 179–99.

[2] K. J. Allison, 'An Elizabethan village "census",' *Bulletin of the Institute of Historical Research*, **36**, 94 (May 1963), pp. 91–103.

[3] A. J. Tawney and R. H. Tawney, 'An occupational Census of the Seventeenth Century', *Economic History Review*, **5** (1934–5), pp. 25–64.

[4] For further comment on this Gloucestershire census, see below, p. 82.

made in England are described below, beginning with the Chantry Certificates of 1547, when the parson and churchwardens of each parish were required to state the number of 'housling' people in the parish.[1] This probably meant the number of communicants, or roughly speaking the number of people over age 14.[2] The age at which communion was compulsory was later, however, fixed at 16.

A second English ecclesiastical count was taken in 1563 at the request of the Privy Council.[3] Families (or households), and not communicants, were the basis of the count this time. A third such enumeration, again of communicants, was the 1603 ecclesiastical census[4] when notice was also taken of recusants for the first time. It is not clear how many of the 1603 returns may still exist (several are in the British Museum, Harleian MSS 280, 594 and 595) but only eleven diocesan returns for 1563 remain. C. T. Smith has published all the 1563 and 1603 data for Leicestershire,[5] and Cornwall has published the 1563 figures for Buckinghamshire,[6] but these enumerations have not so far been much used.

The Protestation Return of 1641-2[7] was in effect a census of all males in the villages of England and Wales over 18 years of age. Some of the returns even give the occupations of the men. This was not a religious census, although it was made in connection with an oath to defend, *inter alia*, the 'true reformed Protestant religion'. A fourth religious census, however, was the so-called Compton census of 1676.[8] It covered only the Province of

---

[1] J. Thirsk, 'Sources of Information of Population, 1500-1760', *Amateur Historian*, 4, 4 and 5 (Summer and Autumn 1959), pp. 129-33 and 182-5.

[2] *Ibid.*

[3] *Ibid.*

[4] *Ibid.*

[5] In the *Victoria County History of Leicestershire*, Vol. III.

[6] J. E. Cornwall, 'An Elizabethan Census', *The Records of Buckinghamshire*, 16, 4 (1959), pp. 258-73.

[7] Thirsk, *loc. cit.* above (footnote 1).

[8] *Ibid.* See also: E. L. Guilford, 'Nottinghamshire in 1676', *Transactions of the Thornton Society*, 28 (1924), pp. 106-13; L. M. Marshall, *The Rural Population*

Canterbury and not that of York, as far as is known, and asked for the same information as in 1603; Nonconformists may (according to Chalkin)[1] have been deliberately understated. According to the returns for 15 parishes of the city of Canterbury itself, 5,054 people over 16 were enumerated, including only 28 papists, but as many as 2,097 Nonconformists. Forty-two per cent of the population of some 8,000 in the town that was the ecclesiastical capital of England were thus apparently outside the established church, even if there were no under-enumeration of Nonconformists. Data of this kind can shake us out of accepting the parish register data as good guides to population trends. Munby[2] also shows that although one-third of the population of Hertford were listed as dissenters in the Compton census, contemporary evidence suggested that the true figure was about a half. Towns generally seem to have contained most of the non-Anglicans, but in Nottingham[3] only about one person in seven was not in the Church of England. The Compton census, however, complete as it seems to have been, is still only available in manuscript except for a few publications of part of its results. The best MS seems to be the one in the Salt Library at Stafford.

Thirsk does not mention the communicants' list of 1688 or 1690 that Dalrymple[4] published. It covers only the Province of Canterbury, but does include Nonconformists and papists. Jones's work on Cumberland[5] and Laslett's and Harrison's on

of Bedfordshire, 1671 to 1921, Aspley Guise (Bedfordshire Historical Record Society, Vol. XVI), 1934; F. G. James, 'The Population of the Diocese of Carlisle in 1676', *Transactions of the Cumberland and Westmorland Antiquarian and Archaeological Society*, **51** (1952), pp. 137–41; C. W. Chalkin, 'The Compton census of 1676: the dioceses of Canterbury and Rochester', *Kent Records*, **17** (*A Seventeenth-Century Miscellany*) (1960), pp. 153–83.

---

[1] *Ibid.*

[2] L. Munby, *Hertfordshire Population Statistics 1563–1801*, Hitchin, 1964.

[3] Guilford, *loc cit.* opposite (footnote 8).

[4] Sir John Dalrymple, *Memoirs of Great Britain and Ireland. From the dissolution of the last Parliament of Charles II until the sea-battle off La Hogue*, Edinburgh and London, 1771–3. Vol. II, appendix, pp. 11–15.

[5] *Loc. cit.* above on p. 77 (footnote 2).

Clayworth[1] show that 1688 was a year in which some list, at least, were being compiled, although Dalrymple himself dated the list as from King William's time. It must be admitted, however, that Clayworth was in the Province of York, and Dalrymple's figures for that Province are mere estimates on the basis of one-sixth of the enumerated totals for the Province of Canterbury, so that no survey of the Province of York may have been made at all. Russell, who is almost the only author to mention the list,[2] thought that 1690 would be its approximate date. However, it seems preferable to believe that the enumeration was done in 1688 by order of King James, but was only compiled into figures for dioceses and provinces in 1689 or 1690, under King William.

Since both the 1603 communicants' list and Dalrymple's list seem to be little known (especially the latter), we give here the raw figures for the dioceses, using the totals of Harleian MS 280 for 1603; and, assuming that 'peculiars' were included with their dioceses, the totals for the provinces and the whole country (see p. 83.) The census did not give diocesan figures until 1831.

The 1603 returns, as given in Harleian MS 280, however, as well as being apparently chiefly concerned with the number of licensed preachers in each diocese and their academic qualifications, undoubtedly contain errors. If we add the parish figures for the diocese of Gloucester that are given in Harleian MS 594, we get a total of 60,957 including 200 recusants, instead of 57,627 including only 64 recusants. Some of the larger parishes, such as Tewkesbury (1,600) and Berkeley (1,400), seem to have only been given in round numbers, suggesting an estimate rather than a count. If the population could be assumed stationary, the evidence of the number of men between 20 and 60 in 1608[3] and

[1] P. Laslett and J. Harrison, 'Clayworth and Cogenhoe', in *Historical Essays, 1600–1750, presented to D. Ogg* (edited by H. E. Bell and R. L. Ollard), London, 1962, pp. 157–84.

[2] J. C. Russell, *British Mediaeval Population*, Albuquerque, 1948, p. 270. Tucker (see footnote, p. 316) also is aware of it.

[3] Tawney and Tawney, *loc. cit.* above on p. 79 (footnote 3).

ENGLAND and WALES : Population over 16 in the seventeenth century

| | 1603 | | 1688 | |
Diocese	All Adults	Non-Anglicans	All Adults	Non-Anglicans
Bath and Wells	84,190	102	151,496*	6,032
Bristol	44,658	213	68,599	2,399
Canterbury	52,791	38	66,026	6,430
Chichester	48,587	262	52,001	2,837
Coventry and Lichfield	117,906	650	162,711	6,991
Ely	30,596	19	32,347	1,430
Exeter	188,873	99	213,274	5,704
Gloucester	57,627*	64	67,225	2,491
Hereford	63,385	431	67,732	1,790
Lincoln	242,845	295	226,322	11,245
London	148,747	318	286,347	22,962
Norwich	147,876	324	177,365	8,605
Oxford	33,761	234	40,292	1,480
Peterborough	54,182	96	93,642*	2,198
Rochester	18,974	18	29,702	1,816
Salisbury	76,801	171	108,294	4,623
Winchester	59,105*	398	159,809	8,872
Worcester	56,735	270	39,533	2,044
Bangor	38,872	32	28,282	266
Llandaff	37,481	381	40,518	1,270
St Asaph	53,438	250	45,998	910
St Davids	83,467	145	70,827	2,585
Provincial total	1,740,897*	4,810	2,238,342	104,980
Carlisle	61,773	74	No published figures	
Chester	180,632	2,442		
Durham	67,805	526		
York	215,190	720		
Provincial total	525,400	3,762	(511,658)*	
England and Wales	2,266,297*	8,572	(2,750,000)*	

* See text for comments.

of all people over 16 in 1603 would allow us to deduce the expectation of life. The calculation, however, is too nice: it comes to 38 years (at birth) if there were only 57,627 people over 16 (using the Princeton 'West' tables, for which see Appendix 1); but it comes to about 58 if there were 60,957. The occupational census of 1608 might seem, therefore, to be under-counted by at least 5 per cent, since an expectation of life much above 38 seems very unlikely, but the population could equally well have not been stationary. This is, in fact, an example where subtle demographic techniques show how inaccurate the data must be, but tell us little more.

The Winchester diocesan figures for 1603, given in detail in Harleian MS 595, are worse; round numbers are given for six out of the seven parishes of the Southwark deanery, in which more than 11,000 communicants were located, and nine parishes of rural Surrey are missing. Worse still, the total of 59,105 given above from Harleian MS 280, which also appears in Harleian MS 595, is a gross error; the whole of Surrey was probably omitted by the clerk who did the arithmetic, although that would still leave a small error. Excluding the omitted parishes, the total number of adults in the Winchester diocese comes to 93,892, of which 1,451 would be recusants and Nonconformists; a distinction was drawn between the two in a few parishes, although the aggregated diocesan figures are only divided into communicants and recusants. The growth of population in the diocese of Winchester was certainly high in the seventeenth century, but not as high as the simple figures of the table would show. Using the corrected figures for the two dioceses of Gloucester and Winchester, the total number of adults in 1603 was 2,304,812. The total population was therefore about 4 million.

One should not use the figures of the table for much in the way of population trends until the 1603 figures have all been checked against the original manuscripts, where they still exist. It is very probable, too, that they are useless for real analysis of the extent of Nonconformity or Catholicism in the country, owing to gross misrepresentation on the part of the returning priests who wanted to show their parishes as being orthodox, as far as they could. However, the totals may be close to the truth.

The figure given for 1688 for the Province of York was calculated so that the total comes to 2,750,000. This was done because the Dalrymple list itself puts York at one-sixth of Canterbury, which must be wrong. In the 1690 Hearth Tax Returns, the Province of York had 27 or 28 per cent of the houses of the Province of Canterbury which would suggest about 600,000 people over 16, and 2,830,000 in the whole of England and Wales. However, the compiler of Dalrymple's list believed that the total population would be double the number over 16, a mistake he could have made from a misreading of Graunt's *Observations* (Graunt believed half the London population was under 16, but preferred 40 per cent for the whole nation); if a lost survey for the province of York had made the total adult population up to 2,750,000, a basis is then also provided for Gregory King's figure[1] of $5\frac{1}{2}$ million people in 1688. Quite possibly, the number of people per house was somewhat lower in the north of England than elsewhere.

It is otherwise difficult to understand, as Glass[2] pointed out nearly twenty years ago, why King did not estimate the population at below 5 million. If the true date of the Dalrymple list is 1688, it would also explain why King uses (or seems to use) the 1690 Hearth Tax Returns combined with the 1695 Marriage Duty data on average numbers per house to calculate the population

---

[1] Gregory King, 'Natural and political observations and conclusions upon the state and condition of England 1696', in G. Chalmers, *An estimate of the comparative strength of Great Britain and of the losses of her trade from every war since the revolution*, London, 1802.

[2] D. V. Glass, 'Gregory King's estimates of the population of England and Wales, 1695', *Population Studies*, III, 4 (March 1950), pp. 338–74; reprinted in *Population in History* (edited by Glass and D. E. C. Eversley), London, 1965, pp. 183–220. For a recent assessment of another part of King's work, see E. Le Roy Ladurie, 'Les Comptes fantastiques de Gregory King', *Annales (E.S.C.)*, **23**, 5 (September–October 1968), pp. 1086–102.

of the country in 1688, and not in 1690 or 1695 as would seem more natural. He also seems to have tried to reduce his 5½ million as much as he could (as well he might), by assuming a slight decline in population and an increase in the number of houses since 1688; Short's parish register data[1] give no warrant for assuming an unusual excess of burials over baptisms at that time, as King claims the assessment data showed him.

It seems possible that King was told (perhaps by Harley) that the population in 1688 was 5½ million, but that the source was kept from him. The basis of the figure could well have been the fairly accurate count of the adult population that Dalrymple found (except for its York component), which seems to have been both official and secret. A demographic mistake, that of doubling instead of adding roughly two-thirds in order to get the total population from the adult population, although King himself knew better, therefore gave a final figure about one-sixth too high. The few who had access to the 1688 returns, would not be at pains, especially in time of war, to point out that England and Wales was less populous than King said.

Lydia Marshall's study of the population of Bedfordshire[2] is also relevant here. She found that Bedfordshire apparently increased more rapidly during the eighteenth century than England and Wales as a whole, which she rightly found puzzling because Bedfordshire had little share in the Industrial Revolution. However, Glass's corrected figure of 4,838,100[3] for the population in 1695 agrees with the Dalrymple list if we assume: (1) that the birth-rate was about 44 per thousand; (2) that the 2,750,000 people over 16 were under-enumerated by about 6 per cent; and (3) that population growth between 1688 and 1695 was about

[1] T. Short, *New observations natural, moral, civil, political and medical on city, town and country bills of mortality. To which are added, Large and Clear Abstracts of the best Authors who have wrote on that subject. With an Appendix on The Weather and Meteors*, London, 1750, pp. 85–9.

[2] *Op. cit.* above on p. 80 (footnote 8).

[3] *Loc. cit.* above on p. 85 (footnote 2).

4 per cent. The national population increase in the eighteenth century will then be much more in keeping with what one would expect on the basis of the Bedfordshire figures. If Gregory King's figures were taken as correct, the rate of under-enumeration in the ecclesiastical census would come to about 20 per cent, which seems improbably high. We might well assume that Glass did not allow quite enough for empty houses (the few figures that do exist suggest this) and that King's secret figure for 1688 was 5,550,000 rather than 5,500,000. Both of these modifications would close the gap between the King–Glass figure for 1695 and the Dalrymple data, leaving under-enumeration in the Dalrymple list at only 3 or 4 per cent.

The implied decline in the Province of York between 1603 and 1688 may seem unlikely, but five of the twenty-two dioceses in the Province of Canterbury also showed declines, and they were all situated a long way from London, whose great growth must have absorbed about half the national population growth of about 700,000 people in 85 years.

The decline of Wales, from 213,258 people over 16 years of age in 1603 to only 185,625 in 1688, is also most interesting. Taken in conjunction with Owen's work,[1] we can sketch the history of the population of Wales and Monmouthshire since the middle of the sixteenth century as follows: growth was rapid after the influenza epidemic of the late 1550's, passing from about 250,000 in 1563 to 350,000 in 1603; but the population was only about 310,000 in 1670, and was the same in 1688; the number of people per house falling from around five when numbers were rising to little over four after decline or stagnation had set in. At the 1801 census, the population was 605,867, a near-doubling in 113 years.

Among the apparently fast-growing dioceses, Bath and Wells and Peterborough stand out, and, as they correspond almost

[1] L. Owen, 'The population of Wales in the sixteenth and seventeenth centuries', *Transactions of the Honourable Society of Cymmrodorion* (1959), pp. 99–113.

exactly to the counties of Somerset and of Rutland and North-amptonshire, a partial check is easily made. The baptisms found by Rickman for these two counties in 1700, when applied to the 1688 figures, yield decidedly low rates, which suggest that these two counties may have had unusually low baptism rates in relation to their births at that period.

OTHER UNOFFICIAL COUNTS

Various places in England had unofficial censuses during the eighteenth century. Manchester and Salford,[1] for instance, had 19,839 inhabitants in 1757 and 27,246 in 1773. Liverpool, too, was counted every decade from 1700 to 1770, and Bolton and other towns near Manchester in 1773.[2] Another such census, of the parish of Manchester outside the two towns, was made in 1775.[3] These counts were made, of course, by enthusiastic local statisticians, proud of their fast-growing city. They can be regarded as substantially correct—and so the interesting point that half the children born in Manchester at the time evidently died before the age of five can be accepted. Moreover, the figure itself suggests little under-enumeration.

Tranter[4] has discussed the listing of the inhabitants of Carding-ton, a parish in Bedfordshire, in 1782. A high level of geographical mobility is implied, because the listing seems to have included, systematically, all persons known to be natives of the parish but living elsewhere (mainly in London), a *de jure* basis, in fact. It is, of course, impossible to tell to what extent these emigrant-listings were complete.

There were also various eighteenth-century ecclesiastical

[1] T. Percival, 'Observations on the state of population in Manchester, and other adjacent places', *Philosophical Transactions of the Royal Society*, **64** (1774), pp. 54–66; **65** (1775), pp. 322–35; and **66** (1776), pp. 160–7.

[2] *Ibid.*

[3] *Ibid.*

[4] N. L. Tranter, 'Population and Social Structure in a Bedfordshire Parish: the Cardington Listing of Inhabitants, 1782', *Population Studies*, XXI, 3 (November 1967), pp. 261–82.

censuses[1] but they have not even been listed, and must be sought in diocesan archives. A good collection of a county's data has been edited by Munby.[2] Hoskins has industriously collected together the various scraps of information that must be the basis of the demographic history of a small area, the Leicestershire village of Wigston Magna, and woven them into a history.[3] It is hard work for what may seem a meagre result, full of qualifications and approximations. Yet all new historical demography must depend, at bottom, on such spadework.

In the middle of the eighteenth century, Webster, a minister in Edinburgh, invited his fellow clergy throughout Scotland to send him returns of their parishioners.[4] As usual in those early days, the returns took many years to complete. Nevertheless, Webster's assessment must be regarded as the real beginning of Scottish demographic statistics. It gives a remarkably detailed picture of the geographical distribution of population in Scotland in the mid-eighteenth century, but it is instructive to notice that Webster himself realized that the population of Glasgow had increased noticeably between the time the first returns came back to him and the date he actually published his account. Kyd has edited Webster's work and published it in a convenient form.[5]

A somewhat similar project to Webster's was carried out in France at much the same time. The Abbé d'Expilly asked for details of baptisms and burials from every parish in 1764,[6] with

[1] Thirsk, *loc. cit.* above on p. 80 (footnote 1).

[2] *Op. cit.* above on p. 81 (footnote 2).

[3] W. G. Hoskins, 'The Population of an English Village, 1086-1801: A Study of Wigston Magna', *Transactions of the Leicestershire Archaeological Society*, **33** (1957), pp. 15-35; reprinted in W. G. Hoskins, *Provincial England. Essays in social and economic history*, London, 1963.

[4] A. Youngson, 'Alexander Webster and his Account of the Number of People in Scotland in the year 1755', *Population Studies*, XV (1961), pp. 198-200.

[5] J. G. Kyd, *Scottish Population Statistics including Webster's analysis of Population 1755*, Edinburgh (Scottish History Society, 3rd Series, Vol. 43), 1952.

[6] Henry, 'The Population of France in the Eighteenth Century', in *Population in History* (edited by Glass and Eversley), London, 1965, pp. 434-56.

the object of measuring both population and natural increase. Unfortunately, most of the results were never published and were in fact eventually destroyed by the Paris mob in 1871. There were other savants interested in population,[1] and their publications are valuable today to the historical demographer. Among these, Duvillard worked out a mortality rate for eighteenth-century France, but Bourgeois-Pichat[2] has discussed his work critically in the light of modern demographic theory; while Moheau's contemporary data[3] on nuptiality have been re-analysed by Henry.[4]

An interesting early census in France, taken in a rural parish in 1691 and giving age, sex and other data, has been recently studied by Noël[5] while Esmonin[6] found a census of Grenoble dating from late 1725 or early 1726, which he had reason to believe was well carried out. Town censuses are relatively rare, and some results are intriguing: 22,622 people were living in 1,320 houses, a rate of 17·1 to every house in Grenoble. Many of the people lived at one room to a family, in fact, which was probably not uncommon in the towns, although almost unknown

[1] See A. Sauvy and J. Hecht, 'La population agricole française au XVIIIe siècle et l'expérience du marquis de Turbilly', *Population*, **20**, 2 (March–April 1965), pp. 269–86; Sauvy, 'A propos du marquis de Turbilly', *Population*, **21**, 5 (September–October 1966), pp. 1027–30.

[2] J. Bourgeois-Pichat, 'Évolution générale de la population française depuis le XVIIIe siècle', *Population*, **6**, 4 (1951), pp. 635–62; reprinted in translation in *Population in History* (edited by Glass and Eversley), London, 1965, pp. 474–97. See also *Population*, **7**, 2 (April–June 1952), pp. 319–29 or *Population in History*, pp. 498–506 for a continuation of the first paper.

[3] Moheau, *Recherches et considérations sur la population de la France*, Paris, 1912 (first published 1778).

[4] Henry, 'La nuptialité à la fin de L'Ancien Régime', *Population*, **9**, 3 (1954), pp. 542–6.

[5] R. Noël, 'La population de la paroisse de Laguiole d'après un recensement de 1691', *Annales de démographie historique* (1967), pp. 197–223. Only about 30 per cent of the population were under 15 years of age, a low figure for such an early date.

[6] E. Esmonin, 'Un recensement de la population de Grenoble en 1725', *Cahiers d'histoire*, II, 3 (1957), pp. 243–78.

in the countryside. It is necessary to be quite certain in a census of town population whether families or houses were being counted, for clearly the several inhabitants of a town house might try to claim that they were all one family for taxation purposes, and it would be difficult for the assessors to separate the few genuine cases from the many spurious ones.

It may seem strange that any individual not directly connected with the Government should ever be in a position to give reasonable estimates of population. In fact, before the days of regular government statistics it was a common practice to allow individuals to investigate population questions with government backing but without government powers. For example, Martin produced his *Statistics of the colonies of the British Empire*[1] in 1839 from the official Blue Books in Downing Street, paying for his assistants by the profits on its sale. The Government had declined the labour of editing the mass of material that was available. In the early years of its rule, the East India Company, too, was often unable to estimate population in India with its own staff and employed outsiders to make surveys on its behalf. Edward Balfour produced two editions of his *Cyclopaedia of India*, for instance, before the first census of 1872, giving numerous population figures.[2] The critical question for us today is how far the investigators were qualified to do the job, and what opportunity and incentives they had to be accurate. The Bhattacharyas have published a list[3] of all the population estimates of India made in the decade 1820–30. Seven further volumes are planned, covering the whole period 1701–1872, which will be invaluable to students of Indian population history.

These early estimates of population by the East India Com-

[1] R. M. Martin, *Statistics of the colonies of the British Empire. With the charters and engraved seals. From the official records of the Colonial Office*, London, 1839.

[2] The two editions appeared in 1857 and 1871; the latter is an immense work of five volumes, comprising 5,814 pages in all, despite the absence of a general census as a source of information. See p. 92 (footnote 4).

[3] Census of India 1961, *Report on the Population Estimates of India, Volume IV (1820–1830)* (edited by D. Bhattacharya and B. Bhattacharya), New Delhi, 1964.

pany's agents provide an interesting study. Martin, for example, published three volumes in 1838 on 'Eastern India', amounting to more than 2,300 pages of print and full of statistics of every kind.[1] The accounts by Hamilton,[2] Thornton[3] and Balfour[4] over the years, and the reports in the *Journal of the Statistical Society of London*[5] together with Martin's and other figures, show how diverse opinions were on Indian population. In 1802, Pinkerton allowed only 60 million people for 'Hindostan'[6] but in 1838, Count Björnstjerna put the population of India at 200 million,[7] possibly based on *The Picture of India* of 1830,[8] although Hamilton had given only 134 million for 1820.[9] Colonel Sykes, around 1850, believed that the estimates had been too high in the past,[10] and gradually informed opinion believed that the Indian population was not much more than 120 million at that date, although

[1] Martin, *The History, Antiquities, Topography, and Statistics of Eastern India; comprising the districts of Behar, Shahabad, Bhagulpoor, Goruckpoor, Dinajepoor, Puraniya, Rungpoor & Assam, in relation to their geology, mineralogy, botany, agriculture, commerce, manufactures, fine arts, population, religion, education, statistics, etc. Surveyed under the orders of the supreme government, and collated from the original documents at the E. I. House, with the permission of the Honourable Court of Directors*, London, 1838.

[2] W. Hamilton, *The East-India Gazetteer*, London, 1815; 2nd edn, 1828.

[3] E. Thornton, *A Gazetteer of the territories under the government of The East-India Company, and of the Native States on the Continent of India*, London, 1854.

[4] E. Balfour, *Cyclopaedia of India*, Madras, 1857 and 1871.

[5] For example, A. Shakespear, 'Statistics of the North-West Provinces,' *Journal of the Statistical Society*, **14**, 4 (December 1851), pp. 345–7.

[6] J. Pinkerton, *Modern Geography, A Description of the Empires, Kingdoms, States and Colonies; with the Oceans, Seas, and Isles, in all parts of the world: including the most recent discoveries, and political alterations. Digested on a new plan*, London, 1802, Volume II, p. 254.

[7] Count Björnstjerna, *The British Empire in the East*, London, 1840 (translated by H. Evans Lloyd from the Swedish, Stockholm, 1838).

[8] *The Picture of India: Geographical, Historical & Descriptive*, London, 1830.

[9] W. Hamilton, *The East-India Gazetteer*, London, 1828, 2nd edn.

[10] W. H. Sykes, 'Revenue Statistics of the Agra Government, or North-Western Provinces', *Journal of the Statistical Society*, **10**, 3 (September 1847), pp. 243–51, and 'Expenditure in India on Public Works from 1837–8 to 1845–6 inclusive', *ibid.*, **14**, 1 (March 1851), pp. 45–7.

150 million or 180 million had been accepted earlier. Milner gave 'probably 130 million' in 1850,[1] Thornton 161·8 million for 1852,[2] Martin 156·5 million for British India in 1859–60,[3] and Blakely 143 million for all-India in 1862.[4] Just before the first census, Balfour gave 212·7 million,[5] but Haushofer put it at only 181·6 million.[6] These figures are important to bear in mind while recalling that the British had been ruling in India for a century or so. There was real surprise when the 1872 census was published showing a much higher figure (206 million) than Sykes and his school believed.[7] It seems that the earlier estimators had been closer to the truth, but it was not widely realized how serious the under-estimation was, although Waterfield[8] did raise the official figure to 239 million (including 48 million in the Feudatory States); the 1872 census itself was proved by 1881 to have been much below the truth in some parts of the country,[9] and by 1891 to have been even more of an undercount. By the

[1] T. Milner, *A Descriptive Atlas of Astronomy, and of Physical and Political Geography*, London, 1850.

[2] *Op. cit.* opposite (footnote 3).

[3] Martin, *The progress and present state of British India. A manual for general use, based on official documents*, London, 1862.

[4] E. T. Blakely, 'On the Commercial Progress of the Colonies and Dependencies of the United Kingdom', *Journal of the Statistical Society*, **28**, 1 (1865), pp. 34–54.

[5] *Op. cit.* opposite (footnote 4), 2nd edn.

[6] *Op. cit.* above on p. 75 (footnote 2).

[7] See H. Beverley, 'The Census of Bengal', *Journal of the Statistical Society*, **37**, 1 (March 1874), pp. 69–107; in the discussion after his paper (pp. 108–13) Mouat, in particular, admitted how far his views had been proved wrong.

[8] H. Waterfield, 'Census of British India of 1871–72', *ibid.*, **39** (June 1876), pp. 411–16. See also *Statistical Abstract for the Colonial and other possessions of the United Kingdom in each year from 1856 to 1870 (As far as the Particulars can be stated)* Eighth Number, London (H.M.S.O.), 1872, p. 1, where British India is given as follows: 1855, 123,931,369; 1861, 143,271,210; 1870: 151,146,516. The Ninth Number of this Abstract (1873) replaced the 1870 figure by a census-based figure for 1871 of 190,663,623, an evident advance of 26 per cent even for the British parts of India.

[9] See Beverley, 'Census of Bengal, 1881', *Journal of the Statistical Society*, **46**, 4 (December 1883), pp. 680–9.

end of the nineteenth century, three things were clear: first, that the 1872 census was about 20 per cent too low; second, that the 1850's estimates were about 50 per cent too low; and third, that the 1820's estimates were certainly not too high and probably rather too low also. The most likely figure for the 1872 population was then thought to be about 240 million. By that time, of course, the controversy was substantially dead, and the early higher estimators were no longer active to defend their ideas, although they had been roughly correct. Davis has summed up the story of the first Indian censuses in a concise form.[1] None before 1931 needed any additions at all for under-enumeration, and his own estimate for the population in 1872 was 255 million. The whole story shows also the general tendency of counters of population to under-count, and for scholars to imagine that there is some virtue, when dealing with population, in guessing figures that are probably rather below the truth. One often hears of a conservative estimate, or a safe estimate, when what is meant is a wrong estimate in which the sign of the error is known to be negative. It would be much better to attempt to produce an unbiased estimate even if the figure seems rather high. Only thus can one avoid such gross mistakes as estimating the population at half its true value.

Even now, such a question as the population of India in the middle of the nineteenth century, or about twenty-one years before the first census, is open to speculation. Shirras suggested 190 million,[2] but at the time Sykes guessed 150 million.[3] Willcox, however, has suggested 205 million,[4] and one feels that 205 to 215 million is probably correct.

Similar errors have often occurred whenever Westerners tried

[1] K. Davis, *The Population of India and Pakistan*, Princeton, 1951.

[2] G. F. Shirras, 'The Population Problems of India', *Economic Journal*, **43** (March 1933), pp. 56–73.

[3] *Loc. cit.* above on p. 92 (footnote 10). (1847).

[4] Willcox, 'Increase in the Population of the Earth and of the Continents Since 1650'. in *International Migrations*, Vol. II Interpretations (edited by Willcox), New York, 1931, pp. 33–82.

to estimate the population of China. As early as 1696, King[1] thought that there were 230 million Chinese, but Higgins[2] thought that 145 million would be high enough for 1790. Martin, who spent some years in China, estimated the population at about 408 million in the 1840's,[3] but Bowring put it at between 350 and 400 million in 1855.[4] Williams[5] belittled Martin and inclined to a population of 337 million or less in 1883, but Haushofer[6] had given 400·5 million in the previous decade. *The North China Herald*[7] seems to give as good a critique of the Chinese sources of this period as any.

Among the deflaters of Chinese population figures, Willcox[8] was the most eminent. He claimed (in 1928) that China's population had never been above 320 million at any time, and Ta Chen[9] supported him. Today, however, Clark is inclined to believe that the 1953 census was substantially accurate,[10] and that all the

[1] *Op. cit.* above on p. 85 (footnote 1).

[2] *Op. cit.* above on p. 75 (footnote 1).

[3] Martin, *China, political, commercial, and social; in an official report to her Majesty's government*, London, 1847. This work, in Vol. II, p. 348, contains this gem: 'There does not appear the slightest probability that under any circumstances Hong Kong will ever become a place of trade.' At the time he wrote, Martin was a member of H.M. Legislative Council in Hong Kong.

[4] Sir John Bowring, 'The Population of China, a Letter, addressed to the Registrar-General', *Journal of the Statistical Society*, **20**, 1 (March 1857), pp. 41–53.

[5] S. W. Williams, *The Middle Kingdom. A survey of the Geography, Government, Literature, Social Life, Arts, and History of the Chinese Empire and its Inhabitants*, London, 1883. Vol. I, pp. 258–88, especially p. 285.

[6] *Op. cit.* above on p. 75 (footnote 2).

[7] 'The Population of China' (extracted from *The North China Herald*), *Journal of the Statistical Society*, **50** (December 1887), pp. 688–96.

[8] Willcox, 'The Population of China in 1910', *Bulletin de l'Institut International de Statistique*, **23**, 2 (Cairo) (1928), pp. 347–61, reprinted in *Journal of the American Statistical Association*, **23** (1928), pp. 18–30; and *Studies in American Demography*, Ithaca, 1940, pp. 511–40.

[9] Ta Chen, *Population in Modern China*, supplement to *American Journal of Sociology*, **LII**, 1 (July 1946).

[10] See C. Clark, 'L'accroissement de la population de la Chine', *Population*, **19**, 3 (June–July 1964), pp. 559–68; 'La population de la Chine depuis 1915', *ibid.*, **21**, 6 (November–December 1966), pp. 1191–9.

official estimates made ever since the Taiping rebellion, or after 1851, are meaningless as they stand.[1]

The Chinese Post Office published estimates of population[2] at various times in the twentieth century, and although it was the one Government service that spread throughout the country, there is no reason to suppose that the counts were 100 per cent complete. It is much more probable that the administration at local levels was inefficient and inclined to be 'conservative' about population questions. A similar tendency can be seen in the eighteenth century in the official Chinese returns.[3]

There are, in fact, contemporary population estimates for most parts of the world since the seventeenth century. Old gazetteers often give figures of population that at least show what was believed at the time. Anderson[4] is a fair example of the late-eighteenth century; Higgins[5] of the early-nineteenth. Before the revival of statistics began at the end of the eighteenth century, there were comparatively few people, however, who understood how to set about making an estimate. Montesquieu, for example, pronounced on population questions[6] without the least idea how they might be resolved. He regarded it as a means of advancing his general argument about the state of France and of Europe at the time, and expected to be believed on a flat statement that the population was much lower in his day than it had been in the distant past.

[1] See also E. H. Parker, 'A Note on Some Statistics Relating to China', *Journal of the Royal Statistical Society*, **62** (1899), pp. 150–6.

[2] For example, see *The China Year Book—1923* (edited by H. G. W. Woodhead), Tientsin, 1923, pp. 4–30.

[3] See Ho, *op. cit.* above on p. 59 (footnote 8), pp. 36–46. For a recent attempt to count the Chinese population, in 1964, see D. Wilson, 'Counting the heads', *Far Eastern Economic Review*, **51**, 1 (6 January 1966), pp. 22–3. A summary of the present state of knowledge is given by A. Lal, 'Population Growth in mainland China: some aspects', *Eugenics Review*, **56**, 1 (April 1964), pp. 29–34.

[4] A. Anderson, *An historical and chronological deduction of the Origin of Commerce, from the earliest accounts*, London (2nd edn), 1787–9.

[5] *Op. cit.* above on p. 75 (footnote 1).

[6] *Lettres Persanes* (1721), Letters CXII to CXXII.

DEMOGRAPHIC ANALYSES

Given a modern census, a number of inferences are ordinarily drawn from it; indeed, with a system of registration of births, marriages, and deaths as well, elaborate demographic analysis can be done. Where the data are few, analysis is no less important; the last ounce, so to speak, must be extracted from what data there are.

As soon as two censuses are available, one important piece of work should be done: a check should be made on the rate of growth or decline of the population. It is hardly credible that a population should grow by more than 3 per cent per annum except by heavy immigration, and even then not for long. This test, applied to Russia in the eighteenth and nineteenth centuries and to China and Japan at various early dates, serves as a mutual check on a pair of censuses. It may be difficult to be sure, however, which census was the really bad one, since both are sure to have been wrong to some extent. A large decline in the population, on the other hand, is always possible, especially in small areas where a disaster—plague, flood or famine—might even wipe out the entire population. Although such things are now almost unknown, we should remember that in the twentieth century the world's demography is in a freak phase. The normal thing is for a decrease in population from one year to the next to be almost as frequent as an increase. Increases in almost all countries in almost every year are quite extraordinary—although in the period for which statistics are good, increases generally do appear.

The actual size of a population—unless unusually large or small—is made interesting by relating it to the size at some other date, not too far away in time, or to the size of some other place. In the abstract, towns of 5,000 and 10,000 seem almost the same; even the relative sizes of towns in the past only have much meaning by comparison with the present. We are interested to know that Naples was for a long time the largest city in Italy just because it is so no longer. Thus either another census, or registration data of births and deaths, are usually required to make a census give us worth-while information.

We can, however, often study the population's distribution by various groupings; one of which, the distribution by age, is of enormous importance in all demographic work. It is more than an interesting feature in itself, for it tells us something about the recent birth- and death-rates. It is not always appreciated that this distribution of the population into age-groups is much better as a guide to the birth-rate than as a guide to the death-rate. If we can ignore migration, and make guesses at the death-rates specific for each age, the births and hence the birth-rates for the previous generation or so can be calculated from the numbers still living at each age as given by a census. It is found that the results are not very greatly influenced by the death-rates actually guessed, provided nothing really extreme is chosen. For example, Sezze (forty-two miles south-east of Rome) in 1708 had 51 per cent of its population under 20,[1] and must have had a high annual birth-rate, say 50 or 55 per thousand. But if we assume birth-rates specific for the age of the mother and try to deduce death-rates from the age-structure, doing the calculation the other way in fact, we run into serious difficulties. We get only the death-rates for the younger ages in the first instance, and have to use trial death-rates for higher ages and then correct them. The dependence on the fertility levels chosen is also very considerable.

A particular aspect of these methods, stable population theory, is the subject of Appendix 1. However, we can give a few illustrations here that scarcely require such careful analysis. Gailey reports[2] a census by age and sex of part of Argyllshire in 1792, for instance, and the distribution implies a rather higher fertility

---

[1] Y.-M. Bercé, 'La population des villes de Sezze et de Narni en 1701 et 1708 d'après les recensements de l'État pontificial', *Population*, **20**, 1 (January–February 1965), pp. 93–108.

[2] R. A. Gailey, 'Settlement and population in Kintyre, 1750–1800', *Scottish Geographical Magazine*, **76**, 2 (September 1960), pp. 99–107.

than in 1881, although emigration must already have affected it. The result agrees with that of the 1821 census, and it is particularly relevant to the question of Highland depopulation[1] to know that high fertility in Argyllshire goes back at least into the eighteenth century.

Although the proportion of the total population that are children gives a fair idea of fertility, we can also often see whether any disaster in the past has disturbed the age-structure by producing a 'bite' out of the population pyramid at a certain age, corresponding to the number of years that have elapsed since the disaster. Thus Iceland in 1703[2] seems to have been in an unhappy state, with few young or old people. One might suspect gross under-enumeration of infants; but Icelandic standards have always been high, and furthermore there was an astonishingly high rate of celibacy revealed by the 1703 census (24 per cent of men and 43 per cent of women aged 50-59 were unmarried). The sex-ratio, too, was unbalanced, with fewer males than females at all ages, reminiscent of the skeletons found of the last survivors of medieval Greenland (see pp. 291-2). The Icelandic population must have been living under extremely difficult conditions, and great efforts were being made to restrain population growth.[3] In actual fact, a smallpox epidemic decimated numbers in 1707 and other epidemics and volcanic eruptions so kept the population down that it was not until 1823 that the 1703 figure was surpassed.

A similar situation may have obtained in Vienna in 1754.[4] Only about half the population aged between 20 and 40 was

[1] There was some controversy about this subject in the nineteenth century. See L. Levi, 'On the Economic Condition of the Highlands and Islands of Scotland', *Journal of the Statistical Society*, **28**, 3 (September 1865), pp. 372–401; Duke of Argyll, 'On the Economic Condition of the Highlands of Scotland', *ibid.*, **29**, 4 (December 1866), pp. 504–35.

[2] Henry, 'La population d l'Islande en 1703', *Population*, **16**, 1 (1961), pp. 122–3.

[3] See Clark, *Population Growth and Land Use*, London, 1967, pp. 92 and 199.

[4] Peller, *loc. cit.* above on p. 73 (footnote 4).

married, and 30 per cent of the women aged 40–50 were single (possibly including widows). There were, as in Iceland, more females than males at all ages, and Peller's calculation of the infant mortality rate is 406 dying in the first year of life per thousand born. Horvath was similarly able[1] to put the infant mortality in Debrecen at 296·1 per thousand births in 1750–4, most of it being caused by diarrhoea. Peller also used the Austrian census of 1754, which seems to be now largely lost, to assess fertility levels in the eighteenth century.

Recent studies in the United States on fertility in the nineteenth century have also relied upon census data. By careful manipulation of the figures, always allowing for mis-statements of age, it is possible to show that the birth-rate in the United States fell almost continuously between 1800 and 1860. More recently Brass[2] has devised methods of calculating fertility from a single set of census data, which have been used widely in underdeveloped countries.[3]

One must expect in general that in a time of acute crisis there will be a lower birth-rate, and the rise in mortality will also affect young children the most. When such a bite in the pyramid is not of the same order for both sexes, it is usually the men that have the bigger loss, and the reason is often war deaths in action. Many countries today, especially Russia, Poland, Germany, and France, show such a feature, with the males much in the minority at the age-groups that fought in the 1939–45 war. The war of 1914–18 showed an even more marked effect at one

[1] R. Horvath, 'The Scientific Study of Mortality in Hungary before the Modern Era', *Population Studies*, XVII, 2 (November 1963), pp. 187–97.

[2] W. Brass, 'The Derivation of Fertility and Reproduction Rates from Restricted Data on Reproductive Histories', *ibid.*, VII, 2 (November 1953), pp. 137–66.

[3] See *The Population of Tropical Africa* (edited by J. C. Caldwell and C. Okonjo), London, 1968. A general survey of these methods is given by Brass, 'Methods of Obtaining Basic Demographic Measures where Census and Vital Statistics Registration Systems are Lacking or Defective', *World Population Conference*, Belgrade, 1965, Background Paper B. 6, No. 409.

time, but it is now so long ago that ordinary mortality has begun to obliterate it.

The 1912 census of China gave an age-distribution by provinces[1] that, whatever guesses may be hazarded as to its accuracy, which both Lieu and Ho[2] recognize was doubtful, shows strong evidence for a falling birth-rate in several of the provinces. Kiangsi, which had the lowest birth-rate, had more people living in each successive quinquennium of age up to 40, so that one might guess that the birth-rate in Kiangsi fell during the years 1872 to 1912 from around 50 per thousand to only about 17, most of the fall probably occurring between 1887 and 1907 because of the sharp changes in the frequency distribution between the ages of 6 and 25 years. On the other hand, the Kiangsi age-distribution between 46 and 75 falls with extraordinary steepness, the numbers halving between 51-5 and 56-60, halving again between 56-60 and 61-5, and falling to less than a third between 61-5 and 66-70, so that there were fewer than one-twelfth as many people aged 66-70 as there were aged 51-5. Unless mis-reporting of ages and omissions were on an immense scale, this can only mean either that the high birth-rate that obtained before 1872 was recently established (since about 1863) or that there was very heavy mortality indeed in Kiangsi some time shortly before 1862. The change is so great that the latter, although unusual, is the less unlikely hypothesis.

The demographer can go thus far from the figures alone and now the historian must look for possible causes of heavy mortality or lowered fertility in Kiangsi in the years immediately before 1862. The task presents no difficulty whatever; the Taiping rebellion, which began in 1851 and ended in 1864, was marked by a slaughter 'on a scale difficult to imagine by modern

[1] D. K. Lieu, 'The 1912 Census of China', *Bulletin de l'Institut International de Statistique*, **26**, 2 (Madrid) (1931), pp. 85–109.

[2] *Op. cit.* above on p. 59 (footnote 8), pp. 73–9. See also W. W. Rockhill, 'The 1910 Census of the Population of China', *T'oung Pao*, **13** (1912), pp. 117–25 and *Bulletin of the American Geographical Society*, **44** (1912), pp. 668–73, who believed the birth-rate might have been no more than 10 per 1,000.

war ethics'.[1] Although we have had an Auschwitz in modern times, it would really seem as though the Germans were only beginning to reach the degree of massacre that the Taipings came to regard as normal, and even if the Jews had been able to retaliate on the same scale, Central Europe would still have scarcely been as desolated as was a large part of China during the Taiping rebellion. Ho gives the figures for the population of Kuang-teh county in Anhwei province: between 1855 and 1865 the numbers declined from 310,994 to 5,078, a loss of more than 98 per cent. The literary chroniclers tell of massacre after massacre, by both sides in turn, but we might be sceptical without these figures. The Paraguayan War of 1864–70 and the Thirty Years War were not more bitterly fought. The Western myth of the 'fiendish Chinese' was presumably born at the time of the Taipings. Kiangsi was, in fact, so hit by the disaster that in 1953 its population was still only 69 per cent of the 1850 figure, although as a whole China had increased a good deal, and there had been in-migration to Kiangsi from less unfortunate parts of the country.

The 1953 census of China gives an age-distribution that does not show any abnormality at ages over 41 as it should if the birth-rate generally fell before 1912. However, the figures have not been published directly nor have they been published by provinces.[2]

A second major demographic use of a census is the information it can give us on marriage-rates and nuptiality in general. Hajnal has gone so far as to propose a 'mean singulate age at marriage' indicator[3] that can be calculated simply from the proportions

[1] Ho, *op. cit.*, pp. 236–57. The crusades were another matter. P. K. Hitti, *History of Syria, including Lebanon and Palestine*, London, 1951, tells (p. 595) of the massacre of 65,000 or 70,000 civilians when Jerusalem was captured on 15 July 1099. Compare also Joshua VIII, especially 24–6.

[2] See Nai-Ruenn Chen, *Chinese Economic Statistics. A Handbook for Mainland China*, Edinburgh, 1967, pp. 8, 134–5.

[3] J. Hajnal, 'Age at marriage and proportions marrying', *Population Studies*, VII, 2 (November 1953), pp. 111–36.

married and single by age and sex at one census. This method has been used in many under-developed countries.[1]

It has been found that the distribution of ages at marriage by sex, the 'marriage pattern' as it is called, often varies little in a society even from century to century. A major change may occur now and then, but such changes are rare, which justifies Hajnal's technique to a large extent. The same is not so true of fertility and mortality; they depend on outside factors a good deal, such as political and economic conditions and public health measures. Nuptiality is largely a matter of social tradition, and tradition is the most stable element in vital human matters; marriage usually occurs at ages that the society thinks suitable. A major upheaval is needed to convince the population of the need for any change in its marriage pattern.

The classic example of a society that did change its marriage pattern is Ireland. Before the Great Famine of 1847, marriage in Ireland was quite early, the bride being apparently in her teens as often as not and the bridegroom not much older. After the Famine, during which one-eighth of the population died within two years and another eighth emigrated, Ireland changed[2] to the present pattern, which is the most extreme in the world. The mean age at first marriage for women is nearly 30 and for men about 35.

At Princeton, Coale and his colleagues have been collecting nineteenth- and twentieth-century data from national censuses so as to produce maps of proportions married for all the 'pro-

[1] S. N. Agarwala has evidently used it for India from 1901 to 1951 in his *The Mean Age at First Marriage from Census Data*, Ph.D. Thesis, Office of Population Research, Princeton University, 1957.

See also T. H. Hollingsworth, 'On the Marriage Rate in Pre-Malthusian Europe; Comparison with the under-developed countries of to-day; the marriage-rate in Europe to-day; comparison with the marriage-rate in former days', *European Population Conference, Strasbourg, 1966*, Paper C. 2, for a use of the pattern of proportions married by age to determine five broad groupings of the countries of the world.

[2] This is, admittedly, an oversimplification. The age at marriage probably rose slowly between 1801 and 1847 and rapidly between 1847 and 1851.

vinces of Europe'—the national administrative subdivisions. Together with a set of fertility maps, it will thus be possible to see at a glance which areas were limiting fertility within marriage as well as which were delaying or forgoing marriage. Livi Bacci, having already done the Italian part, has now gone back to the eighteenth-century censuses for Spain,[1] van de Walle is studying the French-speaking parts of Europe,[2] Demeny the Austro-Hungarian Empire,[3] and Tekse Bohemia, Hungary, and parts of the Balkans.[4]

A third major use of census data for retrospective demographic analysis is to measure internal migration. Information about internal migration is always difficult to obtain from a single enquiry; but, if a man's place of birth is given on his census form as well as his present residence, it is possible to make an estimate of net migration in a lifetime. This is not a very sound method of measurement, but it is often the best that can be done. The age at which migration occurred, return movements to the place of birth, and multiple migrations are, inevitably, ignored. Friedlander and Roshier[5] have recently reworked the data for England and Wales since 1851, using a computer, along similar lines to those of E. G. Ravenstein,[6] who began his study of internal migration as long ago as 1871. Such study confounds migratory movements made almost a lifetime ago with others that were

[1] M. Livi Bacci, 'Il declino della fecondità della popolazione italiana nell' ultimo secolo', *Statistica*, **25**, 3 (1965), pp. 359–452, and *loc. cit.* above on p. 74.

[2] E. van de Walle, 'Marriage and Marital Fertility', *Daedalus* (Spring 1968), pp. 486–501.

[3] P. Demeny, 'Early Fertility Decline in Austria-Hungary: A Lesson in Demographic Transition', *ibid.* (Spring 1968), pp. 502–22.

[4] K. Tekse, 'Some Fertility Patterns in Central and Southern Europe before World War I', *International Symposium on the Problems of Human Reproduction*, Varna, September 1968.

[5] D. Friedlander and R. J. Roshier, 'A Study of Internal Migration in England and Wales, Part I: Geographical Patterns of Internal Migration 1851–1951', *Population Studies*, XIX, 3 (March 1966), pp. 239–78.

[6] His main work is 'The laws of migration', *Journal of the Royal Statistical Society*, **48**, 2 (June 1885), pp. 167–227, and **52**, 2 (June 1889), pp. 241–301.

very recent. Migration patterns change rapidly under conditions of sudden economic development, which usually occurs much more quickly in some parts of the country than in others.

The direct demographic data of Sweden are unique in that they go back to the first half of the eighteenth century. Sweden's migration data, in particular, have been studied more widely[1] than any other country's data and give us a measure of the rates obtaining in pre-industrial Europe. However, the assumptions about migration always affect the results of the calculations so much that it is very dangerous to conclude that the results are in fact correct. In particular, net migration is almost always only a small fraction of the gross, and hence any pattern of net migration flows may be very far from showing the true levels of actual movement.[2]

Buckatzsch suggested using two lists of the population of local areas close together in time to measure migration,[3] but comparatively little can be done because such listings are rare. Laslett and Harrison, however, found a high rate of migration at Clayworth[4] by this method between 1676 and 1688.

More recondite studies can sometimes be made from a complete enough census. For example, Roberts, in a special situation (a population of slaves),[5] was able to calculate a life-table simply from counts of population by age. This is most unusual, since it

---

[1] See, for example, D. S. Thomas, *Social and Economic Aspects of Swedish Population Movements 1750-1933*, New York, 1941; and *Migration in Sweden* (edited by D. Hannerberg, T. Hägerstrand and B. Odering) Lund, 1957.

[2] For a recent assessment of net and gross migration in Britain, see Hollingsworth, 'Internal Migration Statistics from the Central Register for Scotland of the National Health Service', *Journal of the Royal Statistical Society* (Series A), **131** (1968), pp. 340-80.

[3] E. J. Buckatzsch, 'The Constancy of Local Populations and Migration in England before 1800'. *Population Studies*, V, 1 (1951), pp. 62-9.

[4] *Loc. cit.* above on p. 82 (footnote 1).

[5] G. W. Roberts, 'A Life Table for a West Indian Slave Population', *Population Studies*, V, 3 (1952), pp. 238-43; and 'Securing Demographic Data from Limited Historical Material', *International Population Conference*, Ottawa, 1963, pp. 203-9.

depends upon no migration at all. Given an island and slave-owners at a time when the slave trade was abolished, this is not so unlikely as it normally would be. Rubin in a more historical,[1] and Woodruff in a geographic,[2] way have also studied slave populations.

It may be possible to assess the social structure of the population if the data are extensive enough to permit it. That is to say, given the number of rooms in the house, the number of children, the age at marriage, the occupation, and the present age and sex, it may be possible to reach new definitions, by a kind of numerical taxonomy, of social classes. This has not been done for contemporary populations yet, but it will probably be developed as a method by sociologists.

Certain inferences, however, may not be drawn from historical statistics. During the eighteenth century, in particular, it was the custom to tabulate the figures of deaths by age-group (as in a Bill of Mortality), and to discuss the proportions of those dying in each group. A major interest was in the proportion dying under the age of five, but it is not permissible to say that, if 20 per cent of all deaths in one year were children under 5, and in some later year the proportion was only 15 per cent, then the level of children's health had improved.[3] Since adult mortality might be

[1] E. Rubin, 'Les esclaves aux États-Unis de 1790 à 1860. Données sur leur nombre et leurs charactéristiques démographiques', *Population*, **14**, 1 (1959), pp. 33–46.

[2] J. F. Woodruff, 'Some characteristics of the Alabama slave population in 1850', *Geographical Review*, **52**, 3 (July 1962), pp. 379–88.

[3] McKeown and Brown have, in fact, studied the medical evidence for England in the eighteenth century, and concluded that medicine, at least, had no great influence upon demographic trends, even though there is some apparent decline in mortality. As well as poor data, however, an alternative explanation of this decline might still be the spread of the practice of ventilation and cleanliness that seems to have occurred towards the end of the eighteenth century. See T. McKeown and R. G. Brown, 'Medical Evidence Related to English Population Changes in the Eighteenth Century', *Population Studies*, IX, 2 (November 1955), pp. 119–41, and reprinted in *Population in History* (edited by Glass and Eversley), London, 1965, pp. 285–307.

changing as well as child mortality, the only way to analyse child mortality is to base it on the number of births. In most instances, however, both births and deaths will have been under-counted, which makes the task of studying child mortality well-nigh hopeless.

In all the studies that rework census data, the limitations are the comprehensiveness of the census coverage and its accuracy. If the first is inadequate, there is often nothing to be done about it; if there was no question in the census on marital status, no study of nuptiality is possible, clearly. But sometimes there are possibilities. A question may have been asked that was relevant to the subject of interest, and tabulations were made and published although not in the desired form. The census records may still exist, and new tabulations can perhaps be made from them. Alternatively, if the census records have been destroyed, there is still a possibility that the existing tabulations can be made to yield at least part of the answers required. This is a matter of statistical ingenuity and knowledge of what demographic assumptions might be made with safety.

In other instances, there is no doubt about the accuracy and reliability of the census itself. Anyone who has ever organized a field survey knows that errors creep in very readily; a census is no exception, but, because of its official character, the errors are played down to the public. This is quite justifiable in so far as census statistics are among the most accurate that a government produces—probably better than many of its financial data. Yet for detailed demographic work, a census may be unrealiable. Even if something has been counted right down to the last individual, it may not be the right thing. Deliberate falsification of a census is much rarer, the official having no particular motive (as a rule) to disguise the truth. When estimates of population, produced for a particular purpose, are in question, the situation is far different.

New work, of course, is proceeding on the old census material. At Cambridge, Laslett is collecting local census data, and at

Oxford, Miss Anne Whiteman is reported to be working on the Compton census at Lady Margaret Hall. Armstrong, Dyos and others have begun a study of the enumerators' books themselves of the 1851 and 1861 censuses (now released from the archives) in the hope of getting more detailed information than ever before about population trends at the height of the Industrial Revolution. A nominative approach is possible to migration, for example, and if the vital registration data are also available (Drake has them for his present study of Ashford), an unusually complete check on the sources is possible. A further advantage of this approach is that the occupational groupings used in the official census publications of the day need not be followed now; other groupings may prove more meaningful.

The possibilities of further work on old censuses in other countries must be very great. A census is almost always the best source of demographic information; and, in any enquiry, a great effort should be made to find any censuses of interest, partial or otherwise, before turning to less promising sources. If one starts with something less than the best evidence, the work is handicapped from the start.

CHAPTER 4

Taxation Returns and Detailed Surveys

The most common indications of population levels before the period of reliable censuses are given by taxation returns, which have been preserved for almost every part of the world. The Israelite count in Exodus XXX that was mentioned in the previous chapter was really a poll-tax, and tax returns from Egypt may exist for the first century B.C.[1] Some of the better taxation counts have in fact been treated as censuses in Chapter 3.

Wherever money was to be collected, however, the money and not the count would really have been the first consideration of the officials. For this reason, taxation data are somewhat different from less pecuniary sources. Poll-taxes do give a useful guide to total population, of course, provided we can be sure that the great majority of adults were included. But paupers, for instance, were commonly excluded; their number is always difficult to determine, and in many taxations the number who obtained exemption by the plea of poverty must have been enormous. The clergy, in the European middle ages, were also exempt from a poll-tax, but their numbers would scarcely be large enough to disturb any demographic trends that might be calculated. Children, too, were usually excluded, which creates two problems: (1) how to be certain of the age below which children were not taxable, and (2) how to estimate the proportion of children to adults in the population. This latter depends almost entirely on the level and trend of the birth-rate over the past fifty years, and especially on its level over the past fifteen years or so. A high

[1] S. L. Wallace, 'Census and Poll-Tax under the Ptolemies', *American Journal of Philology*, **59**, 236 (1938), pp. 418–42.

recent birth-rate (5 per cent per annum) in an historical population will generally mean that between 37 and 45 per cent of the population were under 15, whilst a low birth-rate (2 per cent per annum) means that only about 18 to 24 per cent were children. One can derive one's own data by comparisons with recent census populations by age for various countries, conveniently published in the *U.N. Demographic Yearbook*, or use various of the published model life-tables.[1]

On rare occasions, we have poll-tax data in which children are also included, so that it amounts to a kind of census; but the dangers in taxation data are revealed in the work of van Xanten and van der Woude,[2] who published the poll-tax data for 's-Hertogenbosch bailiwick between 1695 and 1719. The whole untaxable population as well as the taxables, both adults and children, were counted each year; and, although the figures are incomplete, tax-evasion must have been practised on a very large scale. The poll-tax was only begun in 's-Hertogenbosch in 1687, and although the marked increase in the number of untaxables between 1696 and 1702 may be a genuine increase in poverty, the further increases after 1702 were probably owing to a certain sophistication on the part of the peasants about paying their taxes. The true proportion of poor was probably only 20 to 25 per cent between 1703 and 1715, but the apparent level rose as high as 43·1 per cent. There was evidently an improvement in the system in 1716, and the untaxables fell abruptly from 36·9 per cent to 18·3 per cent in one year. The actual population was extremely stable, as the total figures show. Since these are unusually complete figures, and the United Provinces were not noted for administrative incompetence, grave doubt is cast upon data where the proportion of untaxables has to be guessed.

[1] See Appendix 1, pp. 341–2.
[2] H. J. van Xanten and A. M. van der Woude, 'Het hoofdgeld en de bevolking van de Meierij van 's-Hertogenbosch omstreeks 1700', *A.A.G. Bijdragen*, **13** (1965), pp. 3–96, including an English summary pp. 41–3.

OFFICIAL SURVEYS

The 'extents' of medieval England cannot properly be called taxes, but they can be made to yield rough demographic data. The first extent, in a sense, was the Domesday Book of 1086, which collected information on the men, villeins, cottars, serfs, freemen and socmen (amongst much other data) in each village in England. The extents were surveys, probably intended to bring the Domesday Book up to date in any area where large changes were thought to have occurred.[1] Hallam, for instance, found[2] very rapid population growth in the rich new lands around the Wash, but evidence from places showing little or no change seems scarcer. Extents were rare before about 1250, although that may merely reflect complacency on the part of the officials rather than little population change between 1086 and 1250. They became much more frequent after that, and their value is not so much as a representative sample of England as showing in which places rapid growth took place. Harley showed[3] that there were large variations between different parts of Warwickshire, when he compared the numbers of landholders in 1086 with the number in 1279 as shown by the Hundred Rolls of that date. There is a further weakness in this comparison, however, in that more landholders *suggests* but does not *prove* more population.[4] A certain degree of social change, almost all men becoming landowners in 1279 where only some were in

[1] See J. C. Russell, *British Mediaeval Population*, Albuquerque, 1948, pp. 55–91. He does not suggest, however, that the extents were an up-dating of the Domesday Book.

[2] H. E. Hallam, 'Population Density in Medieval Fenland', *Economic History Review*, 2nd Series, 14, 1 (1961), pp. 71–81; also his book, *Settlement and Society: a Study of the early Agrarian History of South Lincolnshire*, Cambridge, 1965.

[3] J. B. Harley, 'Population Trends and Agricultural Developments from the Warwickshire Hundred Rolls of 1279', *Economic History Review*, 2nd Series, 11, 1 (1958), pp. 8–18.

[4] This point is brought out very clearly by Ohlin in his criticism of a paper by Postan and Titow that had been published in 1959. See G. Ohlin, 'No Safety in Numbers: Some Pitfalls of Historical Statistics', in *Industrialization in Two*

1086, could also account for the data of the Hundred Rolls, although in a somewhat unlikely manner.

Russell believed[1] that almost all men in medieval England held land, or a cottage at least, or else were included in the extents out of official policy. 'It is doubtful if the Conqueror was squeamish about technicalities of landholding,' he writes. 'What he apparently desired to know was the manpower available on the English land.' Even so, the thirteenth- and fourteenth-century extents might have been more interested in taxes than in people, and an impoverished class might have grown up. The question needs careful study, since the population can only be deduced from the extents, even approximately, if its social structure is known fairly well.

Similar sources exist, of course, in other countries, and may be better than the English sources. Kalserová, for instance, used the 1607 register of subjects in her study[2] of part of Southern Bohemia. This may have amounted almost to a census, but it is scarcely possible to know precisely what records exist unless one specializes in a particular country. Almost in passing, Ostrogorsky has shown[3] how a Byzantine *praktikon*, or inventory, can give demographic data at a time and for a place where very little is otherwise known about population. The *praktikon* he cites is for Chilandar, one of the monasteries of Mount Athos, and was compiled in the year 1300. It gives the distribution of 127 families by the number of children, and, presumably because the mean seemed low at 1·69 children per family, it is cited in the *Cambridge*

Systems; Essays in Honor of Alexander Gerschenkron (edited by H. Rosovsky), New York, 1966, pp. 68–90.

---

[1] *Op. cit.*, pp. 37–8.

[2] J. Kalserová, 'Populační vývoj jihočeské vesnice v. 17 st. a v první polovině 18.st.', *Historická Demografie*, 1 (1967), pp. 28–34, and a French summary, pp. 43–5.

[3] G. Ostrogorsky, *Pour l'histoire de la féodalité byzantine* (translated by H. Grégoire), Brussels, 1954, pp. 268–9. D. Jacoby has shown, 'Phénomènes de démographie rurale à Byzance aux XIIIe, XIVe et XVe siècles', *Études Rurales* 5–6 (April–September 1962), pp. 161–86, how numerous these *praktika* are.

Medieval History[1] as evidence for low fertility in Byzantine Greece. Yet if the average number of adults per family be taken as two, which allows some to be widows or widowers and some others to have extra adults in the family beyond a married couple, the average household size will be 3·69, which is much as Russell believed for England at the same period (3·50),[2] where a birth-rate of over 50 per thousand is probable. Alternatively, if the children be taken as under 14, a ratio of 1·69 to 3·69 would mean that about 46 per cent of the population were under 14, which also implies a high birth-rate. If 1·69 had been the mean number of children *ever* born, or the number of children surviving when a woman had completed her child-bearing, 1·69 would indeed be a low average for a family. The Chilander tenants might have been, on average, only two-thirds of the way through the process of raising a family when the *praktikon* was made; the completed family would then tend towards 2·53 surviving children, and not 1·69, suggesting growth and not decline.

Many other kinds of special survey exist, providing all sorts of demographic data. Gille has devoted[3] some sixteen pages to the demographic data contained in the *enquêtes* of the seventeenth and eighteenth centuries in France, and many other countries have similar surveys in their archives.

Lists of movements or transfers of population are sometimes extant; both Parker and Gould have published[4] some of the results of a depopulation enquiry in England in 1607 following several enclosures, and Hardinge has given data[5] of the Irish

---

[1] 1967 edition, Vol. IV, p. 95.

[2] *Op. cit.* pp. 24 *et seq.*

[3] B. Gille, *Les sources statistiques de l'histoire de France. Des enquêtes de XVIIe siècle à 1870*, Geneva and Paris, 1964, pp. 46–62.

[4] L. A. Parker, 'The Depopulation Returns for Leicestershire in 1607', *Transactions of the Leicestershire Archaeological Society*, **23**, 2 (1947), pp. 229–93; J. D. Gould, 'The Inquisition of Depopulation of 1607 in Lincolnshire', *English Historical Review*, **67**, 264 (July 1952), pp. 392–6.

[5] W. H. Hardinge, 'On Circumstances attending the outbreak of the Civil War in Ireland on 23rd October, 1641, and its continuance to the 12th May,

transplanted to Connaught and Clare in 1653. Such figures are, however, rare. There must have been very many migrations of population that are entirely unrecorded, as well as those that are only recorded in non-numerical terms.

The reports of the governors of the eighteenth-century British colonies in North America[1] can provide a basis for estimating population in the prehistory of the United States of America. It is even possible in this instance to estimate internal migration in America in the period before the first U.S. census of 1790, and the heavy net flow to Virginia and the Carolinas between 1753 and 1790 is very striking.

Griffin's special enquiry[2] into mortality among the poor in the city of Limerick is another instance, dating from nearly a decade before the Irish famine. It is particularly valuable because of the originality of his methods; not the least of Griffin's virtues was that he tells us that he interviewed 5 per cent of his 800 Limerick women twice, through inadvertence, and then found a difference of 11 per cent between the number of deaths the women remembered on the two occasions. Retrospective surveys on mortality are always liable to some such error, but it is rarely assessed. Although Limerick's population was rising, its birth-rate seems to have been only about 35 per thousand, which, with the death-rate at about 50, meant that the city must have been gaining by net immigration. Rural Ireland would therefore not necessarily have had such a late age at marriage (mean age for women, 22) as Limerick city. (A completely non-European marriage

1652; the numerical extent and manner of the Transplantation of Irish into Connaught and Clare; the extent, value, and distribution of the Forfeited Lands; their insufficiency to satisfy the Debts and Arrears due to Adventurers and Soldiers; the solution of that difficulty under the Acts of Settlement and Explanation; and the results of these operations', *Transactions of the Royal Irish Academy*, **24**, 3 (Antiquities) (1874), pp. 379–420.

---

[1] E. Vielrose, 'Mouvements migratoires aux États-Unis au XVIIIe siècle', *Annales de Démographie Historique* (1966), pp. 99–103.

[2] D. Griffin, 'Inquiry into the Mortality occurring among the Poor of the City of Limerick', *Journal of the Statistical Society*, **3** (January 1841), pp. 305–30.

pattern for pre-famine Ireland, in which the mean age of marriage of women would be about 17, has sometimes been suggested.) It is also interesting to recall that today Limerick has about 50,000 people, but at the 1821 census it had nearly 60,000, which rose by 14 per cent in the next decade. Moreover, Griffin thought that the 1831 census population was much under the truth.

Chadwick's report[1] on the sanitary condition of the labouring population of Great Britain is much more widely known, but contains few figures that were not taken straight from the census and registration data. Its success lay in the medical interpretation of the statistics, and in the graphic way in which they were presented, not their originality.

HEARTH TAXES

The unit of taxation was often not the individual adult, nor even the individual adult male. The commonest unit of taxation was the family or the hearth. This, no doubt, was because of the overwhelming convenience of assessment and collection; it is much easier to tax houses or families or hearths than to tax individuals. Hearth taxation provides an incentive to live as a single family unit; but, unless the level of taxation were very high, it would presumably not affect the social structure significantly, except possibly in China. The hearth tax returns are usually assumed to be accurate as far as they go; that is to say, the figures produced of hearths are assumed to be the numbers actually taxed. Beloch naturally used tax returns as his main source for European, and especially Italian, population estimates.[2] Controversy revolves mainly around the number of hearths exempt from

[1] E. Chadwick, *Report of an Inquiry into the Sanitary Condition of the Labouring Population of Great Britain*, London, 1842; M. W. Flinn has edited a new edition, 1965.

[2] K. J. Beloch, 'Die Bevölkerung Europas im Mittelalter', *Zeitschrift für Sozialwissenschaft*, **3**, 6 (1900), pp. 405–23; 'Die Bevölkerung Europas zur Zeit der Renaissance', *ibid.*, pp. 765–86; *Bevölkerungsgeschichte Italiens*, Berlin, 1937–39–61.

taxation and the number of people to each hearth, but Herlihy has argued[1] that by the fifteenth century the tax assessments were too far out of date, in part of Italy at least (rural Pistoia), to be any real use for population estimation. If this is true elsewhere, many studies will have lost their point, but one may suppose that it was rare unless the change in total population was not great. A doubling or a halving of numbers would surely stimulate a new taxation assessment survey.[2]

The more important of these uncertainties is the question of the number of people to a hearth, which amounts to the number of people living in a family. There are a few records in which both the number and the total population and the number of hearths or families are preserved, and these have been used to give an indication of the correct multiplier to apply to the hearth figures. These multipliers vary a great deal, and other evidence, such as accounts of the social pattern of the time or the probable method of agricultural production, has been brought in to determine which hearth-ratios are truly representative and which are unusual. It seems that the average family size can vary between $2\frac{1}{2}$ and 10 according to the figures chosen, and since this variation is so wide, some workers have abandoned the use of taxation data altogether.

Krause attempted[3] to estimate the size of the medieval household, using a number of different sources, but his main conclusion was that the correct multiplier varies from place to place and from time to time, a most important advance in our thinking. Although Russell's idea of a universal multiplier of 3·5 must be discarded, it might still be about the lower limit, often reached in practice.

[1] D. Herlihy, 'Population, Plague and Social Change in Rural Pistoia, 1201–1430', *Economic History Review*, 2nd Series, **18**, 2 (August 1965), pp. 225-44.

[2] J. P. Larner makes a similar point in *The Lords of Romagna. Romagnol Society and the Origins of the Signorie*, London, 1965, pp. 209-19.

[3] J. T. Krause, 'The Medieval Household: Large or Small?', *Economic History Review*, 2nd Series, **9**, 3 (1957), pp. 420-32.

The likelihood is that towns had larger households than the country, for Fiumi has given[1] data on hearths and mouths for Prato in 1428-9 that imply this. In the towns, the mean Prato hearth-coefficient was 5·0, although the range Fiumi found for 42 towns was 3·2 to 6·4; for the countryside (including the suburbs of the towns) the mean coefficient was only 3·7, and the range over eight districts was 3·5 to 4·4. A marked difference therefore appeared between town and country, and so it is important to know whether an area was truly urban or more or less rural.

The hearth multiplier also seems to have fallen generally with time, but not without many variations, and Dupâquier has made[2] an important point about how hearth returns vary in relation to population at a period of demographic crisis. After the 1693 epidemic in The Vexin, population really fell sharply, but the number of hearths fell only by a small amount. Moreover, the hearth numbers continued to fall until 1697, although the epidemic was over and the population was really increasing. Dupâquier's ingenious explanation is as follows: the higher mortality of 1693 widowed a great many women (and, to a lesser extent, men). In only a few cases did both husband and wife die. There was an actual *increase* in the number of 'female' hearths, where the head of the family was a woman. In time, these widows died or remarried, their hearths only then disappearing from the enumerations. This illustration demonstrates how erroneous an impression of population movements will be gained from an annual series of hearth data. Dupâquier has also discussed[3] generally the question of the hearth multiplier in France.

[1] E. Fiumi, 'Stato di popolazione e distribuzione della ricchezza in Prato secondo il catasto del 1428-29', *Archivio Storico Italiano*, **123**, III (No. 447) (1965), pp. 277-303.

[2] J. Dupâquier, 'Des rôles et tailles à la démographie historique. L'exemple du vexin français', *Annales de Démographie Historique* (1965), pp. 31-42.

[3] *Idem*, 'Démographie et sources fiscales', *ibid.*, (1966), pp. 233-40.

Hallam has argued[1] that 4·68 was a more likely hearth-coefficient than 3·5, on the basis of the records of the priory at Spalding, Lincolnshire, between 1253 and 1274. Russell riposted,[2] but it now seems agreed that the mean number per hearth in Lincolnshire was high because the population was growing. The coefficient fell sharply after the Black Death, however, and the general rule that rising populations have higher hearth-coefficients than falling populations can be laid down. Bautier found[3] an average household size of 5·2 in Carpentras, a small town near Avignon, in 1473. This can be taken as evidence for a growing population; but if a hearth-coefficient cannot be estimated until it is known whether or not the population is growing, it is likely to be difficult to estimate the population from the number of hearths.

In his work on Alsace in the seventeenth century, Juillard[4] follows Wiebach in using a hearth multiplier of 4·6, but as he uses it both before and after the Thirty Years War, he has probably over-estimated the losses of population.

Laslett and Harrison found[5] a multiplier of 4·09 at Clayworth in 1676, although 41 per cent of the population was then under 16; but the multiplier rose to 4·43 in 1688. In Cogenhoe, another English village, they found hearth-coefficients of over 5 between 1618 and 1628, despite a very low apparent birth-rate according to the parish register. The sources cannot, in fact, be equally reliable, because they are inconsistent with themselves and with common sense.

[1] Hallam, 'Some thirteenth century censuses', *Economic History Review*, 2nd Series, 10, 3 (1958), pp. 340–61; also *loc. cit.* above on p. 113 (footnote 2) (1961).

[2] Russell, 'Demographic Limitations of the Spalding Serf Lists', *ibid.*, 2nd Series, 15, 1 (1962), pp. 138–44.

[3] R. Bautier, 'Feux, population et structure sociale au milieu du XVe siècle. L'exemple de Carpentras', *Annales, E.S.C.*, 14 (1959), pp. 255–68.

[4] E. Juillard, *La vie rurale dans la plaine de Basse-Alsace. Essai de Géographie Sociale*, Paris, 1953, pp. 504–5.

[5] P. Laslett and J. Harrison, 'Clayworth and Cogenhoe', in *Historical Essays, 1600–1750, presented to D. Ogg* (edited by H. E. Bell and R. L. Ollard), London, 1962, pp. 157–84.

The most important use of a count of households, however, is when we have both the number of people and the number of families and can believe their completeness. This is a fairly rare state of affairs, but obviously it gives more than just information on the matter of the multiplier to apply to numbers of hearths in order to obtain a population figure. Medieval family sizes are worthy of study for their own sake, and taxation data sometimes will show us the social patterns as well. We also need complete lists, in varied demographic conditions, as a guide to the interpretation of taxation returns in general. A good set of data exists for Provence[1] in the thirteenth century, and another is the 's-Hertogenbosch data cited above, but doubt has been thrown upon almost all the English lists that have been discovered, even those that refer to small localities. In some of these local returns the number of inhabitants is equated with the number of households, as in Dale's published returns for London in 1638, where the number of households is surely all that is intended.[2] In really good sets of data, children are distinguished from adults and so we can have a rough idea of the birth-rate; sometimes, when lists are compiled at close intervals, we can estimate the death-rate also. Such estimation is best done from a set of model life-tables, or by comparison with a well-enumerated modern population that happens to fit the pattern of age-structures found.

SURVEY OF SOURCES AND STUDIES

In England, the three most important attempts at enumeration of the population before 1801 all had a fiscal purpose: the

[1] See E. Baratier, *La démographie provençale du XIIIe au XVIe siècle, avec chiffres de comparaison pour le XVIIIe siècle*, Paris, 1961.

[2] See T. C. Dale, *The Inhabitants of London in 1638*, London, 1931. This in turn must cast some doubt upon the twelfth-century estimate for London, given by John Stow in his *Survey of London* (London, 1965; originally published, 1598), that it had 40,000 'inhabitants'. The best general assessment of London population before 1801 is C. Creighton, 'The Population of Old London', *Blackwood's Magazine*, **149** (April 1891), pp. 477–96; apart from a few amendments that can be made to it at particular dates, Creighton's work has not yet been superseded.

Domesday Survey of 1086,[1] the Poll-Tax of 1377[2] and the Duty on Marriages, Burials and Baptisms of 1695.[3] In the first of these there was no actual counting of the people, and in the second hearths were not counted, so that the hearth-ratio is only known in isolated instances.

The Domesday Survey and the Extents have been touched upon already; the Poll-Tax of 1377 is the major source of population data on England in the fourteenth century. Children under 14 were omitted, and two counties (Cheshire and Lancashire) were not taxed; nor were the clergy. With adjustments for under-enumeration of all kinds, Russell estimated the total population at 2,232,373.[4] This includes children at one-third of the total population, suggesting (if we try stable population theory[5]) a birth-rate of between 55 and 60 per 1,000, together with a death-rate of 70 to 75. An even higher birth-rate is quite probable, but in the circumstances Russell's figure can be accepted as fairly likely. Russell was sanguine about under-enumeration, believing that rounding to the nearest groat would account for all the errors by the officials, and allowed only 5 per cent for the indigent and for other untaxed persons apart from the clergy. There is a possibility that the adult population could have been under-enumerated by a larger amount—say 15 per cent—so that

[1] See Russell, *op. cit.* above on p. 113 (footnote 1), pp. 34–54.

[2] See J. Topham, 'Subsidy Roll of 51. Edward III', *Archaeologia*, **7** (1785), pp. 337–47; T. Amyot, 'Remarks on the Population of English Cities in the Time of Edward the Third', *ibid.*, **20** (1824), pp. 524–31; R. A. Pelham, 'Fourteenth century England. The Distribution of Population', in *Historical geography of England before 1800* (edited by H. C. Darby), London, 1936, pp. 230–5; Russell, *op. cit.*, pp. 118–46. M. W. Beresford, 'The Poll Taxes of 1377, 1379 and 1381', *The Amateur Historian*, **3**, 7 (Spring 1958), pp. 271–8, reprinted in *Lay subsidies and poll taxes*, Canterbury, 1964.

[3] See D. V. Glass, 'Gregory King's estimates of the population of England and Wales, 1695', *Population Studies*, III, 4 (March 1950), pp. 338–74, and reprinted in *Population in History* (edited by Glass and Eversley), London, 1965, pp. 183–220.

[4] *Op. cit.*, p. 146.

[5] See Appendix 1.

the true 1377 population would have been over 2,400,000.

Several assessments apart from the 1377 Poll-Tax exist that relate to the middle ages.[1] Some have been collected, including all those for Liverpool;[2] other poll-taxes are less complete, however, and their demographic value is accordingly doubtful; but Titow, for one, is undeterred, and uses[3] the hundred penny payments of the thirteenth and early-fourteenth centuries as his main source. Peter's pence, the ecclesiastical taxes paid to Rome, cannot be used for population research[4] because they were arbitrarily fixed and not well recorded, but the manorial death-taxes, or heriots,[5] are more useful. Methods similar to Fisher's on wills[6] might deduce the height of mortality peaks from the heriots, but Ohlin has shown[7] that they are weak as evidence of actual death-rates before 1348, owing to possible splitting of holdings and changes in the age-structure of tenants.

Thrupp had the idea[8] of using the data from the Alien Subsidies in England of the middle of the fifteenth century to estimate the number of foreigners in the country, but the uncertainties as to whether all of them were assessed and the absence of data for

[1] See Beresford, *loc. cit.*; also 'The Lay Subsidies', *The Amateur Historian*, **3**, 8 (Summer 1958), pp. 325–8 and **4**, 3 (Spring 1959), pp. 101–9; all of which are reprinted in Beresford's *op. cit.* (footnote 2, opposite).

[2] See R. Stewart-Brown, *The inhabitants of Liverpool from the 14th to the 18th century*, Liverpool, 1930.

[3] J. Z. Titow, 'Some Evidence of the Thirteenth Century Population Increase', *Economic History Review*, 2nd Series, **14**, 2 (1961), pp. 218–24.

[4] F. Liebermann, 'Peter's pence and the population of England about 1164', *English Historical Review*, **11**, 44 (October 1896), pp. 744–7.

[5] E. Robo, 'The Black Death in the Hundred of Farnham', *English Historical Review*, **44** (October 1929), pp. 560–72; M. M. Postan and J. Titow, 'Heriots and Prices on Winchester Manors', *Economic History Review*, 2nd Series, **11**, 3 (1959), pp. 392–411; J. Longdon, 'Statistical Notes on Winchester Heriots', *ibid.*, pp. 412–17.

[6] See p. 236.

[7] *Loc. cit.* above on p. 113 (footnote 4).

[8] S. L. Thrupp, 'A Survey of the Alien Population of England in 1440', *Speculum*, **32**, 2 (1957), pp. 262–73.

many counties make it a hazardous attempt. However, although the demographic importance of aliens can only be slight, her minimum figure of 16,000 aliens in the working population of England about 1440 does suggest that the proportion of the population that had been born abroad was of the order of 1 per cent, which seems quite high. In modern times, 5 per cent born outside the country is more the order of magnitude, however.

Lay subsidies were latterly a form of tax that fell upon a community rather than an individual, the community deciding for itself how to allot the burden of taxation upon families or individuals. The first lay subsidies to be raised in this way were in 1334, but after the Black Death of 1348, revisions (downwards) of the amount of the assessment were fairly common for about a century, and then ceased. If they are good for nothing else, the fifteenth century lay subsidies do therefore agree with the idea of a population decline until about 1450 followed by an increase, for which there is other evidence.

The Tudor lay subsidies can at least be made to show that migration was probably high,[1] as we saw in Chapter 2. Properly handled, they might fill an important gap in our population estimates for England, for the early-Tudor period is not one of the best documented, and yet an important increase in population probably occurred.

The Hearth Tax of 1662–74[2] is a major source of data. Chamberlayne, a contemporary, may have used it to estimate the total

---

[1] See S. A. Peyton, 'The Village Population in the Tudor Lay Subsidy Rolls', *English Historical Review*, **30**, CXVIII (April 1915), pp. 234–50; J. Thirsk, 'Sources of Information of Population (I)', *The Amateur Historian*, **4**, 4 (Summer 1959), pp. 129–33; J. Cornwall, 'English Country Towns in the Fifteen Twenties', *Economic History Review*, 2nd Series, **15**, 1 (1962), pp. 54–69.

[2] L. M. Marshall, 'The Levying of the Hearth Tax, 1662–88', *English Historical Review*, **51**, 204 (October 1936), pp. 628–46; *Surrey Hearth Tax, 1664* (edited by C. A. F. Meekings), London, 1940; L. Owen, 'The population of Wales in the sixteenth and seventeenth centuries', *Transactions of the Honourable Society of Cymmrodorion* (1959), pp. 99–113; J. Thirsk, 'Sources of Information of Population (II)', *The Amateur Historian*, **4**, 5 (Autumn 1959), pp. 182–5.

population of England at 5,446,000,[1] although ostensibly his method was based upon the 9,725 parishes of England (he allowed 80 families to each, and 7 people in each family).

Marshall used all the seventeenth-century data, especially the Hearth Taxes and the Compton census, to study local population trends in Bedfordshire;[2] she gives a good account of their joint value, and of the practical difficulties of their interpretation. Gregory King[3] apparently used the returns of the preliminary survey for the 1695 Marriage Duty, which was also to tax bachelors and childless widowers (and therefore needed to count the whole population). His object was to calculate not merely the total population of England but its social structure and demographic rates of change. The Hearth Tax Returns of 1690 apparently gave King the opportunity to derive a population estimate from the number of houses and very incomplete data on the household size.[4] However, as we saw in the previous chapter, King may really have done something quite different with these figures. His achievement was his age-structure of the population, using, in particular, data for his native city of Lichfield which he collected himself. Lichfield may, of course, have been atypical, but the birth-rate implied for about 1680–95 is much higher than is usually thought likely. It would seem, however, that King's figures are more to be trusted than Rickman's retrospective

[1] E. Chamberlayne, *Angliae Notitia; or the present state of England, Together with divers reflections upon the antient state thereof*, London, 3rd edn, 1669; 5th edn, 1674. (In the latter, see Vol. I, p. 56.)

[2] L. M. Marshall, *The Rural Population of Bedfordshire, 1671 to 1921*, Aspley Guise (Bedfordshire Historical Record Society, Vol. XVI), 1934.

[3] Gregory King, 'Natural and political observations and conclusions upon the state and condition of England 1696', in G. Chalmers, *An estimate of the comparative strength of Great Britain and of the losses of her trade from every war since the revolution*, London, 3rd edn, 1802.

[4] Extensive use of the 1692 Land-Tax is made in H. Ashworth, 'Statistica Illustrations of the Past and Present state of Lancashire, and more particularly of the hundred of Salford', *Journal of the Statistical Society*, **5** (October 1842), pp. 245–56.

estimates[1] of English population, made in the nineteenth century, because a census is a better basis for calculation than a registration system. Chalmers, who was the first to publish King's pamphlet, is interesting as showing what was believed in the eighteenth century;[2] he amends King's estimates, compounding them with those of Davenant and Halley. An important feature of King's work was that he appreciated that the number of persons per house was higher in towns than in the country, just as Fiumi found[3] in fifteenth-century Italy, and allowed for it in making his estimates. He also thought that the omissions and the returns were greatest in the towns. The Marriage Duties of 1695–1706 should have yielded annual data of births and deaths for eleven years,[4] but very few of the returns exist except for London.[5] These latter may have been very bad indeed after 1700, although the evidence is conflicting.[6] The only other English tax of this period that

[1] *Census of Great Britain 1801*, 'Observations on the Results of the Population Act, 41, Geo. III', London, 1802; *Census of Great Britain 1841*, 'Enumeration Abstract, Preface', London, 1843, pp. 34–7.

[2] Chalmers, *op. cit.* The first two editions (not including King's pamphlet) appeared in 1772 and 1786. We are told: that there were 45,002 parishes in England in 1070 although only 8,700 in 1370; that the mortality in 1349 had little permanent effect, on the ground that armies were considerable and easy to raise; that the 1377 population was 2,811,204; and that the muster of 1574–5 gave a basis for putting the population at that date at 4,690,696, of whom 468,800 should be allowed for Wales.

[3] *Loc. cit.* above on p. 119 (footnote 1).

[4] P. H. Styles, 'A Census of a Warwickshire Village in 1698', *University of Birmingham Historical Journal*, **3** (1951–2), pp. 33–51.

[5] See P. E. Jones and A. V. Judges, 'London Population in the late seventeenth century', *Economic History Review*, **6**, 1 (October 1935), pp. 45–63; Glass, *loc. cit.* above on p. 122 (footnote 3), and introduction to *London Inhabitants within the Walls 1695* (London Record Society Publications, No. 2), London, 1966, pp. ix–xxxviii.

[6] See Sir John Sinclair, *The History of the Public Revenue of the British Empire*, London, 2nd edn, 1790, Part III, p. 11, where the following statistics of the receipts from the Duty are given: 1 May 1695 to 1 May 1700—£258,094; 1 May 1700 to 1 August 1706—£17,422 16s. 2½d. The annual rate of return was therefore exactly £51,618 16s. 0d. during the first five years of the Duty, and

might help the demographer, the window tax of the eighteenth century, is little use; many houses did not pay.[1]

Jersey's tax-lists have been studied by Blench,[2] although his approach includes no new techniques. Dublin has received a good deal of attention in view of its striking apparent growth between 1659 and 1682,[3] and the study of population in seventeenth-century Ireland in general owes much to Petty, who emulated Chamberlayne in his study[4] of Irish population in 1686. His methods are by no means all that could be desired, yet there can be little doubt that his figures are not far from the truth, at least as regards the total population. Connell and Butlin have recently discussed[5] Irish historical population in detail. A contemporary source is South, who published the results of counts of people, houses and hearths in January 1696 and January 1697.[6] A high

almost £2,747 13s. od. during its remaining six and a quarter years. Gregory King had expected the Duty to produce £81,050 a year, although he tells us that it was 'given for' £130,000. According to W. Cobbett, *Parliamentary History of England*, London, 1809, Vol. V, Appendix XIX, however, the latter figure is up to 1 August 1700 only. Even so, King's rule was not achieved.

[1] See W. Brakenridge, 'A letter concerning the present increase of the people in Britain and Ireland', *Philosophical Transactions of the Royal Society*, **49**, 2 (1756), Art. CXIII, pp. 877–90, 'An answer to the account of the numbers and increase of the people of England, by the Rev. Mr Forster', *ibid.*, **50**, 1 (1757), Art. LVIII, pp. 465–79; and R. Forster, 'Letter concerning the number of people in England', *ibid.*, **50**, 1 (1757), Art. LVII, pp. 456–65.

[2] B. J. R. Blench, 'La population et le peuplement de Jersey', *Norois*, **14**, 54 (April–June 1967), pp. 227–39.

[3] R. A. Butlin, 'The Population of Dublin in the late Seventeenth Century' *Irish Geography*, **5**, 2 (1965), pp. 51–66.

[4] *The economic writings of Sir William Petty, together with the Observations upon the bills of mortality, more probably by Captain John Graunt* (edited by C. H. Hull), Cambridge, 1899.

[5] K. H. Connell, *The Population of Ireland*, Oxford, 1950; Butlin, *loc. cit.*

[6] Captain South, 'An Account of the houses and hearths in Dublin, for the years following', *Philosophical Transactions of the Royal Society*, **22**, 261 (February 1700), p. 518, and 'An Account of the number of people in the counties of Ardmagh, Lowth, and Meath, and the city of Dublin; with an estimate of the number of people in the kingdom of Ireland, 10 January 1695/6', *ibid.*, p. 520;

ratio emerges in Dublin: nearly 5 hearths per house, although this figure varied from parish to parish[1] as between 1·5 and 6·7 during the years 1664–95.

The taxation of 1696, as in England and Ireland, is an important source of data on Scotland, although it was not a Duty on Marriages but a poll-tax in Scotland and Ireland. Only Aberdeenshire and Renfrewshire, however, seem to have surviving returns, and on the strength of the former Walton has argued for a nucleated distribution for Aberdeenshire's population at that time.[2] There is, however, no direct way of checking any assumptions we make about the size of the family and hence of the total population, except the evidence (largely given us by King) from the Marriage Duty data, all of which concerns England. Preferring low figures or high can be sometimes a matter of prejudice, rather than evidence, so as to give results that agree with one's preconceptions.

Italy has particularly good sets of taxation data for the medieval period, sometimes providing a social breakdown of the population by occupation. This is particularly true for the kingdom of Naples and Sicily,[3] where extensive research has been done. Felloni has recently considered Genoa,[4] and Fiumi[5] and Herlihy[6] give data on hearth-population ratios in late-medieval Italy.

this latter estimate of the total population comes to no more than 1,034,102, or less than half of what Connell allows.

[1] Butlin, *loc. cit.*

[2] K. Walton, 'The Distribution of Population in Aberdeenshire, 1696', *Scottish Geographical Magazine*, 66, 1 (June 1950), pp. 17–26; 'Population changes in the North-East of Scotland, 1696–1951', *Scottish Studies*, 5 (1961), pp. 149–80.

[3] See Beloch, *Bevolkerungsgeschichte Italiens*, Berlin 1937–39–61, especially Vol. I.

[4] G. Felloni, 'Per la storia della popolazione di Genova nel secoli XVI e XVII', *Archivio Storico Italiano*, 110 (1952), pp. 236–53, and 'Popolazione e case a Genova nel 1531–35', *Atti della società ligure di storia patria*, N.S. IV (78), Fasc. 2 (1964), pp. 305–23.

[5] Fiumi, *Storia economica e sociale di San Gimignano*, Florence, 1961, p. 174.

[6] Herlihy, *Medieval and Renaissance Pistoia. The Social History of an Italian Town, 1200–1430*, New Haven and London, 1967, pp. 55–120.

The 'Polyptyques', lists of tenants and their families, usually of an abbey, are most important sources of early demographic data for France.[1] Lot has written extensively on the main national source for later-medieval France, the 1328 taxation of hearths,[2] and Aquitaine (not then ruled from Paris) is covered by the 1316 Hearth Tax of Edward II of England;[3] the medieval sources for Périgueux have been described[4] in full detail. French demographic sources for the fourteenth century are best south of the Loire and in the towns,[5] but the French Hearth Tax returns for 1664 to 1709 seem to be largely lost. Many areas of France have recently been studied[6] at a local level from old tax data, mostly as part of general local histories.

There have been studies showing a similar picture to Italy and

[1] See: M. Bloch, 'Les invasions: occupation du sol et peuplement', *Annales d'histoire sociale*, **8** (1945), pp. 13–28; C. E. Perrin, 'Note sur la population de Villeneuve-Saint-Georges au IXe siècle', *Le Moyen Age*, **69** (1963), pp. 75–86; N. J. G. Pounds, 'Northwest Europe in the Ninth Century; its Geography in Light of the Polyptyques', *Annals of the Association of American Geographers*, **57,** 3 (September 1967), pp. 439–61. An early article by Lot in *Le Moyen Age* (1921) is useful for its data, but demographically unsound.

[2] F. Lot, 'L'état des paroisses et des feux de 1328', *Bibliothèque de l'École des Chartres*, **90** (1929), pp. 51–107 and 256–315.

[3] Y. Renouard, 'Conjectures sur la population du duché d'Aquitaine en 1316', *Le Moyen Age*, **69** (1963), pp. 471–8.

[4] A. Higounet-Nadal, *Les competes de la taille et les sources de l'histoire démographique de Périgueux au XIVe siècle*, Paris, 1965.

[5] É. Carpentier and J. Glenisson, 'Bilans et méthodes: la démographie française au XIVe siècle', *Annales E.S.C.*, **17,** 1 (January–February 1962), pp. 109–29. This paper also evaluates the various sources that are available.

[6] Such studies include: Baratier, *op. cit.* above on p. 121 (footnote 1): P. Wolff, *Les estimes toulousaines des XIVe et XVe siècles*, Toulouse, 1956, which is critically analysed in J.-N. Biraben, 'La population de Toulouse au XIVe et au XVe siècles', *Journal des Savants*, October–December 1964, pp. 284–300; P. Dollinger, 'Le chiffre de population de Paris au XIVe siècle: 210.000 ou 80.000 habitants?', *Revue historique*, **216** (July–September 1956), pp. 35–44; G. Fourquin, 'La population de la régoin parisienne aux environs de 1328', *Le Moyen Age*, **62** (1956), pp. 63–91. The last two, dealing with Paris, begin with the work of Lot (*loc. cit.*) and of A.-J.-C.-A. Dureau de la Malle, 'L'État des paroisses et feux des baillages et sénéchaussées de France', *Bibliothèque de l'École des Chartres* **2** (1840–1), pp. 169–76.

France in many other parts of Europe.[1] Without a considerable national effort, however, it is not easy to relate the findings of different workers together and so to conclude what the true levels of population are likely to have been. If one could assume that all studies are equally well done and each is of an area thoroughly representative of the country it would be interesting and informative, but it is highly probable that great divergences occur. We must therefore wait until more work has been published before deciding what the patterns truly show. Davídek has recently reviewed the problems of using the various registers of land and revenue and the early censuses in Bohemia for population research between 1557 and 1848,[2] which should greatly help further work on the historical demography of Czechoslovakia.

The sources of Hungarian historical demography have been thoroughly considered,[3] and it is clear that from the eleventh

[1] For the Netherlands, see J. A. Faber, H. K. Roessingh, B. H. Slicher van Bath, A. M. van der Woude, and H. J. van Xanten, 'Population changes and economic developments in the Netherlands: a historical survey', *Afdeling Agrarische Geschiedenis Bijdragen*, **12** (1965), pp. 47–113, or the French summary in *Annales de Démographie Historique* (1965), pp. 199–226. For Spain, see: R. S. Smith, 'Fourteenth-Century Population Records of Catalonia', *Speculum*, **19** (October 1944), pp. 494–501; J. Nadal and E. Giralt, *La population catalane de 1553 à 1717. L'immigration française et les autres facteurs de son développement*, Paris, 1960; Russell, 'The Medieval Monedatage of Aragon and Valencia', *Proceedings of the American Philosophical Society*, **106** (1962), pp. 483–504; A. Castillo, 'Population et "richesses" dans la deuxième moitié du XVIe siècle', *Annales E.S.C.*, **20**, 4 (July--August 1965), pp. 719–33. For Bohemia, see O. Placht, *Lidnatost a společenská skladba. Českého státu, v 16–18 století*, Prague, 1957 (German summary). For Germany, see F. Koerner, 'Die Bevölkerungszahl und -dichte in Mitteleuropa zum Beginn der Neuzeit', *Forschungen und Fortschritte*, **33**, (1959) pp. 325–31. For Belgium, see M. A. Arnould *Les dénombrements de foyers dans le comté de Hainaut (XIVe–XVIe siècles)*, Brussels, 1956.

[2] V. Davídek, 'Statistické příspěvky o osídlení a zalidnení České země v 16. a 17. století', *Demografie*, **7**, 2, (1965), pp. 128–44, and 'Statistické příspěvky o demografii České země v 18. století a do poloviny 19. století (1. část)', *ibid.*, **9**, 2 1967, pp. 142–54.

[3] See *A Történeti Statisztika Forrásai* (edited by J. Kovacsics), Budapest, 1957; and Z. Dávid, 'A történeti demográfiai források értékelésének kérdései' *Demográfia*, **6**, 4 (1963) pp. 515–25. Each has a summary in English.

century onwards, the Hungarian archives are rich and as yet little exploited. As well as the normal state taxations, the lords and the clergy have also left us many fiscal documents. However, they are not always consistent with each other, and there may have been large-scale omissions at times. A census of Hungary in the late-eighteenth century[1] found an average household size of 5·28. There was an immense variation over the country, caused by the seven Croatian counties which averaged 8·33 persons per household, while the other fifty-three counties only ranged between 4·55 and 6·07.

Denmark had a 'Census of Peasants' in 1660, which was really a poll-tax.[2] The sharp decline in Danish population between 1651 and 1662 makes its importance difficult to assess, especially as the Swedish invasion of this period came in the wake of a very severe outbreak of plague. It was, naturally, not uncommon to initiate a census just after important demographic changes had occurred, confusing as it is for us today.

Finland has no documents earlier than the seventeenth century,[3] but there was a farm-census in 1600–10. One of the provinces has lists of taxable people which show violent declines following the famines of the seventeenth century, but lists of proprietors at the same epoch show that most of them escaped the tax. The prime sources of population estimates for eighteenth-century Russia are the Poll-Tax returns,[4] the earliest of which are for 1723. However, the earlier returns are probably incomplete. Nominal

---

[1] J. Tamásy, 'Az 1784–1787, évi elsö magyarországi népszámlálás család- és háztartásstatisztikai vonatkozásai', *ibid.*, **6**, 4 (1963), pp. 526–37, with English summary.

[2] A. Lassen, 'The Population of Denmark in 1660', *Scandinavian Economic History Review*, XIII, 1 (1965), pp. 1–30.

[3] E. Jutikkala, 'Can the Population of Finland in the 17th Century be Calculated?' *Scandinavian Economic History Review*, **5** (1958), pp. 155–72.

[4] See M. Reinhard, 'La population de la Russe au XVIIIe siècle et dans la première moitié du XIXe', *Études et chronique de démographie historique* (1964), pp. 178–83, where he reviews a book in Russian (Moscow, 1963) by V. M. Kabuzan with that title.

lists of proprietors have been collected from six inventories taken between 1828 and 1860 in the Nizhniy-Novgorod government.[1] These must be valuable for showing population trends in detail, especially migration, and they are the first solid evidence we have that the Russians are taking a new interest in historical demography.

Poland presents particular difficulties to the demographic historian, owing to the frequent territorial changes and the migrations of the Polish people.[2] Peter's pence—the church-tax payable to Rome[3]—was raised *per capita* in Poland except in the Poznań diocese, where the tax was on a family basis. The lists were also incomplete owing to law, custom, or abuses. A later source of demographic data for Poland are the registers of the contributions from each messuage, about 1578. It is, however, difficult to convert messuages into numbers of peasants because the seigneurial reserve would be developed to different extents in different parts of the country.

There are numerous taxation returns by hearths for the Ottoman Empire. According to Inalcik,[4] the earliest of the *defter-i hâkâni* record books dates from A.H. 835 (A.D. 1431/2), but they are particularly common in the sixteenth century. Barkan[5] has

[1] I. D. Koval'chenko and V. A. Ustinov, 'La vie rurale en Russie au XIXe siècle: les calculateurs électroniques appliqués aux études rurales', *Annales E.S.C.*, **20**, 6 (November–December 1965), pp. 1128–49; this is a translation by N. Godneff of their article that appeared in *Вопросы Истории*, 5 (1964), pp. 54–68.

[2] W. Kula, 'Stan i potrzeby badań nad demografją historyczną dawnej Polski (do początków XIX wieku)', *Roczniki dziejów spolcznych i gospodarczych*, **13** (1951), pp. 23–106, with a summary in French.

[3] See also Russell, *Late Ancient and Medieval Population, Transactions of the American Philosophical Society*, New Series, **48**, 3 (1958).

[4] H. Inalcik, 'Ottoman methods of conquest', *Studia Islamica*, **2** (1954), pp. 103–29.

[5] Ö. L. Barkan, 'Essai sur les données statistiques des registres de recensement dans l'Empire Ottoman aux XVe et XVIe siècles', *Journal of the Economic and Social History of the Orient* **1** (1957–8), pp. 9–36. For some comments in English on the same data, see Russell, 'Late Medieval Balkan and Asia Minor Population', *ibid.*, **3** (1960), pp. 265–74.

analysed a certain amount of this material, but since it is written in Turkish (and in Arabic script at that) it is difficult of access to most scholars. The Turkish administration of the Balkans, however, was probably more efficient at that time than the administrations of the early-nineteenth century in those countries soon after independence. Only after some decades of separate government would the civil service be able to enumerate the households competently. A considerable vein of rich ore here awaits the enterprising polyglot demographer, or the energetic Turk such as Barkan himself. Two Bulgarians, N. Todorov and V. Katsarkova, have made a promising start on some of the later Ottoman data,[1] using the census of population and property in 1866 of the vilayet of the Danube. The wide difference in the mean age at marriage of the two sexes (26 to 31 for men, 15 to 21 for women) is especially interesting. Jacoby, studying the Byzantine Empire during the 350 years before the Turkish conquest,[2] found hearth-coefficients varying between 3·2 and 5·2 for the same localities, a warning of pitfalls ahead for researchers in this field.

China, as usual, has very many figures, but they conflict. The ratio of mouths to families varies remarkably with time, and also sometimes from province to province. The basis of taxation must in fact have been changed from time to time, since this is the only way of explaining the discrepancies in the figures. It is also probable that large-scale migration or the absence of control by the government over parts of the country at certain times,

[1] N. Todorov and V. Katsarkova, 'Някои данни за семейството и възрастовата структура на градското население в Дунавския вилает през XIX век *International Symposium on the Problems of Human Reproduction*, Varna, September 1968.

[2] D. Jacoby, 'Phénomènes de démographie rurale à Byzance aux XIIIe, XIVe et XVe siècles', *Études Rurales*, **5–6** (April–September 1962), pp. 161–86. See also P. Charanis, 'Observations on the Demography of the Byzantine Empire', *Proceedings of the XIIIth International Congress of Byzantine Studies* (edited by J. M. Hussey, D. Obolensky and S. Runciman); London, 1967, pp. 445–64.

have caused the data to be useless for retrospective demographic research, although no doubt effective enough as a means of raising money at the time.[1]

Very little is known about ancient Indian population, or indeed about Indian population before roughly 1820, and even the early censuses of India are incomplete and somewhat unreliable. The prospects for further research in India depend largely upon what data the Census of India and the Socio-Economic Research Institute of Calcutta can collect.[2] Martin's figures for the District of Southern Concan in 1821,[3] for instance, seem to suggest a population with a birth-rate of about 67 and a normal death-rate of about 48 per thousand, but in which one baby girl in three was exposed; but this is mere speculation, based simply upon the relative proportions of the sexes under age 12 and model life-tables. Several other models would fit equally well.

Burney estimated the population of the Burman Empire[4] on the basis of the lists of houses in 1783 and 1826. His multiplier of 7 persons to a house and his guess of 10 per cent omitted returns seem arbitrary, and his results diverged a great deal from his predecessors'. The range (Symes arrived at a figure four times as large as Burney) serves to remind us how uncertain even near-contemporaries could be about population.

In Africa, Ganiage used the *mejba* to estimate the population of

[1] Since population statistics for China turn upon the distinction between a census and a poll-tax, which is not always clear, we have discussed the taxation data already in chapter 3, and give no further references here.

[2] There are some older studies; for example, C. Finch, 'Vital Statistics of Calcutta', *Journal of the Statistical Society*, 13 (May 1850), pp. 168–82. This is based upon the house-tax of 1793, 1822, and 1837, as well as other data. It is interesting that over 50 years, 1793–1843, Finch in fact found a continual decline in population, or at least in houses.

[3] Census of India 1961, *Report on the Population Estimates of India*, Vol. IV (*1820–1830*) (edited by D. Bhattacharya and B. Bhattacharya), New Delhi, 1964, pp. 161–4.

[4] H. Burney, 'On the Population of the Burman Empire', *Journal of the Statistical Society*, 4, 4 (January 1842), pp. 335–47.

Tunis in 1860.[1] (The *mejba* was a tax that the bey had instituted in 1856.) However, any attempt to assess the African population in general before 1920 is almost hopeless except for the area north of the Sahara. Without any system of civilization, in the sense of a tax-collecting government, there is no written evidence to go on.

Returns of taxation from New Spain in the sixteenth century have been deeply studied by Cook, Simpson, and Borah.[2] They show that the only possible explanation of the steadily diminishing value of each part of the country is that the population was declining very rapidly between 1519 and 1608. Original archives that had not previously been studied showed that the total decline in population in Central Mexico came to the order of 90 per cent of the original level, numbers dropping from 25 million to $2\frac{1}{2}$ million. This is so large a figure—even over a century or so—that it was disbelieved at first in some quarters, but it is now generally accepted; it must count as the greatest change in our ideas of the demography of any past era that has been made in the last twenty years, although not everyone had accepted a pre-conquest population as low as Cook originally preferred.[3] The

[1] J. Ganiage, 'La population de la Tunisie vers 1860. Essai d'évaluation d'après les registres fiscaux', *Population*, **21**, 5 (September–October 1966), pp. 857–86.

[2] S. F. Cook and L. B. Simpson, *The Population of Central Mexico in the Sixteenth Century*, Berkeley and Los Angeles, 1948; W. Borah and Cook, 'The Rate of Population Change in Central Mexico, 1550–1570' *Hispanic American Historical Review*, **37**, 4 (1957), pp. 463–70; Borah and Cook, *The Population of Central Mexico in 1548*, Berkeley, 1960; Cook and Borah, *The Indian Population of Central Mexico, 1531–1610*, Berkeley, 1960; Borah and Cook, *The Aboriginal Population of Central Mexico on the Eve of the Spanish Conquest*, Berkeley and Los Angeles, 1963. Their work has been reviewed by P. Chaunu, 'La population de l'Amérique indienne', *Revue Historique*, **88**, 232 (July–September 1964), pp. 111–18.

[3] S. F. Cook, 'Human Sacrifice and Warfare as Factors in the Demography of pre-colonial Mexico', *Human Biology*, **18**, 2 (May 1946), pp. 81–102; the pre-conquest population is put (p. 93) at only two million. But a decade earlier, six million had been suggested; see D. Camavitto, *La Decadenza delle popolazione messicane al tempo della Conquista*, Rome, 1935, p. 242.

Spanish Government of the day was presumably aware of the population trend but regarded it as such a poor advertisement for their rule that they made sure that the facts were not generally known. It does not matter much here what multiplier is used to convert taxation returns into population, since only if the number of persons per household had multiplied by ten during the century would it be possible that the population had not declined. In such an event, the Spaniards would no doubt have reorganized the basis of collection. One must suppose that there is more unclassified evidence for North and South America in the sixteenth, seventeenth and eighteenth centuries existing in Spanish archives that awaits editing and analysis.

CONCLUSION

The prospects for further advances in historical demography from taxation sources are twofold. First, several sets of tax returns remain largely unexploited, although a few pioneer studies on local areas have proved that they can be used. There are probably many others that would at least give the relative geographical distribution of the population at the time. Second, a better understanding of how the proportion of children or the mean household size tends to vary is gradually enabling us to make a better conversion of the taxed population into total population.

CHAPTER 5

Vital Registration Data

INTRODUCTION

Even if we do not have direct knowledge of the population size itself, the rate of its natural change is often available from registers of births and deaths. Naturally, if both census and vital registration material are available, as in England for more than 130 years past, analysis can go much deeper than from either source by itself.

In historical research, two kinds of vital registration are frequently encountered, and need to be distinguished sharply. Civil registers, kept by state officials, are the modern basis of most demographic analyses; ecclesiastical registers, however, kept by religious officials, are often all that exist for the centuries we want to study. The practical importance of the distinction, clear as it is in principle, will emerge in the course of this chapter.

ORIGINS AND STATE OF THE REGISTERS

Civil registration is in force very widely today, and in most parts of Europe it dates from a reform of the church register system, generally in the nineteenth century. While civil registration is familiar, the parish registers have not been used for demographic research to any great extent, bearing in mind the millions of vital events that they jointly record. The earliest of those still in existence is for Givry in Burgundy,[1] which begins in 1334. Registers were generally instituted during the Renaissance in most countries of Europe, and a large number of them have been preserved

---

[1] R. Mols, *Introduction à la démographie historique des villes d'Europe, du XIVe au XVIIIe siècle*, Louvain, 1954–6, Vol. I, p. 78.

until the present day.[1] The vital events—births, marriages and deaths—thus recorded still await detailed analysis except in a few hundred parishes at the most. These records are highly disparate, both in their physical completeness and in the comprehensiveness of their information. In some parishes full information is given about the occupations of bridegrooms at the time of their marriage, for example, or of the ages of the individuals at death. In other parishes a minimum of information is given, so that a person is scarcely identifiable at all. Again, the registers of many parishes show gaps which may be explained either by the death of the incumbent and his non-replacement for a period of years, or, more often, by the physical loss of the records themselves.

Most of the English registers were begun because of Thomas Cromwell's Ordinance of 1538, but a very few exist from slightly earlier.[2] A scheme was proposed[3] in 1849 for making a general index to all the English parish registers that would only have cost £70,000, but nothing was done, and it would be much more expensive today and less complete as well. The keeping of parish registers was legally required, but there was no real means of enforcing it; hence, particularly in the earlier centuries, many parishes kept their records in a slovenly way. The Injunction of 1538 required: 'that every Sunday, in the presence of at least one of the church-wardens, the parson, vicar, or curate should enter in the said book a written record of the dates and names of the weddings, christenings, and burials of the preceding week'.[4]

---

[1] See also Mols, 'Les origines pastorales de quelques relevés démographiques', *Studi in onore di Armintore Fanfani*, Vol. 5, Milan, 1962.

[2] The best general account of the English parish registers, although now somewhat out of date, is J. C. Cox, *The parish registers of England*, London, 1910.

[3] E. Wyatt-Edgell, 'Proposals for preserving and making a general index of Parish Registers anterior to 1837', *Journal of the Statistical Society*, **13** (August 1850), pp. 218–21.

[4] G. Seton, *Sketch of the history and imperfect condition of the Parochial Records of Births, Deaths and Marriages in Scotland, in illustration of the important advantages which would be derived from the introduction of compulsory registration*, Edinburgh, 1854, p. 2.

This requirement could not work well, because in many parishes half the weeks might be blank, and the habit of writing up the register would never get established.

The present state of the English registers is described by Walne[1] and, from a more demographic point of view, by Wrigley.[2] Mardon[3] gives an illuminating account of the whole development of registration from 1538 to the present which is valuable because, as a superintendent registrar himself, he brings out the points that occur to the man who does the job.

It is particularly revealing to see how poorly the ecclesiastical machinery worked in parts of the country. The bishops' transcripts for the 142 Surrey parishes, which should have been sent to Winchester every year between 1597 and 1800, for instance, were found to be almost wholly incomplete by the Committee on Public Records in 1800. Only twenty registers were in the registry at Winchester and 28,206 transcripts were missing.[4] Henderson[5] has stressed how badly the system of 'searchers' worked, especially in London. Although they were officially appointed to check on registration, they were usually needy old women, open to bribery and often drunk on gin.[6]

One must also appreciate that parish registers do not cover the entire population. In England, it is known from other sources,[7]

[1] P. Walne, 'Parish registers and the registration of births, marriages and deaths in England and Wales', *Archivum*, VIII (1958), pp. 79–87.

[2] E. A. Wrigley, 'Parish Registers and Population History', *The Amateur Historian*, 6, 5 (Autumn 1964), pp. 146–51, and 6, 6 (Winter 1965), pp. 198–203.

[3] C. H. Mardon, 'A History of the Registration of Births, Deaths, and Marriages in England and Wales', *Population Registration*, 5, 3 (September 1967), pp. 3–22.

[4] Cox, *op. cit.*, p. 240.

[5] L. O. Henderson, 'Parish Registers', *The Amateur Historian*, 4, 6 (Winter 1959–60), pp. 232–4.

[6] See also D. V. Glass, 'Notes on the Demography of London at the End of the Seventeenth Century', *Daedalus* (Spring 1968), pp. 581–92.

[7] See, for example, F. Beckwith, 'The population of Leeds during the industrial revolution', *Publications of the Thoresby Society, Miscellany*, 12, 2 (1948), pp. 118–96. The period is 1734-1800.

and obvious on close analysis, that the proportion of persons baptized of those who were actually born was substantially below 100 per cent, at least by 1780.[1] The reasons are diverse: Nonconformity is the most obvious, anti-clericalism and slackness on the part of the clergy also contributed. Registration was especially bad in the towns; Hammond has pointed out[2] that two-thirds of the Manchester burials in 1821–30 were of Dissenters and only one-third of Anglicans. This rate could lead to a death-rate of not 14 per thousand but 48, which she calls 'fantastic'; but 14 would be more fantastic than 48 for the death-rate of Manchester in the midst of the Industrial Revolution.

The Scottish registers are very poor, and their state is best described by Seton.[3] A provincial council was held at Edinburgh in 1551, which ordained that every curate should henceforth keep a register of all baptisms and of proclamations of marriage.[4] A General Assembly in 1565 added a register of deaths to the requirements, and in 1574 every kirk was enjoined to present its list of deaths to the General Assembly. Other ecclesiastical injunctions were made in subsequent years, which were obviously highly necessary; unfortunately, the state of the registers must be assumed poor from the very need for so many injunctions and the evidence of many contemporaries. A few registers may have been maintained in good order, but most were chronically incomplete. For example, Seton cites[5] Arnot's *History of Edin-*

---

[1] See J. T. Krause: 'Changes in English Fertility and Mortality, 1781–1850', *Economic History Review*, 2nd Series, **11**, 1 (1958), pp. 52–70; 'English Population Movements between 1700 and 1850 (I)', *International Population Conference* (New York), 1961, Vol. I, pp. 583–9; 'The Changing Adequacy of English Registration, 1690–1837', in *Population in History* (edited by Glass and D. E. C. Eversley), London, 1965, pp. 379–93; and 'Some Aspects of Population Change, 1690–1790', in *Land, Labour and Population in the Industrial Revolution. Essays presented to J. D. Chambers* (edited by E. L. Jones and G. E. Mingay), London, 1967, pp. 187–205.

[2] B. Hammond, 'Urban deathrates in the early Nineteenth Century', *Economic Journal*, Supplement, *Economic History*, **3** (January 1928), pp. 419–28.

[3] *Op. cit.* above on p. 140 (footnote 4).

[4] *Ibid.*, p. 5.   [5] *Ibid.*, p. 15.

burgh (1779): 'In our calculation, therefore, of the populousness of Edinburgh, we set aside entirely any consideration of the parish registers.' Sir John Sinclair's *Statistical Account of Scotland*, dating from the 1790's, frequently alludes to the unsatisfactory state of the parish registers, and the tax put upon parochial registration in 1783 apparently caused dissenters in Scotland to stop registering the births of their children.[1] Although this tax was removed in 1794, not more than one-third of the births were entered on the parish registers afterwards. Death registration was usually in the hands of the grave-digger,[2] who might even be illiterate, and only the marriage records were anywhere near accurate.

The British Association had to collect vital statistics for the large towns of Scotland as late as 1840[3] in an attempt to fill a gap where registration was so incomplete. The birth-rates they found were useless, however—less than half of what they must have really been, as Cowan had already shown was true of the Glasgow birth registers.[4] Bisset-Smith has estimated[5] that only 46 per cent of births in Scotland were being registered shortly before civil registration began in 1855.

As well as being deficiently kept, most of the old Scottish parish registers are now lost. Seton lists several examples:[6] Abertarff (Inverness-shire) lost its register when it was accidentally dropped into a rapid stream; the Halkirk (Caithness)

[1] J. Stark, 'Contribution to the Vital Statistics of Scotland', *Journal of the Statistical Society*, **14** (March 1851), pp. 48–87.

[2] *Ibid.*

[3] W. H. Sykes, Lord Sandon, G. R. Porter, J. Heywood, W. P. Alison, and E. Chadwick, 'Vital Statistics of Large Towns in Scotland. Report of a Committee of the British Association for the Advancement of Science', *Journal of the Statistical Society*, **6**, 2 (May 1843), pp. 150–66.

[4] R. Cowan, 'Vital Statistics of Glasgow, illustrating the Sanatory condition of the Population', *ibid.*, **3** (October 1840), pp. 257–92.

[5] G. T. Bisset-Smith, 'A Statistical Note on Birth Registration in Scotland previous to 1855; suggested by Inquiries as to Verification of Birth for Old Age Pensions', *Journal of the Royal Statistical Society*, **72**, 3 (September 1909), pp. 618–23.

[6] *Op. cit.* above on page 140 (footnote 4), pp. 21 *et seq.*

parish register was destroyed by 'some ill-disposed persons'; the Kirriemuir (Angus) registers were 'removed by a certain clergy-man in 1713' and were never recovered; the early Yetholm (Roxburghshire) registers were destroyed by the family [perhaps the children?] of a minister of the parish; a leaf from a long-lost seventeenth-century register for Kirkden (Angus) was casually sent from a shop in the neighbourhood to the minister, enabling him to recover what was left of the register itself. The Tiree and Coll (Argyll) registers, at some time prior to 1775, were sent to Edinburgh to help in a case at law, and were never returned; the baptisms and marriages for 1711 to 1748 for a Fife parish were sent to London as evidence in a law suit and never came back. Fire was probably the most frequent cause of loss, however, in Seton's opinion; the house where the registers were normally kept was burnt down on a number of occasions. This was often the schoolmaster's house or the school itself, rather than the manse or the kirk.

Poor standards of church registration outside Great Britain are probably more a matter of anti-clericalism than anything else. Krause has discussed the matter[1] for England after 1690, arguing that adequacy was fairly good about 1700 but grew much worse by the end of the century. While the deficiencies in the data around 1800 are undoubted, 1700 may not have been much better if what Chalkin[2] and Munby[3] have found for Canterbury and Hertford in 1676 is at all typical of country towns. Burial figures are certainly highly incomplete in London, too, where private burial grounds were very commonly used in the eighteenth century.[4] The Society of Genealogists has begun to publish its

[1] *Loc. cit.* above on p. 142 (footnote 1).

[2] C. W. Chalkin, 'The Compton census of 1676: the dioceses of Canterbury and Rochester', *Kent Records*, **17**, *A Seventeenth-Century Miscellany* (1960), pp. 153–83. See also above, p. 81.

[3] L. Munby, *Hertfordshire Population Statistics, 1563–1801*, Hitchin, 1964, p. 24.

[4] M. C. Buer, *Health, wealth and population, in the early days of the industrial revolution*, London, 1926, pp. 16–17.

index[1] of parish registers, which contains a recent opinion on their value as source-material.

BILLS OF MORTALITY

Parish registrations can obviously be aggregated to give total figures for baptisms and burials week by week or year by year; and this, or its equivalent from other sources, was done in many European towns at an early date. The results were published under the name (in England) of Bills of Mortality. They were begun in order to give an indication of the normal level of mortality as contrasted with the plague levels.[2]

There may perhaps seem no proper distinction between Bills of Mortality and the data that can be obtained from parish registers by aggregative methods, and in some studies it is not clear which were the original source. Bills exist for many of the towns of Western Europe from about the same period as the parish registers begin, and may sometimes antedate them, although it is sometimes hard to tell how Bills could have been compiled if there were no church registers.

There are, however, five points to make about Bills of Mortality. First, they are ostensibly complete; there is no difficulty about Nonconformity that causes the English parish registers, for instance, so often to understate births and deaths by important amounts. Second, they have been aggregated already; labour can be saved there, but no alternative groupings by age or period or area other than the published ones, are, of course, possible. Third, they normally give something about causes and ages of death, since they were begun so that the plague deaths per week would be known. Fourth, only towns generally (and not all towns) had

---

[1] Society of Genealogists, *National Index of Parish Registers, Vol. I* (edited by D. J. Steel), 'Sources of Births, Marriages and Deaths before 1837 (I)', 1968.

[2] J. Graunt, *Natural and Political Observations upon the Bills of Mortality*, originally London, 1662; the 3rd edn (1665) has been reprinted in *The Journal of the Institute of Actuaries*, **90**, 384 (1964), pp. 4–61, and the 5th edn (1676) in *The economic writings of Sir William Petty* (edited by C. H. Hull), Cambridge, 1899.

Bills of Mortality, so no rural analyses can be made. Finally, all the information the Bills give is purely statistical, and so there can be no question of anything but aggregative analysis.

However, Maitland found sixty-five burial places in London that had never been taken into the Bills, which accounted for about 10 per cent of all London burials; half of them belonged to the Established Church.[1] If the Bills for the metropolis were so inaccurate in the middle of the eighteenth century, can they have been better in the seventeenth? The very size of London, and its fairly recent growth to that size, had possibly caused higher mortality rates and a worsening of the civic organization; yet by 1750 the plague had been absent from England for seventy-one years, removing from living memory the very *raison d'être* of the Bills.

The extensive series of Bills of Mortality that exist for many towns in Europe[2] must, in fact, be treated with care. Although they show the number of burials and baptisms, and often also of marriages, these are most inadequate unless the total population is known or unless some assumptions about the total population can be made. Thus London had more burials than baptisms for more than a hundred years, including most of the eighteenth century, and some writers wrongly supposed that the population of London really declined. It is by no means easy to distinguish

[1] T. Short, *New observations natural, moral, civil, political and medical, on city, town and country bills of mortality. To which are added, Large and Clear Abstracts of the best Authors who have wrote on that subject. With an Appendix on the Weather and Meteors*, London, 1750, p. 176.

[2] Some of them have been published in English. C. J. Sprengell: 'Bills of Mortality of several considerable towns in Europe. Beginning with the Year 1717, i.e. from Christmas 1716, to Christmas 1717. Extracted from the Acta Breslaviensia', *Philosophical Transactions of the Royal Society*, 32, 380 (November–December 1723), pp. 454–69; 'The Bills of Mortality for the Town of Dresden, for a whole Century, viz. from the Year 1617 to 1717, containing the Numbers of Marriages, Births, Burials, and Communicants', *ibid.*, 38, 428 (April–May–June 1733), pp. 89–93; and 'The Bills of Mortality for the Imperial City of Augsburg, from the Year 1501 to 1720 inclusive, containing the Number of Births, Marriages, and Burials', *ibid.*, pp. 94–7.

between the times when the population was really increasing, stagnant, or decreasing, since the Bills of Mortality taken at their face value show decline throughout. In England, furthermore, baptisms do not represent even a close approximation to births from at least 1770 onwards, since church adherence had become weak, especially in the towns, to which the Bills of Mortality refer.[1]

In his memorable pamphlet, *Natural and Political Observations upon the Bills of Mortality*, Graunt realized that, with sufficient care, calculations could be made that would yield valuable information on the state of the population. He showed that the population of London was increasing; that there was considerable net migration to London from the country; that the western parts of the city were gaining at the expense of the eastern parts; that the total population was not as high as many people thought; and that in the central parts the density of population was tending to decline. At the same time, he made several perceptive remarks about the plague.

Coming first in the field, Graunt had the great distinction that almost any observation he validly made was new. But Halley, celebrated as Secretary of the Royal Society and as the discoverer of the famous comet, is no less distinguished as a demographer, for he invented the life-table, the whole basis of actuarial insurance today. He published his observations on the mortality of Breslau[2] as early as 1693, using the data of deaths in age groups

[1] See also W. Ogle, 'An inquiry into the trustworthiness of the old Bills of Mortality', *Journal of the Royal Statistical Society*, 55, 3 (September 1892), pp. 437–60. Among much interesting information, he tells us of a bye-register at Reading kept between 1696 and 1706 in which 101 unbaptized births are given along with 488 baptisms, suggesting that baptisms understated natality by about 20 per cent.

[2] E. Halley, 'An Estimate of the Degrees of the Mortality of Mankind drawn from curious Tables of the Births and Funerals at the City of Breslaw; with an Attempt to ascertain the Price of Annuities upon Lives', *Philosophical Transactions of the Royal Society*, 17, 196 (January 1692/3), pp. 596–610, and 'Some further Considerations on the Breslaw Bills of Mortality', *ibid.*, 198 (March 1693), pp. 654–6.

to calculate the chances of dying that a person would have as he came to each age group. It was hence possible to calculate an average length of life, or the expectation of life, at any age; the expectation of life at birth is used today as the phrase that commonly summarizes mortality conditions. It is beside the point that Halley's methods were, in fact, wrong. He had the essential idea of what deductions to make from the data.

Amongst eighteenth-century writers, White used the York Bills of Mortality[1] to estimate the changes in York's population, but, since the births had increased and the burials diminished, his calculations were particularly difficult. White's methods are interesting: he began by taking the 2,285 houses liable for tax in 1781; assumed the total was 3,000 houses in all; allowed 4·25 persons per house; and was still forced to assume that the birth-rate was constant, in order to get a population figure for 1728–35 from the information he had available. He was under no illusions about how limited was the value of Bills of Mortality alone.

AGGREGATIVE ANALYSIS ON PARISH REGISTERS

Early work on parish registers was almost entirely done on the basis of the total numbers baptized, married or buried in a given year, and such aggregative analysis is still valuable. Considerable interest was shown in eighteenth-century England in this matter, since the general question of whether the population was rising or falling was in debate and it was thought that parish registers might help to solve it. Short used them[2] a great deal, endeavouring to discover the best conditions for health. His data are now more interesting than his conclusions, since they give us an idea of which years between 1555 and 1749 were worst for mortality and to what extent. Where both parish registers and the Bills of Mortality existed, comparisons between them showed fairly close

[1] W. White, 'Observations on the Bills of Mortality at York in 1782', *Philosophical Transactions of the Royal Society*, **72** (1782), pp. 35–43.

[2] *Op. cit.* above on p. 146 (footnote 1).

agreement, and hence it was not unjustifiable to lean upon parish registers in demographic research. Apart from Short's book, there are many smaller studies in England for the period: on Stoke Damerell[1] (Devon) for 1733; on Bristol[2] for 1741–51; on Great Shefford[3] (Berkshire) for 1747–57; on Holy Cross,[4] a parish

[1] Barrow, 'An Account of Births and Burials, with the Number of Inhabitants at Stoke Damerell, in the County of Devon', *Philosophical Transactions of the Royal Society*, **39**, 439 (October, November, December 1735), pp. 171–2. In 1733, the parish had a population of 3,361 and 122 baptisms, a rate of more than 36 per thousand. The burial rate, however, was remarkably low, only 18 per thousand.

[2] J. Browning, 'The number of people in the city of Bristol calculated from the burials for ten years successively, and also from the number of houses', *ibid.*, **48**, 1 (1753), pp. 217–20. His method relies essentially on the proposition that 'in great cities a twenty-fifth part of the people die yearly'. He then has to adjust his figure for the number of houses so as to find the six people per house that he expects.

[3] R. Forster, 'An extract of the register of the parish of Great Shefford, near Lambourne, in Berkshire, for ten years; with observations on the same', *ibid.*, **50** (1757), XLIII, pp. 356–63. The baptism rate was nearly 35 per thousand, but the burials under the age of two years were only 17 per cent of the baptisms, which suggests that baptisms were customarily delayed, preventing any children who died in the first weeks of life from being baptized at all.

[4] R. More, 'An extract of the register of the parish of Holy-Cross, in Salop, from Michaelmas, 1750, to Michaelmas, 1760', *ibid.*, **52**, 1 (1761), pp. 140–1; W. Gorsuch, 'An extract from the register of Holy-Cross, in Salop, from Michaelmas, 1760, to Michaelmas, 1770', *ibid.*, **61** (1771), pp. 57–8; Gorsuch, 'Extract of the register of the parish of Holy Cross, from Michaelmas 1770 to Michaelmas 1780, *ibid.*, **72** (1782), pp. 53–7. The population was remarkably constant: 1755, 1,049; 1760, 1,048; 1765, 1,096; 1770, 1,046; 1775, 1,057; 1780, 1,113. Moreover, the high figure for 1765 can be partly explained by four large families that moved into the only empty houses in the parish between 1760 and 1765. On the other hand, nine houses were pulled down in 1767 to make space for a new bridge that was being built over the Severn. The apparently small increase between 1770 and 1775 was caused by a fire in 1774, after which 24 of the homeless inhabitants left the parish altogether.

One might suppose that the baptisms would be equally steady, but in fact the rate rises from 31·6 per thousand in 1750–60 to 35·0 in 1760–70 and 36·5 in 1770–80. Before jumping to the conclusion that the birth-rate was rising, however, we should consider the burials under one year of age as a proportion of the baptisms: 13·3 per cent, 19·1 per cent and 16 per cent in the successive decades.

adjoining Shrewsbury, for 1750–80; on five parishes in Anglesey[1]
for various periods between 1547 and 1771, but more especially
1710–71; on Manchester for 1717–75[2] and 1573–1841;[3] on
Chester[4] for 1764–74; on Blandford Forum[5] (Dorset) for 1733–72;

Although some rise in fertility may have occurred, therefore, it is remarkable
that the lowest baptism-rate coincides with the lowest proportion of infant
mortality, especially as this is the earliest of the three decades, when knowledge
of methods of preventing birth and death might be expected to be less, on
balance, than later.

---

[1] P. Panton, 'Extract of a letter concerning the increase of population in
Anglesey', *ibid.*, **63** (1773), XXIV, pp. 180–4. His idea is to take a few years'
baptisms and burials for each parish at three or four widely separated periods.
Although this does give a rough guide to population trends, it is no use for
detailed analysis.

[2] T. Percival, 'Observations on the state of population in Manchester, and
other adjacent places', *ibid.*, **64** (1774), pp. 54–66, **65** (1775), pp. 322–35, and **66**
(1776), pp. 160–7. The death-rate in Manchester and Salford in 1754–61,
allowing for dissenters, was 39 per thousand. See also Hammond's work,
mentioned above on p. 142 (footnote 2).

[3] R. Parkinson, 'On the Origin, Custody, and Value of Parish Registers, with
an Abstract of the Registers of the Collegiate Church of Manchester', *Journal
of the Statistical Society*, **5** (1842), pp. 256–63. The rate of increase of population
is so high that there can be little doubt that the Manchester-Salford township
grew rapidly from 1691 onwards; the era of most rapid growth would be about
1771–90.

[4] J. Haygarth, 'Observations on the bill of mortality in Chester for the year
1772', *Philosophical Transactions of the Royal Society*, **64** (1774), pp. 67–78, 'Bill
of mortality for Chester, for the year 1773', *ibid.*, **65** (1775), pp. 85–90, and
'Observations on the population and diseases of Chester, in the year 1774', *ibid.*,
68 (1778), pp. 131–54. There can be little doubt that Chester was a relatively
healthy place, although the various figures for the age at death, the baptisms,
and the age distribution of the population produce no clear pattern. As a town
of 14,713 inhabitants (in 1774), Chester must have had a considerable migration
both inwards and outwards that will make close demographic analysis impossible. However, the birth-rate seems to have been quite low as well as the
death-rate.

[5] R. Pulteney, 'An account of baptisms, marriages, and burials during forty
years, in the parish of Blandford Forum, Dorset', *ibid.*, **68** (1778), pp. 615–21.
The baptism-rate, at only 27 per thousand in 1763–72 after allowing for dissenters, seems extraordinarily low; it might have been about 33 in 1733–42. However, Pulteney gives no data on deaths by age, and seems chiefly interested in

on a parish in Southwark[1] for 1602–1839; and on Tavistock[2] for 1617–1836. Price also has parish register data scattered throughout his book,[3] as well as in his articles,[4] and Eden's classic work[5] draws on the registers of some 180 parishes.

burials. The ratio of baptisms to marriages is less than three, which certainly suggests that the marriages were fully recorded.

---

[1] G. Weight, 'Statistics of the Parish of St George the Martyr, Southwark', *Journal of the Statistical Society*, 3 (April 1840), pp. 50–71. This parish, being a suburb of London, naturally had a different demographic history from most parts of England. A great change took place between 1697 and 1722, when the number of rated houses in the parish rose from only 409 to 1,503. But all the statistics Weight gives need care in their interpretation, which he does not himself provide. St George's seems to have been a good church for a cheap marriage in the seventeenth century; in 1667, for instance, there were 379 marriages registered, but only 138 baptisms. However, the Act of 1695 seems to have changed matters, and in 1700 there were only 28 marriages but 282 baptisms. The figures vary thereafter in an eccentric way, and at last we have the comparison (p. 59) between civil and parochially registered events in 1839. The marriages at St George's church were 6 per cent *above* what took place according to the civil register, but both baptisms and burials were about 60 per cent *below* what the civil register of births and deaths gave. This is, surely, enough to prove that the parish registers for London are liable to almost any degree of under-enumeration of vital events.

[2] C. Barham, 'Remarks on the Abstract of the Parish Registers of Tavistock, Devon', *ibid.*, 4 (April 1841), pp. 34–49. His analysis is on modern lines (although he could not know that) in that he discusses 'crises', the most severe of which at Tavistock was from August to October 1626, when 331 people died, mainly of plague. Minor crises occurred in 1643 (about May), 1644 (September), 1690 (February), and 1740 (February). The ratio of baptisms of legitimate children to marriages fell after 1686 (p. 42), and was especially low in the middle of the eighteenth century; however, a certain falling-off in religious observance might account for it. In view of the baptism-rate of only 27·4 per thousand that emerges for the period 1777–86 and 26·3 for 1827–36, we might accept this.

[3] R. Price, *Observations on Reversionary Payments; on Schemes for Providing Annuities for Widows, and for Pensions in Old Age; on the Method of Calculating the Values of Assurances on Lives; and on The National Debt. Also, Essays on different Subjects in the Doctrine of Life—Annuities and Political Arithmetic; a Collection of New Tables, and a Postscript on the Population of the Kingdom*, London (6th edn), 1803.

[4] *Idem.*, 'Observations on the expectations of lives, the increase of mankind, the influence of great towns on population, and particularly the state of London

Edmonds, who studied the parish of Madron[1] in the extreme west of Cornwall, using the registers and such local material as he could find, gave an interesting account of life there in 1760, when conditions had evidently been very primitive. The improvement, he thought, began in this parish about 1778, which is important to more than his own study, since Madron was presumably almost the last parish in England to benefit from any social or economic changes that may have been spreading. One would therefore expect that population growth in England accelerated in the years before 1778, but accelerated little more afterwards.

When the first census of Great Britain was taken in 1801, interest in parish registers was so strong that Rickman, the organizer of the census, instructed all parish clergy to return the baptisms and burials from their registers for each of the preceding twenty-one years (that is, back to 1780) and for each tenth year back to 1700, as well as marriages annually since 1754 and

with respect to healthfulness and number of inhabitants', *Philosophical Transactions of the Royal Society*, **59** (1769), pp. 89–125. His method of calculating the population of London from the current (1758–68) bills is interesting: the 15,710 baptisms a year are assumed to be equivalent to a population of 314,200 who are natives of London (a rate of 50 per thousand!), and the 22,956 burials mean that an annual net immigration of 7,246 is needed to keep the population stationary; these, Price argues, have an average expectation of life at the time of their arrival of 30 years, so a further 217,380 Londoners can be put down as immigrants, making 531,580 people in all. However, as Price admits, the baptism and burial figures were each defective to a different degree, the population was not stationary, and the assumed baptism-rate of 50 per thousand is a mere guess.

See also 'Observations on the difference between the duration of human life in towns and in country parishes and villages', *ibid.*, **65** (1775), pp. 424-45. In all his writings, Price takes the view that English population was low, or falling, or only stationary, in opposition to the general belief that it was increasing fast, and is much opposed to the growth of the new towns, because they were bad for health.

⁵ Sir F. M. Eden, *The State of the Poor; or, An History of the Labouring Classes in England . . .*, London, 1797.

¹ R. Edmonds, 'Statistical Account of the Parish of Madron, containing the borough of Penzance, in Cornwall', *Journal of the Statistical Society*, **2** (July 1839), pp. 198–232.

decennially back to 1700. This was clearly regarded as the best way of determining the trend of population in England and Wales in the eighteenth century. He thought the baptisms would yield better results than the burials because deaths were more liable to fluctuation in bad years. He therefore assumed a constant baptism rate, based on 1801 experience, and multiplied the baptism totals by it to get population estimates.[1] In the 1811 census report,[2] these baptism totals were scaled up by about 3 per cent, so as to allow for late returns and a few duplicate returns.

Rickman later asked for similar information for the years 1569 to 1571, 1599 to 1601, 1629 to 1631, 1669 to 1671, 1699 to 1701, and 1749 to 1751. This series of figures has now been lost, apart from the rather meagre calculations, presumably made to Rickman's posthumous satisfaction (he died in 1840), that were made on them and appeared[3] in the report on the census of 1841. The method was, in effect, to calculate a figure for population based on each of the three rates, and then to average the three figures. Many historians have relied on Rickman's calculations, directly or indirectly, as their source of data,[4] but he did not appreciate all the difficulties of demographic analysis from baptismal and burial data, and in the present century Griffith has attempted to correct his work.[5] Griffith was something of a pioneer, and his work must now be regarded as superseded; he was altogether too credulous of the value of the baptism figures, and took too little account of the work of the nineteenth-century statisticians. However, he also published[6] some additional data

[1] *Census of Great Britain 1801*, Observations on the Results of the Population Act, 41. Geo. III, London, 1802.

[2] *Census of Great Britain 1811*, Preliminary Observations, pp. xviii–xx.

[3] *Census of Great Britain 1841*, Enumeration Abstract, London, 1843, preface, pp. 34–7.

[4] E.g. K. F. Helleiner in *The Cambridge Economic History of Europe*, Vol. IV, London, 1967, pp. 1–95.

[5] G. T. Griffith, *Population Problems of the Age of Malthus*, Cambridge, 1926.

[6] *Idem*, 'Rickman's Second Series of Eighteenth-Century Population Figures', *Journal of the Royal Statistical Society*, **92**, 2 (1929), pp. 256–63.

on Rickman's methods, found in a manuscript. Marshall[1] and Krause[2] have attempted to rectify Griffith's work; Brownlee's ingenious early work,[3] too, is really more worth reading today, with Gonner's straightforward essay,[4] than Griffith's. Glass' summary of the controversy[5] should also be read in order to understand the situation.

At the important period of changeover from parochial to civil registration in England and Wales, the 1841 Census Commissioners made an abstract of the parish register data for the decade 1831–40, comparing them with the civil registration figures for 1839–40. It appears in the State Papers in Volume XXV of the *Reports of Commissioners* in 1845, but seems to have been left out of the index to State Papers as printed. It has not, therefore, received the attention it deserves. Many of the discrepancies are large, and some areas actually show more baptisms than births.[6] Regional variation was great; in Wales the baptisms were only 52 per cent of the births registered in 1839–40, while in Shropshire they were actually 102 per cent. The great peak of baptisms registered in 1837, however, which rose 18 per cent above the average of 1836

[1] T. H. Marshall, 'The Population problem during the Industrial Revolution: A Note on the Present State of the Controversy', *Economic Journal*, Supplement, *Economic History* I, 4 (1929); reprinted in both *Essays in Economic History* (edited by E. M. Carus-Wilson), 1954, and *Population in History* (edited by Glass and Eversley), 1965, pp. 247–68.

[2] *Loc. cit.* above on p. 142 (footnote 1).

[3] J. R. Brownlee, 'The History of the Birth- and Death-Rates in England and Wales taken as a whole, from 1570 to the Present Time', *Public Health*, **29** (June 1916), pp. 211–22 and (July 1916) pp. 228–38.

[4] E. C. K. Gonner, 'The population of England in the eighteenth century', *Journal of the Royal Statistical Society*, **76** (1913), pp. 261–96, followed by a discussion.

[5] Glass, 'Population and Population Movements in England and Wales, 1700 to 1850', in *Population in History* (edited by Glass and Eversley), London, 1965, pp. 221–46.

[6] Births were themselves substantially under-registered in England and Wales until 1860 or later. See Glass, 'A Note on the Under-Registration of Births in Britain in the Nineteenth Century', *Population Studies* V (1951), pp. 70–88.

and 1838, amounted to less than 5 per cent in Wales, and was actually a trough, below the surrounding years' level, in Shropshire. The highest 1837 baptism peaks, which were certainly not caused by fertility fluctuations, were in Leicestershire (55 per cent above the mean of 1836 and 1838), Bedfordshire (47 per cent), the metropolitan division as a whole (41 per cent), and the East Riding with York City (40 per cent); Suffolk, Northamptonshire and Warwickshire also show the effect in a marked degree. It would seem that these were the counties where casual conformity rather than open Nonconformity was very common, and a certain alarm at the prospect of civil registration prompted thousands of baptisms.

The intricate question of the distribution of population and migration from one part of the country to another has hardly been studied even in contemporary Britain, although Deane and Cole have attempted to calculate it for the eighteenth century.[1] Their methods are not very critical of their sources, the chief of which are Brownlee and Gonner. This is, however, perhaps the most interesting demographic aspect of eighteenth-century England, when the first Industrial Revolution in the world was getting under way, even more interesting than possible changes in the vital rates. It is by no means easy to calculate migration rates properly, for not only are the baptism and burial figures somewhat unreliable and migration taking place on a large scale, but there is reason to suppose that death-rates fell in some manner during the century, and quite possibly birth-rates actually rose. Thus it is not possible to reach more than rough conclusions by simply assuming that birth- and death-rates were approximately constant for any part of the eighteenth century, and Deane and Cole's brave attempt really pushes the data too far. Some of their results could easily be the reverse of what really happened.

Loschky has attempted an assessment of the variability of

[1] P. M. Deane and W. A. Cole, *British Economic Growth, 1688–1959*, Cambridge (2nd edn), 1967, pp. 98–135.

parish registers in England,[1] using the baptism series of twenty Lancashire parishes over the entire eighteenth century. His main aim was to calculate how large a study must be in order to establish vital rates with reasonable accuracy, but his most useful point is that the larger parishes tended to be less completely registered, presumably owing to the burden of work on the incumbent.

Loschky's statistical method relies on coefficients of variation, which come out relatively high for the fastest-growing parishes when compared with his calculations based on a constant parish size and a constant baptism-rate. This was inevitable, however, if the fastest-growing parishes had increasing baptism-rates, which is possible; consequently much of his subsequent argument is not necessarily valid. A relationship between the baptism/birth ratio and the coefficient of variation of the baptism series, of the kind Loschky looks for, would emerge if a change of religious practice occurred during the eighteenth century in several of the parishes, but most of the relatively large coefficients of variation amongst the twenty baptism series might be accounted for by changes in birth-rates.

NOMINATIVE RESEARCH METHODS ON PARISH REGISTERS AND SIMILAR MATERIAL

Louis Chevalier seems to be the true father of the recent wave of parish register studies, for he outlined how historical demography in France might proceed, advocating their use, as early as 1946.[2] Progress, however, was slight until 1956, when Fleury and Henry published a manual[3] explaining in detail just how a parish register

[1] D. J. Loschky, 'The Usefulness of England's Parish Registers', *Review of Economics and Statistics*, XLIX, 4 (November 1967), pp. 471–9.

[2] L. Chevalier, 'Pour une histoire de la population', *Population* I, 2 (April–June 1946), pp. 245–56; translated and reprinted in *Population in History* (edited by Glass and Eversley), London, 1965, pp. 70–8.

[3] M. Fleury and L. Henry, *Des registres paroissiaux à l'histoire de la population: manuel de dépouillement et d'exploitation de l'état civil ancien*, Paris, 1956.

could be ransacked systematically and all its useful demographic information extracted. This is not as simple a matter as it might seem, since all possible contingencies have to be allowed for in advance. There has to be a way of recording all information that may be found, and at the same time for showing what information was not there. It is also highly desirable to have standard forms on which the data are recorded that can be shuffled for the subsequent analysis. The chief point, indeed, of the Fleury–Henry method is family reconstitution, which depends upon knowing the names of the individuals baptized or married or buried and the names of their parents or children. It has proved possible, in a remarkable number of instances, to identify individuals in a parish register at many points in their lives, and thus to reconstitute their family history. This amounts to compiling one's own genealogy, and if it could be done perfectly, the genealogical situation would apply (see Chapter 6). But naturally there are many omissions, and Fleury and Henry supply criteria for determining at what point the work of reconstitution can be deemed complete. It is not strictly possible, however, to be certain that all the children of a marriage were indeed baptized at the same church, and thus even with the most careful research work, it is possible that a family was reconstituted to show five baptized children that should really have shown six. Nevertheless, the method has the immense virtue that it enables workers in many parts of France, and now in many other parts of Europe, to work in a uniform way and thus produce comparable results.

The manual published in 1956 by Fleury and Henry has reappeared in a revised edition.[1] It sets out a systematic way of choosing suitable registers, filling in a slip for each event, reconstituting families and calculating various demographic indices. As yet there is no translation into English, but this has not prevented a school of historical demographers from arising in Cambridge and already a number of works has appeared from this

[1] *Idem, Nouveau manuel de dépouillement et d'exploitation de l'état civil ancien,* Paris, 1965.

group. *An Introduction to English Historical Demography* (London, 1966), edited by E. A. Wrigley, gives an account of the work that this group has been doing, and the methods that they employ, and Wrigley's own chapter in it acts as a translation and adaptation of part of Fleury and Henry's manual.

Henry has also written a manual of historical demography[1] in which methods of analysis appropriate to parish register material are well described, including a section on testing the quality of the data. Beyond this, Blayo and Henry have evolved an interesting method of estimating mortality as part of their study of certain parishes in Brittany and Anjou.[2] They use the proportion of newly-weds whose parents were living; this index may be available frequently from the marriage contracts, even though the dates of death of their parents, or even their ages, may be missing. The average level of adult mortality over the previous generation affects the proportions of living parents at their children's marriages very markedly in practice, so that it should at least be a useful check on other figures. Under modern or very primitive conditions of mortality the index would be too close to unity or zero to be much help. The only doubt about the method must be sociological: having a dead father may sometimes have greatly increased the chances of a son's marriage, owing to his inheritance. Even so, the same should be less true of daughters with dead mothers; it may even be that by calculating both indices, as Blayo and Henry do, we could have an indication of the significance of being an orphan in the marriage stakes.

A different use of parish registers was made by Buckatzsch,[3] who was able to find the occupations of most of the people who were married or died in Sheffield from the registers for 1655 to

---

[1] Henry, *Manuel de démographie historique*, Geneva and Paris, 1967.

[2] Y. Blayo and Henry, 'Données démographiques sur la Bretagne et l'Anjou de 1740 à 1829', *Annales de Démographie Historique* (1967), pp. 91–171, especially p. 127.

[3] E. J. Buckatzsch, 'Occupations in the Parish Registers of Sheffield, 1655–1719', *Economic History Review*, 2nd Series, I (1949), pp. 145–50.

1719. By comparing the occupations of bridegrooms and of brides' fathers, he showed that the cutlery trade was predominant in Sheffield even at that time, although the cutlery workers were often immigrants from agricultural areas.[1] In a similar way, Keller, on Darmstadt, and Sieber, on Besigheim, have also been able to study immigration,[2] using the parish register deaths from plague during the Thirty Years War.

Marriage contracts have an obvious value in estimating the extent of migration,[3] literacy wherever a signature was required from bride or groom, and social class wherever occupations were always given. Van Nierop, for instance, used the data about the bridegrooms of Amsterdam[4] between 1578 and 1601 to assess both the social composition of the city and its rate of growth. One must suspect, however, that the completeness of her study changed over the period, for a trebling within twenty years is a very rapid rate of growth indeed.

FAMILY RECONSTITUTION BEFORE 1956

In the years before 1914, historical demography was pursued in Germany much more thoroughly than elsewhere, yet it still comes as a surprise to find that Roller, in his study[5] of Durlach in the eighteenth century, seems to have reconstituted the lives of all the 24,342 people who lived in the town (near Karlsruhe) at any time during the period. He called his method 'genealogisch',

[1] *Idem*, 'Places of Origin of a group of immigrants into Sheffield, 1624–1799', *ibid.*, **2** (1950), pp. 303–6.

[2] See G. Franz, *Der Dreißigjährige Kreig und das deutsche Volk*, Stuttgart, 1961, pp. 6–7.

[3] J. P. Poussou, 'Expérience aquitaine et méthodologie des contrats de mariage au XVIIIe siècle', *Annales du Midi*, **76**, 1 (1964), pp. 61–76.

[4] L. van Nierop, 'De bruidegoms van Amsterdam van 1578 tot 1601', *Tijdschrift voor Geschiedenis*: **48**, 4 (1933), pp. 337–59; **49**, 2 (1934), pp. 136–60; **49**, 3 (1934), pp. 329–44; **52**, 2 (1937), pp. 144–63; and **52**, 3 (1937), pp. 251–64.

[5] O. K. Roller, *Die Einwohnerschaft der Stadt Durlach im 18. Jahrhundert in ihren wirtschaftlichen und kulturgeschichtlichen Verhältnissen dargestellt aus ihren Stammtafeln*, Karlsruhe, 1907.

and he certainly used the parish registers as his main source, but the precise details escape a mere tyro in German. Roller felt able to measure in- and out-migration, as well as fertility and mortality on an annual basis, but he wrote before the modern emphasis on intervals between births as a guide to possible birth control, and his analysis is rather disappointing, although copious. One suspects that the Durlach data might be worth re-working.

A few other attempts were made at family reconstitution before 1956. One of these was by Morrell[1] in 1935, who was able to show that the family size was relatively low, at least for two English parishes, and the age at marriage relatively high in the later-Tudor period. Hyrenius[2] studied the Swedish population of Estonia from 1841 to 1900, also using parish registers and family reconstitution. This is as good a piece of work as any done since, and was actually carried out before 1956, but similar examples are extremely rare.

It may be of interest that some 2,700 names were recently extracted from parish registers in the Parma valley for a study of human genetics.[3] The period of study was the middle of the sixteenth century, and the record linkage was to be done by computer. It seems, therefore, that the basic work of family reconstitution has been done in an entirely different context, but the methods might be applicable to demographic studies.

PARISH REGISTER SOURCES AND STUDIES IN DIFFERENT COUNTRIES

France

Mols has described some of the oldest French registers,[4] many of

[1] C. C. Morrell, 'Tudor Marriages and Infantile Mortality', *Journal of State Medicine*, **43** (1935), pp. 173–81.

[2] H. Hyrenius, 'Fertility and Reproduction in a Swedish Population Group without Family Limitation', *Population Studies*, XII, 2 (1958), pp. 121–30.

[3] I. Barrai, L. L. Cavalli-Sforza and A. Moroni, 'Record linkage from parish books', in *Mathematics and computer science in biology and medicine*, London (Medical Research Council), 1965, pp. 51–60.

[4] *Op. cit.*, above on p. 139 (footnote 1), Vol. I, p. 79.

which antedate the ordinance of 1539 of Villers-Cotterêts, which prescribed that they should be kept. The general state of them today has been described by Léonardi,[1] and Goubert has discussed their value for sixteenth-century demographic research.[2] Biraben, Fleury, and Henry[3] make a key date of 1668 in their consideration of the quality of the data that they contain. The general standard apparently improved at about that time, although in some respects the French registers are thought still to be deficient before about 1740.

An elaborate national system for sampling the French parish registers has been devised, and is explained in full by Fleury and Henry[4] and Biraben, Fleury, and Henry.[5] The aim, of course, is to discover the way in which French population developed between about 1670 and 1830; these dates were chosen because at an earlier period the data are unreliable and at a later date the civil registration system is adequate. Several progress reports have appeared,[6] and Blayo and Henry[7] have already produced one of the principal regional studies, relating to Brittany and Anjou between 1740 and 1829, while Henry and Lévy's interim study[8] of the region around Paris has been available for some

[1] P. Léonardi, 'L'état civil en France', *Les cahiers français*, **27** (March 1958), pp. 2–8.

[2] P. Goubert, 'Registres paroissiaux et démographie dans la France du XVIe siècle', *Annales de Démographie Historique* (1965), pp. 43–8.

[3] J.-N. Biraben, Fleury, and Henry, 'Inventaire par sondage des registres paroissiaux de France', *Population*, **15**, 1 (1960), pp. 25–58.

[4] Fleury and Henry, 'Pour connaître la population de la France depuis Louis XIV. Plan de travaux par sondage', *Population*, **13**, 4 (1958), pp. 663–86.

[5] *Loc. cit.*

[6] Henry, 'Dépouillement de registres d'état civil', *Population*, **15**, 3 (1960), pp. 545–7; J. Houdaille, 'État d'avancement d'une enquête sur la population de la France de Louis XIV à la restauration', *ibid.*, **20**, 2 (March–April 1965), pp. 293–5; Blayo, 'L'enquête de l' I.N.E.D. sur la population de la France avant 1830', *Annales de Démographie Historique* (1966), pp. 193–7.

[7] *Loc. cit.* above on p. 158 (footnote 2).

[8] Henry and C. Lévy, 'Quelques données sur la région autour de Paris au XVIIIe siècle', *Population*, **17**, 2 (1962), pp. 297–326.

years. Goubert gives a general account of recent French research on sixteenth- and seventeenth-century populations,[1] but the recent French studies relate principally to the eighteenth century.

The first study to appear in the recent wave was done by Gautier and Henry[2] on Crulai, a village in Normandy. It was mainly confined to a relatively short period, 1674–1742, but all the techniques of ransacking a parish register were used and it can be regarded as an archetype. The most elaborate study in France, however, is that of Beauvais by Goubert.[3] He attempted to show how the population had responded to economic changes over a long period (nominally 1600–1730, but he also took notice of the years 1730–89), and in particular to show the exact courses of the crises of subsistence that recurred in the area. His wealth of economic and social data and his discussion of their interrelationship with the demographic conditions make Goubert's study the best of its kind; its 750 pages enable him to touch upon every aspect of Beauvais life and to throw some light upon the credibility of his results.

One cannot confidently give a complete list of French local studies in historical demography that have appeared in the past decade, but the following at least includes the best-known: (1) Sotteville-lès-Rouen (1760–90), by Girard;[4] (2) Ingouville (a suburb of Le Havre) for 1730–90, (3) Saint-Angan (in the Morvan) for 1730–93, and (4) Boulay (in Moselle) for 1617–1850,

[1] Goubert, 'Recent Theories and Research in French Population between 1500 and 1700', in *Population in History* (edited by Glass and Eversley), London, 1965, pp. 457–73.

[2] E. Gautier and Henry, *La population de Crulai, paroisse normande. Étude historique*, Paris, 1958.

[3] Goubert, *Beauvais et le Beauvaisis de 1600 à 1730, contribution à l'histoire sociale de la France du XVIIe siècle*, Paris, 1960; see also M. Reinhard, 'La population française au XVIIe siècle', *Population*, **13**, 4 (1958), pp. 619–30, which is a review of Goubert's work.

[4] P. Girard, 'Aperçus de la démographie de Sotteville-lès-Rouen vers la fin du XVIIIe siècle', *ibid.*, **14**, 3 (1959), pp. 485–508. A high level of child mortality, late but nearly universal marriage, and no evidence of birth control were among the findings.

the first by Terrisse, the other two by Houdaille;[1] (5) La Rochelle for 1610–85, by Pérouas;[2] (6) the Paris region (1670–1829), by Henry and Lévy;[3] (7) the Ile-de-France in the eighteenth century, by Ganiage;[4] (8) Sainghin-en-Mélantois, near Lille (1665–1851), by Deniel and Henry;[5] (9) two villages, Thézels and St Sernin,

[1] M. Terrisse, 'Deux mongraphies paroissiales sur la population française au XVIIIe siècle. I, Un faubourg du Harve: Ingouville', *ibid.*, **16**, 2 (1961), pp. 285–300. The infant mortality (286 per thousand live births) and the bastards (5·7 per cent in 1774–90) seem the most noteworthy features. Houdaille, 'Deux monographies paroissiales sur la population française au XVIIIe siècle. II, Un village du Morvan: Saint-Agnan', *ibid.*, **16**, 2 (1961), pp. 301–13; and 'La population de Boulay (Moselle) avant 1850', *ibid.*, **22**, 6 (November–December 1967), pp. 1055–84. A notable crisis from plague occurred in Boulay in 1635–6, when about 23 per cent of the population died within four months. Celibacy after the age of 50 was very rare early in the eighteenth century, but rose steeply to a peak in the early-nineteenth, going with relatively late marriage. An interesting feature of this study was the use of the marriage register to estimate the level of literacy (because the register had to be signed). Only 15 per cent of brides and 59 per cent of bridegrooms were literate in 1670–1719, but by 1750–79 the corresponding rates were 46 per cent and 79 per cent, and they rose higher after the Revolution.

[2] L. Pérouas, 'Sur la démographie rochelaise', *Annales E.S.C.*, **16**, 6 (November–December 1961), pp. 1131–40. The change from being 80 per cent Protestant in 1610 to 80 per cent Catholic in 1676 is especially interesting, and the great decline in its population between 1610 and 1628 (roughly 75 per cent) owing to sieges, famine, and an epidemic has many sad parallels.

[3] *Loc. cit.* above on p. 161 (footnote 8). As well as giving practical details about the amount of work required, Henry and Lévy discuss the reliability of the methods and results. As usual in urban parishes, infant mortality comes out quite high (about 230 per thousand live births).

[4] J. Ganiage, *Trois villages d'Ile-de-France au XVIIIe siècle*, Paris, 1963. Some attempt to estimate migration was done here, but the matter it affects most, adult mortality, was impossible of proper study because too many ages at death were unknown. Infant mortality was 210 per thousand, and fertility rather above the Crulai levels.

[5] R. Deniel and Henry, 'La population d'un village du Nord de la France, Sainghin-en-Mélantois, de 1665 à 1851', *Population*, **20**, 4 (July–August 1965), pp. 563–602. This village was characterized by net emigration from 1740 onwards and possibly earlier still. Marriage, as usual in eighteenth-century France, was late (about 27 or 28 was the median age for women's first marriages), and fertility very high before 1770; in the Revolutionary period, family

in Bas-Quercy, in the eighteenth century, by Valmary;[1] (10) the south suburb of Paris (1774–94), by Galliano;[2] (11) three Breton villages in the eighteenth century, by Goubert.[3] All these are fairly consistent in their methods and approach.

More varied examples would be the summary analysis by Jacquart[4] of the effects of the Fronde of 1652 on the Paris region, where mortality was evidently 4 to 10 times normal for a time, or Le Roy Ladurie's use of parish register baptism data[5] to assess the extent of contraception in Languedoc just before the French revolution. Two studies reaching into the sixteenth century limitation does seem to have been practised however. Infant mortality was over 200 for the most part, but did fall after 1770.

---

[1] P. Valmary, *Familles paysannes au XVIIIe siècle en Bas-Quercy*, Paris, 1965. In this economically backward area, with scattered settlement, the registers were not good until about 1747, but with the help of some other local data it was possible to show that marriage was late and fertility low. Child mortality was also low, which seems strange in a remote area. The nature of the settlement may have weakened the Church, however, with the possibility of some under-registration.

[2] P. Galliano, 'La mortalité infantile (indigènes et nourrissons) dans la banlieue Sud de Paris à la fin du XVIIIe siècle (1774–1794)', *Annales de Démographie Historique* (1966), pp. 139–77. This study provides much more detail about infant mortality than any other of the period, and perhaps the general average level of only 177 per thousand is surprising. However, those families that could afford to send their children out of the city to be brought up might be a socially privileged class to some extent, with the money to afford better care. No other demographic topics are touched upon.

[3] Goubert, 'Legitimate Fecundity and Infant Mortality in France During the Eighteenth Century: A Comparison', *Daedalus* (Spring 1968), pp. 593–603. A classic pattern emerges of very high fertility and late marriage. Hardly any women had children before the age of 26, for which the legal age of majority, 25 in most places, might be the original cause. Infant mortality was high in these remote rural areas, about 250 per thousand live births. Although there was no trace of birth control, the population seems to have been declining between 1770 and 1787, so late was marriage and so high mortality.

[4] J. Jacquart, 'La Fronde des Princes dans la région parisienne et ses conséquences matérielles', *Revue d'histoire moderne et contemporaine*, **7** (1960), pp. 257–90.

[5] E. Le Roy Ladurie, 'Révolution française et contraception: Dossiers languedociens', *Annales de Démographie Historique* (1966), pp. 417–36.

should be mentioned, since the poor data before 1668 makes them the more precious: one of Ermont, in the Paris region,[1] and the other of the Nantes country.[2] The very low proportion of reconstitutable Nantes families (only 4, out of 750 people) suggests that omissions were fairly common at this early date, and so the birth-rate for the sixteenth century in particular, ostensibly about 36 or 40 per thousand, should probably be somewhat higher.

Finally, because it presents more analysis of the causes of the observed demographic phenomena than is usually offered, as well as a comparison with some of the above studies, we must mention Leymond's work on Duravel[3] in Haut-Quercy. She took two disjoint periods, 1693–1720 and 1770–1800, and found a rise in the mean ages at first marriage and a fall in the mean intervals between births. The ratio of endogenous to exogenous infant mortality (for which see our remarks on p. 183) at Duravel was about 2 to 1, as at Crulai, but it was nearly 1 to 2 at Sotteville-lès-Rouen. We suggest how far errors in the data might account for this kind of result at the end of the chapter.

Crises of subsistence, or occasional years in which mortality rises to five times its normal level with concomitant falls in the baptism and marriage rates, come up in almost every French study of parish registers, and in Belgium Ruwet[4] has considered crises at Liège between 1590 and 1790 and related them to high prices. They are much less common in English registers,

---

[1] Société historique et archéologique de l'arrondissement de Pontoise et du Vexin, *Le premier registre paroissial de l'état civil d'Ermont (1558–1557)* (edited by A. Vaquier), 1962. [I have only seen Houdaille's review of this, in *Population*, 19, pp. 1003–4.]

[2] A. Croix, 'La démographie du pays nantais au XVIe siècle', *Annales de Démographie Historique* (1967), pp. 63–90.

[3] D. Leymond, 'La communauté de Duravel au XVIIIe siècle. (Démographie —Économie)', *Annales du Midi*, 79, 4 (October 1967), pp. 363–85.

[4] J. Ruwet, 'Crises démographiques, problèmes économiques ou crises morales? Le pays de Liège sous l'ancien régime', *Population*, 9, 3 (July–September 1954), pp. 451–76.

however, so that it would seem that the English were not living quite so close to the margin of subsistence.

England

Before 1956, as parts of larger local history studies, Jones studied population in Broughton-in-Furness[1] for the whole eighteenth century, but was unable to do more than suggest the trend, and Wood used parish register data[2] for various towns in Nottinghamshire, ostensibly to estimate their eighteenth-century population, but really following their demographic histories from 1570 to 1801 as far as he could.

Among aggregative parish register studies in England in recent years are Eversley's on fifteen parishes in Worcestershire[3] in 1660–1850, and Chambers' on Nottingham[4] in the eighteenth century; both used constant conversion ratios to get the number of births from the number of baptisms, and to get the deaths from the burials. This assumption, in view of the high rates themselves, is obviously very dangerous, but at that time there seemed little alternative. The apparent rise in the birth- and death-rates, for instance, that Chambers found[5] around 1725

---

[1] G. P. Jones, 'The Population of Broughton-in-Furness in the Eighteenth Century', *Transactions of the Cumberland and Westmorland Antiquarian and Archaeological Society*, **53** (1954), pp. 136–48.

[2] A. C. Wood, 'A Note on the Population of Nottingham in the Seventeenth Century', *Transactions of the Thoroton Society*, **40** (1936), pp. 109–13; and 'A Note on the Population of Six Notts. Towns in the Seventeenth Century', *ibid.*, **41** (1937), pp. 18–26.

[3] D. E. C. Eversley, 'A survey of population in an area of Worcestershire, 1660–1850', *Population Studies*, X (1957), pp. 253–79, and reprinted in *Population in History* (edited by Glass and Eversley), London, 1965, pp. 394–419.

[4] J. D. Chambers, 'The Vale of Trent 1670–1800. A Regional Study of Economic Change', *Economic History Review, Supplement*, **3** (1957), and partly reprinted as 'The course of Population Change' in *Population in History* (edited by Glass and Eversley), London, 1965, pp. 327–34; *idem*, 'Population Change in a Provincial Town, Nottingham 1700–1800', in *Studies in the Industrial Revolution: Essays presented to T. S. Ashton* (edited by L. S. Presnell), London, 1960, and also reprinted in *Population in History*, pp. 334–53.

[5] *Loc. cit.* (1960).

could equally well be caused by a strengthening in Anglican church adherence at that time. Krause has argued[1] that the completeness of registration varied widely between 1780 and 1850, and one must agree with him; he is probably over-optimistic about the average level of completeness before 1780, however, which could have been quite high while still being below the level of 1820.

Of the later studies not using family reconstitution, Drake[2] worked on parts of the West Riding of Yorkshire, 1540–1699; Sogner[3] used seventeen parishes in Shropshire, 1711–60, to study population trends early in the Industrial Revolution; and Hair[4] studied bridal pregnancy, 1540–1835.

The Cambridge Group for the History of Population and Social Structure, however, is now studying a large number of parishes. Their plan covers a sample of all the parishes of England, and a large number of amateur workers is helping to complete this project, which will take many years. It reflects exactly the project started rather earlier in France, where, although the registers do not go back quite so far as the English ones, they are more complete in some ways.[5] Studies on parish registers along the same lines have been attempted in almost all European countries within recent years, which we shall come to presently, but it is believed that no country has such a comprehensive plan as England or France.

[1] *Loc. cit.* above on p. 142 (footnote 1), especially (1958).
[2] M. Drake, 'An Elementary Exercise in Parish Register Demography', *Economic History Review*, 2nd series, **14**, 3 (1962), pp. 427–45.
[3] S. Sogner, 'Aspects of the Demographic Situation in 17 Parishes in Shropshire, 1711–60', *Population Studies*, XVII, 2 (1963), pp. 126–46.
[4] P. E. H. Hair, 'Bridal Pregnancy in Rural England in Earlier Centuries', *ibid.*, **20**, 2 (November 1966), pp. 233–43. He took 77 parishes, and found that a proportion of between a third and a sixth of all brides must have been pregnant at marriage. It was lower before 1700 than after, and the North of England had the highest rates.
[5] For a description of the Cambridge methods, see *An Introduction to English Historical Demography: From the Sixteenth to the Nineteenth Century* (edited by E. A. Wrigley), London, 1966. Their approach is largely geographical, by way of local historians.

England's progress is, of course, well behind that of France, and at present only one study of a parish has appeared that uses family reconstitution, Wrigley's work[1] on Colyton in Devon. The results show rather better conditions in England than in France; the usual pattern[2] of late marriage and relatively infrequent marriage; and a surprisingly high expectation of life, especially in the sixteenth century. A serious plague in 1646 is the main crisis, but at Colyton crises of subsistence in the French manner are absent. At the end of the chapter, we show that Wrigley's mortality estimates are probably too low, although the expectation of life at birth is still about 32 to 35 in the sixteenth century, which is higher than it was in the seventeenth.

The most interesting result from Colyton is the evidence of family limitation that Wrigley found after the plague of 1646, together with a tendency for the age at marriage to rise. It apparently reached a point where, around the end of the seventeenth century, women were markedly older than their husbands, and married at an average age of over thirty. The pattern gradually seems to have reverted to normal, and by the time registration became civil and not ecclesiastical in 1837, had entirely changed to the familiar one of both being under twenty-five and the wife about two years younger than her husband.

Germany

The oldest parish registers in Germany are apparently to be found in Saxony,[3] but the Reformation really caused their spread, and

[1] Wrigley, 'Family Limitation in Pre-Industrial England', *Economic History Review*, 2nd Series, **19**, 1 (April 1966), pp. 82–109; and 'Mortality in Pre-Industrial England: The Example of Colyton, Devon, Over three Centuries', *Daedalus* (Spring 1968), pp. 546–80. See also below, pp. 186–95.

[2] The European marriage pattern, as known from the seventeenth century or before until 1914 or later, has been little studied for its own sake, despite its enormous importance. See J. Hajnal, 'European Marriage Patterns in Perspective', in *Population in History* (edited by Glass and Eversley), London, 1965, pp. 101–43.

[3] Mols, *op. cit.* above on p. 139 (footnote 1), Vol. I, p. 82.

Nuremberg has the oldest that is beyond all doubt, dating from
1524. The first registers are mostly Protestant; there was some
delay before the Catholics also commonly had registers.[1] There
have long been historical studies based upon the German registers.
Before 1939 Münter had studied Dilsberg[2] (near Heidelberg), in
detail, showing the relative changes of the Protestant and Catholic
communities there, and he could hence put the date at which the
Catholics became the majority in Dilsberg at between 1708 and
1737. Several aggregative studies in Southern Germany have been
made by Professor Kisskalt[3] and his colleagues at Munich, assessing mortality in the seventeenth and eighteenth centuries for the
most part: Bäumler[4] worked on Weiden (Oberpfalz) for 1551–
1800; Ehrhart[5] on Kempten for 1606–24 and 1686–1870; Hail[6]
on Memmingen, 1644–1870; and the Schmölzes[7] on Landsberg
am Lech 1585–1875. Heckh uses parish registers in rural parts of
Württemberg[8] to study class fertility since 1650, and Schade[9]
seems to have reconstituted families for eight communes in
Schwalm over the period 1600–1900. Livet[10] discusses the further

[1] See *ibid.*, where Mols discusses the reasons for this.
[2] H. Münter, 'Church Registers, as Sources for the History of Rural Communities', *English Historical Review*, **52**, 1 (January 1937), pp. 98–103.
[3] K. Kisskalt, 'Epidemiologisch-statistische Untersuchungen über die
Sterblichkeit von 1600–1800', *Archiv für Hygiene und Bakteriologie*, CXXXVII,
1 (March 1953), pp. 26–42.
[4] G. Bäumler, 'Medizinalstatistische Untersuchungen über Weiden/Ober-
pfalz von 1551–1800', CXX (1938), pp. 195–243.
[5] W. Ehrhart, 'Die Sterblichkeit in der Reichsstadt Kempten (Allgäu) in
den Jahren 1606–1624 und 1686–1870', *ibid.*, CXVI (1936), pp. 115–30.
[6] A. Hail, 'Die Sterblichkeit in Memmingen in den Jahren 1644 bis 1870',
ibid., CXVIII (1937), pp. 67–87.
[7] F. Schmölz and T. Schmölz, 'Die Sterblichkeit in Landsberg am Lech von
1585–1875', *ibid.*, CXXXVI, 7 (28 October 1952), pp. 504–40.
[8] G. Heckh, 'Unterschiedliche Fortpflanzung ländischer Sozialgruppen aus
Südwestdeutschland seit dem 17. Jahrhundert', *Homo*, **3**, 4 (1952), pp. 169–75.
[9] H. Schade, 'Neue statistische Ergebnisse einer Bevölkerungserhebung in
der Schwalm', *ibid.*, **9**, 1 (1958), pp. 13–20.
[10] G. Livet, *La Guerre de Trente Ans*, Paris, 1963, pp. 49–55.

use of parish registers for studying the mortality of the Thirty Years War.

The Low Countries

The oldest Belgian parish register is that of marriages at Brussels,[1] which dates from 1482. It is common in Brabant, too, for marriage-registers to be the oldest. Most registers in the Netherlands start between 1573 and 1585.[2] The earliest began in 1524, with the exception of some doubtful registers from Delft going back to 1367. In both Belgium and Holland there has been considerable activity of late, and several urban parishes have been studied. The Dutch results for the seventeenth century seem to be especially good,[3] and there is evidence of the decline, that students of political history know well, after 1700. Morineau remarks[4] on the difficulty of family reconstitution in Holland because there are fewer surnames in use (Spain and Portugal, he claims, also suffer from relatively few surnames).

In Belgium, Ruwet's work on Liège was mentioned above in relation to the crises in France; he also made a study of St Trond,[5] a parish in Limburg. This latter was done on the basis of a listing of the population in 1635 and the parish register data of baptisms. Almost all the children under 10 in the 1635 list were also in the baptismal register, although after the age of 10 migration seems to have been quite frequent. With such a high degree of evident completeness of registration, Ruwet could easily estimate child

---

[1] Mols, *op. cit.* above p. 139 (footnote 1), Vol. I, p. 80.

[2] *Ibid.*, p. 81.

[3] See, for example, A. M. van der Woude and G. J. Mentink, *De demografische ontwikkeling te Rotterdam en Cool in de XVIIe en XVIIIe eeuw*, Rotterdam, 1965, which they summarized in French in 'La population de Rotterdam au XVIIe et au XVIIIe siècle', *Population*, **21**, 6 (November–December 1966), pp. 1165–90.

[4] M. Morineau, 'Démographie ancienne: monotonie ou variété des comportements?' *Annales E.S.C.*, **20**, 6 (November–December 1965), pp. 1185–97.

[5] Ruwet, 'La population de Saint-Trond en 1635', *Bulletin de la Société d'Art et d'Histoire du Diocèse de Liège*, **40** (1957), pp. 151–93.

mortality rates and so show that half the children born in the parish were not reaching the age of nine, which, together with the figure of 34·8 per cent non-communicants (under 15 years of age in this instance) and the parish register birth-rate of 44 per thousand, gives an adequate demographic picture of the parish. Model life-tables (see Appendix 1) would suggest a stationary population and an expectation of life at birth of about 23 years.

Van Assche-Vancauwenberg has studied two villages in Brabant[1] that had good parish registers and a few local censuses, and found a decline in population during the seventeenth century but a doubling during the eighteenth century. Such violent changes should not be regarded as unusual. The pre-documentary past was not a period during which nothing happened except minor fluctuations. On the contrary, the changes were probably more rapid and violent than they are today. Thus a halving or doubling of a population during a century should almost be regarded as normal, and constancy regarded with suspicion. Wyffels similarly studied Bruges[2] from 1606 to 1795, where the decline in numbers occurs chiefly between 1700 and 1760. This contrasts strikingly with England, for instance, at that time; but in Flanders there seem to have been many different socio-economic systems in the eighteenth century, which Deprez has summarized in demographic terms.[3]

---

[1] D. van Assche-Vancauwenbergh, 'Deux villages du Brabant sous l'Ancien Régime: Bierges et Overyse. Étude de démographie historique', in *Cinq études de démographie locale* (*XVIIe–XIXe siècles*), Brussels, 1963. [I have only read Houdaille's review on *Population*, **19**, (1964) p. 1002 of this.]

[2] A. Wyffels, 'De omvang en de evolutie van het Brugse bevolkingscijfer in de 17de en de 18de eeuw', *Revue belge de Philologie et d'Histoire*, **36** (1958), pp. 1243–74.

[3] P. Deprez, 'The Demographic Development of Flanders in the Eighteenth Century' (translated by M. Hilton), in *Population in History* (edited by Glass and Eversley), London, 1965, pp. 608–30. Deprez also gives the results of some of the other Belgian family reconstitution studies in this article.

Northern Europe

Norway has a fairly good series of parish registers, originating in 1685.[1] Figures from 1735 onwards have been published, and can be used to estimate population trends for Norway[2] between 1735 and the first thorough census in 1801 and beyond. Michalsen has described the Norwegian parish registers[3] from the archivist's point of view, as Jørgensen has outlined the state of the Danish parish registers.[4] These last were first kept in Schleswig towards the end of the sixteenth century, and spread to Denmark early in the seventeenth. Although all parishes had to keep them after 1645, uniformity in their compilation was not achieved until 1812. Lassen used data from 52 parishes in Zealand[5] for 1651–66 to illustrate mortality conditions in the seventeenth century, which were sometimes very bad (about 12 per cent of the population evidently died during the year 1657).

Sweden has a fine tradition of geographical research, so that it is perhaps not surprising that Friberg, a geographer, should have provided some of the most painstaking pieces of local historical demography[6] that have appeared anywhere. He was

[1] See J. E. Backer, 'Population Statistics and Population Registration in Norway. Part 1, The Vital Statistics of Norway: an Historical Review', *Population Studies*, I, 2 (1947), pp. 212–26.

[2] Drake, 'The growth of population in Norway, 1735–1855', *Scandinavian Economic History Review*, 13, 2 (1965), pp. 97–142. The birth-rate for the whole country seems remarkably low at about 30 per thousand before 1816. The Trondheim diocese, in particular, seems to suffer from understatement of births in the years 1735–44, when a birth-rate of only 20 per thousand emerges.

[3] F. Michalsen, 'Church registers in Norway', *Archivum*, VIII (1958), pp. 43–53.

[4] H. Jørgensen, 'Les registres paroissiaux et d'état civil au Danemark', *ibid.*, VIII (1958), pp. 37–41.

[5] A. Lassen, 'The Population of Denmark in 1660', *Scandinavian Economic History Review*, 13, 1 (1965), pp. 1–30.

[6] N. Friberg, 'Dalarnas befolkning på 1600-talet. Geografiska studier på grundval av kyrkböckerna med särskild hänsyn till folkmängdsfohållandena', *Geografiska Annaler*, 35 (1953), pp. 145–414 (including an English summary), and 'The Growth of Population and its Economic-Geographical Background

especially fortunate in having several catechetical lists to use as checks on his parish registers; five were made between the years 1663 and 1731 in one area, the last four listing the entire population. As well as his careful checks on completeness, a low birth-rate during the Thirty Years War emerges from the age-distribution of one parish in 1666, and a very rapid population growth (doubling in about 25 years) appears for another district just before the disastrous harvests in Sweden at the end of the seventeenth century. Considerable variations in the birth-rate, as well as very great variations in the death-rate, were evidently the main features of Swedish population change in the seventeenth and eighteenth centuries. Unfortunately, Friberg made no attempt at family reconstitution, but it could presumably be done very well from his data.

Jutikkala[1] studied the Great Famine in Finland of 1696 and 1697 from, amongst other sources, the death registers of twenty-five parishes. Again, this is a subtle piece of historical demography, using also other local records of the period, so that Jutikkala's conclusion that the population was reduced by 39 per cent is really confirmed, rather than established, by the parish registers. Oja has described[2] the Evangelical Lutheran Church registers in Finland, the earliest of which begins in 1599. A great deal of detail is available in them, and there are also many lists of tax-payers that will be useful in demographic research. Jutikkala explains how the clergy returned the population movements to the government from 1736 onwards in differing degrees of detail.[3] These returns are now, of course, in Stockholm, because Finland was then under Swedish rule.

in a Mining District in Central Sweden 1650–1750. A methodological study', *ibid.*, **38** (1956), pp. 395–440.

[1] E. Jutikkala, 'The Great Finnish Famine in 1696–97', *Scandinavian Economic History Review*, **3**, 1 (1955), pp. 48–63.

[2] A. Oja, 'Finnlands Bevölkerungsregister', *Archivum*, VIII (1958), pp. 55–9.

[3] Jutikkala, 'Finland's Population Movement in the Eighteenth Century', in *Population in History* (edited by Glass and Eversley), London, 1965, pp. 549–69.

Eastern and Central Europe

Rosiak has described the parish registers of Poland,[1] which were universal by the second half of the sixteenth century. The partition of Poland late in the eighteenth century disrupted this system, so that thereafter the Austrian, Prussian and Russian parts all had different amounts of state control.

Czechoslovakia now has a few parish register studies on an aggregative basis. Kryl is the chief writer on the subject,[2] but the small amount of space allowed to Kryl's articles in *Demografie* suggests that until recently Czech historical demography was not encouraged as much as in, say, Hungary, where the parish registers begin as early as 1576,[3] and state control over them began as early as 1770. No inventory exists, however, and they remain in the churches' hands. Civil registration only began in 1895. Kovacsics does not expressly regard the registers as sources of historical statistics,[4] but Fallenbüche used the baptisms at Pest in the eighteenth-century[5] to estimate the town's population—assuming, of course, accurate statistics and constant fertility. The census of 1771 gave Fallenbüche his base figure, but net immigration and faulty registration might cause a certain error in his series at times. There was, however, a negligible non-Catholic community, which does remove one common difficulty.

Jäger-Sunstenau has described[6] the Austrian parish registers,

[1] S. Rosiak, 'Les registres paroissiaux et les registres d'état civil sur les territoires de la Pologne', *Archivum*, VIII (1958), pp. 31–6.

[2] For example, R. Kryl, 'Pohyb obyvatelstva ve farnosti Trhový Štěpánov v letech 1690–1755', *Demografie*, 4, 2 (1962), pp. 187–8.

[3] F. Endrényi, 'Les registres paroissiaux et d'état civil en Hongrie', *Archivum*, VIII (1958), pp. 15–22.

[4] *A. Történeti Statisztika Forrásai* (edited by J. Kovacsics), Budapest, 1957. There are several taxation and conscriptional sources for Hungary, however.

[5] Z. Fallenbüche, 'Adatok Pest varos XVIII, szagadi népességének fejlödéséhez', *Történeti Szatisztikai Közlémenyek* (1958), 1–2, pp. 65–72. [I have only seen the review in *Population* 15 (1960), p. 752, of this.]

[6] H. Jäger-Sunstenau, 'Die pfarr- und standesamtilichen Register in Österreich', *Archivum*, VIII (1958), pp. 3–14.

seventy-eight of which go back to the sixteenth century (excluding territory no longer Austrian). The proportion of parishes covered, however, only reaches near-completeness after 1800. Mols, writing of the old Austro-Hungarian Empire, remarks[1] that the registers began in the parts under Italian influence.

Vaucher has given an account[2] of parish registers in Switzerland, and the oldest Swiss register, Porrentruy, dates from 1481.[3] The different cantons followed different rules, largely determined by their religious bias. In the Catholic areas, most of them do not begin before the Council of Trent, but the main towns were Protestant, and Zurich (1525), Basle, Berne, Schaffhausen and Geneva all have church registers dating from the first half of the sixteenth century. Geneva's records were collected and published long ago by Mallet in the form of vital statistics.[4]

Southern Europe

Some interesting social data has been found in Portugal on two parishes, one in Lisbon[5] and one in a country town.[6] The Lisbon parish is particularly interesting in that it relates to the first quarter of the eighteenth century, before the famous earthquake of 1 November 1755. At that time Lisbon appears to have had a considerable foreign population and a very varied social structure.

[1] *Op. cit.* above on p. 139 (footnote 1), Vol. I, p. 82.

[2] G. Vaucher, 'Registres paroissiaux et d'état civil dans la Confédération suisse', *Archivum*, VIII (1958), pp. 61–77.

[3] Mols, *op. cit.*, Vol. I, p. 82.

[4] E. Mallet, 'Recherches historiques et statistiques sur la population de Genève, son mouvement annuel et sa longévité, depuis le XVIe siècle jusqu'à nos jours (1549–1833)', *Annales d'hygiène publique et de médecine légale*, XVII, 1 (January 1837), pp. 5–172. Less than a third of this very comprehensive study deals with the period before 1814, but much of Mallet's early data seem worth reworking. *Journal of the Statistical Society* (1851) contains an English epitome.

[5] M. de L. A. da C.M. do C. de Silva Neto, *A freguesia de Santa Catarina de Lisboa no 1° quartel do seculo XVIII. (Ensaio de demografia histórica)*, Lisbon, 1959.

[6] C. M. Gonçalves Borges Landeiro, *A vila de Penamacor no 1° quartel do seculo XVIII*, Lisbon, 1965. [I have only seen Cailar's review of this in *Population*, **21** (1966), p. 420.]

The rates of baptism, marriage and burial vary considerably, even in a period without a plague epidemic, which suggests that disease was fairly common and occasional good years, without any major epidemic, might result in very low mortality. It is clear that a good deal of further work is possible here, and only lack of interest in the past has held it up. Felix has described[1] the Portuguese parish registers; the oldest existing is a baptismal register dating from 1529, and from 1563 onwards they were kept in an orderly way.

As long ago as 1767, Thomas Heberden published a note[2] on the eighteenth-century population of the island of Madeira, which illustrates some rather different problems. Using a census of 1743 of people aged 7 and upwards and the parish registers between 1759 and 1766, he could deduce that the population over 7 had grown since 1743 at 8·2 per thousand per year, while since 1759 the rate of natural increase had been nearly twice as high. This could be explained either by net emigration over the period 1754–66 of about 10,000 people (the population was about 60,000 in all), or by a rate of natural growth between 1743 and 1759 of only about 5 per thousand per year as compared with 15 for 1759–66. Since the burial-rate varied much more than the baptism-rate over these eight years, one is inclined to guess that at some point between 1743 and 1758 an epidemic reduced the population by, say, 15 per cent in a single year. The records may have been incomplete, although in a small island that is not so likely to happen. Perhaps, however, there was a movement to Lisbon following its partial destruction in 1755.

In Spain, Nadal and Giralt used parish registers, together with various other sources, in their study[3] of French migration to

[1] E. Felix, 'Les registres paroissiaux et l'état civil au Portugal', *Archivum*, VIII (1958), pp. 89–94.

[2] T. Heberden, 'On the increase and mortality of the inhabitants in the island of Madeira', *Philosophical Transactions of the Royal Society*, 57 (1767), pp. 461–3.

[3] J. Nadal and E. Giralt, *La population catalane de 1553 à 1717. L'immigration française et les autres facteurs de son développement*, Paris, 1960.

Catalonia in the second half of the sixteenth century. Marriage registers, in particular, were useful as showing the frequency of migrants in the population. A Barcelona register existed from 1457.[1]

Certain Italian parish studies have appeared recently, and in the main agree with other results. The registers begin, in the small towns and villages, almost as early as in France. Siena seems to have the longest set of data;[2] from 1381 to 1817 there is a continuous series. But the best sources appear to be for Bologna, where Bellettini[3] was able to study baptismal records from 1459 to the nineteenth century, and for the Veneto, and in particular for Venice itself.[4] In Bologna, there was a considerable increase in baptisms between 1510 and 1590, but the peak level was not reached again until about 1825. The plagues of Venice in the seventeenth century stand out clearly, and a tendency for the birth-rate to be lower in the eighteenth century and for marriage ages to rise is also apparent in both Bologna and Venice. Conditions of life, in fact, seem to have been somewhat worse, apart from the plague, in the eighteenth century than in the seventeenth, as well as being worse (with the plague) in the seventeenth than in the sixteenth, which is a salutary check to our customary notion that positive progress always occurs. Bellettini's figure for the birth-rate in Bologna is only about 30 to 35 per thousand, which, if not merely caused by underregistration of baptisms, could reflect the large proportion of priests and servants (all normally unmarried) that the town no doubt held.

Yugoslav registers generally begin soon after the Turkish

[1] See R. S. Smith, 'Barcelona "Bills of Mortality" and Population, 1457–1590', *Journal of Political Economy*, XLIV, 1 (February 1936), pp. 84–93.

[2] Mols, *op. cit.* above on p. 139 (footnote 1), Vol. I, p. 80.

[3] A. Bellettini, *La popolazione di Bologna dal secolo XV all'unificazione italiana*, Bologna, 1961.

[4] D. Beltrami, *Storia della popolazione di Venezia, dalla fine del secolo XVI alla caduta della repubblica*, Padua, 1954, and 'Précis historique de la population de la Terra Ferma vénitienne pendant le XVIIIème Siècle', *International Population Conference*, New York, 1961, Vol. I, pp. 544–55.

withdrawal,[1] so that in Dalmatia and Istria they date from the late-sixteenth century, but in Slavonia they begin early in the eighteenth century. They were not looked after with particular care, and many were destroyed or otherwise lost as recently as the Second World War. Mikić has published a study[2] on one of the villages of the Istrian coast for 1772 to 1956, based on parish registers.

Rumania[3] has parish registers going back only to the middle of the eighteenth century, except in Transylvania where they began in the seventeenth century. The recent official history of Transylvania[4] includes a good deal of population data. The registers were kept by the clergy without any official directives until 1831, but there is the compensation that all registers for before 1883 are in the State Archives.[5]

Other parts of the world

Ganiage was able to produce a study[6] of the parish register of Tunis, at least in the nineteenth century; the Christian population, however, was European and only a small fraction of the total for the town. This seems to be the only study of its kind that has been made in Africa; the rates are colonial in that fertility recalls French Canada rather than France.

[1] I. Karaman, 'Protection of old parish registers in the territory of Federative People Republic Yugoslavia', *Archivum*, VIII (1958), pp. 115–16.

[2] F. Mikić, 'Prirodno gibanje stanovništva u selu Brseč 1772–1956 (prilog biodemografiji mikrorajona)' *Stanovništvo*, **2**, 3 (July–September 1964), pp. 197–256. [I have only seen a review of this.]

[3] I. Comânescu and G. Ungureanu, 'Les registres paroissiaux et d'état civil de la République populaire roumaine', *Archivum*, VIII (1958), pp. 23–9.

[4] *Din istoria Transilvaniei* (edited by M. Constantinescu), Bucharest, 1960–1. See Volume I, pp. 161–3, 200–3, and 275–8.

[5] Some Moldavian statistics evidently appear in: C. Turcu, 'Cele mai vechi statistici moldoveneşti', *Studii şi cercetări ştienţifice*, **8**, 2 (1956), pp. 57–88. They are based on sixteenth-century registers, but I have not been able to study this article, and the registers are probably taxational.

[6] Ganiage, *La population européenne de Tunis au milieu du XIXe siècle. Étude démographique*, Paris, 1960.

America has a few historical studies based on parish registers, of which one of the most interesting concerns the Indian missions in Lower California between 1752 and 1814. Aschmann, who did not use the Fleury–Henry method which was then just beginning to be used widely in Europe, tells the sad story[1] of how the mission populations died out. By about 1770, all the local population had been converted to Christianity, and the priests kept complete registers of all their flock. At a typical parish, Santa Gertrudis, the numbers fell from 1,360 in 1768 to 117 in 1821. There is no evidence of emigration (indeed there was nowhere for the Indians to go), but the burial-rate was nearly always over 60 per thousand per year and occasionally as high as 100, which easily exceeded the baptism-rate. The population died out through disease, especially syphilis; occasionally typhus, malaria or smallpox also visited the missions. Two decades earlier, Cook studied[2] a similar group, the California Mission Indians, between 1769 and 1834. There was an irregular growth until about 1824, and then a very rapid fall, so that there were only 14,900 people in 1834 where there had been 20,300 as early as 1805.

Within the last few years, some study of seventeenth-century New England has been begun and it appears clear that the family size was, as has long been suspected, extremely large, with 7 or 8 children per family growing to adulthood. The normal birth-interval was two years, the age at marriage was low, and mortality was apparently remarkably low, since the mean expectation of life at 21 is calculated by Demos[3] at about forty-five years. (English national cohorts only reached this level about 1890.) It is interesting that the men appear to have lived longer than the

---

[1] H. Aschmann, *The Central Desert of Baja California: Demography and Ecology*, Berkeley and Los Angeles, 1959.

[2] S. F. Cook, *Population Trends Among the California Mission Indians*, Berkeley and Los Angeles, 1940.

[3] J. Demos, 'Notes on Life in Plymouth Colony', *William and Mary Quarterly*, 3rd Series, 22 (April 1965), pp. 264–86.

women; no doubt frequent child-bearing had a marked effect. It is hoped that further studies will appear to confirm these patterns. Lockridge has studied Dedham, Mass., for the first century of its existence (1636–1736) from the parish registers,[1] but his main concern was merely to establish total population and approximate rates of vital increase.

Houdaille[2] used three parish registers in what is now Haiti for the period 1722 to 1790, employing orthodox Fleury–Henry methods. In the rest of America, Lodolini has described the origin and the state of the parochial registers in eight countries of Latin America,[3] while Sánchez-Albornoz has made a preliminary attempt[4] to appraise the Latin American registers as sources of historical demography.

The Cocos-Keeling Islands, in the Indian Ocean, happen to provide suitable data for family reconstitution, which Smith analysed[5] for the years 1873–1947. There was almost no migra-

---

[1] K. A. Lockridge, 'The Population of Dedham, Massachusetts, 1636–1736', *Economic History Review*, 2nd Series, **19**, 2 (August 1966), pp. 318–44.

[2] Houdaille, 'Trois paroisses de Saint-Domingue au XVIIIe siècle. Étude démographique', *Population*, **18**, 1 (1963), pp. 93–110. Special features of this population were the low proportion of white women, and (consequently) the great difference between white men and women in their mean age at first marriage—31 versus 20 or 21. Under-registration of deaths in childhood seems certain, and the mean age at baptism is estimated at about four months. A large number of coloured people figure in these three parish registers, and interracial marriages were fairly frequent; but 56 per cent of the coloured children were illegitimate by 1760.

[3] E. Lodolini, 'Los libros parroquiales y de estado civil en América Latina', *Archivum*, VIII (1958), pp. 95–113.

[4] N. Sánchez-Albornoz, 'Les registres paroissiaux en amérique latine. Quelques considérations sur leur exploitations pour la démographie historique', *Revue suisse d'histoire*, **17**, 1 (1967), pp. 60–71.

[5] T. E. Smith, 'The Cocos-Keeling Islands: A Demographic Laboratory', *Population Studies*, XIV, 2 (November 1960), pp. 94–130. The birth rate averaged 55·8 per thousand over a period of 60 years, 1888–1947. Marriage, as one might then expect, was early; the median age was about 18 at first marriage for girls, but it evidently rose somewhat during the period of study from only 17 to nearly 19. Bridal pregnancy was usual (about 70 per

tion, unlike eighteenth-century Madeira, and very good vital registration records; a full-scale analysis was therefore possible, and although the material used was not strictly a parish register, Smith's thorough methods would apply equally well to any similar community that kept good records and had no migration over a considerable period.

COMMENTS ON FAMILY RECONSTITUTION METHODS

(1) *General*

The proportion of families that have been reconstituted in any parish by the Fleury–Henry method is usually disappointingly small. It rarely reaches 10 per cent, and the main reason for this seems to be migration from parish to parish. Thus the bride or bridegroom very often came from a parish other than the one of the marriage, and hence the baptism record cannot be found. It is hoped that a study of a group of neighbouring parishes will soon be done, which should show the frequency with which couples from adjacent parishes got married. The proportion of families that can be reconstituted should then rise substantially, perhaps to 30 or 40 per cent. Kenyon[1] showed, from marriage licence data, that only 40 per cent of the marrying residents of Kirdford, a large parish in Sussex, married within the parish between 1575 and 1800, but another 40 per cent of them married with ten miles of Kirdford. The class that married by licence may have been somewhat elevated, but it was hardly extremely so, which augurs well for the success of a study of neighbouring parishes.

cent of first births were within nine months of marriage). Infant mortality, however, was also high: about 375 per thousand before 1912, although only about 86 after 1918. In partial compensation for this drop in mortality under the age of one year, mortality in the second year of age rose.

---

[1] G. H. Kenyon, 'Kirdford Inventories, 1611 to 1776. With particular reference to the weald clay farming', *Sussex Archaeological Collection*, 93 (1955), pp. 78–156.

The pioneer French studies are not without their French critics. Poussou[1] has pointed out the large amount of information contained in local documents other than the parish registers, and complained that Henry and his followers often neglect everything except the acts of baptism, marriage, and burial. In principle, Henry would agree with Poussou that the full range of local data ought to be exploited; the fascination of family reconstitution for its own sake may have led some of his disciples to premature publication of their results without checking them against other sources. Poussou believed that the study of internal migration in France is likely to be difficult from the parish registers alone, which will affect one's conclusions about many other matters. Nuptiality might, in particular, be affected by selective emigration from their native village of girls who had no intention of marrying young; the marriage rates of the ones who stay at home will then seem falsely high.

It is unfortunate, too, that most French parish registers are inadequate, or even non-existent, before about 1668. This is a relatively late date, in that the patterns of modern life were already laid down in England by then, and it is the period before 1640 that is especially interesting. For France, there is no immense difference shown at the time of the French Revolution, and it might be that it is Henri IV and not Louis XVI whose reign was the turning point in France.

(2) *Infant and child mortality*

Once the number of families in a parish that have been reconsituted is large enough to avoid the worst troubles from random variation in the data, mortality under the age of 15 is measurable by the methods of Fleury and Henry. (Between 15 and about 25 they are unable to suggest any way of circumventing the uncertainties owing to migration.) Illustrations of the method are found in the studies of Crulai and, in English, of Colyton. A more refined approach is advanced in Blayo and Henry's work[2] on

[1] *Loc. cit.* above on p. 159 (footnote 3).   [2] *Loc. cit.* above on p. 158 (footnote 2).

Brittany and Anjou between 1740 and 1829. A sharp distinction is drawn between endogenous and exogenous infant mortality, and the biometric method (invented by Bourgeois-Pichat) of distinguishing between them can also be used to suggest the degree of undercounting of very early deaths. The original articles must be consulted in order to form an opinion on the reliability of the Bourgeois-Pichat method,[1] but it should certainly be tried in every parish study so that any unusual features in the course of infant mortality will be noticed. There is already some evidence[2] that breast-feeding practices may have an enormous influence on infant mortality.[3] There are three questions that can, however, be raised on Henry's method of calculating mortality between 0 and 15 years.

First, the interval between birth and baptism is very short in Catholic countries (such as France), whereas in Protestant countries (and certainly in England) it is longer. The exact length seems to be a matter of custom, and in France there was even a tendency sometimes to baptize retrospectively if a child was stillborn or died within a few hours of birth. Since the risk of mortality is much higher on the day one is born than on any other day of one's life under the age of 80 years (and probably under 100), the importance of knowing exactly what the baptismal practice was is very great.

In the European ruling families,[4] nearly 9 per cent of all

[1] A good summary of it is in R. Pressat, *L'analyse démographique: méthodes, résultats, applications,* Paris, 1961, pp. 83–93. Bourgeois-Pichat's original articles appear in *Population,* **6,** 2 and 3 (1951).

[2] J. Knodel and E. van de Walle, 'Breast Feeding, Fertility and Infant Mortality. An analysis of some Early German Data', *Population Studies,* XXI. 2 (September 1967), pp. 109–31.

[3] A useful analysis of infant mortality patterns in modern Africa, where high rates are found, is contained in *The Population of Tropical Africa* (edited by J. C. Caldwell and C. Okonjo), London, 1968; R. Clairin's chapter (pp. 199–213) is especially valuable.

[4] S. Peller, 'Births and Deaths among Europe's Ruling Families since 1500', in *Population in History* (edited by Glass and Eversley), London, 1965, pp. 87–100.

children who were born in the sixteenth century died in the first week of their lives, so that a delay of only a week in the normal practice of baptism would, with that rate of mortality, produce an apparent birth-rate that would require an inflation of 10 per cent to be correct. The French baptism figures, as Henry is aware, may include a considerable number of stillborn children, and might therefore overestimate the birth-rate. The English figures, on the other hand, will tend to under-estimate it, but the probability that the delay between birth and baptism tended to increase between 1600 and 1800 makes any allowance for this form of error particularly hazardous, since the endogenous infant mortality rate was also probably changing.

Second, omissions from the parish registers, through careless-ness of the registrar or non-conformity to the prevailing form of religion, can scarcely be estimated very well except if we know that they were negligible. We have suggested elsewhere[1] the extent to which this could have happened at Colyton, and can here only reiterate that English parochial registration was *certainly* very poor between 1801 and 1821, and almost as bad between 1821 and 1841.[2] Before 1801, Krause would agree that it was getting worse from 1780 onwards, and while we accept his evi-dence that overt Nonconformity before 1780 was rare, which would imply rather better registration, there is little evidence that it was as complete as he believes. The main arguments for sup-posing that English parochial registrations between about 1650 and 1780 were well below the numbers of corresponding vital events taking place are: (i) the 1695 Marriage Duty raised only £50,000 a year at first, and even the revising Act of 1698 only led to the raising of £70,000 a year, whereas £80,000 at least should have come in (see above pp. 126-7); (ii) King's age-distribution for 1695 implies a high birth-rate (much higher than the 34·5 per

---

[1] T. H. Hollingsworth, 'The Importance of the Quality of the Data in Historical Demography', *Daedalus* (Spring 1968), pp. 415-32.

[2] Krause, *loc. cit.* above on p. 142 (footnote 1), should be consulted if the point seems debatable.

thousand that King himself assumed), which would mean that Rickman's baptism total for 1700 was far below the births unless the rate had dipped suddenly; (iii) French experience is that registration is only really good after 1740, and yet France's general level of culture in the age of Louis XIV was commonly thought to be higher than England's and one might expect that a superior standard of registration would go with it, especially since in the Catholic church both priest and peasant would be more amenable to the discipline of registration; (iv) it is, *a priori*, odd that the completeness of registration should get worse in an age of enlightenment, and doubly so if at the same time both birth- and death-rates are apparently rising—although this is merely suspicion, not real evidence.

Third, migration under the age of 15 is assumed rare. However, at St Trond in Belgium early in the seventeenth century, as we have seen, migration was fairly common after the age of 10, rather than 15. The rate of child mortality between the ages of 10 and 15 would be under-stated by the procedure of the Fleury–Henry manual in any parish where children left in any numbers after the tenth birthday. Further to this, temporary absences from the parish by a family, which Henry has studied[1] in relation to estimates of fertility, will also affect child mortality rates as calculated. It is important to realize that *any* amount of migration will have the effect of producing apparent mortality rates that are too low. This may explain why the Colyton child mortality rates, when compared with a model life-table, seem to become lighter as one proceeds from ages 1 to 4 up to 5 to 9 and to 10 to 14.

(3) *Adult Mortality*
The Fleury–Henry method of reconstitution of a parish register was originally intended for measuring natural fertility. It can

[1] Henry, 'The Verification of Data in Historical Demography', *Population Studies*, XXII, 1 (March 1968), pp. 61-81.

study infant and child mortality as a fairly simple extension, but its inconvenience for measuring adult mortality is considerable. The period during which adults are at risk is impossible to determine with confidence, and single people cannot be considered at all. In some of the French studies, despite the method of measuring adult mortality given in the manual, it was deemed impossible to make sensible estimates, and only infant mortality was considered.

In Gautier and Henry's pioneer study of Crulai, migration could largely be discounted by keeping only to those married couples both of whom had been baptized in the parish. Only 14 per cent of men and 22½ per cent of women were then left whose age at death was unknown, and only 3 per cent of men and 5 per cent of women had no indication at all of their subsequent careers after marriage. Henry's method is to allot the unknown ages at death according to two hypotheses, taking optimistic or pessimistic views of the mortality of the missing cases. Now the Crulai data may seem to be well-nigh complete already, but even the best group (men whose wives' birth-dates were also known) comes out, by this method, with a mean age at death that is somewhere between 52·7 (pessimistic) and 55·2 (optimistic), or an expectation of life at age 27 (the mean age at marriage of the group) between 25·7 and 28·2. In terms of the Princeton model West life-tables, these in turn correspond to levels of about 3·21 and 5·43, or expectations of life at birth of 23·42 and 28·71. In terms of the expectation of life at birth, therefore, the range of uncertainty is no longer a mere 3 per cent on either side of the mean, but more than 10 per cent each way.

Naturally, the other groups at Crulai fare considerably worse; for Colyton, Wrigley was obliged[1] to modify Henry's pessimistic hypothesis for estimating the ages at death, since otherwise the pessimistic figures would have been absurdly low. It seems advisable to think about adult mortality in a reconstituted parish population with more care.

[1] Wrigley, *loc cit.* above on p. 168 (footnote 1) (1968).

The cause of the absence of ages at death is always that no entry in the burial register can be positively identified as referring to the person in question. Now if William Bagshaw was buried on a certain day according to the Colyton register, it may be impossible to know whether it was a father or his son, and neither can be credited with the burial. But this ensures also that neither will ever be given an age at death, although at least one of them died in the parish. The same difficulty can easily arise with first cousins, who will usually be about the same age, moreover.

A second snag is that migration from the parish will not occur uniformly over a lifetime. Modern research on migration has shown that a man (or woman) is more likely to emigrate at the age of about 25 than at any other time in his life, the frequency falling steadily until the age of about 55, after which it stays roughly constant at a level of perhaps one-third of its peak. There is also an extra tendency to move at around the time of a man's marriage, and as many as 10 per cent of all the changes of address in Britain today are associated with a recent marriage, or (less often) an impending marriage. If such a pattern of migration in relation to age and marriage applied in past centuries, it should be possible, in principle, to allot the unknown ages of adults at death in a more useful way than the Fleury–Henry manual propounds.

A third snag to the use of parish registers is the old one of outright omissions. These may have been rather rare in France, but in England Nonconformity was very common by 1800; and the known burial grounds undoubtedly accounted for a large number of burials that never reached the parish registers. Moreover, the completeness of recording of Anglican burials in a given parish register is not clear. (See our remarks about the Ottery St Mary parish register between 1689 and 1700 on pages 191–3.)

Let us only consider migration here, since it is certainly a frequent cause of missing ages at death, and is the only one of the three that must always be present. The distribution of ages at which migration took place will certainly be skew, with its peak quite young, whereas the distribution of ages at death will have an older peak. Now, Henry's optimistic hypothesis supposes that all the people whose age at death is missing reached the age of 60, and that they then died off with the same frequency distribution as those whose actual age at death was known. This hypothesis amounts, in fact, to assuming that everyone migrated on his 60th birthday, which is so unlikely, even as an average of what happened, as not to be worth considering. It is, in short, *too* optimistic.

The mean time spent in the parish after marriage before migrating from it, given that migration was going to take place before death, can scarcely exceed fifteen years, and could well be less than ten. Let us see how this affects a case where there is a large number of missing ages at death, Colyton in 1538–1624.[1]

Out of 345 married people whose spouses' age was known and whose marriage took place at Colyton between 1538 and 1624, we do not know the date of burial of as many as 118 (34 per cent); and no more information of any kind, following their marriage, could be found for 88 of these. The mean age at marriage was 25·4 years (the sexes are combined), so it is not absurd to take 14·6 years as the mean interval between marriage and migration from Colyton. This enables us to simplify the calculations by assuming that everyone who migrated left on his 40th birthday, unless we know he was certainly still in the parish then, in which case he migrates when he completes his next decade of life. Five of the unknown cases seem definitely to have died in the parish, but their ages at death are no problem to distribute. The effect of the operation is to assume a mean interval before migration of rather over fifteen years, which is probably too long, but the eventual distribution of ages at death is shown opposite:

[1] *Ibid.*

Vital Registration Data

| Age at death | Known age | Died in Colyton | Migrated Population | | | | Total |
			At any time	After 40	After 50	After 60	
Under 40	48	2					50
40–49	28	$1\frac{1}{2}$	14				$43\frac{1}{2}$
50–59	51	1	25	6			83
60–69	46	$\frac{1}{2}$	$22\frac{1}{2}$	6	2		77
70–79	40	0	$19\frac{1}{2}$	5	$1\frac{1}{2}$	$1\frac{1}{2}$	$67\frac{1}{2}$
Over 80	14	0	7	2	$\frac{1}{2}$	$\frac{1}{2}$	24
Total	227	5	88	19	4	2	345

This method will certainly tend to understate mortality under 40, and possibly also to overstate it at 40–49, but it should be fairly close to the truth when we take the whole set of figures. Now let us consider the age-specific survivorship rates:

Age-range	Probability of survival per 1,000	Corresponding expectation of life at birth in U.N. model life-tables
25 to 40	850*	41
40 to 50	852	40
50 to 60	670	29
60 to 70	543	34
70 to 80	262	32

* The survival rate of 855 per thousand for ages 25.4 to 40 was converted for convenience of comparison.

The mean expectation of life at birth of the five estimates from the adult mortality rates is 35 years. It seems possible that migration was really earlier than we assumed, which would make mortality in the range 25 to 40 higher, and would depress the expectation of life to perhaps about 32 years, as the rates of survival over the age of 50 seem to indicate. However, model life-tables, which are necessarily based on the mortality experience of nineteenth- and twentieth-century populations, may not be applicable to the sixteenth and seventeenth centuries, a point we discuss in Appendix 1 (pp. 342–4).

189

(4) *Further remarks on the Colyton results*

There is therefore some discrepancy in the Colyton data for people born 1538–99 between mortality up to the age of 15 and mortality over the age of 25, for while an expectation of life at birth of about 45 is indicated by the former, the latter points to about 35. Infant mortality at Colyton is especially odd, as has been mentioned elsewhere,[1] and the state of the parish register could account for it if frequent omissions are thought possible. It is certainly true that if we take King's figure[2] of 1,554 for the population of Colyton in 1695 and consider the seven years or so prior to 1695,[3] the baptism rate is about 20 per thousand, the burial rate about 30, and the marriage rate about 1 (11 marriages in seven years, 1688–94). This last is frankly absurd, since seven years is a long time in a young adult life and the numbers of young unmarried people in Colyton would have become overwhelming. There was a sharp rise after 1695 to about 4 marriages per thousand inhabitants per year (43 in seven years, 1695–1701), still a very low figure but perhaps a possible one. It would seem, however, that about 70 per cent of the marriages at Colyton between 1674 and 1694 were clandestine if we expect 7 per thousand of the population as the normal rate, the average rising to 85 per cent in 1688–94. Between 1695 and 1715, only 50 per cent would have been clandestine.[4]

The apparently low birth-rates of about 1670–1700 at Colyton

[1] Hollingsworth, *loc. cit.* (above on p. 184); Wrigley, *ibid.*, makes a reply. Spontaneous abortions and unrecorded still-births may likewise have been considerable; we have, however, no knowledge of them.

[2] Glass, 'Gregory King's Estimate of the Population of England and Wales, 1695', *Population Studies*, II (1950), pp. 338–74, reprinted in *Population in History* (edited by Glass and Eversley), London, 1965. See p. 199 of the reprint. The spelling 'Culliton' was customary at that time.

[3] Using the Devon and Cornwall Record Society's printed transcript of the Colyton register, edited by A. J. P. Skinner, Exeter, 1928.

[4] Compare Steel, *Sources of Births, Marriages and Deaths before 1837 (I)*, London, (National Index of Parish Registers, Vol. I) 1968, p. 296.

are less obviously wrong, but they do not agree very well with King's one other datum about the parish,[1] the number of houses inhabited in 1695, which was only 237. This means that there were more than 6·5 people per house, as compared with less than 4·5 in King's national average for towns other than London. A parish with such a low birth-rate as 20 per thousand would hardly contain many children, and we must assume that the 237 houses were full of lodgers, immigrating to Colyton at an unusually high rate, at a time when the natives were having few children. There was a Nonconformist chapel at Colyton that was old at the time of the diocesan enquiry early in the nineteenth century, but we cannot well discover how many of the inhabitants were Nonconformists in the 1690's. The failure of the 1695 Marriage Duty Act to raise much during its first three years of operation, and even after the revising Act of 1698 to raise as much as expected, suggests strongly that the attitude of priest and public all over England towards parish registration was very indifferent then. The absence of any change in the ostensible levels of registration at Colyton over the period 1690–1706 (apart from the jump in the marriages mentioned already) rather suggests that a fairly low standard of completeness existed throughout, although the possibility that it was one of a handful of good parishes cannot be disproved. A qualification for being registered at all was, perhaps, merely that of being in good standing with the vicar. Since church enthusiasm tends to be least in young adulthood and most in old age, this would explain why Colyton mortality does not fit the model life-tables. (Such an explanation cannot explain the ruling families' rates, however; see pp. 343–4.)

Ottery St Mary, about ten miles from Colyton, provides a good example of what can happen when a register is kept in various ways.[2] In 1689 and 1690, the vicar (Thomas Gatchell)

---

[1] Also given by Glass, *loc. cit.* opposite.
[2] The Ottery figures are taken from the Devon and Cornwall Record Society's transcript of the register, edited by H. Tapley-Soper, Exeter, 1908–29.

signed the burial register regularly, and the annual totals of burials were 114 and 111. A new vicar (William Hull) came to the parish in May 1691, and for nearly a year followed the old practice. However, he gave up signing in March 1691/2, and the burials fell from 90 in 1691 to 49 in 1692. This apparent improvement in the health of the Ottery parishioners was continued in 1693 and 1694, with only 62 and 63 burials respectively, so that an average of 58 burials a year was maintained over the three years 1692–4 as compared with 105 a year in 1689–91, when the vicar had been signing the register. The first four months of 1695 saw 27 burials, only 4 more than in the corresponding period of 1694, but there is a note in the register after the last entry for April saying that a new law taxing burials is about to come into force. (This, of course, is the Duty on Marriages, Burials, and so on that we met on pp. 125–6.) From then on, two witnesses sign each burial entry. No fewer than 89 burials appear between 1 May and 22 September 1695 (there had only been 28 in the same period in 1694), and then the signing stops, without any comment in the register to explain it. Only 17 more burials took place in the remainder of the year and only 22 and 29 in the whole of the two succeeding years, but the rate of burial did recover to an average of 59 burials per year in the last three years of the century.

Four different régimes, therefore, appeared within the twelve years we have considered, none of which seems explicable by the vagaries of epidemic diseases. First, under Gatchell and during the first months of Hull, only about 60 per cent of all Ottery St Mary burials were probably recorded in the parish register. This might be the numbers actually buried in the parish graveyard. Second, from March 1691/2 to April 1695 and from 1698 to 1700, about 33 per cent were registered, probably corresponding to burials where the relatives asked for registration. Third, for just 145 days in 1695, there was 100 per cent registration of every kind of burial by loyal tax-paying subjects of King William. Fourth, from 23 September 1695 to the end of 1697, about 17 per cent registration of burials only, corresponding to a level agreed by parson and people (and woe betide informers!) of what they could afford to pay in burial taxes at four shillings a time, which would be reminiscent of the lay subsidies of the later Middle Ages, but was strictly illegal in 1695. No one signed anything, and if questions were ever asked they could then plead carelessness. By 1698, when the parish realized that the Marriage Duty was not going to be collected from them, the more natural practice of before 1 May 1695 returned. The Ottery marriages jumped in 1695, but to less than twice their old level, while the baptisms rose, for a couple of years, by about 50 per cent.

Now it may be that, ten miles away at Colyton, a deep respect for the parish register was universal, at least among those few who married at the parish church; but it will be difficult to find many of the burials (and hence the ages at death) of any Colytonians who migrated to Ottery and died there. The excellent physical appearance of the Colyton register, with few reversals of date amongst the entries, might, in short, merely bespeak the pride of the vicars; a proud vicar would regard a reversal of dates as too serious a blemish on his precious register to justify making a late entry (except perhaps for someone who insisted upon it). The class that married in Colyton parish church was highly selective at the period when family limitation and late marriage appear in the reconstituted family records, and one must wonder as to their social status and whether even they adhered strictly to the Anglican forms for the whole of their married lives.

In his first article on Colyton, Wrigley remarks[1] that three particular points need to be met by an alternative explanation to family limitation for the results he found at Colyton: (i) the steeper fall in fertility in the later years of the fertile period than in the earlier; (ii) the rise in the mean age at first marriage for women; and (iii) the eventual near-reversion to the earlier fertility pattern.

[1] *Loc. cit.* above on p. 168 (footnote 1), (1966), p. 100.

Now only a half, or fewer, of the girls who married in Colyton evidently did so at the parish church at the relevant period, and only about a third of that half could be found in the baptism register. Marriage often seems to have been brought about at Colyton by pregnancy, even among the older brides, and one could suppose that older girls in this position might be more successful in getting an expensive parish wedding than were their younger sisters. The younger girls, whether pregnant or not, would probably be more inclined to economize and use one of the marriage shops that there must have been in the neighbourhood. A bride older than her groom, especially if born in the parish, might almost always have brought him to the church. The answer to point (ii), therefore, could be that marriages at higher ages appear disproportionately often in the minority of marriages that can be used for reconstitution. This train of thought also leads to a possible answer to point (i). The first child, often the immediate cause of the marriage itself, had a very good chance of baptism; but religious enthusiasm, or the desire for respectability, no doubt wore thinner with age, which, coupled with the threat of the baptism tax for some of the time, caused the apparent birth-intervals to increase as women grew older. Yet the women who married after 30 were apparently more than usually keen to have their very last baby baptized, so that the cynic's theory that religion is a matter for young girls and old women might have a grain of truth. If a really late child were unusually likely to be recorded (the same as an early one), but the penultimate child had a poor chance, we should get very much the Colyton pattern of fertility as reconstituted.

The apparent reversion to the pre-1646 pattern (really pre-1630) would then be illusory. Slowly, two changes would occur affecting registration in the eighteenth century: an increase in overt Nonconformity and a decrease in occasional Nonconformity. Those who adhered to the Anglican Church seem to have become a better-defined group, and Henry's method of family reconstitution would only then begin to work properly, because the conditions for which it was designed were beginning to be fulfilled. Not all the Nonconformists would belong to a chapel, no doubt; that would not matter, as long as the Anglican church was an integrated community, with all its members consistently obeying its rules.

All this detailed criticism of one parish may seem disproportionate in a book of wide scope, but Colyton is the first English parish to be studied with the full intensity of Henry's methods, and Wrigley's work is likely to be taken as a model for other studies. We cannot yet decide how far the results can be accounted for by family limitation, occasional Nonconformity, overt Nonconformity, temporary absences, migration, or unregistered infant mortality, but it is a great piece of luck that Gregory King should have given us the population of Colyton in 1694 or 1695. If almost any other parish in England had been chosen to be the first to be reconstituted, we should have no means of checking the register by determining the baptism, burial, and marriage rates. It is doubly lucky that 1695 is at the height of the extraordinary period in Colyton's demographic history.

It would be very illuminating to test the parish registers of all English parishes where local censuses exist for before 1740. If this showed that very few parish registers are reliable, England will only, after all, be as bad as France in that respect, and it might save much heartbreaking effort if the worst were known soon. There is no reason why the English should not have practised deliberate birth control in the seventeenth century, but it is not going to be easy to disentangle its effect from the other influences working upon the parish registers of the time.

CONCLUSION

While the French parish registers after 1668 seem reasonably complete, and the English ones are arguably incomplete at all periods, there has been little careful study of ecclesiastical register-keeping in other countries. The easy-going attitude of eighteenth-century English clerics is perhaps well-known, but parallels to it may emerge elsewhere. The civil registers, moreover, which exist for much of the nineteenth century in many countries, are themselves not beyond suspicion,[1] although in general they are much more reliable and would repay further scrutiny. Indeed, nominative studies on these, rather than the church registers, might prove the more profitable line of research into demographic laws and tendencies. For purely historical purposes, of course, we must try to use what data relate to our period.

[1] R. Gutman, 'The Birth Statistics of Massachusetts during the Nineteenth Century', *Population Studies*, X, 1 (July 1956), pp. 69–94, illustrates the difficulty of establishing the size of the errors, which were evidently immense in Massachusetts before 1850. See also his 'Birth and Death Registration in Massachusetts. I—The Colonial Background, 1639–1800', *Milbank Memorial Fund Quarterly*, XXXVI, 1 (January 1958), pp. 58–74, and 'Birth and Death Registration in Massachusetts. II—The Inauguration of a Modern System, 1800–1849', *ibid.*, XXXVI, 4 (October 1958), pp. 373–402.

CHAPTER 6

Closed Populations

(1) *General*

Many of our difficulties over the demography of the past disappear if we are lucky enough to find a complete genealogical record of the births, marriages, and deaths of a random sample of the population. The vital rates can then be calculated directly, although in generation or cohort form rather than as current rates. If we suspect such a peculiarity as, for example, late marriage for younger sons and early marriage for eldest sons, we can easily look to see if it occurs. A completely defined population suffices better, however, than a more vaguely limited quasi-random sample, a consideration which is frequently overlooked in the enthusiasm of any demographer who comes across a genealogy. Unless the population is rigorously defined in some way, independent of the genealogy itself, the sample must be self-selected to some extent. Of course, genealogies give us no idea of the true size of the population of which they might be assumed to have been representative; but on the other hand, they can give good indications of the levels of demographic rates then prevailing and of any changes in those levels. The absolute level of population is very often of less moment than its rate of change.

The degree to which the special population of a genealogy can be regarded as typical of any population other than itself must always be uncertain. Often enough, a social or religious group keeps its own genealogical data just *because* of its sense of separateness. The English Quakers, for example, have good registers, with the necessary genealogical links indicated; but, since they felt themselves to be a people apart, their fertility, say, or their age at marriage, might also have been markedly different from the general population.

There is always a certain doubt about the completeness of genealogical records, too, even though they may appear to be perfectly complete. The methods of the chronicler or archivist, however, are no different from those of the genealogist, and the genealogy's compiler is unlikely to have been much interested in demography. Many infants who died within a day or two of birth will probably have been omitted altogether, and some method of allowing for them must be found, or fertility study will be liable to bias. Children who died unmarried are sometimes omitted, and it is always difficult to know what 'died young' really means in a genealogy. It is certain that 'died in infancy' in English genealogies can merely mean died under 21, the age of the end of legal infancy.

(2) *Ordinary People*

There is an excellent register for Quebec, compiled by Tanguay, which amounts to a genealogy of the whole French-Canadian population. It is particularly useful for the period before 1759, and a small part of it has been studied closely by Henripin.[1] However, he did not concern himself with mortality in adult life, and concentrated upon fertility, taking about one-seventh of all the marriages recorded in the years 1700–30. The rise in the French-Canadian death-rate[2] that appears when one compares the years 1711–40 with 1741–70 from about 25 per thousand to about 36 per thousand might be worth further investigation, using the same register.[3]

A local genealogy in South China that seems to have been of good quality was used by Yuan[4] nearly forty years ago, and it is

[1] J. Henripin, *La Population Canadienne au Début du XVIIIe Siècle. Nuptialité—Fécondité—Mortalité infantile*, Paris, 1954.

[2] *Ibid.*, p. 14.

[3] See also J. Sutter, 'Deux instituts de population: de génétique, au Danemark, de généalogie, au Canada', *Population*, 8, 2 (April–June 1953), pp. 339–52.

[4] Yuan I-chin, 'Life tables for a southern Chinese family from 1365 to 1849', *Human Biology*, 3, 2 (May 1931), pp. 157–79; and 'The Influence of Heredity upon the Duration of Life in Man, based on a Chinese Genealogy from 1365 to 1914', *ibid.*, 4, 1 (1932), pp. 41–68.

said that many thousand other Chinese genealogies exist;[1] however, Yuan was careful to ignore his data with regard to young children. The most attractive European genealogies to the demographer are usually those referring to people of high social position, but the English Quakers are a group that is not far different from the common people in wealth and also has excellent records.[2] Certain American families have also furnished the raw data for studies,[3] but it would appear that these families were largely upper-middle class. There must be more doubt about the degree of completeness and of the definition of the population under study when, as with these assorted genealogies, the data are not chosen *by* the demographer, but presented *to* him. It is much more satisfactory if there is an independent criterion that determines who ought to be included, as in the case of the Quakers. Small-scale studies of this kind must be numerous; even in the U.S.S.R., Bunak has been able to make

[1] See W. Eberhard, 'The Leading Families of Ancient Tun-huang', *Sinologica*, 4, 4 (1956), pp. 209–32, and in *Settlement and Social Change in Asia*, Hong Kong (1967), pp. 102–29. Hu Hsien-chin, *The Common descent group in China and its function*, New York, 1948, evidently contains much useful information also.

[2] For studies of the English Quakers, see J. J. Fox, 'On the Vital Statistics of the Society of Friends', *Journal of the Statistical Society*, 22 (1859), pp. 208–31 and pp. 481–3. M. Beeton, G. U. Yule and K. Pearson, 'Data for the problem of evolution in man. V, On the correlation between the duration of life and the number of offspring', *Proceedings of the Royal Society*, 67 (1900), pp. 159–79, and Beeton and Pearson, 'Inheritance of the Duration of Life and the Intensity of Natural Selection in Man', *Biometrika*, I (1902), pp. 50–89, both also include Quaker data amongst other sources. D. E. C. Eversley is at present engaged in a full-scale study of the Quaker records.

[3] Beeton, Yule and Pearson, *loc. cit.*, used data of the Whitney family of Connecticut; E. B. Wilson and C. R. Doering, 'The elder Peirce's', *Proceedings of the National Academy of Sciences*, 12 (1926), pp. 424–32, used the Peirce family records; S. Winston, 'Birth Control and Sex Ratio at Birth', *American Journal of Sociology*, 38, 2 (September 1932), pp. 225–31, worked from the *Abridged Compendium of American Genealogy*; and B. C. Freeman, 'Fertility and Longevity in Married Women dying after the end of the reproductive period', *Human Biology*, 7 (1935), pp. 392–418, worked from eleven published genealogies for United States families.

a demographic study[1] of a small rural Russian population.

(3) *The Upper Classes*

Upper-class studies that do not attempt to be anything else can be very valuable. Henry's study of the Genevan bourgeoisie[2] is of the first importance, giving us a demographic analysis covering four centuries. The detail of the investigation is much greater than is commonly done, and the methods can scarcely be questioned. Although they were a group of high position, the bourgeois families of Geneva were probably not greatly different from the prosperous townsfolk of many parts of Europe, and their records seem to have been tolerably complete as far back as 1550. Other upper-class genealogy-based studies have been made by Guy,[3] Darwin,[4] Beeton, Yule and Pearson,[5] Rodenwaldt,[6] Jalavisto[7] and Forster,[8] each using published material for a bourgeois or petty noble class. Miss A. von Nell, at Bochum, is at present making a retrospective sociological study of similar data from

[1] V. V. Bunak, 'Демографическое изучение малых популяций по материалам посемейно-генеалогических исследований *World Population Conference*, Belgrade, 1965, Session B.12, paper 204.

[2] L. Henry, *Anciennes familles genevoises—Étude démographique: XVIᵉ–XXᵉ siècle*, Paris, 1956. He had a genealogy to hand for nineteen bourgeois families that Choisy (Geneva, 1947) had compiled.

[3] W. A. Guy, 'On the Duration of Life of the English Gentry, with additional observations on the Duration of Life among the Aristocracy', *Journal of the Statistical Society*, **9** (1846), pp. 37–46.

[4] G. H. Darwin, 'Marriages between First Cousins in England and their Effects', *ibid.*, **38** (1875), pp. 153–82.

[5] *Loc. cit.*

[6] E. Rodenwaldt, 'Untersuchungen über die Biologie des venezianischen Adels', *Homo*, **8**, 1 (1957), pp. 1–26. He ascribes the decline of the Venetian nobility to marriage changes, both older and less frequent marriage having the effect of producing lower fertility even though actual fecundity may have been unimpaired.

[7] E. Jalavisto, 'Inheritance of longevity according to Finnish and Swedish genealogies', *Annales Medicinae Internae Fenniae*, **40**, 4 (1951), pp. 263–74.

[8] R. Forster, *The Nobility of Toulouse in the eighteenth century: A Social and Economic Study*, Baltimore, 1960. See especially p. 129.

Germany, mainly for the nineteenth century, but beginning in 1770.

Mortality levels were much worse, even for the highest classes of society, in the seventeenth century than they are in almost any part of the world today for the general population. Indeed, in McCulloch's *Survey of the British Empire*,[1] the remark was fairly made that the common man enjoyed a longer length of life in the mid-nineteenth century than the English nobility had endured in the past. If it was true then, it is much more true today. The family limitation that is such a feature of French demographic history has been shown to have begun amongst the French aristocracy early in the eighteenth century,[2] and an interesting parallel trend appeared for a time amongst the British aristocracy;[3] but after about 1740, the British fertility levels turned upwards again while the French continued to fall. By the time of the revolutionary period at the end of the eighteenth century, the British aristocrats were having families more than twice as large as their French counterparts. The age at marriage, too, was very different in the two societies after the seventeenth century, when the French began to marry extremely young and the British remarkably late. A French duke would commonly be married by the age of 21 or so, but an English one would probably be over 30 before he was married. Here we are not in the position of having to depend on background sociological evidence, but can actually supply it from the data.

There is, in fact, no lack of studies of the nobility proper. It was

---

[1] 1854 edition, Vol. II, p. 556; quoted in the *Annual Report of the Registrar-General for England and Wales* for 1872.

[2] Henry and C. Lévy, 'Ducs et pairs sous l'ancien régime', *Population*, 15, 5 (1960), pp. 807–30.

[3] T. H. Hollingsworth: 'A Demographic Study of the British Ducal Families', *Population Studies*, XI, 1 (July 1957), pp. 4–26, reprinted with revisions in *Population in History* (edited by D. V. Glass and D. E. C. Eversley), London, 1965, pp. 354–78; *The Demography of the British Peerage*, supplement to *Population Studies*, XVIII, 2 (November 1964); 'The Demographic Background of the Peerage, 1603–1938', *The Eugenics Review*, 57, 2 (June 1965), pp. 56–66.

realized in the last century that the records of noble families in the various countries were a useful source for demographic research, and one can cite (in chronological order): Sadler,[1] Edmonds,[2] Doubleday,[3] Simpson,[4] Guy,[5] Benoiston de Chateau-

[1] M. T. Sadler, *The Law of Population: a treatise, in six books; in disproof of the superfecundity of human beings, and developing the real principle of their increase*, London, 1830. See Vol. II, pp. 270–82; pp. 340–8; and pp. 593–607. His methods were justly attacked by T. B. Macaulay in his review of the book, *Edinburgh Review*, 51, cii (July 1830), pp. 289–321. The controversy, unwisely for Sadler, did not end there; he twice defended himself in pamphlets of refutation and rejoinder, Macaulay's final reply appearing in the *Edinburgh Review* of January 1831.

[2] T. R. Edmonds, 'On the Duration of Life in the English Peerage', *The Lancet*, 10 February 1838, pp. 705–9. The age at death of 243 out of 675 peers had to be guessed, but his method is essentially sound. The rate at which mortality increased with age was apparently greater than in the general population, but Edmonds could hardly have known it at such an early date.

[3] T. Doubleday, *The True Law of Population, shown to be connected with the food of the people*, London, 1842. See pp. 31 *et seq.* However, his conclusion (p. 34) that the extinction of baronetcies (more than 80 per cent in about 220 years) was especially rapid is not valid, although the calculation itself is correct.

[4] Sir James Simpson, 'On the Alleged Infecundity of Females born co-twin with males, with some notes on the average proportion of marriages without issue in general society', *Edinburgh Medical and Surgical Journal* (January 1844), pp. 107 *et seq.*, and reprinted in his *Obstetric memoirs and contributions*, Edinburgh, 1855, Vol. I, pp. 324 *et seq.* He attempted to estimate the frequency of human infertility from the recent marriages of the British Peerage in 1833, finding that about 16·4 per cent were childless after five years of marriage. His method, however, was inaccurate to some extent; any marriages that had children by 1832 were counted as such, but only those married before 1833 who remained childless for the first five years (provided the husband was under 56 at marriage) were counted as childless. It should be appreciated, nevertheless, that fertility was high amongst the peerage at that time, and yet 16 per cent cannot be very far from the true proportion of childless marriages, which is much higher than would be found in most populations with high fertility.

[5] Guy, 'On the Duration of Life among the Peerage and Baronetage of the United Kingdom', *Journal of the Statistical Society*, 8 (1845), pp. 69–77. This was only one of many papers Guy wrote on mortality, and we comment on his work in the text on pp. 216–17.

neuf,[1] Bailey and Day,[2] Galton,[3] Oliphant,[4] Darwin,[5] Sprague,[6]

[1] Benoiston de Chateauneuf, 'Mémoire sur la durée des familles nobles de France', *Mémoires de l'Académie des sciences morales et politiques*, 2nd Series, V (1847), pp. 753–94. Despite his diligence in collecting data of 13,179 children in 3,330 families, the sex-ratio of 152 boys to 100 girls that he obtains (p. 762) must mean massive underenumeration of girls.

[2] A. H. Bailey and A. Day, 'On the Rate of Mortality prevailing amongst the Families of the Peerage during the 19th Century', *Journal of the Institute of Actuaries*, IX (1861), pp. 305–26, and reprinted in *Journal of the Statistical Society*, 26 (1863), pp. 49–71. They made a proper study of mortality between 1800 and 1855, and came to the conclusion that the mortality amongst peerage families was roughly equivalent to that of Farr's Healthy Districts. The widest divergence was at ages under 10, where the nobles enjoyed only one-third of the national mortality rate; males aged 20 to 29, on the other hand, fared worse than the general population.

[3] F. Galton, *Hereditary Genius*, London, 1869, pp. 130–40. This has become famous for his theory that English peerages were tending to die out because of frequent marriages with heiresses (who, having no brothers and often no sisters as well, might be supposed to carry genes detrimental to procreation in some sense). In fact, however, Galton did not have enough data to settle whether the rate of extinction of hereditary titles really was remarkably high following a marriage with an heiress. See also Gatton's *Natural inheritance* (London, 1889), pp. 241–8, in which, helped by H. W. Watson, he made some progress in the theory of extinction of surnames. 'Branching processes', of which this is an example, are important in modern physics, and many textbooks now explain the mathematical theory in detail.

[4] T. L. K. Oliphant, 'Was the old English Aristocracy destroyed by the Wars of the Roses?', *Transactions of the Royal Historical Society*, I (1872), pp. 351–6. His conclusion seems to be that the Wars of the Roses did have a destroying effect, but the evidence that the old families would not have declined similarly without the Wars of the Roses is not convincing.

[5] *Loc. cit.* above on p. 202 (footnote 4). The aristocracy had a high rate of first cousin marriage, about 4½ per cent, but the effects seem to have been negligible.

[6] T. B. Sprague, 'Note on the Probability that a Marriage entered into by a Man above the Age of 40 will be Fruitful', *Proceedings of the Royal Society of Edinburgh*, 10 (1879), pp. 202–8. The weaknesses of this study are manifold: it used peerage data only; it took no account of possible changes in fertility during the previous century or two; and (crucially) it ignored the age of the wife. After a refinement of this work that appeared in *Journal of the Institute of Actuaries*, XXV (1885), pp. 160–94 (with 8 pages of discussion after the paper), Sprague's final analysis appeared as 'On the Probability that a Marriage

Wall,[1] Pearson, Lee and Bramley-Moore,[2] Fahlbeck,[3] Westergaard,[4] Beeton and Pearson,[5] Punnett,[6] Rosenfeld,[7] Whetham

entered into by a Man of any Age, will be Fruitful', *Proceedings of the Royal
Society of Edinburgh*, **14** (1887), pp. 327–46, and was reprinted in *Journal of the
Institute of Actuaries*, XXVII (1888), pp. 195–214. The work was by now much
more careful and less ambitious. It recognized, too, the special nature of
peerage data. Slightly higher proportions of childless noblemen were found
in the latest generation than in the previous one, keeping age at marriage
constant, which indeed reflected a real fall in fertility between about 1820
and 1880. There was also some tendency for brothers of peers to be childless
more frequently than the peers themselves who had married at the same age,
an important social fact amongst the aristocracy.

---

[1] A. J. Wall, 'Some considerations in regard to the causation of sex', *The
Lancet* (5 February 1887), pp. 261–3, and (12 February 1887), pp. 307–9. As
well as British peerage data, Wall used Royal, Princely, and 'Countly' families
from the Continent. The correct answer to the question he studied is now
known (the age of the mother does not matter, except in so far as the child
may die before birth; the proportion of females conceived rises with the age of
the father), so Wall's figures, which do not clearly provide any conclusion, probably show up the weaknesses of omissions in the data more than anything else.

[2] Pearson, A. Lee, and L. Bramley-Moore, 'Mathematical Contributions to
the Theory of Evolution. VI, Genetic (Reproductive) Selection: Inheritance
of Fertility in Man, and of Fecundity in Thorough-bred Racehorses, *Philosophical Transactions of the Royal Society*, Series A, **192** (1899), pp. 257–330. The
landed gentry, as well as the aristocracy, were used in this study, because
a really large number of cases was needed. The conclusion was that the effect,
although small, does exist.

[3] P. E. Fahlbeck, *Der Adel Schwedens (und Finnlands). Eine demographische
Studie*, Jena, 1903. This is more of a sociological study (of the Swedish nobility)
than the English papers mentioned previously. There is a very interesting age-
distribution by sex of the 12,737 members of the nobility resident in Sweden
on 1 January 1895 on page 351, which shows that the birth-rate must surely
have fallen a good deal between 1865 and 1894, and probably began its decline
about 1850.

[4] H. Westergaard, *Die Lehre von der Morbidität und Mortalität*, Jena, 2nd edn,
1901. As well as his own data on ruling families, Westergaard includes some
of Fahlbeck's early results and G. Bang's work on the Danish nobility.

[5] *Loc. cit.* above on p. 201 (footnote 2).

[6] R. C. Punnett, 'On Nutrition and Sex-Determination in Man', *Proceedings
of the Cambridge Philosophical Society*, **12** (1903), pp. 262–76. Much the same
comments might be repeated from the remarks on Wall's paper (footnote 1).

and Whetham,[1] Wagner-Manslau,[2] Fisher,[3] Furtak,[4] Vielrose,[5]
Punnett found a rising proportion of boys with higher social position, which
might well have been brought about by fewer stillbirths; and, amongst the
peerage families, a declining proportion with position in the family, much as
one would expect.

[7] S. Rosenfeld, 'Zur Frage der vererblichen Anlage zu Mehrlingsgeburten',
Zeitschrift für Geburtshilfe und Gynäkologie, **50** (1903), pp. 30–52. Although he
had a large body of data (from the Yearbook of the German nobility), its
quality is doubtful. The results he found on the frequency of twinning were
too low: one birth in about 130 was a twin birth according to his figures, with
no change in frequency since before 1800. In reality, one birth in about 80
or 90 should be twins.

---

[1] Sir William C. Dampier Whetham and C. D. Whetham, *The Family and
the Nation. A study in natural inheritance and social responsibility*, London, 1909,
pp. 138 *et seq*. A decline in the fertility of the peerage families, beginning by
1841 or earlier, is indubitable.

[2] W. Wagner-Manslau, 'Human Fertility. A Demonstration of its Genetic
Basis', *Eugenics Review*, **24** (1932), pp. 195–210, and 'Human Fertility II. A
Further Study on German Women', *ibid*., **24** (1932), pp. 297–304. His data
came entirely from the published Gotha almanacks and the court calendars.
He found that the proportion of middle-class wives was increasing, but that
they were less fertile than the wives from the old nobility. Much of the decline
in overall fertility could then be explained by marrying middle-class wives
for money, who he thought had a low hereditary fertility. The age at which
wives were married might, of course, have depended on their social position;
social factors, conceivably, could have caused the differentials in fertility also.
However, in so far as one can ever separate heredity from environment, there
is a case for preferring heredity here. Wagner-Manslau also wrote several
articles in German on similar subjects in: *Archiv für Sippenforschung*, VIII,
4, and X, 1; *Archiv für Soziale Hygiene und Demographie*, VI, 5 (1931); *Eugenik*
(1932); and *Archiv für Rassenhygiene*, XXV, 2 (1932).

[3] This is a critique of Wagner-Manslau by the outstanding geneticist of the
day. R. A. Fisher, 'The Inheritance of Fertility. Dr Wagner-Manslau's Tables',
Annals of Eugenics, **6** (1934–5), pp. 225–51. His verdict is favourable to Wagner-
Manslau's conclusions. However, the great secular decline in fertility between
1834 and 1932 must complicate the story; 'other things' were not equal during
the period to which the data relate, which may or may not matter, depending
on the precise manner of the decline.

[4] T. Furtak, 'Kilka zagadnień z demografii historycznej szlachty polskiej',
Rocznik dziejów spotecznych i gospodarczych, **6** (1937), pp. 31–58. This article is
cited by W. Kula in 'Stan i potrzeby badań nad demografją historyczną dawnej
Polski', *ibid*., **13** (1951), on p. 95, and also by E. Vielrose in *Die Bevölkerung*

Cooper,[1] Hollingsworth,[2] Henry and Lévy,[2] and Fügedi.[4] The subjects investigated in these studies, including as they do such recondite topics as the frequency of twinning, the sex-ratio at birth and what influences it, the span of life, the inheritance of fecundity and longevity, and the rate of extinction of noble lines, show how important the data are; but it is fair to say that most of the techniques used by the earlier men would not stand close scrutiny, and we have better data now to answer most of their non-historical questions. Strangely enough, few gave any thought to the possibility that vital rates might have changed with time, and hence most of them did not split up their statistics of the nobility into time-periods. The points of interest to us today were thus scarcely touched upon.

Polens vom X bis XVIII Jahrhundert, Marburg, 1958, p. 19. Although I have not seen Furtak's paper on the Polish nobility myself, it appears that their records are by no means complete. However, there is a strong likelihood that Furtak's conclusion that women had the shorter lives in the eighteenth century is in fact correct.

5 E. Vielrose, 'Przyczynek do demografii szlachty polskiej', *Przeglad Statystyczny* (1939), pp. 328–42. This is a work that is only known to the author through Vielrose, *op. cit.*, p. 10.

---

[1] J. P. Cooper, 'The Counting of Manors', *Economic History Review*, 2nd Series, 8 (April 1956), pp. 377–89. This uses data on the rate of extinction of various titles in England between 1307 and 1798, and some of Fahlbeck's early material on Sweden. No clear conclusions emerge, except that titles always are extinguished at a rate that seems to the outsider very high.

[2] *Loc. cit.* above on p. 203 (footnote 3).

[3] *Loc. cit.* above on p. 203 (footnote 2).

[4] E. Fügedi, 'A 15. századi magyar arisztokrácia demográfiai viszonyai', *Történeti Statisztikai Évkönyv* (1963–4), pp. 35–72. It would appear that Fügedi's work on the fifteenth-century Hungarian aristocracy may founder, because the aristocracy itself is ill-defined (as it was in England not much earlier), and infant mortality comes to an absurdly low figure. Because the ostensible intergenesic intervals are so long, he was tempted to assume that nearly one-third of all births may have been omitted from the genealogies he employed, and the sex-ratio at birth of 144 boys per 100 girls that he found certainly suggests that something of the sort must have occurred. The age at marriage of men was apparently getting later in the second half of the fifteenth century, which might be a pointer towards European marriage patterns at that time.

The best genealogies of all, however, are those of the kings and sovereign princes of Europe. Goehlert,[1] Kisch,[2] Wall,[3] Woods,[4] Kemmerich,[5] Sundbärg,[6] Savorgnan,[7] Diepgen,[8] and

[1] V. Goehlert, 'Die Zwillinge. Ein Beitrag zur Physiologie des Menschen', *Virchow's Archiv*, **76** (1879), pp. 457–74, seems to be one of the earliest. Rosenfeld's study, above, seems rather more satisfactory in its methods.

[2] E. H. Kisch, 'Zur Lehre von der Bedeutung des Geschlechtes', *Zentralblatt für Gynäkologie*, **11** (1887), pp. 49–51. Although I have not seen this article, its main conclusion, that the sex of a child depends on the *relative* ages of husband and wife, would seem to be a statistical artefact of no real significance.

[3] *Loc. cit.* above on p. 206 (footnote 1).

[4] F. A. Woods, *Mental and Moral Heredity in Royalty. A Statistical Study in History and Psychology*, New York, 1906. This is a fascinating study, although, scientifically speaking, it is of doubtful value. Some 700 people of royal birth were arranged in ten classes for intelligence and ten for virtue. William the Silent, Isabella I of Castile, and Queen Louisa Ulrica of Sweden are all awarded double first classes; Ivan, son of Anthony Ulric of Brunswick, Alphonso VI of Portugal, Philip, son of Charles III of Spain, and Anne of Saxony, William the Silent's second wife are all put in the lowest class on both scores. Only one person is given marks at opposite ends of the scale on the two counts: Catherine the Great of Russia (clever but bad).

See also Woods, 'The Non-Inheritance of Sex in Man', *Biometrika*, V (1906–7), pp. 73 *et seq.*, which is based upon von Behr's genealogy of the ruling families and on *Burke's Peerage*.

[5] M. Kemmerich, 'Die Todesursachen innerhalb der deutschen Kaiser- und Königsfamilien', *Saluti senectutis* (Leipzig) (1909), pp. 105–94. I have not seen this paper, but according to E. Vielrose, *op. cit.* above on p. 207 (footnote 4), Kemmerich produces figures for the expectation of life of males in medieval Germany, and the results are lower for the most part than amongst the English landholders of the same period.

[6] G. Sundbärg, 'Maisons Souverains de l'Europe, en 1841–1890', *Ekonomisk Tidskrift*, **6** (1909), pp. 195–237. My source for this is Savorgnan's (1962) article cited below, footnote 7. Apparently the survivorship rates were worse than for Sweden between 1891 and 1900, which either shows how very fortunate the Swedes were, or else that Swedish statistics (never questioned normally) may be inaccurate.

[7] There are many papers by Savorgnan that produce demographic data from the genealogies of the ruling families of Europe, the first of which appeared at least as early as 1923; however, I have not traced them all. One of the most interesting appeared first in *Rivista internazionale di scienze sociali* (1941), and subsequently as F. Savorgnan, 'La longevità dei principi della Chiesa e dei principi laici', *Rivista italiana di economia, demografia e statistica*, **16**, 3–4 (July–

Peller[1] used this material, the three last-named using Isenburg's *Stammtafeln*[2] as source. There has, in fact, been some attempt to follow demographic trends through time in many of these studies, and more particularly in that of mortality by Guy[3] who studied all the Christian sovereigns he could find from A.D. 1 onwards. The gravest weakness in Guy's method of analysis is that he did not consider the age at which these monarchs acquired their thrones, which must have varied a good deal. However, Guy's conclusion is certainly interesting in that they apparently had shorter lives than the aristocracy, at least if they were born between the thirteenth and sixteenth centuries. It is also interesting that up to 1600 there seems very little variation in the monarchs' mortality, as far as it can be judged; the thirteenth century was slightly the worst.

December 1962), pp. 255–64. His method is not wholly sound, for the age at entry of cardinals to office is implicitly assumed not to exceed 60. It is not, therefore, surprising that he found low apparent mortality for cardinals between the ages of 60 and 65 as compared with lay princes.

[8] L. Diepgen, 'Statistisches über Fürstenehen 1500–1900', *Archiv für Hygiene und Infektionskrankheiten*, CXX (1938), pp. 192–4. The very large families (nine or more children) were apparently becoming steadily rarer over the four centuries, falling from 32·3 per cent in the sixteenth century and 25·9 per cent in the seventeenth to only 14·9 per cent in the eighteenth and 7·1 per cent in the nineteenth; but infertility, age at marriage, and mortality make the fertility pattern complex.

---

[1] S. Peller: 'Studies on Mortality since the Renaissance', *Bulletin of the History of Medicine*, XIII, 4 (April 1943), pp. 439–61; *ibid.*, XVI (1944), pp. 362–81; *ibid.*, XXI, 1 (January–February 1947), pp. 51–101; 'Mortality, Past and Future', *Population Studies*, I, 4 (March 1948), pp. 405–56; 'Births and Deaths among Europe's Ruling Families since 1500', in *Population in History* (edited by Glass and Eversley), London, 1965, pp. 87–100. In the final paper, evidence appears for a steadily rising mean age at first marriage, especially for men; but the proportions never married at any given age tend to fall with time, suggesting both later and more universal marriage.

[2] Wilhelm Karl, Prinz von Isenburg, *Stammtafeln zur Geschichte der Europäischen Staaten*, Berlin, 1936–7.

[3] Guy, 'On the Duration of Life of Sovereigns', *Journal of the Statistical Society*, 10 (1847), pp. 62–9. His source was *L'Art de vérifier les dates*.

A useful source of the ages of oriental rulers is de Guignes' *General History*.[1] If due allowance were made for the age at entry, actuarial tables of mortality could be constructed for the various periods, and we should then also have comparable data on a non-European population of princes. One further piece of research might be mentioned here, Coolidge's note[2] on the fertility of women of the ancient Near East. The data are liable to errors of many kinds, but are probably closer to completeness than any other from their period. She found, using male births only, that Hellenistic queens had a fertility not much above a comparable group today, but that women found in the Bible had a much higher level of fertility. Other evidence supports the view that the higher classes in the later Greek world scarcely reproduced themselves, whereas the Israelites of old had expanded fast. Coolidge has thus added genealogical evidence to what we were already inclined to suspect. The matter will probably always remain beyond complete demonstration, but it looks as if it can be regarded as probable.

The main limitation of genealogical work is that it depends entirely upon the existence of a good and representative genealogy. Material relating to a high social class is really only applicable to that class, and genealogies that exist for lower social classes and have no self-selection bias are very rare. It is all too easy to take a family that happens to have survived to the present day and study its historical records, but in a random sample there ought to be a considerable number of families that died out long ago. The actual records of extinct families have had no one to preserve them and must normally be presumed lost. In a case where the records exist but have not been compiled into a

---

[1] J. de Guignes, *Histoire générale des Huns, des Turcs, des Mogols, et des autres Tartares occidentaux, &c. avant et depuis Jésus-Christ, jusqu'à présent; précédée d'une introduction contenant des tables chronol. et historiques des princes qui ont régné dans l'Asie*, Paris, 1756-8.

[2] S. Coolidge, 'Note on the Fertility of a Number of Women of the Ancient Near East', *Human Biology*, **25**, 3 (September 1953), pp. 203-5.

genealogy, there is an enormous labour in doing so; work of this kind is being attempted in the reconstitution of families from parish registers, but a genealogy must strive for complete reconstitution.

An intermediate situation arises when some of the genealogy is published and the gaps have to be filled in. This is true of the British peerage families, where the wives' birthdays and the families into which the daughters married usually have to be found by hunting through various local, professional, or general publications and archives. A large proportion cannot be found although many do turn up after a while.

The intervals between successive births in a family might, however, yet be studied in some of these élite groups and throw light upon the extent of birth control at different periods. While it is possible to fill in the gaps in the genealogical data, it should be recognized that there are dangers in doing so. It is possible to calculate age-specific mortality rates for each generation of birth, but if short age-periods are needed, some of them may acquire biases because of the method of completing the records. For example, if 5 per cent of women are known to have died unmarried at an unspecified age, they may all have to be given the same age at death; the five-year age-group that includes that age will then get a mortality rate that is about 50 per cent too high, other mortality rates being lowered. One cannot fit a model life-table[1] to such rates very easily. Ideally, the difficulty might be avoided by randomizing the ages at death that are to be arbitrarily assigned to the unknown cases; this would, however, be difficult to manage in practice.

PROFESSIONAL DIRECTORIES

A fairly good set of data is yielded by professional lists for physicians (Casper,[2] Neison,[3] Guy[4]) or lawyers (Guy[5]) or clergy

[1] See Appendix 1.

[2] Casper, 'De la durée vitale probable chez les médecins', *Annales d'Hygiène Publique*, XI (1834), pp. 375–84. Only 24 per cent of the physicians that this

(Deparcieux,[1] Guy,[2] Savorgnan[3]), which were often studied in the nineteenth century to answer questions such as the relative mortality of one profession as opposed to other classes of society. Since most entrants to a profession were in their early twenties, it is fair to use the lists in this way.

Soldiers and sailors were also studied in the nineteenth century

Berlin professor studied during the decade 1823–33 reached the age of 70, assuming an age of 23 at entry, but 42 per cent of theologians did so. Yet after the age of 62, the physicians had the lower age-specific mortality rates, presumably because they took fewer risks than when younger and had more idea than the theologians of how to avoid infection.

[3] F. G. P. Neison, 'On the Rate of Mortality in the Medical Profession', *Journal of the Statistical Society*, **15** (1852), pp. 193–223. From various sources, he comes to the conclusion that the medical profession had higher mortality rates at all ages than the general population.

[4] Guy, 'On the Duration of Life among Medical Men', *ibid.*, **17** (1854), pp. 15–23. Guy's less accurate methods show a rather more favourable picture for the medical men, although the general practitioners fare rather worse than the physicians and surgeons, which may be related to exposure to infection.

[5] Guy, 'On the Duration of Life among Lawyers; with additional observations on the Relative Longevity of the three Learned Professions', *ibid.*, **20** (1857), pp. 65–72. It appears that medical men had been gaining in duration of life since the sixteenth century, whereas lawyers had been losing slightly and the clergy remaining the same. Unfortunately, one cannot do Guy's study rigorously since the age at entry to a profession, and even more to eminence, is ill-defined and yet important to the results to a certain extent.

---

[1] A. Deparcieux, *Essai sur les probabilités de la vie humaine*, Paris, 1746. The heavily English bias of the lists of works mentioned reflects the author's limited reading. As well as Deparcieux, many other eighteenth-century writers (such as Wargentin and Süssmilch) made what studies they could of population. But although the Statistical Society's *Journal* may be tedious to meet in extended précis, one must not too often refer the reader to works (as Deparcieux') one has not read.

[2] Guy, 'On the Duration of Life among the Clergy', *Journal of the Statistical Society*, **14** (1851), pp. 289–98. The varied sources (county histories, the *Annual Register*, Chalmers' *Biographical Dictionary*, and the *Gentleman's Magazine*) make it impossible, as usual with Guy's studies, to determine just what universe of people was under study.

[3] Savorgnan, *loc. cit.* above on p. 209 (footnote 7).

from the official returns by Christie,[1] Lever,[2] Tulloch,[3] and Sykes,[4] and the interest was often in such matters as the relative mortality of different stations (Tulloch,[5] Balfour,[6] and Clarke[7])—

[1] R. Christie, 'On the rate of mortality amongst officers retired from the Indian army', *Journal of the Statistical Society*, 1 (September 1838), pp. 279–83. He considered all officers who had retired between 1760 and 1836, and assumed that all of them were commissioned at 18 in order to calculate his life-table.

[2] J. W. C. Lever, 'On the Sickness and Mortality among the Troops in the United Kingdom. Abstract of the Statistical Report of Major Tulloch', *ibid.*, 2, 4 (July 1839), pp. 250–60. This refers to the period, 1830–7, since regiments had been returning their annual numbers of deaths to the War Office. The official reports themselves might, of course, also be consulted.

[3] A. M. Tulloch, 'Comparison of the Sickness, Mortality, and Prevailing Diseases among Seamen and Soldiers, as shown by the Naval and Military Statistical Reports', *ibid.*, 4, 1 (April 1841), pp. 1–16. The sailors were both better fed and better paid than the soldiers, which explains the death rates (11·1 and 20·4 per thousand per year respectively).

[4] W. H. Sykes, 'Vital Statistics of the East India Company's Armies in India, European and Native', *ibid*, 10, 2 (May 1847), pp. 100–31. Mortality in Bombay Presidency, at least, seems to have not depended on age within the range (21 to 52 years) that included almost all the soldiers, the general average rate being 27·29 per thousand per year. The native troops, however, had a much lower rate of mortality (12·91) than the European troops (50·78) in Bombay. In Madras, the European death rate was nearly twice the native, and in Bengal more than four times. Without adequate explanations of these differences, one must wonder how far the army mortality figures were, in fact, correctly kept. Infectious diseases could account for everything, but the detailed study necessary to demonstrate whether this was so would be laborious.

[5] Tulloch, 'On the Sickness and Mortality among the Troops in the West Indies', *ibid.*, 1 (July 1838), pp. 129–42; (August 1838), pp. 216–30; and (November 1838), pp. 428–43. The *average* death-rate for the Tobago station over 20 years was 15·28 *per cent* per year, and it was nearly as high on several other islands. In the seventeenth century it was recorded that two-thirds of some 800 troops arriving in Jamaica had died within a fortnight, and heavy mortality upon arrival was still common.

[6] E. G. Balfour, 'Statistical Data for forming Troops and maintaining them in Health in different Climates and Localities', *ibid.*, 8, 3 (September 1845), pp. 193–209. The main conclusion of this paper was that elevation was very important in lowering mortality. The worst localities were Sierra Leone, the Bahamas, and Jamaica.

[7] R. Clarke, 'Short Notes of the Prevailing Diseases in Sierra Leone, with a Return of the Sick Africans sent to Hospital in Eleven Years, and Classified

the annual deaths from disease were sometimes 30 per cent of the strength sent to a tropical station—the chances of being drowned at sea,[1] and the risks of dying in battle[2] or in prison.[3] Clearly,

Medical Returns for 1853–54; also Tables showing the Number of Lunatics admitted to Hospital, 1842–53', *ibid.*, **19**, 1 (March 1856), pp. 60–81. Although there is little data here that may be useful to the historical demographer, it is interesting that as early as 1855 the phrase 'White Man's Grave' (p. 76) was being used of West Africa.

[1] F. G. P. Neison, 'Mortality of Master Mariners', *ibid.*, **13** (August 1850), pp. 193–209. The data came from an insurance company, the Master Mariners' Society, and related to the years 1835–48. Only 165 of the 270 deaths of master mariners in these 14 years were from natural causes, and Neison detected a tendency for wrecks to be more likely with younger captains, no doubt through their inexperience.

[2] W. B. Hodge, 'On the Mortality arising from Naval Operations', *ibid.*, **18** (September 1855), pp. 201–21, gives a general summary of British experience between 1775 and 1843, with particular reference to the Napoleonic Wars; *idem*, 'On the Mortality arising from Military Operations', *ibid.*, **19** (September 1856), pp. 219–71, the counterpart of the previous paper for the British army. R. T. Jopling, 'On the Mortality among Officers of the British Army in the Crimea', *ibid.*, **20**, 1 (March 1857), pp. 54–60, makes a few comparisons of the four chief battles in the Crimean War with some others, and there is no doubt that Waterloo was the most fatal battle for officers, both relatively and absolutely, that Great Britain had fought for a long time; Sebastopol and Inkerman did, however, surpass any of the Peninsular War battles. As many as 148 of the 372 deaths of officers in the Crimea were from disease, and the overall mortality was as high as $11\frac{1}{2}$ per cent.

[3] Sykes, 'Analysis of the Report of Surgeon F. P. Strong to the Bengal Government for 1847, of the Mortality in the Jails of the 24 Pergunnahs, Calcutta', *ibid.*, **12** (1849), pp. 48–59. An interesting conclusion was that permanent prisoners in these jails were better off than temporary prisoners, but no explanation seems satisfactory.

F. J. Mouat, 'On Prison Discipline and Statistics in Lower Bengal', *ibid.*, **30**, 1 (March 1867), pp. 21–57 and **35** (1872), pp. 57–106. Again, after age 30, there seems little effect of age upon the mortality rates (1867, p. 54), which are very high because of sickness. Detailed study of age-specific mortality in such a population might be useful in showing how an epidemic affects different age-groups in the population, a point that is in dispute, for instance, over the Black Death in England. (See Ohlin's criticism of Russell's life-tables, mentioned later in this chapter, p. 221.)

there is no reason why retrospective research[1] of this kind, rather on the lines of an insurance company's records, should not still be done, wherever suitable records can be found. So keen was interest in such affairs at one time that the Statistical Society of London set up a committee in 1838 to enquire[2] into sickness and mortality among the troops in Madras during the previous forty-five years.

William Guy was the pioneer in occupational mortality in Great Britain and was presumably instrumental in getting the detailed information provided by the census and registration systems that eventually enabled Farr to calculate occupational mortality exactly. But for Guy, working in the 1840's and 1850's, there were no data to use except the records of insurance companies, biographical collections, genealogies, and the lists of such institutions as the Law Society or the army and navy. From such data it is not strictly possible to calculate mortality rates, but the orders of magnitude can generally be estimated. The fact that clergymen generally have a higher expectation of life than physicians, for instance, was established before accurate registration of death data had appeared. The accident risk of the armed forces and the apparent over-indulgence of the aristocracy were also discussed by Guy. Yet since he could not tell for certain at what age men entered an occupation and he could not say how many left it for another in the prime of life, Guy was unable to produce fair expectations of life. He had to assume that such contingencies were rare, or at worst would compensate each other. A more serious weakness, however, was that Guy was restricted to the professions in the broadest sense, and was quite

[1] As, for example: P. M. Tait, 'On the Mortality of Eurasians', *ibid.*, **27**, 3 (September 1864), pp. 324–55; S. Brown, 'On the Rates of Mortality and Marriage amongst Europeans in India', *ibid.*, **27**, 4 (December 1864), pp. 566–79.

[2] 'Report of a Committee of the Statistical Society of London upon the Sickness and Mortality among the European and Native Troops serving in the Madras Presidency from 1793 to 1838', *ibid.*, **3** (July 1840), pp. 113–42, and **4** (July 1841), pp. 137–55. This should be read in conjunction with Tulloch's work cited above.

unable to estimate mortality amongst the general population. In the summary[1] of his work in this field, some evidence, however, does emerge for a relatively low mortality in the sixteenth century. The general trend over five centuries was towards longer and longer lives, the eminent men born in the fourteenth century dying at a mean age of 53·50 years, whereas those born in the eighteenth reached 63·41. However, while the sixteenth century might have been expected to afford only about 58·8 years if it fitted neatly into the progression, Guy's calculated mean figure was 64·23, the highest of all five centuries. There is the logical weakness in all these studies that we do not know the true age at entry into eminence, but it is unlikely to have varied in such a way as to negate the conclusion that the sixteenth century was a favourable period to be born, at least for the middle-to-upper class of eminent people. Mortality here is wholly adult mortality, and therefore seems to have been relatively low between about 1550 and 1650.

At an early period, nominative lists may give us information on migration and social structure that are better than complete ignorance. Thrupp has used[2] lists of London merchants to make population estimates of London for the late-medieval period, but the approach is too indirect to be very useful. Thrupp's social analysis, on the other hand, must surely be valid but does not help the demographer.

The nominative lists of the kind found in a standard work of reference are, of course, similar to the professional lists already mentioned. For example, the *Dictionary of National Biography* lists people with their birth and death dates; if allowances were made for the age at entry to the work, information on mortality in the past might be obtained. A similar method has been

[1] Guy, 'On the Duration of Life as affected by the Pursuits of Literature, Science, and Art: with a Summary View of the Duration of Life among the Upper and Middle Classes of Society', *ibid.*, **22** (1859), pp. 337–61.

[2] S. L. Thrupp, *The merchant class of medieval London (1300–1500)*, Chicago, 1948.

Historical Demography

used[1] to estimate fertility amongst the Philadelphia aristocracy of the twentieth century, by considering how many children each of them reported, and Harvard graduates have also been studied[2] in this kind of way. The main difficulty is that the exact reasons for being recorded in the work of reference are often imprecise, and in these cases there is a serious risk of bias towards the long-lived and sometimes towards the highly fertile. On the other hand, information compiled from sending questionnaires to distinguished people may omit previous marriages or children altogether. There may be more sense in Li Chi's idea[3] of using famous men with one of ten common Chinese surnames to study migration, the area from which they came in each epoch showing roughly how far the families had then spread. The same idea, however, probably would yield little in a society with many more different surnames than China has.

An interesting little piece of early longitudinal demography that deserves to be noticed is Tennent's article[4] on his own class of Glasgow schoolboys. He had kept in touch with most of them throughout the previous sixty years, and let us see how rapidly

[1] E. D. Baltzell, 'Social Mobility and Fertility within an Elite Group', *Milbank Memorial Fund Quarterly*, 31, 4 (October 1953), pp. 411–20. See also: Benoiston de Chateauneuf, 'De la Durée de la Vie chez les Savants et les Gens de Lettres', *Annales d'Hygiène Publique*, XXV (1841), pp. 241–68; Guy, 'On the Duration of Life of the members of the Several Professions', *Journal of the Statistical Society*, 9 (1846), pp. 346–53; M. E. Bernstein, 'Studies on the Human Sex Ratio', *Journal of Heredity*, 45, 2 (March–April 1954), pp. 59–64.

[2] G. T. Bowles, *New Types of Old Americans at Harvard and at Eastern Women's Colleges*, Cambridge, Mass., 1932. [I have not seen this work, but it is cited by E. Huntington in his *Mainsprings of Civilization*.]

[3] Li Chi, *The Formation of the Chinese People. An anthropological study*. Cambridge, Mass., 1928.

[4] A. Tennent, 'Statistics of a Glasgow Grammar School Class of 115 Boys', *Journal of the Statistical Society*, 18 (1855), pp. 364–6. About a quarter of them survived for 60 years from the age of 8 or 9 (around the year 1795), but more than 20 per cent had died before they were 30. This suggests, using the Princeton 'West' model life-tables, that the expectation of life of these boys, who were born about 1787, was then 30 years or less; but that conditions apparently improved, corresponding to a figure of nearly 35 years in the event.

they died off. The important points here are that *all* Tennent's schoolmates were counted (including a few that he had lost touch with), and that he did not think their mortality or longevity was especially interesting. They should therefore be representative of late-eighteenth-century middle-class Glasgow boys. Here again, there must be many parallel sets of data in existence.

Rather similar calculations have been made in France on the survivorship of former pupils of the Ecole Polytechnique.[1] Here the group is very clearly defined and a truly cohort approach is possible.

HOSPITAL AND INSURANCE DATA

The relative contributions of different causes of death aroused a great deal of controversy in the nineteenth century. Hospitals are an important source of the earlier data,[2] but there was no agreement on diagnosis that would yield really comparable figures. Important questions, such as the relative influence of altitude upon infectious disease, or of occupations upon particular diseases, remained subjects of controversy. It is still instructive to study these controversies, because although the situation is now more satisfactory there are still many examples of dubious

[1] R. Giraud, 'Probabilités de survie des Polytechniciens (contribution à leur estimation)', *Journal de la Société de Statistique de Paris*, **104**, 7– 8– 9 (July–September 1963), pp. 199–210. I regret not having studied this work except in review.

[2] R. Bland, 'Some Calculations of the Number of Accidents or Deaths which happen in consequence of parturition; Midwifery reports of the Westminster General Dispensary', *Philosophical Transactions of the Royal Society*, **71** (1781), pp. 355–71. Five out of twelve children born apparently died within two years, and another one of those twelve by the age of four, which was therefore the median age of survival. However, hospitals seem to have been a liability at about that time, since patients very often caught diseases from other patients. The population at large might have fared better.

A century later, Steele collected and considered hospital statistics in an essay that won him a medal: J. C. Steele, 'The Mortality of Hospitals, General and Special, in the United Kingdom, in Times Past and Present', *Journal of the Statistical Society*, **40**, 2 (June 1877), pp. 177–261.

classification of a cause of death. For example, when a person dies of more than one cause it is not obvious which is the immediate cause, and there has often been a tendency for diseases to be apparently more associated with the doctor rather than with the locality, a given doctor being prone to ascribe his favourite disease disproportionately often as the cause of death.

In addition to these lists, the early records of life insurance companies are a source of mortality data that has been exploited from time to time.[1] The social class that had life insurance at an early period is, of course, uncertain, and we can scarcely tell what the results really mean apart from showing general upper-middle class levels and trends of mortality.

INQUESTS AND WILLS

Russell, in his well-known book, used[2] the *inquisitiones post*

[1] J. Milne, *A treatise on the valuation of annuities and assurances on lives and survivorships; on the construction of tables of mortality; and on the probabilities and expectations of life*, London, 1815. The Carlisle Life-Table, based on 1774–87 experience in that city, appears in vol. II, p. 404. Neison, as well as his work on Master Mariners *loc. cit.* above on page 215 (footnote 1), used insurance data frequently; see his 'Contributions to Vital Statistics, especially designed to elucidate the Rate of Mortality, the Laws of Sickness, and the Influences of Trade and Locality on Health, derived from an extensive Collection of Original Data, supplied by Friendly Societies, and proving their too frequent instability', *Journal of the Statistical Society*, **8**, 4 (December 1845), pp. 290–343, and **9**, 1 (March 1846), pp. 50–76; and 'Mortality of the Provident Classes in this Country and on the Continent', *ibid.*, **13** (December 1850), pp. 313–58. A more recent example of historical work with life insurance data is Sir William P. Elderton and M. E. Ogborn, 'The Mortality of Adult Males since the Middle of the Eighteenth Century as shown by the Experience of Life Insurance Companies', *Journal of the Royal Statistical Society*, **106**, 1 (1943), pp. 1–20. Although the death-rates by age for 1863–93 were not much lower at adult ages than they had been in 1838–54 (say) for the general population, a marked reduction emerges for the Equitable Life Assurance Society's clients when that period is compared with 1762–1829. It would appear, therefore, that about 1830–7 or thereabouts a reduction in English adult mortality should be found, and in Appendix 1 we show that there is strong evidence for such a reduction in mortality between 1821 and 1841.

[2] J. C. Russell, *British Mediaeval Population*, Albuquerque, 1948, pp. 92–117.

mortem and proofs of age as his sources for a series of male life-tables for England from 1250 to 1450. The date of the man's death and the age of his heir were required, as well as the value of the estate he left. From two sources, a man's age at death can often be found (provided identification is possible), since each heir presumably will die in turn as a vassal holding land from the king. Age-specific mortality rates can then be calculated for males (assuming that the ages were given correctly), the procedure being much as for an insurance life-table.

There is some difficulty about these ages, particularly when the heir was over 21 and felt no need to be exact about his age. In fact there is a tendency, noted by Russell (and also found in the aristocratic families), for men to give their age to the nearest round number *below* their true age; a 44-year-old, for example, might well call himself 40. However, if one knows of this bias, it can be allowed for; the bias owing to their selectivity as an élite is more serious. They all held land, and must have had better chances in life than the common people. It is only a remote possibility that their travels exhausted them or that their food surfeited them, as Russell suggests.[1] Land-holding may, of course, have been distributed more widely in the past than it is now, so that half the population, say, held land.

A further weakness of the inquisitions as a source for constructing life-tables is the small numbers of men at risk at the low ages, as is inevitable. Ohlin has discussed[2] the consequences of these small numbers to great effect, as indeed he discusses Russell's other procedures in compiling his life-tables. Ohlin's critique must be read for itself, but an important point is his adjustment of the estimated population, getting declines at the four epidemics of 1348–50, 1360–1, 1369, and 1374 of not 16·6 per cent, 12·7 per cent, 10·0 per cent, and 8·6 per cent (as Russell),

[1] *Ibid.*, p. 117.
[2] G. Ohlin, 'No Safety in Numbers: Some Pitfalls in Historical Statistics', in *Industrialization in Two Systems: Essays in Honor of Alexander Gerschenkron* (edited by H. Rosovsky), New York, 1966, pp. 68–90.

but 22 per cent, 18 per cent, 10 per cent, and 12 per cent respectively—significantly greater mortalities in all except the third epidemic. If we combine these, the population in 1375 would be not 60 per cent of the 1348 figure, but 51 per cent. On Russell's calculation of the population of England in 1377 at 2,223,000, the 1348 population would then become about 4,360,000 and not 3,693,500. In Appendix 3, we reach a rather different figure again for the population in 1348, but by an entirely different method—although using what are essentially the same source data.

A comparison can be made with the expectation of life of the sons of dukes and kings at this period,[1] which comes to 24·0 at birth (born 1330–1479) versus Russell's 24·9. High mortality through violent deaths can more than account for this, although child mortality is dubiously calculable at this date, even for the sons of the aristocracy. Only an estimated 44 per cent of their deaths under the age of five have even been mentioned in the published accounts of the genealogy of the nobility.

Thrupp has attempted to estimate the changes in population in medieval England[2] by using manor court rolls and wills to calculate male generation replacement rates. Although the adult male replacement rates that she found did indeed fall after the Black Death, the probability of having any direct male heir is not a good estimator of population change unless we know much more than a crude figure. If her approximate figures are anywhere near the truth (and one always has the difficulty that they can only refer to a class above the lowest, labouring, level), then between 1259 and 1348, the population would have been rising at about 25 per cent per generation, say by 9 per thousand per year; and between 1349 and 1492 falling at about 60 per cent per generation, say by 17 per thousand per year. On this basis, we might have 2,850,000 people in 1259, 5,560,000 on the eve of the

[1] Hollingsworth, *loc. cit.* (1957) above on p. 203 (footnote 3).
[2] S. L. Thrupp, 'The Problem of Replacement-Rates in Late Medieval English Population', *Economic History Review*, 2nd series, **18**, 1 (August 1965), pp. 101–19.

Black Death and 2,230,000 in 1377, all of which is likely enough; but only 890,000 about 1408; 356,000 about 1439; and a mere 142,000 about 1470. Clearly, some explanation is necessary. Illegitimacy, as Thrupp suggests, may have increased; certainly, collateral heirs were normally available, which makes any massive decline in numbers even within this class out of the question.

Russell had tackled[1] a similar set of data to Thrupp's but in much more detail. A mistake in method when he had nearly solved an intricate problem prevented him from calculating in detail a basis for the whole population trend in England between the first half of the thirteenth century and the end of the fifteenth. Because his book is well known and his explanation of his procedure is difficult to follow, we have devoted a thorough analysis to it in Appendix 3.

Generation rates of change are relatively little used in demography, although they do arise naturally out of genealogical studies.[2] The replacement rate per generation, however, depends upon the length of a generation only to a small extent, and this length, moreover, varies little. One can therefore assume a length of a generation (about 32 years is normal), and convert generation replacement rates to rates of natural increase and *vice versa*.

CONCLUSIONS

The strength of dealing with a closed population is that migration is removed from consideration automatically. The people may have migrated, but they will have been followed by the genealogist or the compiler of records for some yearbook or insurance

[1] *Op cit.*, pp. 240–2.

[2] Hollingsworth, *op. cit.* above on p. 203 (footnote 3) (1964), and, especially, *loc. cit.* (1965). A rather unnecessary use of replacement rates can be seen in E. Cavaignac, 'Notes de démographie antique', *Journal de la société de statistique de Paris*, **76**, 1 (1935), pp. 4–9. He showed that the Babylonians could have increased from 36,000 to 216,000 between the twenty-eighth century B.C. and about 2450 B.C., but this does not require a calculation of replacement rates.

company. The convenience of using closed populations is that this hard work has very often already been done.

The main weakness of a closed population for the historical demographer is that it may not be representative of any group other than itself, since it often is a special social group in some sense. Omissions in the data, lack of rigid definition of the group itself, and ambiguity about the moment of entry to observation, can also sometimes reduce the intrinsic value of such studies.[1]

Nevertheless, the work of the early pioneers of demography in this field reminds us how fruitful further study might be. It is to be hoped that the efforts Princeton University has recently made to store the data on the British peerage families will be repeated for the continental aristocracy and the European ruling families, for the major part of most of the earlier studies has been simply collecting data that had been used by someone else before.

[1] Some degree of standardization in the compilation of a genealogy has recently been urged by M. Peronnet, 'Généalogie et histoire: approches méthodiques', *Revue Historique*, **92**, 239 (January–March 1968), pp. 111–22.

CHAPTER 7

Other Written Evidence

INTRODUCTION

It might be supposed that when our information is not fully adequate the best thing to do is to discard it. When we can be sure how far it is accurate and complete, however, it is foolish to discard any possible source of demographic knowledge for it would often mean discarding the entire body of data and regarding all questions of population as unanswerable. It is very often possible to make worth-while deductions from what appear to be unpromising facts. In this chapter, we give several examples of what can be done. Rules can hardly be laid down, since the diversity of material is wellnigh endless, but there are limits to be observed nevertheless. The reader will discover for himself, through the examples, where some of these implicit limits lie; and, although the methods we cite do not exhaust the ingenuity of the historical demographer, all the more widely used methods, and several more eccentric ones, are included.

MILITARY SOURCES

The size of armies[1] yields an obvious rough estimate of the size of the population of a country, at least as giving a minimum figure for the total. The chief difficulty is to determine what proportion of the population was represented by the army, and there is a further question of how far the figure quoted was (if not a mere guess) the nominal strength of the army or its effective strength. A Roman legion, for example, had 6,000 men nominally, yet it is known that a fighting legion normally had little more than half that figure.

[1] See, for example, F. Lot, *Recherches sur les effectifs des armées françaises des Guerres d'Italie aux Guerres de Religion, 1494–1562*, Paris, 1962. [I have not read this work myself.]

The size of the army that was defeated or that won a victory is sometimes recorded in ancient inscriptions. Such figures have been questioned (invariably as being too large), but there seems less reason to doubt the figure than to doubt whether it really meant the size of the army, or its nominal strength, or its strength including all supporting services. This latter in any modern army is many times the number of the fighting men, and in a large organization, such as the Persian army of Xerxes, there may well have been a similar multiplier.[1]

Elaborate use of army data has been made for estimations of the size of the population of India. Moreland, when assessing the population level at the death of Akbar in 1605,[2] made extensive use of the estimates of total army size in the southern part of India. A notional strength of 1 million in the sixteenth century (or 650,000 as the practical maximum) suggested 30 million people in the Deccan and Vijayanagar. For Northern India, the area under cultivation was less than in 1920, but the total population of India cannot have been less than 100 million.[3] Moreland corroborated his result by evidence of city comparisons: Lahore must have been above half a million if the travellers' tales were true, and Agra not far behind. Even more adventurous calculations have been made for the population of India in 200 B.C. by Nath,[4] and in 320 B.C. by Datta.[5] The political structure of

[1] See Sir F. Maurice, 'The Size of the Army of Xerxes in the Invasion of Greece 480 B.C.', *Journal of Hellenic Studies*, **50** (1930), pp. 210–35. He, however, estimates that the whole body of men cannot well have exceeded 175,000, and not the two million that Herodotus mentioned, by a detailed consideration of how it must have crossed the Hellespont on the bridge of boats.

[2] W. Moreland, *India at the death of Akbar: an economic study*, London, 1920, pp. 9–22.

[3] See also J. M. Datta, 'A Reexamination of Moreland's Estimate of Population in India at the Death of Akbar', *Population Bulletin of India*, **1** (1960), pp. 165–82, who raises the figure from 100 million to 110 million.

[4] P. Nath, *A study in the economic conditions of ancient India*, London, 1929, pp. 117–23.

[5] J. M. Datta, 'Population of India about 320 B.C.', *Man in India*, **42**, 4 (October–December 1962), pp. 277–91.

Mauryan India was highly elaborate, but by each of six methods[1] Nath reached about 126 million in 200 B.C. A figure for 320 B.C. can be found from the number of men conscripted from each unit and if only about 2 per cent of the entire population can have been soldiers, a population is obtained for 320 B.C. that is much higher than for A.D. 1605 (181 million versus 110 million).[2]

It is worth recalling that the anonymous author of *The Picture of India* thought that the population was about 200 million and had changed little since earliest times,[3] a sentiment that Johnston echoed[4] when he said that the population in 400 B.C. was at least as great as at the time the British conquest began.

There are extensive Chinese data on army size at the time of the warring states in the late Chou dynasty, and they yield such high probable figures for population that they have been discarded by many scholars. However, it is important to know the general considerations behind such a calculation before deciding whether or not to discard the figures also. At the time of the Magyar conquest of Hungary, the number of knights able to bear arms (actually obtained from Moslem sources) has been used[5] to make an estimate of the population as high as half a

[1] These were: (i) the number of estates multiplied by the average population per estate; (ii) the number of estate-owners estimated for the whole country from a part of it, and similarly multiplied; (iii) population of part of the country multiplied by its notional share of the total; (iv) calculation from the area of land required to support one person and the proportion of the total that was cultivated; (v) nominal strength of the army multiplied by 15 or 20; (vi) Greek estimates of the forces opposed to Alexander. We encounter some of these methods again later in this chapter.

[2] Datta, *loc. cit.* (1962).

[3] *The Picture of India: Geographical, Historical & Descriptive*, London, 1830, Vol. I, pp. 14–21.

[4] J. Johnston, 'Education in India, and the India Commission on Education', *Journal of the Statistical Society*, **46**, 2 (June 1883), pp. 225–74. See especially pp. 250–1.

[5] A. Armengaud, 'L'histoire de la population hongroise', *Études et chronique de démographie historique* (1964), pp. 151–4; a review of *Magyarország történeti demografiája: Magyarország népessége a honfoglalástól 1949-ig* (edited by J. Kovacsics), Budapest, 1963.

million. There are also series of numbers of men conscripted by Edward III for his French wars[1] which provide useful information on the relative population of different parts of England in the fourteenth century, and in particular of the relative size of the towns.

It is essential to realize that in these examples nothing approaching the present-day situation arose, where 10 per cent of a national population might often be on active service in a war. In Serbia in the First World War, as many as a quarter of the population may have joined the armed forces;[2] but although there was conscription in France between 1841 and 1864, of 7,378,610 men who reached the age of 20, 31·75 per cent were exempted and 34·66 per cent of the remainder were rejected on physical grounds.[3] Only some 3 million soldiers were thus found, or 128,000 a year. Lane, in an interesting article[4] on the economics of warfare, leads one to suppose that in historical societies one or two situations usually seems to have obtained, radically different as they are for a historical demographer: either armour was both so expensive and so effective that only a small number of men was required to fight, each heavily armed; or almost the whole population fought for a short period while not needed for the harvest, because superiority of numbers was all-important. Campaigns could not continue for more than a few months with the latter type of army, of course, since it was not possible to absent large numbers of people from agricultural work. A highly equipped army, however, could undertake a very long campaign, as when Alexander's Macedonians conquered much of Asia during eleven years away from home (334–23 B.C.). The Mongols,

[1] Given in T. Rymer, *Foedera, Litterae & Acta Publica*, London, 1821–5.

[2] G. Diouritch, 'A Survey of the Development of the Serbian (Southern Slav) Nation. An Economic and Statistical Study', *Journal of the Royal Statistical Society*, **82**, 3 (May 1919), pp. 293–334.

[3] Sir George Balfour, 'On the Military Conscription of France', *Journal of the Statistical Society*, **30**, 2 (June 1867), pp. 216–92.

[4] F. C. Lane, 'Economic Consequences of Organized Violence', *Journal of Economic History*, XVIII, 4 (December 1958), pp. 401–17.

on the other hand, were not an agricultural people, and a large part of the population might count as the army.[1]

An alternative source to actual sizes of armies, which exists for Tudor England, is the muster rolls.[2] It is obvious that the muster definition of 'able' men actually allowed many men to dodge the roll, and later the payment of a mustering bounty[3] would obviously tend to lead to inflated totals in the muster. The able tended to move frequently,[4] too, so the value of the rolls to a demographer is slight, since the general indications of distribution of population they do give are known better from other sources—the Chantry Certificates of 1545, the Ecclesiastical Census of 1563, the Communicants' Lists of 1603, or even Rickman's retrospective estimates for 1570 and 1600. This is less true of Rymer's data on the armed forces of Edward III, but their exploitation is far from easy and has scarcely been attempted. In the eighteenth century, Forster was able to argue from the militia levies[5] that the population of England was then about 7,200,000, which in retrospect seems on the high side. Brakenridge disagreed with him at the time,[6] using, however, Halley's life-table (which was wrong) to bolster his argument.

Juillard assumed[7] that the military rolls of 1618 in Alsace would

---

[1] See also H. Delbrück, *Numbers in History. How the Greeks defeated the Persians, the Romans conquered the World, the Teutons overthrew the Roman Empire, and William the Norman took possession of England*, London, 1914.

[2] E. E. Rich, 'The Population of Elizabethan England', *Economic History Review*, 2nd Series, **2**, 3 (1950), pp. 247–65.

[3] L. Boynton, *The Elizabethan Militia*, London, 1967, p. 27. A bounty of 8*d.* per day spent at the muster was introduced in 1573, increased to 1*s.* by the seventeenth century.

[4] Rich, *loc. cit.*

[5] R. Forster, 'Letter concerning the number of people in England', *Philosophical Transactions of the Royal Society*, **50**, 1 (1757), LVII, pp. 457–65.

[6] W. Brakenridge, 'An answer to the account of the numbers and increase of the people of England, by the Rev. Mr Forster', *ibid.*, **50**, 1 (1757), LVIII, pp. 465–79.

[7] E. Juillard, *La vie rurale dans la plaine de Basse-Alsace. Essai de Géographie Sociale*, Paris, 1953, pp. 504–5.

include all men aged between 20 and 40, and guessed a multiple of 6·5 to calculate the total population from them. As he said, the figure of 3 that had also been suggested is clearly too small, and indeed 6·5 seems to be about right. However, 20 to 40 is less than the usual range of ages at which men are assumed to be potential recruits.

Militia data can also be useful when the population is changing rapidly, as in Whitney's estimations of New England local population in the late-seventeenth century.[1] Both the numbers of families and the numbers of militia are known, and the varied and changing age-structure of these colonial populations mean that neither figure on its own can be used as an adequate guide to the population size. Whitney therefore used a two-stage method, using both indicators in combination.

DEATHS OF OFFICE HOLDERS FOR MORTALITY IN EPIDEMICS

The plague mortality in 1348 and later years has to be estimated from a wide variety of sources: the diminution of taxation levels after a plague; calculations on the number of benefices of the church that were instituted in different years; calculations based on inquisitions after death that give statements of age; and of course, the estimates of contemporary chroniclers are also worth attention. In Appendix 2, we discuss an epidemiological approach. Each method taken separately is open to suspicion, but confidence increases if together they give a consistent picture. The historical demographer must try to paint this picture, and see if the sources can be reconciled.

The most direct evidence published on plague mortality in England comes from ecclesiastical sources. Thompson[2] has given,

[1] H. A. Whitney, 'Estimating precensus populations: a method suggested and applied to the towns of Rhode Island and Plymouth colonies in 1689', *Annals of the Association of American Geographers*, **55**, 1 (March 1965), pp. 179–89.

[2] A. H. Thompson, 'The Registers of John Glynwell, Bishop of Lincoln, for the years 1347–50', *Archaeological Journal*, **68** (1911), pp. 301–60; and 'The

for two large dioceses, Lincoln and York, the numbers of benefices that had new clergy instituted to them during 1347–50, 1361–2, and 1368–9. This is not quite the same as the number of new institutions made, since some of the benefices fell vacant more than once; nor is either the same as the number of deaths of incumbents, since a number of benefices were resigned. Moreover, the beneficed clergy were probably somewhat older than non-beneficed clergy, and obviously considerably richer. The two were almost equal in numbers,[1] so that much of the visitation of the sick to perform the last rites would probably have been done by the non-beneficed.[2] The possibility that the clergy were especially liable to infection must, however, be weighed against their better education and, no doubt, less arduous way of life compared with the common man, both of which might tend to reduce their risks of death somewhat; while Boucher, for instance, thought that the mortality of the clergy of Bristol in 1348 was higher than that of the rest of the city[3] (which nevertheless lost between 35 and 40 per cent of its population), one cannot truly tell whether the clergy always died in larger proportions than other people, but one can sometimes tell how rapidly they died.

The diocese of Lincoln contained 1,857 benefices at this period. In the 18 months up to 25 March 1349—before the Black Death had touched the diocese—212 institutions were made by John Glynwell, the new bishop; 76 were caused by resignations, 72 by deaths, and the causes of the institutions of the remaining 64

Pestilences of the Fourteenth Century in the Diocese of York', *ibid.*, **71** (1914), pp. 97–154.

---

[1] J. Topham, 'Subsidy Roll of 51 Edward III', *Archaeologia*, **7** (1785), pp. 337–47. He gives the figures (for 1377) as 15,380 beneficed and 13,781 non-beneficed clergy. The latter would probably have been relatively more numerous before the Black Death; in 1377, they were more than twice the beneficed in Cornwall, less than half of them in Sussex.

[2] See Thompson, *loc. cit.* (1914), p. 98.

[3] C. E. Boucher, 'The Black Death in Bristol', *Transactions of the Bristol and Gloucester Archaeological Society*, **60** (1938), pp. 31–46.

(almost all in a single archdeaconry) have been lost. However, we can assume that there were about 109 resignations and 103 deaths in 18 months—say 69 deaths a year. The pre-plague death-rate comes to 36·5 per thousand per year, and although this figure is for adult males, the death-rate of the whole population was probably similar. In the following 12 months 1,025 institutions were made, 201 being because of resignations and 824 because of deaths. The increase in the resignations seems to have been caused by the chance of quick preferment as some of the richest livings were becoming available. The true clerical death-rate for the year of the Black Death must be rather higher than 824 out of 1,857 (443·7 per thousand), since there must always have been an interval between the death of an incumbent and the institution of his successor. At least one month[1] seems to have been the practice, which makes an important difference to the calculations, reducing the numbers at risk in 1349–50 considerably. In 1347–9, the 212 institutions give a 'dead time' of 17·7 years at one month for each, so it is as if 12 of the benefices were not at risk at all. The annual death-rate before the Death must be raised from 36·5 per thousand to 37·3 to allow for this 'dead time' between incumbents. In 1349–50, however, 85·4 benefices can be regarded as not at risk, and the annual death-rate is 465·1 per thousand.

Mortality thus rose for these clergy of Lincoln diocese to 12·5 times its previous level, and in order to apply this figure to the general population we need an estimate of its normal rates of birth and death. If, for example, we had had a population with annual birth- and death-rates equal at 30 per thousand, numbers would have fallen by 34 per cent within the year 1349–50. Previous rates of 35 per thousand would suggest a 40 per cent fall in population. Alternatively, we might suppose that $465·1 - 37·3 = 427·8$ per thousand was the extra mortality owing to the Black Death, and, because pneumonic plague is an infectious disease, that the the extra liability should be added to that of the general

[1] Thompson, *loc. cit.* (1911), p. 317.

population. On this hypothesis, the reduction in numbers would be 42·78 per cent.

Thompson himself, and Russell[1] following him, calculated not an annual death-rate but an annual life-table mortality rate from the same data. If a benefice was vacated more than once in the year (and this was frequent), they ignored the later deaths. In this way, they found that some 40 per cent of beneficed clergy living on 25 March 1349 were dead one year later. This seems a less reliable way of calculating the mortality, since in a parish where the plague raged for a long time only one clergyman can possibly be counted as dying; nor is it clear what corrections Thompson made to the rates for the dead time after clergy resigned their benefices, although Russell ignored it. Only 76 of the benefices were in fact vacant more than once, whereas one might have expected rather more; this reflects not the relative youthfulness of the many new incumbents so much as the short period of the Black Death, during which no doubt a successor was sometimes designated within a few days of a death, but died before he could be instituted to the benefice. By the time a successor was installed, the plague might well have left the parish.

Jessop,[2] on the Norwich diocese, and Dimock,[3] who covered several parts of England, provide data similar to Thompson's, although less precisely. It should be possible to estimate the Black Death mortality by region from such data.

WILL TOTALS

Similar methods can be used on Mollat's data of legacies at Paris.[4] Seventy-eight items appear on the register of accounts of

---

[1] J. C. Russell, *British Mediaeval Population*, Albuquerque, 1948, pp. 220–2.

[2] A. Jessop, 'The Black Death in East Anglia', in *The Coming of the Friars and other Historic Essays*, London, 1906, pp. 166–261.

[3] A. Dimock, 'The Great Pestilence: A Neglected Turning Point in English History', *Gentleman's Magazine*, **283** (1897), pp. 168–88.

[4] M. Mollat, 'Notes sur la mortalité à Paris au temps de la Peste Noire, d'après les comptes de l'oeuvre de Saint-Germain-l'Auxerrois', *Le Moyen Age*, **69** (1963), pp. 505–27.

St Germain-l'Auxerrois between January 1340 and June 1348—a period of 8½ years. The mean annual number was therefore only 9·2. In the 21 months July 1348 to March 1350, 449 legators appear, an annual rate of 256·6, or almost 28 times what it was before. A rise in the death-rate of 28 times is scarcely credible, however; if only 2 per cent of the population survived the Black Death (to take an absurd extreme), the 98 per cent who died in 21 months would represent an annual death-rate of 56 per cent, and a 28th of that is 2 per cent, or 20 per thousand, for the normal annual pre-plague death-rate. It is, of course, possible that the 78 legacies in the years 1340–8 were unusually few; or that pre-plague mortality was genuinely low for the legacy-leaving class; or that many more legacies were left when the Black Death was raging, as people became frightened. On a more conceivable mortality rate for the Black Death of 76 per cent, the pre-1348 death-rate would have to be only 15 per thousand for this class.

Fisher has recently drawn attention[1] to a similar source of epidemic mortality data, the wills proved in the various diocesan courts of England. In seven dioceses between 1551 and 1570, a marked constancy appears except for the years 1556–60, which were more than two and a half times the level for the other years (Quinquennial totals: 1,772; 4,543; 1,721; 1,786). Each diocese was affected, although Worcestershire and Gloucestershire seem hardest hit. The chroniclers speak of an epidemic of influenza in 1557 and 1558 that followed two years of bad harvests, and Short[2] and Creighton[3] also noticed it. The epidemic was spread over more than just these two years, but they were apparently the worst. Changes in the propensity to make a will, or in the courts' procedures for proving wills, cannot possibly account for such a large rise and fall; and the mortality of the will-making

[1] F. J. Fisher, 'Influenza and inflation in Tudor England', *Economic History Review*, 2nd Series, **18**, 1 (August 1965), pp. 120–9.

[2] T. Short, *New observations natural, moral, civil, political and medical, on city, town and country bills of mortality*, London, 1750, p. 85.

[3] C. Creighton, *A History of Epidemics in Britain*, Cambridge, 1891–4. See 1965 reprint, Vol. I, pp. 401–4.

class (largely middle-class adult males, one supposes) must have risen generally to about 2·58 times normal, and during 1557 and 1558 considerably higher, probably to more than four times normal. Supposing that the same applied to the whole population, and taking 35 and 31 per thousand as the normal rates of birth and death (as Fisher does, although we should prefer higher figures), we should have death-rates of 153 per thousand per year during 1557 and 1558; and, if the birth-rate had not changed, the total decline in population would have been 23·7 per cent during those two years, instead of the usual increase of 0·4 per cent per year. Presumably this decline was made up more quickly than the 50 years it would have taken at the old rates of increase, but one would certainly like to know more about the demography of that period.

Fisher's evidence suggests that 1557–8 was the last great English mortality, perhaps only surpassed by 1348–9 since written records began. Short's data[1] merely suggest that this might have been so, but the period is too early for his parish register approach to work very well. A large number of wills have been indexed and calendared for the various dioceses of England, and they could be used systematically to trace the course of year-to-year mortality since about 1400. They would be particularly valuable for the period before the parish registers become adequate about 1560. Preliminary counts of wills have already suggested that Creighton's account of the mortality waves of the fifteenth and early-sixteenth centuries[2] can be revised.

We can illustrate the value of wills by taking an example, the London wills proved in the Court of Hustings during a period that includes the Black Death.[3] Naturally, only the upper classes are included, but it is obvious that they were greatly affected. The numbers of wills proved each decade run as follows (records

[1] *Loc. cit.*

[2] *Op. cit.* See also below, p. 387.

[3] R. R. Sharpe, *Calendar of Wills proved and enrolled in the Court of Husting, London, A.D. 1258–A.D. 1688*, London, 1889–90.

covering parts of 1360, 1361, and 1380–5 being unfortunately missing):

1271–1280	172	1351–1360	141*	1431–1440	71
1281–1290	226	1361–1370	300*	1441–1450	51
1291–1300	245	1371–1380	140	1451–1460	45
1301–1310	285	1381–1390	60*	1461–1470	43
1311–1320	310	1391–1400	126	1471–1480	31
1321–1330	290	1401–1410	100	1481–1490	22
1331–1340	261	1411–1420	77	1491–1500	23
1341–1350	579	1421–1430	80		

* Incomplete decade.

The figures show that the Court of Hustings was much less used in the fifteenth century than the fourteenth. Unless we can believe that the upper-class population of London declined very greatly, the explanation must chiefly be that the practice of proving London wills changed.

Nevertheless, the change appears to have been slow. Suppose we define a 'poor' year as any year with more than twice the wills of the decadal average. We shall then get nine poor years: 1349, 1361, 1375, 1433, 1442, 1473, 1480, 1481, and 1497. The last six, however, might be spuriously poor years, caused by the random variation of a small annual number. If we now define as 'bad' years all years with three times the decadal average of wills, we are left with only two: 1349 and 1361. The former year's wills are six times, the latter year's wills four times as high as average. The practice of leaving London for the country in time of plague may have developed among these highly favoured people in 1361, which would then account for the absence of great peaks of mortality afterwards. We cannot study the course of mortality in 1361 very well because some of that year is missing, but 1349 is complete, and we now concentrate upon that year, which is, of course, the most interesting of all. The annual totals of wills proved run as follows:

1345	17	1349	356
1346	15	1350	49
1347	26	1351	20
1348	23	1352	16

In 1349 itself, the four successive quarters saw 101, 152, 51, and 52 wills proved, and these figures and the fairly high total for 1350 show that the Court could not keep pace with the deaths. The dates when wills were made, rather than proved, are a better guide to the course of mortality. Using an almanac of saints' days (almost all the wills were dated in the form of 'Monday after the feast of St Gregory' rather than '16 March'), we can elucidate the most probable dates of death, since wills were traditionally almost always made on one's deathbed.[1] The following shows how the first wave of the Black Death struck upper-class Londoners:

Wills made		*Wills made*	
September 1348	5	March 1349	90
October	5	April	101
November	12	May	57
December	22	June	13
January 1349	34	July	4
February	51	August	3
		Total	397

Two hundred and twelve wills were proved in the ten years 1339–48, and presumably about that number of deaths occurred, so the mortality of 1348–9 was more than 18 times as high as in a normal year. In the peak months of March and April the weekly deaths run as follows:

[1] It might be objected that the figures of wills are deficient, but it is no objection that only a sample of deaths are recorded when we merely wish to trace the course of the plague. Comparisons between widely different years are impermissible, of course, but comparisons over a short period are instructive. The delay between the date of the will and the proof of the will is less than a year in all but a few cases, and in almost all instances this must have occurred after the death.

Week	Wills made
4 March–10 March	27
11 March–17 March	22
18 March–24 March	23
25 March–31 March	16
1 April – 7 April	32
8 April –14 April	29
15 April –21 April	17
22 April –28 April	19

There was therefore a double peak, as in many other plagues, and the highest number of wills made on any one day was 9, on 12 March and 7 April.

This illustration shows how valuable even a few thousand wills can be in showing us the effect of epidemics. We do not get absolute figures, but we can deduce the general course of events. Similar techniques should be applicable in many countries for the whole of the later-medieval period.

NOMINATIVE DATA

Given lists of names of men at the period when surnames had recently been adopted, we can sometimes deduce the origin of many of them because their surnames were place-names. This has obvious dangers and can at best only work for a short time after surnames became used. Higounet has reviewed[1] the possibilities of doing it in France, where Metz, Paris and Toulouse had already been studied.

In his study of Arras, Lestocquoy[2] used three such lists: a list of tenants of St Vaast Abbey at Arras drawn up about 1170; a list of tenants of Arras Cathedral, which also gave the names of

[1] C. Higounet, 'Mouvements de populations dans le Midi de la France, du XIe au XVe siècle, d'après les noms de personne et de lieu', *Annales (E.S.C.)*, 8, 1 (January–March 1953), pp. 1–24.

[2] J. Lestocquoy, 'Tonlieu et peuplement urbain à Arras aux XIIe et XIIIe siècles', *ibid.*, 10, 3 (July–September 1955), pp. 391–5.

previous tenants, and dating from 1261; and an Arras obituary roll, giving nearly 10,500 names of people who died between 1194 and the middle of the fourteenth century. From these lists, Lestocquoy could say that around 1160 to 1230 few people had come to Arras from long distances (over 120 km.). This is as one would expect, but the interesting thing is that even fewer people had come from between 30 and 120 km., which is not what we should find in a modern society, where the propensity to migrate falls away steadily with distance. Almost all of those whose surnames were place-names came, in fact, from within a 30 km. radius. Close study of these places and their frequency, together with study of places not far from Arras but unrepresented, convinced Lestocquoy that the radius did not represent a day's journey from Arras—and indeed why should it—but followed the diocesan boundary. The data all fit, therefore, with the theory that the town grew in the Middle Ages almost entirely because of tax privileges granted to people of the diocese who cared to migrate to Arras itself. A careful study of surnames has shown us the migration pattern, which then confirms one theory of the town's growth and contradicts others.

Ekwall studied migrants to London during the years 1100 to 1365 in much the same way.[1] No such extraordinary pattern occurs, but there is no historical reason to expect one. Migration fell away with distance in every direction; but, in relation to population, the counties to the north and east of London (Hertfordshire, Bedfordshire, Cambridgeshire, Suffolk and Norfolk) sent rather more migrants to London than one would expect, while to the west and south, Berkshire, Wiltshire and Sussex sent very few. There was a tendency, too, for migrants from the immediate ring of home counties to become relatively less frequent after 1300, suggesting an increase in the efficiency of communications and a greater unifying of the country. Bücher

[1] B. O. E. Ekwall, *Studies on the Population of Medieval London*, Stockholm, 1956, cited by J. C. Russell, 'Medieval Midland and Northern Migrants to London, 1100–1365', *Speculum*, **34**, 4 (1959), pp. 641–5.

would appear to have used[1] a similar method for getting migration data in his study of Frankfurt am Main in the fourteenth and fifteenth centuries.

FOOD CONSUMPTION

The quantity of food consumed in a city, or less often in a country, has often been used as a source of population estimates, although the results can never be very accurate. Day used the customs duties on imported grain at Genoa[2] to argue that the city had 60,000–65,000 inhabitants in 1348 on the eve of the Black Death. Smuggling, however, might mean that the true population should be put as high as 100,000, and then the 40,000 deaths usually allowed in Genoa in that year would agree with the 40 per cent decline shown by the customs duties.

Another example, using more direct data, concerns the population of the city of Constantinople under the Ottoman Empire. While Charanis has recently discussed the literature on the Byzantine period,[3] we have contemporary estimates for Constantinople in the eighteenth century.[4] The main difficulty was that Islamic tradition forbade the counting of people as an act; yet since the Turkish administration was fairly efficient and in

[1] K. Bücher, *Die Bevölkerung von Frankfurt am Main im XIV und XV Jahrhundert*, Tübingen, 1886; p. 454 is mentioned by Russell (*Journal of Regional Science*, 2 (1960), pp. 55–70) as giving the fractions of immigrants who came from different distances, but I have not been able to verify this myself.

[2] J. Day, *Les douanes de Gênes, 1376–77*, Paris, 1963. (Only 39 of the 983 pages are commentary, the rest are the customs returns themselves.)

[3] P. Charanis, 'Observations on the Demography of the Byzantine Empire', *Proceedings of the XIIIth International Congress of Byzantine Studies* (Oxford, 1966), pp. 445–64. For Constantinople itself, see particularly A. M. Andréadès, 'De la population de Constantinople sous les empereurs byzantins', *Metron*, I, 2 (December 1920), pp. 68–119.

[4] M. Mackenzie, 'Extracts of several letters concerning the plague at Constantinople', *Philosophical Transactions of the Royal Society*, 47 (1751–2), LXIII, pp. 384–95, and LXXXVII, pp. 514–16, and Sir James Porter, 'Answer to some queries respecting Constantinople', *ibid.*, 49, 1 (1755), pp. 96–109.

full control of the city it was possible to calculate the population from the amount of bread baked in the city. The bread baked could not be measured directly, but the amount of wheat taken into the city was measured by the Turkish authorities and the amount of the bread could be calculated from the wheat. It was possible, by this roundabout method, both to estimate the population of the city and to re-estimate it after a plague, and so to have a guide as to the mortality in the plague. The results show that Constantinople was only a little smaller (if at all) than London or Paris at that time, and that the plague was still capable of destroying one-fifth of the population there within a few months.

Giovanni Villani[1] used the same method for the population of Florence in 1337, and a similar method was used by Brakenridge[2] to estimate the population of England in 1755. Although moderate accuracy is possible, such questions as the increase or decrease of numbers are difficult. Food consumption data, in fact, both aggregate and per head, have too wide a margin of error to give more than the right order of magnitude for the population size.

Drink consumption data would seem to be even less reliable; Heckscher[3] managed to show that beer consumption in sixteenth-century Sweden was 40 times higher per head than at present. Similarly, Myatt-Price[4] has shown that ale was drunk at the rate of three to four pints per meal in a house in Suffolk during the fifteenth century, which also seems very high.

[1] G. Villani, *Cronica*, Lib. XI, cap. 94. The peak of medieval population in Florence was apparently reached nearly half a century before the Black Death arrived. See E. Fiumi, 'La demografia fiorentina nelle pagine di Giovanni Villani', *Archivio Storico Italiano*, CVIII (1950), pp. 78–158.

[2] Brakenridge, 'A letter concerning the number of people in England', *Philosophical Transactions of the Royal Society*, 49 (1755), XLV, pp. 268–85.

[3] E. F. Heckscher, *An Economic History of Sweden*, (translated by G. Ohlin), Cambridge, Mass. (Harvard University Press), 1954, pp. 21–2 and 68–70.

[4] E. Myatt-Price, 'A tally of ale', *Journal of the Royal Statistical Society*, Series A, 123, 1 (1960), pp. 62–7.

TRAVELLERS' TALES AND HEARSAY

Although rather vague estimates of population, made casually by untrained persons, must be of doubtful value, they are sometimes the only historical figures we have. In certain parts of the world, nothing better may be available even in the twentieth century; Bharier has used various such estimates of the population of Iran[1] to produce a curve of population since 1900. The bases of estimates of this kind are extremely varied, and we must now give several examples.

Procopius, as well as his estimate of daily plague mortality[2] at Constantinople in 542 (discussed in Appendix 2) is also the source for the figure of 300,000 males[3] put to death at Milan in 539. This presupposes a minimum population of 450,000, with 600,000 or so more probable. Most critics have dismissed the figure entirely. There are many such isolated figures in the literature, and unless we had evidence that Procopius was present we could hardly accept the figure as correct. Moreover, the massacred males (however many they were) need not have been normal residents of Milan.

Some interesting information is contained in the account by Hsüan Ts'ang, the Chinese buddhist who travelled to Nālandā[4] in India in the seventh century A.D. He describes in some detail the monastery, or university as we might call it, where he stayed for the five years, 633–7. Ten thousand monks lived on the site, and the whole surrounding countryside must have been extremely prosperous to support it. One hundred villages, each having 200 households, were Nālandā's endowment, and these people (perhaps 100,000) had to supply the scholars with food. As well as the 10,000 monks, 20,000 servants were attached to Nālandā,

---

[1] J. Bharier, 'A Note on the Population of Iran, 1900–1966', *Population Studies*, XXII, 2 (July 1968), pp. 273–9.

[2] Procopius, *History of the Wars*, Book II, Chaps 22–3.

[3] *Ibid.*, Book VI, Chap. 21.

[4] See J. Mirsky, *The Great Chinese Travellers*, London, 1965, pp. 81–5.

making a total integrated community of about 130,000. Of course, this merely suggests the scale on which Indian life was then organized, not the population.

These last two examples are, of course, scanty; but Marco Polo has left various scraps of demographic information in the account of his travels that are more useful. In particular, what he says implies that Hangchow (which he calls Kinsai) had several million inhabitants in the late-thirteenth century.[1] This sounds unbelievable, but the circumstantial evidence that Marco Polo provides is hard to refute and is the more convincing because he does not make any explicit calculations of the population. He makes four main points.

(1) Forty-three cartloads of pepper, each of 223 pounds (or 101 kg.), were consumed daily in the city according to his informant, an official of the Imperial customs. That is 153,424 ounces (or 4,344 kg.) of pepper a day. Although it may have been lavishly used, it was a taxed article and would hardly be wantonly wasted. Could an average human stomach cope with more than a small part of an ounce of pepper a day, remembering that a considerable fraction must have been young children? It seems unlikely that fewer than 5 million people could possibly have consumed so much, and they would each have had about one gram per day. Built as it was on an archipelago, Hangchow had none of the water-supply problems that might have curbed city-growth elsewhere. The other evidence about Hangchow supports this, and points towards 5 million as a likely population figure unless the Venetian's memory was distorted in an oddly self-consistent way. Hangchow had recently been the capital of the southern Sung dynasty, and Marco Polo was certain that it was the largest city in China and in the world.

(2) Marco Polo says that Kinsai had 12,000 bridges (Soochow, another great city, had 6,000; but Venice had only about 400, although it had 110,000 inhabitants in 1338), and 10 principal

[1] Marco Polo, *Travels* (translated by R. Latham), Harmondsworth, 1958, pp. 184–94.

market-places, each a square covering 160 acres, occurring 4 miles apart along the main thoroughfares. On market-days, 40,000–50,000 people, he says, would gather in each of these ten great squares. The buildings around the squares were high, with shops on the ground floor, and there were many side-streets. We should conclude that 400,000–500,000 people bought and sold in the ten main markets, while obviously most of the population had other work to carry on in the side-streets. There would be plenty of space in the side-streets for the people to live.

(3) The crafts, he says, were organized in 12 main guilds, with many lesser ones. Each of the 12 had 12,000 workshops that employed between 10 and 40 men, and so 144,000 workshops belonging to these guilds employed some 2 million people, allowing around 14 to each. (The average would, naturally, be nearer 10 than 40.) With the lesser guilds, we must surely have 3 million employed people in Hangchow. Even if many women and children are here included, a population of 5 million—including, of course, suburbs—is the lowest that is consistent with the data at their face value.

(4) He also says that there were 3,000 public baths in Kinsai, which could accommodate 100 people at once. People went to the baths 'several times a month', and if they each stayed half a day, on average, 600,000 people bathed daily and 5 million could bath about 4 times a month.

A hearth-tax in the thirteenth century found 1·6 million households in Hangchow,[1] which also suggests 5 million people at least, and 6 or 7 million as more probable. It may be that the civic area comprehended by these accounts extended far beyond what we should consider the truly urban area, but there seems no particular reason to believe this when all the evidence points the other way. Provided the problems of distribution of food and of sanitation could be solved for such a large number, and that the surrounding countryside was extremely fertile (as it seems to have

[1] W. Schneider, *Babylon is Everywhere. The City as Man's Fate* (translated by I. Sammet and J. Oldenburg), London, 1963, p. 169.

been), there is really no reason to doubt the accounts of population that have survived. It was a delicate structure, however, and Hangchow might have dwindled to 2 million or less within a century, as the effort of maintaining so many people in one place began to seem not worth the benefit.

Eberhard prefers to apply a modern Indian or Egyptian population density to Sung cities,[1] guessing 1,000,000 to 1,600,000 for K'aifeng (then called Pienchow) after 1078, at a density of 200 to 300 per hectare. Since Marco Polo says that the 10 principal market-places were each 4 miles apart along the main thoroughfares, we can suppose that the area of the city in the neighbourhood of the market-places was 160 square miles or so, which is 41,450 hectares. Five million people would therefore only require a density of about 120 to the hectare. We are bound to conclude that 5 to 7 million people is the most probable range for late-thirteenth-century Hangchow.

Bernal Díaz, in his *History of the Conquest of New Spain*, tells us that after the conquest of Mexico in August 1521 they could not walk in Tlatelolco (the market-place) without treading on the bodies and heads of dead Indians.[2] Tlatelolco was a large square (it still exists), bigger than the Plaza at Salamanca.[3] Most of the warriors who had crowded in from all the provinces and subject towns, as well as the inhabitants of Mexico itself, had died, and 'the dry land and the stockades were piled with corpses'. Cortés allowed the Mexicans to evacuate the city because of the stench,[4] and 'for three whole days and nights they never ceased streaming out, and all three causeways were crowded with men, women, and children'. These causeways were 8 yards wide.[5] When the Spaniards entered the city they 'found the houses full of corpses'. 'There had been no live births for a long time, because they had

[1] W. Eberhard, 'The Structure of the Preindustrial Chinese City', in *Settlement and Social Change in Asia, Volume I*, Hong Kong, 1967, pp. 43–64, especially p. 49.

[2] B. Díaz, *The Conquest of New Spain* (translated by J. M. Cohen), Harmondsworth, 1965, p. 405.

[3] *Ibid.*, p. 234.   [4] *Ibid.*, p. 406.   [5] *Ibid.*, p. 216 and p. 359.

suffered so much from hunger and thirst and continual fighting.'[1]

The circumstantial evidence again seems sober and convincing, and the city covered a very large area. It had many people from neighbouring towns inside it during the siege, as is clear from the deserted state of the towns Cortés advanced through to get to the capital. However, even though very many had died, the number who walked along the three causeways must have been very great. The maximum number would be a shuffling crowd 6 deep and 2 yards apart, going at half a mile an hour. Every hour, 2,640 people would be leaving the city along each causeway, or 7,920 an hour in all, for 72 hours—making 570,240 people. The smallest number that is believable would be roughly 3 deep and 6 yards apart—only 1 person for every 16 square yards of causeway. It is not really credible that they would have left Mexico less closely packed than that when they at last received the opportunity after a three months' siege. Being less crowded, they would go faster, say at $1\frac{1}{2}$ miles per hour even in their feeble state, for no one walks much slower than his capacity without such a reason as pressure of space. At this rate, 1,320 people would leave the city per hour on each causeway, still half as many as before, or 285,120 in all. Díaz's account therefore suggests 428,000 ($\pm$ 142,000) survivors of the siege, as well as scores of thousands dead. The normal population of the city might have been about 300,000, allowing for an influx before the siege of about 200,000 people from the vicinity.

Striking evidence of recent population decline was produced for eighteenth-century Syria by Chasseboeuf de Volney.[2] He claimed that the number of villages in the Pashalik of Aleppo had fallen by 1785 from more than 3,200 on the old *defter*,[3] or tax register, to scarcely 400, and believed that much of the depopula-

[1] *Ibid.*, p. 407.

[2] Comte C. F. Chasseboeuf de Volney, *Voyage en Syrie et en Égypte, pendant les années 1783, 1784 et 1785, avec deux cartes géographiques et deux planches gravées*, Paris, 1787, 2nd edn, Vol. II, p. 135.

[3] Compare above, pp. 132–3.

tion had occurred since about 1765. The larger towns, he said, had absorbed the agricultural population, who had fled to escape the hand of despotism. On all sides you could see collapsed houses, cisterns smashed in, and abandoned fields.

Although this is a self-consistent account of a general decline in population, with the evidence of an eye-witness to support that of taxation data and with a socio-economic explanation as well, we should not assume that the population of the area declined by seven-eighths within 20 years. The size of Aleppo itself probably increased in this period, and the average size of the surviving villages might also have risen. Moreover, much of the decline probably occurred before 1765. As specific evidence, Volney is not very helpful, but in general terms his remarks are most valuable.[1] Since Aleppo itself evidently had about 100,000 inhabitants,[2] the ratio of rural-to-urban population in the area had clearly fallen very greatly by 1785, since the 400 villages would presumably only contain a similar number of people, making the city population of the pashalik about 50 per cent of the total.

Pankhurst makes good use of early travellers' accounts[3] to estimate the population of many of the towns and villages of Ethiopia in the eighteenth and nineteenth centuries, a valuable achievement in a country that still has never taken a general census. As well as his evidence on the losses caused by war, famine, and disease,[4] the decline of Gondar (the old capital city) from about 65,000 towards the end of the eighteenth century to only a few thousand in 1900 is very striking.

[1] Amongst recent scholars, Issawi refers to the great decline in the population of Syria between Roman times and the eighteenth century in his introduction to *The Economic History of the Middle East 1800–1914* (edited by C. Issawi), Chicago and London, 1966, p. 3.

[2] Volney, *op. cit.*, Vol. II, p. 139.

[3] R. Pankhurst, 'Notes on the demographic history of Ethiopian towns and villages', *Ethiopia Observer*, **9**, 1 (1965), pp. 60–83.

[4] *Idem*, 'The Great Ethiopian Famine of 1888–1892: a new assessment', *Journal of the History of Medicine and Allied Sciences*, **21**, 2 (April 1966), pp. 95–124, and 3 (July 1966), pp. 271–94.

Similar scraps of information from the accounts of old travellers are generally all we have for any part of Africa south of the Sahara. Randles points out the difficulty of assessing the population even of such a well-known town as Kilwa[1] before the Portuguese sacked it in 1505, but things are little better in the nineteenth century.

Hamilton[2] provided estimates of exports of slaves from Africa in 1839-40, as well as some indications of population distribution in Central Africa at that time, based upon the reports of explorers; and almost all the sources we have on the population of tropical Africa before about 1900 are of one or the other type. Curtin and Vansina,[3] however, were able to point out that the languages spoken by West African slaves are sometimes known, and will show the regions from which they came. This is important, not only for assessing which parts of West Africa were relatively most depopulated by the slave trade, but also the density of population itself. Needless to say, attempting to assess the density of settlement on the basis of the number of slaves who came from an area is a very unreliable way of getting population figures.

The population tables of the past themselves do not, of course, necessarily count as reliable evidence. De Dainville quotes a work by Dupain-Triel (père) written in 1782 in which estimation of the current population of the world's cities was attempted.[4] Nanking and Constantinople were thought the world's largest; in the next rank were Peking and Moscow, with Paris, St Petersburg and London close behind; and in the lower rank,

[1] W. G. L. Randles, 'Matériaux pour une histoire du sud-est Africain jusqu'au XVIIIe siècle', *Annales (E.S.C.)*, **18**, 5 (September–October 1963), pp. 956–80. Both 4,000 and 10,000 are suggested figures for Kilwa.

[2] A. Hamilton, 'On the Trade with the Coloured Races of Africa', *Journal of the Statistical Society*, **31** (March 1868), pp. 25–48.

[3] P. D. Curtin and J. Vansina, 'Sources of the nineteenth century Atlantic slave trade', *Journal of African History*, **5**, 2 (1964), pp. 185–208.

[4] F. de Dainville, 'Grandeur et population des villes au XVIIIe siècle', *Population*, **13**, 3 (1958), pp. 459–80. The title of Dupain-Triel's work is *Essai d'une table paléométrique*.

Rome, Venice, Berlin and Vienna. The farther these cities were from Paris, the less Dupain-Triel can have known about them. In particular, it is quite possible that the world's largest city in 1782 was really Jedo (now called Tokyo), in Japan, which he does not mention at all.

Holmes' evidence[1] for a generally lower population after the Turks conquered the Byzantine Empire, circumstantial as it is, is inescapable unless most of the Byzantine figures are regarded as exaggeration. In a more enterprising way, Clarke attempted to assess the actual population trends in the Ottoman Empire during the eighteenth and nineteenth centuries.[2] His information was almost entirely travellers' tales, but was most extensive, and although it has not received much attention, it seems valuable. In the towns at least, the numbers of Turks were declining slowly, while the Greeks were increasing quite rapidly. For 16 large towns, we can deduce the following populations from Clarke's figures, interpolating or extrapolating where necessary:

Date (approx.)	Total	Turks	Armenians	Greeks	Jews	Others
1770	778,000	658,500	50,500	36,900	11,100	21,000
1820	753,000	605,600	61,300	52,400	13,200	20,500
1864	729,000	538,500	58,100	110,800	15,500	6,100

In 176 Asian towns of the Ottoman Empire, the total population in 1864 apparently came to 1,844,000 (1,383,290 Turks, 256,570 Greeks, 173,590 Armenians, and 30,550 Jews and others). We should not assume that these data are valueless, but rather regard them as our first basis of knowledge until something better is found. The evidence for a decline between 1770 and 1864 should correct any belief that these were years of world-wide population growth.

[1] W. G. Holmes, *The Age of Justinian and Theodora: a history of the sixth century, A.D.*, London, 1912, Vol. I, p. 137.

[2] H. Clarke, 'On the Supposed Extinction of the Turks, and Increase of the Christians in Turkey', *Journal of the Statistical Society*, **28**, 2 (June 1865), pp. 261–93.

To summarize these isolated fragments, we must decide whether they were mere gossip or propaganda, or whether they were the result of actual counts, whether of people or of quantities of material of some kind. It is not enough to determine whether the author could have known the facts; we need to decide whether what he says is likely to have been true, and then to recall that copying errors are by no means uncommon. The general conclusion is likely to be in most cases that the information only gives a broad estimate of population levels and says nothing about population trends.

INSCRIPTIONS

Inscriptions on monuments are undoubtedly among the most reliable sources of population data that have still not been mentioned. There is little room for explicit lying when a monument is publicly erected within a few years of the event, and there is every opportunity for the authority erecting the monument to have ascertained the facts in advance. But although the facts can usually be regarded as accurate, they rarely bear directly upon population. An inscription in the church at Yarmouth gave the mortality in the Black Death in 1348 in the town, but this is a rare example and (as often happens) the monument is no longer in existence and we have to rely upon secondary sources for it.[1]

An inscription of the Hellenistic period from Ilium[2] mentioned 101 adult males, of whom 66 were celibate and the other 35 had only 27 children between them. While this is certainly evidence of a very low birth-rate, there is quite a high probability that the people whose names were inscribed were unrepresentative. However, since one could assume as many adult females as adult males, it means that in some population of 229 persons there were only 27 who could be classified as children, or 11·8 per cent. Even

[1] Creighton, *op. cit.* above on p. 236 (footnote 3), pp. 130–1.
[2] A. Landry, 'Quelques aperçus concernant la dépopulation dans l'antiquité gréco-romaine', *Revue historique*, **61**, 177 (1936), pp. 1–33.

if only those under 10 were counted as children, it is difficult to see how the birth-rate could possibly have been more than about 20 per thousand, and 15 would be more likely.[1] A high rate of mortality must be assumed, and consequently a rapid decline in population.

Frank found a strong tendency, in some 4,485 Roman inscriptions that he studied,[2] for fathers with Greek names to give Latin names to their sons, but very little tendency for the opposite to take place. While this is probably evidence for immigration of Greeks to Rome, we cannot calculate a rate at which it might have happened from Frank's data.[3] His information on the dying out of noble families is more useful, however: out of 400 families of senators of A.D. 65, half had gone by A.D. 96; and out of 45 patrician families in Caesar's day, only one, the Cornelii, remained in A.D. 117. Since the second period is about five times as long as the first, a constant rate would have produced a reduction to one-thirty-second if collateral heirs could be ignored, and so the two rates of decline are roughly equivalent. One must conclude that an average of about one child grew up per family among upper-class Romans of the time; even two children per family would,

---

[1] Polybius, *Histories*, Book 37, para. 9 (translated by E. S. Shuckburgh), London, 1889, says that all Greece was visited in his time (about 150 B.C.) by a dearth of children and generally a decay of population. The cause, moreover, was not war or disease in his opinion, but more celibacy and a reluctance to rear more than one or two children on the part of the married.

[2] T. Frank, 'Race mixture in the Roman Empire', *American Historical Review*, 21, 4 (July 1916), pp. 689–708. See also, for a criticism, E. Cicotti, 'Motivi demografici e biologici nella rovina della civiltà antica', *Nuova Rivista Storica*, 14, 1–2 (January–April 1930), pp. 29–62.

[3] More recent work on these inscriptions is now showing that most of the lower classes of Imperial Rome were slaves or of recent slave origin. This in turn would suggest higher fertility amongst the lower classes. See L. R. Taylor, 'Freedmen and Freeborn in the Epitaphs of Imperial Rome', *American Journal of Philology*, LXXXII, 2 (1961), pp. 113–32. Further research on the lower classes may clarify the class patterns; see B. Rawson, 'Family Life among the Lower Classes at Rome in the first two centuries of the Empire', *Classical Philology*, 61, 2 (April 1966), pp. 71–83.

in theory, lead to complete extinction in the long run.[1] The implied rate of population decline, however, is less than 2 per cent per annum; we might guess a death-rate of 45 per thousand and then the birth-rate would have to be 27, or else 35 and 17, or of course other combinations. The rate of decline of the senatorial families under the Flavians, however, probably did not equal that of the Hellenistic Greeks of Ilium discussed above.

ECONOMIC EVIDENCE

Hardly any less reliable as guides to demographic change are the various economic indicators. There is some connection between modern marriage-rates and economic activity,[2] and migration is also affected by economic changes over the short run. Mortality in advanced countries varies more with climate than with economic variables, however, presumably because it depends so much upon the susceptibility of the elderly to extra strains in cold weather, while fertility seems almost impervious to economic changes, only being affected via the marriage-rate and that to a weak degree. Clark argues for population decline in Roman Egypt from the evidence of rents;[3] but the effect, although probable enough, has not yet been demonstrated properly in a context where the demographic facts are known.

In historical populations, it is idle to speculate on whether, say, the fall in real wages in Europe in the sixteenth century really reflects a rising population. The market was flooded with

[1] A full discussion is given by T. E. Harris, 'Branching processes', *Annals of Mathematical Statistics*, **19** (1948), pp. 474-94. Briefer and easier is W. Feller, *An Introduction to Probability Theory and its Applications, Vol. One*, New York and London, 1950, p. 224.

[2] D. V. Glass, 'Marriage Frequency and Economic Fluctuations in England and Wales, 1851-1934', in *Political Arithmetic* (edited by L. Hogben), London, 1938, pp. 251-82; M. Silver, 'Births, marriages, and income fluctuations in the United Kingdom and Japan', *Economic Development and Cultural Change*, **14**, 3 (April 1966), pp. 302-15; R. H. Hooker [Bibliography, p. 420].

[3] C. Clark, *Population Growth and Land Use*, London, 1967, p. 65.

American bullion at the same period, and wages might have fallen because, so to speak, the populace were forced to compete against long-dead Peruvian miners, and not simply against each other. The effect would wear off, but only after many decades. It is therefore a confused problem, and the evidence from economic conditions is difficult to apply. Yet the curve derived in Appendix 3 for English population between 1234 and 1489 agrees remarkably well with a curve for real wages derivable from Slicher van Bath's data,[1] the population minimum tallying quite well with the maximum of real wages in the fifteenth century. It is therefore plausible to assume rapid population growth in England in the sixteenth century, probably reaching a peak early in the seventeenth century. If the method could be pushed further, a minimum would follow about 1730; but industrialism and importing of food must, obviously, disturb such tidy relationships eventually, and possibly did so much earlier than 1730.

NUMBERS OF CITIES

An unusual method of historical demography was employed in FitzGerald's calculations on the population of China in the T'ang period.[2] Chinese cities being definite, walled, administrative and military centres, it was not altogether unreasonable to deduce that a high rate of foundation of new cities implied an expanded population, nor even that the number of inhabited cities in an area was closely related to the size of the population. In 618, at the beginning of the T'ang dynasty, FitzGerald credited north China with about 762 cities and south China with only about 181. This reflects the relatively recent colonization of the south, and the 1644 figures of 728 and 712 respectively reflect equally the more even balance between north and south China achieved by

[1] B. H. Slicher van Bath, *The Agrarian History of Western Europe, A.D. 500–1850* (translated by O. Ordish), London, 1963, p. 327. See also his diagrams on pp. 102–3.

[2] C. P. FitzGerald, 'A New Estimate of the Chinese Population under the T'ang Dynasty in 618 A.D.', *The China Journal*, 16, 1 (January 1932), pp. 5–14 and 2 (February 1932), pp. 62–72.

the end of the Ming dynasty. However, unless there were a change in the average population to be allowed to a city and the region dependent upon it, north China must have lost population between 618 and 1644, since the number of northern cities had declined from 762 to 728, whereas most authorities assume a considerable increase in population.

FitzGerald went on to find 817 cities in north China in 1911 and 744 in south China, making only a modest increase since 1644. Assuming that there had been again no change in the average population ruled from each city, FitzGerald showed that the total population of China in 1644 would have had to be 250 to 300 million, or twice as high as is usually thought the maximum possible at that time. Even in 618, the population would have been nearly 130 million, again about double the accepted figure.

The weakness in this reasoning is that the cities, once built, probably tended not to be multiplied unduly. Although from time to time one city was abandoned and another founded, the administrative structure was conservative and disinclined to allow more offices to be created. As technology advanced and peace continued during the 267 years of the Ch'ing dynasty, it may have become possible to administer twice as many people from a city as before—while the people became more densely settled on the land. If this were so, FitzGerald's 618 and 1644 estimates of population should be halved, giving figures that are by no means incredible. Any other change than a doubling in a city's administrative capacity would, of course, mean a different adjustment to the population figures FitzGerald produced. He himself studied the ratio of the population of a province to the number of cities it contained (using 1885 and 1910 data) and found a wide variation between different parts of the country. Where such geographical variations exist, historical variations might well exist also, which would, of course, demolish the value of FitzGerald's idea.[1]

[1] Most of FitzGerald's figures can be found in Li Chi, *The Formation of the Chinese People. An anthropological inquiry*, Cambridge, Mass., 1928. Li Chi used them himself, however, to study migration. (See above, p. 218.)

LOST VILLAGES

Population trends in medieval Europe may be assessed, to some extent, by an analysis of the place-names on maps or in lists at different dates. Beresford, Allison, and others, for instance, have made a series of studies of different counties of England with a view to determining when villages were deserted.[1] The total proportion of villages that were ever deserted is fairly considerable, and may reach one-third. One does not know the populations of these villages, but the very fact that large numbers of settlements were abandoned, taken in conjunction with the continental evidence that under a similar social system abandonment of villages was rare there, suggests a certain amount of social change in England. The population was not necessarily decreasing or increasing between 1300 and 1700, however, on this evidence; for, as we shall see presently, abandonment of a village may sometimes actually be connected with population growth and not decline.

Duby has discussed the demography of desertion of villages in France in some detail.[2] Population movements cannot easily be related to the desertion of villages, since at the period when it was most common in France there are few other sources of demographic information to act as a check, and even they are mainly fiscal returns. There is no doubt, however, that the deserted villages of the fourteenth and fifteenth centuries do correspond to a local fall in population.

Relatively few French villages of the fourteenth century were no longer inhabited in the eighteenth, compared with the English ratio.[3] Local differences in the quality of the land meant

[1] M. W. Beresford, *The Lost Villages of England*, London, 1954; K. J. Allison, 'The Lost Villages of Norfolk', *Norfolk Archaeology*, **31**, 1 (1955), pp. 116–62. See also Beresford, *New Towns of the Middle Ages*, London, 1967.

[2] G. Duby, in *Villages désertés et histoires économiques XIe–XVIIIe siècle*, Paris, 1965, pp. 14–24.

[3] See J.-M. Pesez and E. Le Roy Ladurie, 'Les villages désertés en France: vue d'ensemble', *Annales (E.S.C.)*, **20**, 2 (March–April 1965), pp. 257–90.

that whole communities ceased to exist when the population fell in a region; the survivors of the epidemic might be spread in proportion to the previous population, but if the distances were short they would at once migrate from bad lands to good, refilling the villages in the good areas and abandoning the villages in the bad ones. Repopulation of the region required re-establishment of these villages, which usually took place eventually.

However, Allison has shown that at least 34 Norfolk villages existing in 1086 had disappeared by 1316, or 4·6 per cent. Since this is generally regarded (with good reason) as a period of demographic growth, the simple assumption that population invariably relates to the number of settlements in an obvious way cannot be maintained. Duby gives other instances of the same thing;[1] and, indeed, since there are still many lost villages today and since population today is undoubtedly higher than ever before, the argument cannot be gainsaid. A village might well be lost in a temporary decline, and not be resettled when the population recovered. The number of lost villages would then reflect the periods of temporary decline and give no indication of whether or not they were interspersed with rapid growth. Lost villages, in fact, are merely indicators of *possible* decline in population.

Duby also pointed out that lists of places in old records are sometimes misleading, since a name might refer to a villa or to a village. The abandonment of a villa would be much more common than that of a village, and much less important demographically. Archaeological evidence for a village's existence is therefore much more useful than its mere listing in a document, for its size can be estimated if its remains can be found. Finally, Duby's opinion was that the size of the population was far from the most important factor in determining the pattern of rural settlement. The rural economy underwent modifications continually, making some village sites more attractive, others less.

[1] *Loc. cit.*

It is this that will have been the main cause of deserting villages, and not population.[1]

A more promising recent approach is described by Lunden,[2] who tries to calculate the actual number of farms in a part of Norway at the time immediately preceding the Black Death. Checking the figures against the land register and taxation data on grain produced leads to a fair level of agreement between the different estimates of the population, and one hopes similar careful work may be successful elsewhere.

LEVEL OF CULTURE

There are, however, even more general and vague methods of assessing the size and trend of population, to which we must now turn. The aggregate supply of food is determined by the area inhabited and the method of obtaining food, and this does give us an upper limit to the population.[3]

For example, a few simple assumptions about the rate of population growth and the carrying capacity of the land, based on three studies of small islands in modern times, led Birdsell to suggest[4] that Australia, although able to support 300,000 aborigines, might have been peopled to that number some 2,204 years after first colonization. Since the Pleistocene period in Australia ended about 6544 B.C. ($\pm$150 years), according to Birdsell, aboriginal occupation that began then would have been complete

[1] For an illustration of this in Yorkshire, see J. A. Sheppard, 'Pre-enclosure field and settlement patterns in an English township, Wheldrake, near York', *Geografiska Annaler*, 48, B, 2 (1966), pp. 59–77.

[2] K. Lunden, 'Four Methods of Estimating the Population of a Norwegian District on the Eve of the Black Death (1349–1350)', *Scandinavian Economic History Review*, XVI, 1 (1968), pp. 1–18. The population of 1665 in this area was evidently still only about 80 per cent of its 1350 figure.

[3] See R. J. Braidwood and C. A. Reed, 'The Achievement and Early Consequences of Food-Production: A Consideration of the Archaeological and Natural-Historical Evidence', *Cold Spring Harbor Symposia on Quantitative Biology*, XXII (1957), pp. 19–31.

[4] J. B. Birdsell, 'Some population problems involving pleistocene Man', *ibid.*, pp. 47–59.

by about 4340 B.C., or by 4190 B.C. at the latest. This calculation seems more precise than it is, however, for even at a very low rate of population growth a very large population size will be reached from a single small tribal group if thousands of years are available. At a growth rate of 4 per thousand per annum, less than in the United Kingdom in recent years, a population doubles itself in about 175 years; it will reach 1,000 times its original size in less than 1,750 years. If we were to guess the aboriginal growth rate in prehistoric Australia at one-third of Birdsell's figure, which it would be if the death-rate were only about 5 per cent higher, the latest date by which we should expect to find Australia still short of complete habitation up to Birdsell's limit of 300,000 would advance from 4190 B.C. to A.D. 297. There is little to choose between two rates of population growth that are both small and positive, and other evidence is needed to determine the date by which the aborigines had spread right throughout Australia. One should note, too, that Carneiro and Hilse,[1] in determining the rate of population growth in the Neolithic age (8000–4000 B.C.), found that the average rate must have lain between 0·8 and 1·2 per thousand, or well below Birdsell's estimate for Australian aboriginal growth.

Cumberland[2] has described the population trend of New Zealand before 1843, too, on no more than broad ecological evidence, but his results are more interesting. The Moa-hunters arrived about A.D. 750 and lasted until about 1450, by which time they had been destroyed by the agricultural Maoris, who began to arrive about 1350. At their height, the Moa-hunters would only have numbered 12,000–15,000, while the Maoris would have been 200,000 or even 400,000 by the eighteenth century.

[1] R. L. Carneiro and D. F. Hilse, 'On determining the probable rate of population growth during the Neolithic', *American Anthropologist*, **68**, 1 (February 1966), pp. 177–81.

[2] K. B. Cumberland, 'Neuseeland in den Epochen der Moajäger und Maori. Ein Beitrag zur prähistorischen Geographie', *Die Erde*, **98**, 2 (1967), pp. 90–114. I understand that Cumberland (of the University of Auckland) has written about the Moa-hunters in English elsewhere.

Captain Cook's estimate of 100,000 Maoris, made in 1769–74, was in fact based on very little evidence. A knowledge of the terrain of the North Island (where almost all the Maoris then lived), of their manner of life, and of how long they had been there, are better guides to population than the keenest inspection from a ship. A rate of increase of 1 per cent per annum from 1450 onwards, they then being about 12,500 (the same as the vanishing Moa-hunters), would suffice to produce about 400,000 Maoris in 1800.

Steward[1] made a very thorough analysis of the various estimates that have been made of the total population of America in 1492, again mainly by broad arguments from cultural patterns. His $4\frac{1}{2}$ million for Mexico, however, would now need revision, and his total of 15,490,000 is far too low. Steward, although very careful in his comparisons, used nineteenth-century data for some areas, arguing by analogy from them to areas for which he had no early estimates at all. If, as in Mexico, city-dwelling was common before 1492, this is a very bad approach, because changes in the populations of cities are sometimes very great within a century or two.

We can sometimes see just how misleading arguments from similarity of culture may be, however carefully done. For instance, Sir Richard Temple argued[2] that if China were inhabited in 1885 at Indian densities of population, matching similar areas in the two countries, there would only be 297 million Chinese, compared with 253 million Indians, in the 1880's. He therefore thought that China's population was much less than the 400 million often then claimed for it. But if China 'ought' only to have surpassed India by about 17 per cent in those days, the same argument today, when India and Pakistan have a combined population of about 625 million people, implies that China would

[1] J. H. Steward, 'The Native Population of South America', *Bureau of American Ethnology Bulletin*, **143**, V (1949), pp. 655–68.
[2] R. Temple, 'Population Statistics of China', *Journal of the Statistical Society*, **48**, 1 (March 1885), pp. 1–9.

have about 730 million, which is not far from the general view. The explanation seems to be that India was underpopulated relative to China in 1881.

When one is hoping to assess the population of Africa for any period before about 1920, it is necessary to base most of the calculations upon general ideas about cultural level, these being gained from travellers' tales and similar sources. At earlier dates, we must apply such methods to other parts of the world, although knowledge of the culture cannot be very certain. However, in principle, if we know the general level of culture, that it depended upon hunting wild animals or fishing, for example, then we can roughly estimate the density of population. More precisely, we can say that the total population could not have exceeded a certain level. Alternatively, if we know that food crops were cultivated in a systematic manner, as in the early Babylonian and Nilotic civilizations, for example, we can assume that the density of population, at least in the area that was cultivated and its immediate surroundings, was much higher and so that the total population level was higher also.

Deevey has suggested[1] that population tends, in fact, to rise in steps when viewed over the long term and not in a smooth way, the steps corresponding to revolutions in the method of food production and the social arrangement appertaining to it. For the world as a whole, the steps are relatively steep and do not last for many centuries. Three would occur: (1) before 100000 B.C. (toolmaking discovered); (2) about 6000 B.C. (agriculture); (3) about A.D. 1750 (scientific and industrial way of life). The history of North American population since 1492 is then a rise of a step; the population of China between the Han and the Ming dynasties is a tread of a step, of much longer duration. In an intriguing calculation, Deevey estimated that about 110,000 million people have ever lived: 36,000 million would have been palaeolithic hunters and another 30,000 million would have lived

[1] E. S. Deevey, Jr., 'The Human Population', *Scientific American*, 203, 3 (September 1960), pp. 195–205.

before the invention of agriculture, leaving 44,000 million since 6000 B.C. Using rather different assumptions, Desmond estimated[1] the total number of humans at only 77,000 million: according to him, only 12,000 million lived before 6000 B.C., another 42,000 million lived between then and A.D. 1650, and 23,000 million have lived since 1650. The discrepancies are, of course, large, and depend on the assumptions chosen. One cannot estimate the population that may have lived in prehistoric times to within a factor of three or four, because of our absence of knowledge.[2]

Yet, even in quite recent times, the area of land under cultivation and the method of agriculture used are sometimes almost the only clues to the fundamental demographic statistic, total population size. The useful study by Slicher van Bath[3] suggests general levels of production and consumption in Western Europe since the Middle Ages; for Eastern Europe, Warriner has made a beginning,[4] but our knowledge is much less. The margin of error in all such calculations must be fairly wide.

A controversy in 1865 and 1866 over the population of England before the Black Death illustrated the difficulties in the method. Thorold Rogers believed[5] that 2½ million was the utmost limit of English population before modern times, and that the probability was that the medieval population was less than 2 million even in 1348. Since he had studied 8,000 accounts of farm-bailiffs relating to the period 1259–1400, his view cannot be

[1] A. Desmond, 'How Many People Have Ever Lived on Earth?' *Population Bulletin* (February 1962), and reprinted in Ng, *The Population Crisis*, Bloomington, Ind., 1965, pp. 20–38.

[2] For further details on these and some similar methods of research, see D. Brothwell and E. Higgs (editors), *Science in Archaeology. A Comprehensive Survey of Progress and Research*, London, 1963, pp. 325–64.

[3] *Op. cit.* above on p. 255 (footnote 1).

[4] D. Warriner, 'Some Controversial Issues in the History of Agrarian Europe', *Slavonic and East European Review*, **32** (December 1953), pp. 168–86.

[5] J. E. T. Rogers, 'England before and after the Black Death', *Fortnightly Review*, **3**, 14 (29 November 1865), pp. 191–6.

taken lightly. His argument was: (1) foreign trade in grain can be ignored; (2) the average rate of production was four times the seed; (3) the rate of seeding had never altered, right up to 1865; (4) 12 million quarters of grain were produced annually in England in the 1860's at 30 bushels per acre; (5) if agriculture, at 8 bushels an acre, had been fully spread over England in 1348, 2½ million people at most could have then been fed with corn at the rate of one quarter per person per year; (6) meat and other foodstuffs were unimportant; (7) the West, North, and North Midlands were *not* fully developed agriculturally; and so (8) 2 million people is a likely maximum population figure. He went on to remark that since the 1377 Poll-Tax data lead to a population larger than 2 million, the Black Death must have had very little effect, and the population was almost equally pressing on the resources in 1348 and 1377.

Frederic Seebohm, however, who had begun[1] by asserting that half the population died in 1349, replied[2] to Rogers as follows: (1) 7,200,000 acres were sown in 1859; (2) only one-seventh was needed for seed, so 25,100,000 quarters were produced annually, not the 12 million Rogers supposed; (3) a further 5,500,000 acres were growing non-corn crops; (4) allowing some deduction for thinly settled counties, 8 million acres were probably under cultivation in 1348; (5) if these 8 million acres were seeded at 2 bushels an acre and yielded four times the seed, the average yield would be one quarter an acre; (6) 5 million people could thus easily have been fed, and indeed, half as many again.

Seebohm was largely right; Rogers had equated the acreage sown with wheat in the 1860's with the total acreage sowable with any type of corn. Bennett has suggested[3] 8·2 bushels per acre as the average yield of wheat about 1348, and if only 60 per

[1] F. Seebohm, 'The Black Death and its Place in History', *ibid.*, 2, 8 (6 September 1865), pp. 149–60, and 9 (20 September 1865), pp. 268–79.

[2] *Idem*, 'The Population of England before the Black Death', *ibid.*, 4, 19 (15 February 1866), pp. 87–9.

[3] M. K. Bennett, 'British wheat yield per acre for seven centuries', *Economic Journal*, Supplement, *Economic History*, 3 (February 1935), pp. 12–29.

cent of the 12,700,000 acres sown in 1859 were sown in 1348,
7,620,000 acres were still sown, and their harvest would be
62,484,000 bushels. A quarter would be needed for seed, leaving
46,863,000 bushels or 5,857,875 quarters of corn. A population of
over 5 million would therefore be attainable. Since the population
was almost certainly lower, the area sown must have been less than
60 per cent of the area sown in 1859—probably only 40 or 50 per
cent of it, in fact. Although a substantial part of the fields were
sown with rye, barley and oats, the yields were fairly similar
and so it should not greatly affect the calculations.[1] Famines often
occurred, but they would be local, poor transport making
effective relief impossible, or else a blight of the crops would
cause a general dearth in particular years.[2] Pressure on *ultimate*
resources of land did not exist in the classic Malthusian way, or
all the available land would surely have been used. England, in
fact, had no need to improve the yield on corn before the
eighteenth century. The area-agriculture method, therefore, here
tells us nothing about population that was not known already;
population data, rather, inform our ideas about the spread of
agriculture.

Davis has argued[3] that ancient agriculture was highly labour-
intensive, and so between 50 and 90 peasants would have been
needed to support each townsman. Consequently, he believed
that ancient cities must have been quite small. The rich soils of
the Nile or the Yellow River, however, do not require much
tilling to make a crop grow, and the marginal productivity of
agricultural labour cannot have been high. Even today, the hours
worked per year by a farmer in tropical Africa are only about
half of those worked by anyone in a northern industrial society.

[1] See Slicher van Bath, *op. cit.*, above on p. 255 (footnote 1), pp. 170–4.
[2] For descriptions of universal famines see H. S. Lucas, 'The Great European
Famine of 1315, 1316, and 1317', *Speculum*, 5 (1930), pp. 343–77, and K. S.
Gapp, 'The universal Famine under Claudius', *Harvard Theological Review*,
28 (1935), pp. 258–65.
[3] K. Davis, 'The Origin and Growth of Urbanization in the World',
American Journal of Sociology, 60, 5 (March 1955), pp. 429–37.

We cannot therefore limit ancient cities on these grounds very much. By measuring the area of a city it is possible that we may be able to estimate its population (see pp. 279–88), although the reliability of our estimate can hardly be high.

Similarly, the area of cultivated land can sometimes be measured and a figure of rural population reached.[1] It is always necessary, however, to know the prevailing culture; and this, it must be emphasized, is as true for the cities as it is for the countryside. While many scholars have calculated population in the Palaeolithic, Neolithic or Bronze Age period on the basis of an assumed level of cultivation of crops, similar considerations really apply to the towns also. Hogg, for example, estimated[2] that at least 4,000 people would have lived in the three north-west counties of Roman Wales, simply on the basis of hut-groups that have been discovered. Wide variations of population density within a town are known, however, to have occurred at later periods, making anything more than a minimum population estimate hazardous.

THEORIES

When we have very little useful data about a country, as in the Dark Ages for Europe, or in the Middle Ages for the Near East, for example, we may have to fall back on theory in order to produce any population figures at all. The figures are then scarcely more than tentative estimates, to be overturned without hesitation should any more solid evidence emerge. We here give a single extended illustration.

[1] For the method of measuring areas inhabited by different groups, see A. Rosenblat, *La población indígena y el mestizaje en América*, Buenos Aires, 1954. He works by analogy wherever information is lacking, and eventually produces estimates of American population in 1492, 1570, 1650, 1825, and 1950. The two first figures for Mexico must certainly be amended in the light of the research done by Cook and the University of California group. See Bibliographical reference on p. 407 for Rosenblat's latest figures.

[2] A. H. A. Hogg, 'Native Settlement in Wales', in *Rural Settlement in Roman Britain* (Council for British Archaeology, Research Report, 7) 1966, pp. 28–38.

Russell has advanced the principle[1] that, in a pre-modern socio-economic system, a metropolis will normally have $1\frac{1}{2}$ per cent of the population of the area it serves. There is a shaky theoretical justification for this principle, but geographers know very well that in many countries today rules about the sizes of cities both in relation to the whole state and to each other are very unreliable. This did not daunt Russell, however, and in his monograph he was able to make the rule work fairly easily by his somewhat Procrustean methods of defining the rural hinterland of a city and by interpreting the meagre facts in a suitable way. In a later article[2] he attempted to show how the rule was obeyed by English population in 1377. In the midst of the depopulation caused by the Black Death, 1377 is hardly an auspicious date for finding conformity to any theoretical law; but, with some adding together of neighbouring cities, he managed to convince himself of its validity. Unfortunately, any one of several similar such 'laws' would fit the data equally well, and the theoretical basis for it is not convincing. Any intractable evidence can, as a last resort, be discarded as an 'obvious exaggeration' or as 'hopelessly deficient'. Were the laws relating metropolitan size to the national community better substantiated, Russell's procedure would be justified; as it is, we are unable to distinguish one type of society from another by his method. Modern Thailand would, on his theory, have to be a much more unified economic unit than modern Italy. It seems more convincing to argue that, at a certain point in their histories, some countries have experienced extreme concentration of national energies in the capital, corresponding to good internal communications and little foreign trade except with the metropolis itself. England in 1700 would be an example.

A more extreme example of juggling with scanty data is in

[1] Russell, *Late Ancient and Medieval Population*, Philadelphia *Transactions of the American Philosophical Society*, 1958, p. 68.

[2] *Idem*, 'The Metropolitan City Region of the Middle Ages', *Journal of Regional Science*, 2, 2 (Fall, 1960), pp. 55–70.

Historical Demography

Russell's article[1] on the population of thirteenth-century Ireland. Some light, admittedly, is thrown on this dark subject; but it is mostly a false light. Towns had to be grouped together, and about half the slight evidence there is had to be distorted. No demographer would be surprised to learn that Ireland was untypical, moreover; as the one country in the world with a long history today of population decline, Ireland's anomalous character is, demographically speaking, established.

Russell put the population of Ireland around A.D. 1275–85 at about 650,000, which, while it is unlikely to be very far wrong, he achieved only by making an analogy with Wales or England on the basis of the area, number of clergy, and number of political units, parishes or churches. Since no population estimates can be made for England between 1086 and 1377 except by interpolation or striking an average density from some small area's population, the base from which the analogy is made (the Welsh data are even weaker than the English) is not strong. Moreover, even in 1086 and 1377 the English population figure is not directly known, but has to be calculated from the Domesday Survey and the Poll-Tax returns. The population of Ireland in the late-thirteenth century could be put between 400,000 and 800,000 with a good chance of being correct, but to do so would take most of the meaning from Russell's study of the urban population before it had been done.

The urban population, however, received Russell's finer efforts. His main bases were the taxes paid by the burgesses (at an assumed rate of one shilling per burgess and five times as many people as burgesses) and the area enclosed by the town walls (multiplied by an arbitrary factor of 100 or so persons to the hectare). Galway, apparently the third largest city in Ireland, did not fit the pattern and most of the people of Galway were assumed to live outside the walls. Russell's estimate of cottagers and women and children, on which the figure of five for the ratio of population to burgesses depends, is clearly imprecise, and the density of population in a

[1] Idem, 'Late Thirteenth-Century Ireland as a Region', Demography, 3, 2 (1966), pp. 500–12.

medieval city is almost certainly much less standard than Russell believes.

When he turned to the population of Dublin in detail, Russell seems to have had to make some effort to get his estimate down to the 10,000 people that his theory required. The 112 hectares of the city, for example, was nearly half the size of London (288 hectares) at that period, for which the population could easily have been 50,000. The number of new members of the Dublin guilds was 220 in 1226, 65 in 1256, and 140 in 1257; these three are the only years in the thirteenth century for which figures can be derived. The fluctuations were, obviously, very great, but Russell discarded the first (and largest) figure, and, taking the average of the other two, assumed that an average member stayed in his guild for 20 years, giving 2,050 guild members in the city and so perhaps 10,000 people or so in the town. An alternative calculation, however, would be to take all three figures, the average of which is 141·7; assume that the average man remained a guild member for a generation (about 32 years for the average child, but less for the eldest son, so take it as only 25), and so get 3,542 guild members altogether. With their wives and children, there might be four times as many people in Dublin of this class, or 14,167. There would also be clergy, soldiers, apprentices, servants, and beggars, making perhaps 20,000 people in all. The average being of the three years 1226, 1256 and 1257, this population estimate would best apply to Dublin about 1246, whereas we are really interested in the city a generation later. The city was probably increasing in numbers at the time, and so 25,000 in 1280 or so does not seem unreasonable, although we have now raised Russell's estimate to $2\frac{1}{2}$ times his figure. The evidence of the area of the city does not conflict with this if London held 50,000 people at the same period. It is also pertinent that Clyn said[1] that 14,000 people died in the Black Death of

[1] See Creighton, *op. cit.* above on p. 236 (footnote 3) (1965 edition), Vol. I, p. 131, and A. Gwynn, 'The Black Death in Ireland', *Studies*, 24 (1935), pp. 25–42.

1348–9, a figure that Creighton thought was obviously wrong, but which we can now see to be possible. However, we can hardly regard the population of thirteenth-century Dublin as being definitely nearer 25,000 than 10,000 on such slight evidence as is given here.

In order to fit his pattern of the theoretical distribution of Irish cities, Russell had not only to estimate Dublin's population at only 10,000 and to assume that most of the people of Galway lived outside that city's walls; the second city, Waterford, was not large enough, and had to be assumed to fulfil the joint function with New Ross, fifteen miles away. Clearly, if we make enough adjustments to the scanty data, almost any 'law' about population distribution can seem to apply. The interesting thing about thirteenth-century Ireland, however, would seem to be exactly the opposite of what Russell claimed: the rank-size rule does not apply either way, Dublin being too large and Waterford and Galway too small. Dublin probably had 3 to 4 per cent of the total Irish population, and several times as many as any other town in the whole country. If there is anything in the theory of city-size distribution, Dublin was already part of a London-centred economy, which, however, would have imprecise boundaries, possibly including parts of the Low Countries.

AD HOC ARGUMENTS

The number of Jews, 15,000, leaving England[1] when they were expelled in 1290 suggests the following rough calculation. The Jews must have lived in the towns, and we know that a large community lived in London. If we estimate the London Jews as low as 5,000 (and Lincoln, York and the other provincial cities together are unlikely to have had twice as many as London), and we argue that the London ghetto seems to have covered rather less than one of the 24 wards within the city's walls, then unless the Jews were unusually crowded—and they seem to have been

[1] Given by C. Roth, *A History of the Jews in England*, Oxford (3rd edn), 1964, Chapter 4.

relatively rich, which makes this unlikely—London would have to have at least 120,000 inhabitants. If so, it must have decreased between 1290 and 1348 by about half. Perhaps the rise of Norwich hurt London at that time (see below, p. 364), but the figures are, of course, only rough guesses.

Lestocquoy has discussed[1] the very difficult task of tracing population development in France between the fifth and ninth centuries, with particular stress on the towns. Building of abbeys, in particular, was noticeable at this period, but it is not certain how far their construction reflected anything more than a transference of power from the state to the church. However, there was undoubtedly a tendency for towns to grow around the nucleus of an abbey, so some population growth is presumably implied by the foundation of the abbeys.

Any evidence for the colonization of new land is also, of course, evidence of increased population. The very endings of place-names can sometimes show the approximate date of the founding of a settlement,[2] and Lamprecht[3] made a detailed study of the dates of foundation of certain German villages with a view to estimating population trends. The inaccuracy of such a method, however, can be great.

Considerations of climate are uncertain, but could be important,[4] and Walford provides a list and a discussion of the principal

[1] Lestocquoy, 'Le paysage urbain en Gaule du Ve au IXe siècle', *Annales* (*E.S.C.*), **8**, 2 (April–June 1953), pp. 159–72.

[2] V. O. Hansen, *Landskab og bebyggelse i Vendsyssel: studier over landbebyggelsens udvikling indtil slutningen af 1600-tallet*, Copenhagen, 1964, English summary, pp. 210–22.

[3] K. Lamprecht, *Deutsches Wirtschaftsleben im Mittelalter. Untersuchungen über die Entwicklung der materiellen Kuttur des platten Landes auf Grund der Quellen zunächst des Mosellandes*, Leipzig, 1886, especially Vol. I, pp. 161–4, and Vol. II, p. 20. For comments, see G. Ohlin, 'No Safety in Numbers: Some Pitfalls of Historical Statistics', in *Industrialization in Two Systems: Essays in Honor of Alexander Gerschenkron* (edited by H. Rosovsky), New York, 1966, pp. 68–90, especially pp. 81–4.

[4] See E. Le Roy Ladurie, 'Climat et récoltes aux XVIIe et XVIIIe siècles', *Annales* (*E.S.C.*), **15**, 1 (1960), pp. 434–65. I regret, however, not having seen

disasters.[1] Checking population changes against climatic evidence is worth the trouble, since it may cause us to reassess some of our demographic calculations.

TOMBSTONES

It might be thought that mortality tables for the past can be drawn up if we are lucky enough to find a large number of tombstone inscriptions giving age at death of the people buried, as there are of the population of ancient Greece and of the Roman Empire. Unfortunately, the great precision of such calculations is not matched by their reliability. A very large number of inscriptions has, nevertheless, been collected[2] and the ages at death have been analysed many times.[3] They suggest that in the city of Rome itself mortality was higher than elsewhere, while the most favour-

his book, *Histoire du climat depuis l'an mil*, Paris, 1967. Henry's review (in *Population*, 1967, pp. 945–6) leaves no doubt as to its great range, even though it is rather discursive.

[1] C. Walford, 'The Famines of the World: Past and Present', *Journal of the Statistical Society*, **41** (September 1878), pp. 433–526, and **42** (March 1879), pp. 79–265.

[2] See B. E. Richardson, *Old Age among the Ancient Greeks. The Greek Portrayal of Old Age in Literature, Art and Inscriptions, with a Study of the Duration of Life among the Ancient Greeks on the Basis of Inscriptional Evidence*, Baltimore, 1933. Her diligence, however, is misplaced from the demographic point of view; she probably lost about 1,000 infant and child deaths owing to the selectivity of those who received a memorial. Some improvement on Richardson's methods was achieved by V. S. Valaoras, 'Ἡ Μέση Διάρκεια τῆς Ζωῆς εἰς τὴν Ἀρχαίαν Ἑλλάδα', Πρακτικα τῆς Ἀκαδημιας Ἀθηνων, **13**, (12 May 1938), pp. 401–9.

[3] A. G. Harkness, 'Age at Marriage and Death in the Roman Empire', *Transactions of the American Philological Association*, **27** (1896), pp. 35–72; W. R. MacDonell, 'On the expectation of life in Ancient Rome, and in the Provinces of Hispania and Lusitania, and Africa', *Biometrika*, **9** (1913), pp. 366–80; W. F. Willcox, 'The Length of Life in the Roman Empire: A Methodological Note', *Congrès international de la population* (Paris, 1937), 2, Démographie historique, pp. 14–22; M. Hombert and C. Préaux, 'Note sur la durée de la vie dans l'Egypte gréco-romaine', *Chronique d'Égypte*, **20**, 39–40 (January–July 1945), pp. 139–46; A. R. Burn, 'Hic Breve Vivitur: A Study

able mortality rates appear in the remote provinces of North Africa. Eberhard also had some data, relating to China in the period A.D. 500–750, of this type.[1] They suggest light mortality, but can do no more than that.

The most telling criticism of graveyard research of this kind has been made by Henry.[2] He took the cemetery of Loyasse at Lyons for a period in the nineteenth century when the true mortality rates are known, and compared the results of using the cometery data with the true figures from death registration.[3] The difference in the proportions buried under the age of 15 was immense, it being about 40 per cent of all deaths but less than 10 per cent of the inscriptions. Clearly, no great assistance is rendered by the advantage of inscriptions; the results of using the skeletons themselves (see pp. 289–93) would have been scarcely any worse, and might conceivably have been better, supposing that some children were buried without tombstones.

Henry also found that there were too few young men and too many young women buried in the cemetery. Two possible reasons suggest themselves for this: differential migration and differential propensity to have a tombstone. The former may have been the case in the past, and would indeed yield erroneous results in terms

of the Expectation of Life in the Roman Empire', *Past and Present*, 4 (1953), pp. 2–31; J. D. Durand, 'Mortality Estimates from Roman Tombstone Inscriptions', *American Journal of Sociology*, 65, 4 (1960), pp. 365–73; M. K. Hopkins, 'The Age of Roman Girls at Marriage', *Population Studies*, XVIII, 3 (March 1965), pp. 309–27; *idem*, 'On the Probable Age Structure of the Roman Population', *ibid.*, XX, 2 (November 1966), pp. 245–64. (This is not an exhaustive list.)

---

[1] Eberhard, 'Notes on the Population of the Tun-huang Area', *Sinologica*, 4, 2 (1954), pp. 69–90, reprinted in *Settlement and Social Change in Asia*, Hong Kong, 1967, pp. 70–87, especially p. 77.

[2] L. Henry, 'La mortalité d'après les inscriptions funéraires', *Population*, 12, 1 (1957), pp. 149–52, and 'L'âge au décès d'après les inscriptions funéraires', *ibid.*, 14, 2 (1959), pp. 327–9; also his criticism of L. R. Nougier's paper in *ibid.*, 9, 2 (April–June 1954), pp. 272–4.

[3] *Loc. cit.* (1959).

of mortality rates, but Henry was able to eliminate it in this case, and showed that the number of young women who received a tombstone was a very high proportion of the total number of young women who actually died. It therefore follows that in all past societies, we must look out for a tendency to sentimentalize the death of a young wife but to ignore the death of a young son and perhaps also a young husband whose wife could not afford a tombstone. Whatever the reasons, the graveyard material has very little value for calculating vital rates.[1] Hopkins, however, was at least able to show[2] that the age at marriage in ancient Rome was almost certainly much lower than in post-Renaissance Europe.

CONCLUSION

The sources and methods described in this chapter are evidently very diverse. Moreover, other sources probably exist and the methods that might be devised are surely not yet exhausted. Although the results must be less accurate than those described in earlier chapters, one should bear these less reliable sources in mind as possibly worth using even when something better seems available, for corroboration of one's findings is always desirable.

When good bases of data are available, it might be possible to parallel Henry's research on the cemetery of Loyasse in some of the other kinds of data, as for instance the numbers of wills proved per year or the number of settlements in an area. This would greatly improve our confidence (or lack of it) in the methods themselves.

---

[1] See also R. J. Myers, 'An instance of the pitfalls prevalent in graveyard research', *Biometrics*, **19**, 4 (December 1963), pp. 638–50.

[2] *Loc. cit.* (1965), above on p. 272 (footnote 4).

CHAPTER 8

Non-Written Sources

Although in the previous five chapters we have exhausted the written sources of historical population data, there are still a few ways in which estimates can be made, using non-written sources. These vary greatly, and savour even more of Sherlock Holmes than the devices described in Chapter 7. The three groups of sources on which our ingenuity may be expended are pictures, ruins, and skeletons, but the value of the results is hardly commensurate with the effort of imagination required. Pictures, moreover, are rarely our sole source of information on population, and there cannot be many examples of their being the best source available. The other two kinds of sources, ruins and skeletons, take us into the realm of archaeology. They are often not merely the best demographic source of information about a society, but may be the only evidence for its very existence. The problem of their interpretation is then acute, and a good deal of thought has gone into it. Although we cannot hope for much accuracy compared with the work described in Chapters 3 to 6, it may compare favourably with the kind of work described in Chapter 7.

PICTURES

Occasionally we may have pictures of cities, drawn in detail, for periods when no better base for making a population estimate can be found. As a test of their value, we give the result of an experiment done on a book[1] that shows contemporary views of

[1] G. Braun and F. Hogenberg, *Old European Cities*, London, 1965. This is a modern reprint and translation of 32 maps and texts from *Civitates Orbis Terrarum* (1572–1618).

32 European cities, dating from between 1572 and 1618.

A purely subjective impression, which can be little more than the total volume of buildings that seem to have been used for dwellings, allowing something for the apparent areal density of windows to walls, would make the 19 largest depicted cities the following (in order): Naples, Paris, Amsterdam, Antwerp, Breslau, London, Lyons, Constantinople, Granada, Rome, Strasbourg, Toledo, Barcelona, Brussels, Prague, Vienna, Königsberg, Milan and Danzig. A twentieth city, Venice, is described but not depicted in the book, and there is little doubt that the compilers thought these 20 were the largest 20 cities in Europe. Some of the remaining 13 cities were very small and may have been included for reasons other than their size.

Now 1572–1618 is an era when quite good population statistics for European cities are available, so we can check the method against the relative sizes that are approximately established by the statistics. Constantinople should have come second and not eighth (or ninth, if Venice were thought larger), and Milan should have come about fifth and not eighteenth or nineteenth. But Breslau's size is probably overestimated, and the Spanish cities also seem to be too large. One might say, however, that if one could get the scale of subjective impression to actual numbers right, the population of the various cities could probably be estimated to within 20 per cent of the true figure by this method as often as not. The difficulty of comparing two very different city views is considerable, since the artist was normally trying to display not the size of the city, but its chief landmarks.

RUINS

Duncan-Jones,[1] discussing Roman cities in Africa, remarked that there are five ways in which their population can be assessed:

1. the productivity and area of the land supplying the city;
2. the water supply—rivers and aqueducts;

[1] R. P. Duncan-Jones, 'City Population in Roman Africa', *Journal of Roman Studies*, **53**, 1–2 (1963), pp. 85–90.

3. the area, as compared with the area of some city of known population;
4. the density of the existing ruins of houses within the city;
5. the size of the amphitheatres and theatres.

The first of these belongs to the previous chapter; of the others, the area of the city is much the most commonly available. The density of population in an ancient city has been assumed[1] to have never been more than 200 people to the hectare, and usually 100 or less if the city was not a metropolis. But this is too simple a rule; Clark's studies of urban population densities[2] show the differences between different kinds of city and suggest that very high densities in pre-industrial cities might have arisen. This is borne out by study of the present density of population in Erbil,[3] in Iraq, which has changed relatively little since ancient times, which is estimated at about 213 to the acre (526 per hectare). Allowing for a large market-place and a bigger temple than the present mosque, 200 to the acre (494 per hectare) has been suggested as the probable maximum density for an ancient mesopotamian city. Similarly Hong Kong, although industrial, has most of the older features still, and the density of population in its towns is very high indeed (Kowloon had 725,177 people in 1961 at 755 per hectare; 6,980 per hectare was reached in two parts of Hong Kong Island that each contained more than 10,000 inhabitants).

[1] By J. C. Russell, in *Late Ancient and Medieval Population*, Philadelphia (Transactions of the American Philosophical Society), 1958, p. 68.

[2] C. Clark, 'Urban Population Densities', *Journal of the Royal Statistical Society*, Series A, **114**, 4 (1951), pp. 490–6. See also Chapter IX of his *Population Growth and Land Use*, London, 1967, pp. 339–87, and J. E. Brush, 'Spatial Patterns of Population in Indian Cities', *Geographical Review*, **58**, 3 (July 1968), pp. 362–91.

[3] R. J. Braidwood and C. A. Reed, 'The Achievement and Early Consequences of Food Production: A Consideration of the Archaeological and Natural–Historical Evidence', *Cold Spring Harbor Symposia on Quantitative Biology*, XXII (1957), pp. 19–31.

Similarly, Lot has assumed[1] that city population in the past was subject to an upper limit equal to that of the density of population in Paris in 1806. He describes how Paris was then choked with people and how close together the buildings were prior to Napoleon's re-drawing of the town plan and constructing the famous boulevards of Paris. Lot's assumption has been widely accepted and Russell, in particular, has used it to justify his general assumption that no medieval cities can possibly have exceeded 100,000 inhabitants except for Constantinople and possibly Naples. Mumford[2] takes a different view, accepting Venice, Milan and Paris as also reaching this size. Florence and Cordova should perhaps be included too. However, the city of London within the walls certainly had a higher density of population during the seventeenth century than Lot and Russell believed the maximum, and although at that time London had many suburbs outside the walls that together made up most of the metropolitan population, it does not follow that London within the walls had markedly fewer people before 1550 than a hundred years later. It was possible to get the people into the area at the later date, and so it may have been possible to do so earlier.[3]

Striking examples of high population density can be found in Bombay, where a part of Bombay island has had very high densities for at least the past 100 years, as well as in Hong Kong, where the highest densities in the world are recorded. It surprised Schmitt, an American visitor, to discover[4] that although Hong

[1] F. Lot, 'Capitales antiques, capitales modernes. Rome et sa population à la fin du IIIe siècle de notre ère', *Annales d'histoire sociale*, VIII (1945), pp. 29–38.

[2] L. Mumford, *The Culture of Cities*, London, 1942.

[3] The best account of London's population before 1801, not superseded apart from a few points, is still: C. Creighton, 'The Population of Old London', *Blackwood's Magazine*, 149 (April 1891), pp. 477–96.

[4] R. C. Schmitt, 'Implications of density in Hong Kong', *Journal of the Institute of Planners*, 29, 3 (August 1963), pp. 210–17. Kowloon City had a population density eight times New York City. Tracts of some acres in extent in Victoria and Kowloon exceeded the density of population of mere blocks in Manhattan.

Kong has few tall buildings, it had in 1961 a higher density of population in its cities than the United States had anywhere, even in Manhattan. Wanchai, a census division of Hong Kong island, had a population of 186,169 on less than one square kilometre—or 2,092 per hectare. Lot's theoretical maximum is hence proved too low by a factor of at least ten, and consequently all his and Russell's assumptions about, for example, ancient Rome do not hold.

The walls of the city of Rome could, therefore, have contained 2 million inhabitants at the height of the Roman Empire, if they lived at the highest modern Asian densities; nevertheless, Russell argued[1] that Imperial Rome could not have exceeded 300,000 people because of the problem of supplying them. There is no doubt that supplies were important, as the Roman roads and aqueducts bear witness, and they were probably the factor that limited the size of the city, but it is not clear why 300,000, rather than any other figure, should be taken as the limit. Von Gerkan suggested[2] 600,000 to 700,000 inhabitants as the maximum size of the city of Rome, which contained 1,386·9 hectares in all, but only 693 hectares that could be regarded as the built-up area. The density, excluding the open spaces within the city walls, would then be about 1,000 per hectare. Three contiguous wards of Hong Kong island (Central, Sheung Wan and Wanchai) had 376,783 people[3] living on only 250 hectares in 1961, a density of 1,507 per hectare. Meyer has, in fact, argued[4] that the population of ancient Rome cannot be estimated accurately, a conclusion

[1] Russell, 'The Metropolitan City Region of the Middle Ages', *Journal of Regional Science*, 2, 2 (Fall, 1960), pp. 55–70; see p. 68.

[2] A. von Gerkan, 'Die Einwohnerzahl Roms in der Kaiserzeit', *Mittheilungen des Kaiserlichen Deutschen Archaeologischen Instituts, Römische, Abtheilung*, 55 (1940), pp. 149–95.

[3] K. M. A. Barnett, *Hong Kong. Report on the 1961 Census*, Volume II, p. 11. (This is the official government report, Barnett being the Census Commissioner.)

[4] F. G. Meyer, 'Römische Bevölkerungsgeschichte und Inschriftenstatistik', *Historia*, 2, 3 (1954), pp. 318–51.

that implies that almost all the ancient cities of the world must be inaccessible to precise demographic study.

The crucial difference would seem to be between a 'horse and cart society' and a 'man with a yoke society'. If the standard means of carrying anything from place to place is on the shoulders of a man, as it still is in Hong Kong, there is an enormous pressure to restrict the physical area on which a population lives in a city. Adding even a quarter of a mile to the distances that must be travelled adds very greatly to the time, trouble and expense of every journey and therefore to the cost of carrying on a business of any kind. This was not true in nineteenth-century Paris, but probably was true in first-century Rome. Thus the ancient writers may not have been exaggerating and the modern ones may have been too sceptical.

The ancient cities of central America, notably in the Yucatan peninsula, had areas that are so large that it is difficult to accept them as cities in the normal sense. Morley found[1] by a survey of part of Uaxactun, a second-rank Mayan city, that 43 per cent was swampy and uninhabitable, 15 per cent contained cere-monial and governmental precincts, and in the remaining 42 per cent were 52 house-mounds and 50 reservoirs. A density of only about 1,100 people per square mile of habitable land was indi-cated for this supposed city. Mayan cities were, in fact, as large in area as the modern cities of Europe; the civic centre alone at Tikal covered one square mile.[2] It seems possible that these cities really might have been city states in the sense that the city was co-terminal with the state and everything outside was alien country. All the food might be grown within the city limits on a kind of market gardening system, and consequently the buildings had to be relatively far apart and the population density, although enormous for a rural area, was very low for a city. Nevertheless, Morley remarks that in the eighth century the Yucatan peninsula

[1] S. G. Morley, *The Ancient Maya*, Palo Alto, 1947, p. 313.
[2] *Ibid.*, p. 320. The area of Tikal seems to have been about 30 square miles, or roughly the size of Nottingham.

must have had three or four times the population that it has today, and it would have been much higher (as high as 53 million) if all the sites found were occupied at the same time. Similarly, it is interesting that Oldenburg quotes Tavernier as saying[1] that Isfahan and Paris were about the same size in the seventeenth century, but Paris had ten times the population of Isfahan. Variability in urban population density is no newly-found thing.

Measurements have been made of most of the ancient and medieval cities of Europe, which have been studied by Mols[2] and also discussed in detail by Russell.[3] Certain cities have received special attention: Huntington, for example, believed[4] that Cyrene's ruins suggested 100,000 inhabitants, whereas J. W. Gregory had calculated 25,000 at the most; Torres-Balbas has dealt with the cities of medieval Spain;[5] and similar figures for area are available for some ancient Asian cities, such as Anshan, Mohenjo-Darro, Babylon and Harappa. The level of culture is likely to be decisive in determining whether the population of these cities was relatively small or relatively large. Beloch is said

[1] H. Oldenburg, 'Observations concerning some of the most considerable parts of Asia from Tavernier's voyages', *Philosophical Transactions of the Royal Society*, **11**, 129 (20 November 1676), pp. 711–15, and 130 (14 December 1676), pp. 751–8. Tavernier made his six oriental voyages between 1631 and 1668.

[2] See R. Mols, *Introduction à la Démographie Historique des Villes d'Europe du XIVe au XVIIIe siècle*, Louvain, 1954–6, Vol. II, pp. 50–100. This is, of course, much more elaborate a treatment than we can offer here.

[3] Russell, *op. cit.* above on p. 279 (footnote 1) (1958), pp. 59–71.

[4] E. Huntington, 'Climatic change and agricultural exhaustion as elements in the fall of Rome', *Quarterly Journal of Economics*, **31** (February 1917), pp. 173–208.

[5] L. Torres-Balbas, 'Extension y demografía de las ciudades hispanomusulmanes', *Studia Islamica*, **3** (1955), pp. 35–59. He is inclined to believe that many of the higher figures that are sometimes mentioned are the result of the Moorish or Andalusian love of hyperbole. Nevertheless, the population of Spain at the beginning of the tenth century was evidently higher (at $7\frac{1}{2}$ or 8 million) than it was 800 years later.

to have argued[1] for a decline in population East of Baghdad after the irrigational system ceased to function, in the twelfth century; the cities would presumably have declined with the rest of the country. The evidence from Baghdad at the time of the caliphs is only slightly less vague. Lassner has tried to study the area of the city,[2] but its destruction by the Mongols in 1258 makes modern archaeological work unfruitful. Baghdad's total extent was at least 7,000 hectares, or five times that of Constantinople; but it was a spacious city, having none of the natural limitations of Constantinople. Lassner followed Jacoby[3] in assessing the population of Constantinople at 360,000 in the city proper and 15,000 more in the suburbs, and reached a tentative 280,000 to 560,000 for Baghdad on a comparative basis. Russell, however, believed[4] that Constantinople had a population of no more than 150,000 about A.D. 400; this seems too low for the sixth century, although his 35,000 at the time of the Turkish conquest in 1453 seems reasonable. (Schneider, too, allowed[5] only 40,000 to 50,000 by 1437, and 60,000 to 70,000 in 1477; he remarked that the city was not fully built up as early as the Comnenan period.)

The contemporary literary evidence for the population of Baghdad[6] is two-fold: that there were 860 doctors in the city, and

[1] K. J. Beloch, 'Die Bevölkerung im Altertum', *Zeitschrift für Sozial-wissenschaft*, 2 (1899), pp. 505–14, pp. 600–10, and pp. 610–21. Although I have been referred to this set of articles for this statement, my German has not perhaps been adequate for me to discover it in them.

[2] J. Lassner, 'Massignon and Baghdad: The Complexities of Growth in an Imperial City', *Journal of the Social and Economic History of the Orient*, 9 (1966), pp. 1–27.

[3] D. Jacoby, 'La population de Constantinople à l'époque byzantine: un problème de démographie urbaine', *Byzantion*, xxxi (1961), pp. 81–109.

[4] Russell, *op. cit.* above on p. 279 (footnote 1), p. 77, and *loc. cit.* above on p. 281 (footnote 1).

[5] A. M. Schneider, 'Die Bevölkerung Konstantinopels am XV Jahrhundert', *Nachtrichten der Akademie der Wissenschaft in Göttingen*, Phil.-Hist. Klasse (1949), pp. 233–44. [I have only seen H. Ritter's review of this in *Oriens*, 3 (1950), p. 147.]

[6] Lassner, *loc. cit.*

that there were 120,000 bath-houses. The latter yields an apparent population of 96,000,000 people, and it is evident that there is some mistake. One doctor per thousand inhabitants, however, is still quite a high figure, and so at least 860,000 inhabitants must be probable. Other accounts of the number of bath-houses (some of which may be their total capacity for simultaneous bathing rather than the number of establishments) suggest a figure of 1,500,000, and it would seem that Baghdad's population should be placed in a range about three times as high as Lassner allows— 860,000 to 1,500,000. Perhaps the figure of 96 million should be divided by 100, an easy possibility in Arabic where unless numbers are written out the zeros are indicated by dots which could easily be confused with smudges. Hamdan[1] puts the population of Abbasid Baghdad at 2 million, but without discussion.[2]

The sociologist, Sjoberg, however, agrees[3] generally with Russell that although some ancient cities were no doubt fairly large they rarely exceeded 100,000, but his precise reasons for preferring low figures are unclear. It may be that it was usual in pre-industrial, yet highly urbanized, societies for the principal city to surpass all the rest by an enormous margin—just as London was roughly twenty times the size of the next English city in 1700. A stranger who had travelled around provincial England at that date, visiting Exeter and Bristol, Gloucester and Lichfield, York and Newcastle upon Tyne, Lincoln and Norwich, would have been unable to believe that the capital city had much more than 50,000 or 70,000 inhabitants—but London really had about 600,000. Cairo, similarly, accounted for about 12 per cent of the population of Egypt in 1798.

[1] G. Hamdan, 'The Pattern of Medieval Urbanism in the Arab World', *Geography*, 47 (1962), pp. 121–34.

[2] See also W. Schneider's book, *Babylon is Everywhere. The City as Man's Fate* (translated by I. Saminet and J. Oldenburg), London, 1963, for comments on Baghdad and other cities. It is particularly useful for the various facts about ancient cities that it contains.

[3] G. Sjoberg, *The Preindustrial City*, New York, 1965, p. 83.

Duval, discussing Paris[1] under the Roman Empire, discounted the 15,000 or more that the amphitheatre could hold (the theatre only held 3,000), assuming that visitors would be expected in town for the larger shows. He did so, however, in order to support Lot's view that a density of 150 people to the hectare would be correct, making only 8,000 in the city proper. Including suburbs, Paris could not, he thought, then have exceeded 20,000 people. He estimated that an aqueduct could have supplied water for between 4,000 and 5,000, but since it may not have been the only Paris aqueduct and since many people may have drunk the Seine, the information is little help.

A casual remark by Plato, early in the *Symposium*, to the effect that 30,000 people had been present that day in the theatre at Athens, can be regarded as a piece of information for assessing the population of Athens at the height of its power. It has been disputed whether the figure is accurate, however, and in view of its casual context it might be as well to put it on a plane with Plato's story of The Lost Continent of Atlantis.

Collingwood was one of the first to estimate[2] the population of Roman Britain and arrived at 500,000, but the data are so scanty that it is really a guess rather than an estimate. Methods that lead to definite results, depending upon assumptions that are more than merely plausible, do not exist. Nevertheless, several further attempts have been made. Usher argued[3] that Collingwood's guess was too low, but Foord had given[4] a figure (3 to 3½ million south of Hadrian's Wall) as high as any for the area before about 1600. Frere advances[5] a total population for Roman Britain

[1] P.-M. Duval, *Paris antique, des origines au IIIe siècle*, Paris, 1961, p. 249.

[2] R. G. Collingwood, 'Town and country in Roman Britain', *Antiquity*, **3**, 11 (1929), pp. 261-76. Roman London, according to him, might have had 25,000 inhabitants, or 5 per cent of the total he allowed for Britain.

[3] A. P. Usher, 'A new estimate of the population of Britain in Roman times', *Geographical Review*, **20**, 4 (1930), pp. 674-6.

[4] E. A. Foord, *The Last Age of Roman Britain*, p. 66, quoted by Usher, *loc. cit.*

[5] S. Frere, *Britannia: a history of Roman Britain*, London, 1967, pp. 261-3 and 309-11. London for him had 30,000 to 40,000 people.

of 2 million, and also figures for some of the towns, but his sources include the 1377 Poll-Tax returns as well as the areas of the Roman city ruins. Thomas, however, has obtained[1] a density for the native population in Cornwall in Roman times by a semi-direct method. He counted the 'rounds' in that county, guessed the number of people living in each, and allowed 50 per cent more for the 'non-round' population. This is obviously a very inexact method, but is at least a base from which to work. The population of Cornwall in Roman times was about 70 per cent of the figure found from the Domesday Book, according to Thomas; if so, of course, we shall regard Collingwood as being too low, Foord and Frere as too high, and possibly Usher as about right.

In a similar spirit, Nougier tried to assess the size of the population of France before 1000 B.C.[2] He came to the conclusion that there were 5 million inhabitants after 3000 B.C., but his methods are in reality highly speculative. When he tried to be more quantitative, he had to rely on the evidence of skeletons, which, as we shall see, are often extremely misleading as sources of demographic data.

Krzywicki gives a general discussion[3] on the demographic rates of primitive communities which convinces one of the need to understand such a society a little before making more than a rough guess as to its demography.

Although population figures for ancient or medieval cities tend to be exasperatingly imprecise, it is a fair assumption that when new walls were constructed, enclosing a larger area, this is evidence of an increased population. In medieval Europe, in contrast to ancient America, the city can never have grown all its food within its walls. The expense of extending the wall would

[1] C. Thomas, 'The Character and Origins of Roman Dumnonia', in *Rural Settlement in Roman Britain* (edited by C. Thomas), London, 1966, pp. 74–98.
[2] L. R. Nougier, 'Essai sur le peuplement préhistorique de la France', *Population*, **9**, 2 (April–June 1954), pp. 241–71.
[3] L. Krzywicki, *Primitive Society and Its Vital Statistics*, London, 1934.

only be borne if a much larger population was in a position to demand such an extension. The actual increase in the enclosed area, of course, does not provide a very exact indicator of the extent to which the population had risen, but it will suggest the periods at which expansion occurred. In this connection it is interesting that the city of London seems to have had the same area, except for trivial amendments, from the tenth to the sixteenth centuries. Unless the wall-builders of the Anglo-Saxon period were extremely wasteful of effort, it would therefore seem that the population of London at the time of the Norman Conquest may have been quite large. The question is very difficult to settle, because the Domesday Book does not include the city of London. Perhaps this itself is evidence that London was not merely a large town like other towns, but was of a different order of magnitude from any other city in the kingdom, even as early as 1086. It is certainly true that in Edward III's edicts for troops and supplies for the Hundred Years War, London is usually treated in quite a different way from all the other cities of the kingdom, and is regarded as though it were a county, although a county of a very special kind. However, we believe that the maximum medieval population was not greatly over 60,000 on the balance of the evidence.[1]

Cook had an unusual method[2] of assessing the population of the Teotihuacan (or Toltec) civilization at its height, around A.D. 900, that is worth a mention. The pyramid at Teotihuacan, not far from Mexico City, is so big that it would have required, Cook thought, a community of 150,000 people to build it. Three similar pyramids, on the same assumptions, would have required 250,000, 75,000 and 150,000 people in their respective communities. The local density of population in these four regions (625,000 people), assuming the area of settlement can be deline-

[1] See pp. 364 and 368-9.
[2] S. F. Cook, 'The interrelation of population, food supply, and building in pre-conquest central Mexico', *American Antiquity*, **13**, 1 (July 1947), pp. 45-52.

ated, Cook then calculated at 13·3 per square kilometre. If the rest of the region had only half this density, the whole would contain 2,700,000 people, which is still, of course, a minimum figure. But the four communities were almost certainly not, say, three times as large as Cook calculated, or they would surely have built larger pyramids. The remainder of the region was quite probably less densely populated, since pyramid-building was no doubt a pursuit of the wealthier and more numerous groups, so that a population between 1,600,000 and 4,500,000 is in fact very probable for the whole area.

SKELETONS AND SKULLS

Many attempts have been made in recent years to determine the population and mortality rates of the past from careful study of human skeletons found in old burial places. We shall consider these in turn. The medieval population in parts of Hungary, Spain, Sweden and Poland has been considered within the last fifteen years, and in each case some of the figures were based upon a comparatively small number of skeletons. In Mexico the problem is slightly different, but there are records of skull counts there after the elaborate sacrifices that were common in the fifteenth century.

The first difficulty is that the sample of skeletons that is found may not be representative of the population. However, we know enough about social conditions in the Middle Ages to be fairly certain that the whole population would be buried in the same cemetery, which means that there is less risk in medieval Europe of a non-representative sample; but the estimates of age are uncertain nevertheless. Death data by ages are a poor guide to real mortality by age, although Halley used them[1] as long ago as

---

[1] E. Halley, 'An Estimate of the Degrees of the Mortality of Mankind, drawn from curious Tables of the Births and Funerals at the City of Breslaw; with an Attempt to ascertain the Price of Annuities upon Lives', *Philosophical Transactions of the Royal Society*, **17**, 196 (January 1692/3), pp. 596–610, and 198 (March 1693), pp. 654–56. See also Henry's criticism (1957) cited on p. 410.

1693; his results were not as satisfactory as they would have been from a modern system of census and death registration. We do not know the true size of the population, and to estimate it from the cemetery data is impermissible when the mortality rate is unknown and its determination is in fact the purpose of the investigation.

However, some of the results are intriguing even if others are almost certainly wrong. In Hungary, Acsádi and Nemeskeri found[1] a growing population between A.D. 900 and 1120, with the death-rate tending to rise slowly and males having much lower mortality than females. All three of these are possible, and even probable, but their infant mortality rate of only 66 per thousand children born is incredible, unless we suppose that the early Magyars had an exceptional level of obstetrical skill and public health, equivalent to that of England about 1918. Acsádi has, more recently, summarized[2] all the latest Hungarian work on the demographic evidence of cemeteries (3,531 skeletons in all), making careful allowances for missing data. However, the expectation of life at birth of 28·73 that the combined results suggest still seems rather high, although infant mortality is raised to 200 per thousand born. Perhaps life was relatively easy for these new Magyar settlers, and became harder in the later-Middle Ages as the Hungarian plain became more thickly populated.

Russell provides[3] more comprehensive data of the same kind, covering the whole of Europe (except Russia) about the fourteenth century, and similar criticisms may be made. The evidence,

---

[1] G. Acsádi and J. Nemeskeri, 'Paläodemographische Probleme am Beispiel des frühmittelalterlichen Gräberfeldes von Halimba-Cseres Kom. Vezprem/Ungarn', *Homo*, **8**, 3 (1957), pp. 133–47.

[2] Acsádi, 'A középkori magyar halandóságra vonatkozó paleodemográfiai kutatások eredményei', *Történeti Statisztikai Evkönyv* (1963–4), pp. 3–34 and 295–7. In September 1968, Dr Acsádi told me that a book in English was then in preparation on the demography of ancient Hungary from the evidence of skeletons.

[3] Russell, 'Effects of Pestilence and Plague, 1315–85', *Comparative Studies in Society and History*, **8**, 4 (July 1966), pp. 464–73.

however, that female mortality was higher than male seems hard to refute, since the difference is large. Child-bearing, presumably, is the explanation; the same is true of twentieth-century India. In Sweden, Gejvall[1] found a much more likely infant mortality-rate at a slightly later period (1100–1350) than the first Hungarian study mentioned above. One-third of his 364 skeletons were of children under one year, and half were under the age of 8. The average length of life was less than 20 for each sex. The women had the better expectation of life; but although this is commonly found in modern populations, it is interesting that Gejvall found many more women than men, and it is probable that adult men often died somewhere else. This emigration would have produced a biased sample, and the true average length of life for his group might have been nearer 25 than the 15 or 18 years that he found.

A rather more remote society was studied by Churcher and Kenyon[2] in Canada, dating from about A.D 1250. It consists of American Indians, about whose social behaviour at that time we know very little. Churcher and Kenyon had a particularly difficult problem in that over 2,000 bones were found (some only partially preserved) but the number of individuals that was represented was not clear. The anatomical problems were so acute, in fact, that demography had a very limited scope, and in this example little more could be done than assume a possible death-rate and then estimate the size of the population on the assumption that the ossuary was only in use for a short time.

Some interesting work has also be done[3] on the extinction of the medieval Norse settlement in Greenland. The skeletons have been studied in detail, but they only amount to 38 in all. The

[1] N. G. Gejvall, *Westerhus. Medieval Population and Church in the Light of Skeletal Remains*, Lund, 1960, pp. 35–44; cited by Russell in 'Recent advances in mediaeval demography', *Speculum*, 40, 1 (January 1965), pp. 84–101, p. 86.

[2] C. S. Churcher and W. A. Kenyon, 'The Tabor Hill Ossuaries: A study in Iroquois Demography', *Human Biology*, 32 (1960), pp. 249–73.

[3] C. Gini, 'The extinction of the Norse settlement in Greenland', *Acta Genetica et Statistica Medica*, 6 (1956–7), pp. 404–5, and 'Sulla scomparsa delle colonie normanne in Groenlandia', *Genus*, 13, 1–4 (1957), pp. 62–131.

excess of women, who were 26 as against 12 men, suggests that the final disaster may have come suddenly, but on such a small sample it is dangerous to base very much.

Stloukal has studied[1] some thousand skeletons from Moravia, dating from the eighth and ninth centuries A.D., but the high sex-ratio of 130 males per 100 females amongst those found precludes the sample from being wholly representative. The males lived rather longer than the females in adult life, and one might suppose that there was a certain amount of lost female neonatal deaths (or else lost female infanticide) that would account for the high sex ratio.

Skeletons referring to Greece give the longest series for one area that has been studied. Angel devoted a great deal of research[2] to the expectation of life in ancient Greece, removing the infant deaths altogether by only considering the expectation of life at the age of fifteen years. This device indeed avoids trouble over the absence of many infant skeletons, but allows nothing for migration by adults, which at some periods may have been high. However, it is likely that the general trends he found are correct; the decline in expectation of life he found between classical and Hellenistic Greece on the one hand (about 40 more years at age 15) and Turkish Greece (only 31) on the other seems not unlikely, and the old level was quite probably not regained until the nineteenth century. For most parts of Europe, of course, it is well-nigh certain that by 1800 expectations of life were the highest that had ever been known. [But see pp. 217, 343-4.]

[1] M. Stloukal, 'Pokus o palaeodemografii starých Slovanů', *Demografie*, 4, 1 (1962), pp. 37-42, and 'Demografické zvláštnosti staroslovanských pohřebišť', *ibid.*, 7, 1 (1965), pp. 58-60.

[2] J. L. Angel, 'The Length of Life in Ancient Greece', *Journal of Gerontology*, II, 1 (January 1947), pp. 18-24, and 'Human Biology, Health, and History in Greece from First Settlement until Now', *American Philosophical Society Yearbook* (1954), pp. 168-72. We should also mention here the small-scale study of M. S. Senyürek, 'Note on the duration of life of the ancient inhabitants of Anatolia', *American Journal of Physical Anthropology*, V, 1 (1947), pp. 55-66, which was largely based on 112 skulls, without any startling results.

Kurth found[1] some Neolithic remains in Cyprus that suggest a neonatal mortality rate of one in three, with none of the 180 individuals identified living over 50. While there are questions as to the representativeness of such a small population (the reason why their particular remains have been preserved is normally the important one), the mean expectation of life was evidently under 21 years, so that we should conclude that the community had difficulty in maintaining its numbers, which must have been normal in most prehistoric populations.

In the Canary Islands, Schwidetzky has studied[2] a population now wholly extinct but which has left many skeletons in the graves on Teneriffe and Grand Canary. The skulls appear to show that they lived to a relatively advanced age, with almost 10 per cent reaching the age of 60. Here our ignorance of the social pattern of these people is total, and therefore we can make little assessment of how far the population that has been preserved is truly representative. The same criticism applies to the skulls and bones, found by Vallois[3] and also discussed by Datta,[4] which date from the Neanderthal, Palaeolithic and Neolithic periods. Vallois gives full details of the difficulties of estimating the age of skeletal remains, while Datta has made a more realistic adjustment of the data. In particular he suggested that the infant mortality rate was probably about 50 per cent before the advent of modern man. The expectation of life at birth was correspondingly low, about 14 years only. But without a good knowledge of the social structure of the society, we cannot safely make assumptions about which people happen to have been buried in any particular place.

[1] G. Kurth, 'Zur Stellung der neolitischen Menschenreste von Khirokitia auf Cypern', *Homo*, **9**, 1 (1958), pp. 20–30.

[2] I. Schwidetzky, 'In welchem Alter starben die alten Kanarier?', *ibid.*, **8**, 2 (1957), pp. 98–102, and **9**, 1 (1958), pp. 31–3.

[3] H. V. Vallois, 'La durée de la vie chez l'homme fossile', *L'Anthropologie*, **47** (1937), pp. 499–532.

[4] J. M. Datta, 'Demography of Prehistoric Man', *Man in India*, **39**, 4 (October 1959), pp. 257–70.

One final illustration, macabre as it is, must conclude this survey. More than twenty years ago, Cook considered[1] the demographic aspects of the religious system of fifteenth-century Mexico; human sacrifice was at its height, on a very wide scale indeed. Over the whole period, apparently 15 per cent of deaths were human sacrifices; this would now be modified, however, presumably, to only $1\frac{1}{2}$ per cent, since Cook's own ideas of the population of fifteenth-century Mexico have changed radically since 1946. Perhaps, indeed, this study started the search for evidence of a high pre-conquest population. The skull pyramid at Tenochtitlan alone contained more than 136,000 skulls, and was built in only 32 years, 1487–1519, at a rate, therefore, of 4,250 skulls a year. Together with other estimates, at least 20,000 people must have been sacrificed every year just before Cortés arrived. If the population had only been 2 million (which was believed probable in 1946), this would have had a very important effect on the population size.

CONCLUSION

Unwritten evidence, in fact, is rarely as valuable as the written word or figure. The advantage of physical contact with the raw material does enable many kinds of tests to be made upon it, to be sure; but the evidence is always indirect at best, and has to be amplified by fairly bold assumptions to produce any actual estimates of demographic levels or rates at all. The main value of the unwritten evidence is as corroboration of what can be suggested from other sources. On its own, it could be very misleading.

[1] Cook, 'Human Sacrifice and Warfare as Factors in the Demography of pre-colonial Mexico', *Human Biology*, **18**, 2 (May 1946), pp. 81–102.

CHAPTER 9

The Limits of Demographic Research in History

Demography is always concerned with events that have already happened, so that even contemporary demography is historical in a sense. Many countries still take no census at all, and in others the census is highly defective. These countries include, for instance, Afghanistan, Bhutan, Ethiopia, Saudi Arabia and Yemen; and many parts of Africa also have little or no good data. Sample surveys are often taken in such places in an endeavour to collect information that would be impossible to get for the whole population, but they are by no means always satisfactory. We shall never be able to discover even the current population trends for some countries unless some of the retrospective indirect methods now being developed prove to be applicable.

As well as countries that have no census, many important questions are not asked in countries that take a census. In fact, every country's census can be described as defective in some way or other. The International Statistical Institute has been attempting to improve and to standardize international methods of census-taking for more than eighty years, and more recently the United Nations has tried to do the same, but with comparatively little result. Governments are not particularly interested in such matters as international comparability, and the cost of collecting more than the bare minimum of information is generally thought to be excessive.[1]

Defective systems of registration of births, marriages and

---

[1] The 1961 census of Great Britain, which was not especially elaborate, cost just over three million pounds. More than half of this sum was spent in paying the enumerators.

deaths and of recording migration (both internal and external) are very common. A registration system is generally established after the census has worked for some considerable time, and requires a high level of competence, day in and day out, in order to keep it comprehensive and accurate. Births, marriages and deaths are fairly completely recorded in most advanced countries, although the cause of death is still frequently given wrong on the death certificate. Full demographic details about a birth, however, such as the duration of marriage, the number of children previously born, and so on, are often not legally required at the registration of a birth. Internal migration is only recorded in a small number of countries, and at least 5 per cent of movements always seem to be missed by a migration register. Thus few countries (the United Kingdom is not one of them) can claim to have a thorough vital registration system, even today. Birth and death registrations are very poor in many countries, and known to represent only a fraction (in India, about a half) of the real total number of such events. Governments do not feel that the value of a registration system is great enough to justify the trouble and expense of raising the levels of coverage. In the United States of America, for example, registration of at least 95 per cent of births has only been achieved since 1946.[1] Many of the interesting social and demographic factors in history that we would like to study are, in fact, beyond the scope of even contemporary research in many countries, although Great Britain is relatively well supplied with historical data.

Censuses, however, should always be taken as more reliable sources for demographic study than registers of vital events if there is ever any doubt about the completeness of coverage of either of them. This point is extremely important in English demographic history, where the ecclesiastical censuses of 1676 and 1688 must be preferred to the parish registers as far as possible.

A good knowledge of the demography of a country is usually

[1] S. Shapiro, 'Development of Birth Registration and Birth Statistics in the United States', *Population Studies*, IV, 1 (June 1950), pp. 86–111.

only possible for countries with a high standard of living. Many conditions, such as low infant mortality rates, low birth-rates, high real income per head, and a high level of car ownership, are associated; and the accuracy of demographic statistics themselves is also correlated with the other indices of a high standard of living. Thus it is very natural that few societies in the past should have good statistics on population, and, in particular, there are almost no instances of entirely reliable data before 1700.

QUALITY OF HISTORICAL DATA

The quality of the data has been discussed elsewhere[1] in general terms; but, to be specific, the most common errors are probably mistakes in copying. People who have never tried to work with figures for long may not appreciate that 2 or 3 per cent of any figures copied in a hurry will commonly be wrong, and that if the copier has no real interest in the figures he will scarcely realize it when he has made a mistake. Such mistakes must have been very common in the past, since many sets of records were copied and recopied several times before they reached their extant form. As Hume pointed out 200 years ago,[2] a copying mistake in a word usually spoils the grammar and is easily detected, whereas a copying mistake in a figure is often impossible to spot.

The officials who are our sources of information may, of course, have been incompetent, and we should consider whether the officials were interested in getting their returns correct, because if they had the will to do so they might have found the way. It was by no means always impossible to get a good idea of an historical population provided enough trouble was taken, but that in turn would depend upon the concern the officials had for accuracy.

[1] T. H. Hollingsworth, 'The Importance of the Quality of the Data in Historical Demography', *Daedalus* (Spring 1968), pp. 415–32.
[2] In his famous essay, 'Of the Populousness of Ancient Nations'.

The level of literacy sometimes needs to be taken into account, too. In towns, one may assume that the bourgeois were good at book-keeping and therefore were capable of counting their numbers well. But the soldiers and peasants were not necessarily literate and might not have taken a census in the appropriate spirit, because they would not really have known what it was for. If the officials were almost the only literates, they could scarcely have conducted a census of population that was free from guesswork.

The actual collection of data is also very important. It may have been collected on forms, on cards, by simple counts without paper work, or by estimating from a detailed knowledge of only a small part of the total area. Many parts of the world still rely upon information supplied by the local 'headman', which may, as in Nigeria, be open to suspicion. The actual status of the officials, whether they were appointed by the Government or were the products of a civil service examination system, generally determines their attitude towards their work. Population returns based upon taxation records, when the taxation system itself was not under the direct control of the Government but was farmed out, will be liable to grave error owing to the convenience of the tax-farmer. Similar data collected by the officials of the Government will be much more reliable. Further to this, a regular system of collection of information will normally result in improvements of technique. For example, the English system of civil registration of births was begun in 1837, but the figures were poor before 1840 and still markedly wrong in 1860.[1] It is hardly possible to make a complete survey of an area the very first time it is done.

The mere existence of multitudinous records, however, is no indication of reliability, since these records may all be misleading and their sheer weight then tells us no more than a scanty set

[1] D. V. Glass, 'A Note on the Under-registration of Births in Britain in the Nineteenth Century', *Population Studies*, V (1951), pp. 70–88. The registration of births cannot be regarded as complete until about 1870, or even 1876.

would. Historical examples of this are China, Italy and Germany, where many small areas have extensive sources of population returns, but we are ignorant of the bases on which these returns were compiled and hence are in no position to judge their real value. What are always wanted are good records rather than many. It is not uncommon to find annual returns in China that were, in fact, copied from one year to the next without change, or else with a few trivial changes for verisimilitude. This would have been done because of laziness, indifference, and slack supervision from the central authority, which were all too common when there seemed no immediate reason why the information should be kept accurate. The Emperor of China issued edicts at times in the hope of raising the standard of Chinese population returns, but although there was an effect on the next year's results, it is impossible to know whether the earlier or the later figure is closer to the truth, since a Chinese official was primarily concerned to please the Emperor, secondarily interested in simplifying his own work, and scarcely at all bothered by truth in the abstract.

It may sometimes be that many records existed at one time but have been lost, and it is then possible that they were checked against each other at the time and thus that the few pieces of information that have come down to us could be trusted. It is, however, usually difficult to discover whether such completeness ever happened in any particular case, but if the opposite is true and there never were many records, we can be sure that the few that there are have comparatively little value.

Although malice is not a common reason for error, whenever false returns are suspected one must always consider what might be the motives for exaggerating or minimizing the size of the population. If there are sufficient data, it may be possible to check wilful misrepresentations of population, which are scarcely ever mutually consistent. Moreover, malice itself suggests that a truer figure was known by the false witness, and so it may be possible to guess what his more honest figure would have been.

It is often said, for instance, that population estimates in the past were commonly exaggerated. However, if one is considering an oriental village, it may well be that the local official deliberately *understated* its population, partly to avoid responsibility and partly to give himself a margin of people to return in some future year if population increase should become fashionable with the Government. Actual accuracy was of less importance to him than administrative convenience, and he might fail to show change when change would need explanation, and show change when change was expected of him. There is evidence that this might have been commonly done in China.

In contrast, an official of a township in the American west in the nineteenth century would overstate its population as a matter of course. He would be quick to explain that the latest census had undercounted his area, and that the population had risen very fast since the census. His motives are perhaps easier for us to understand, but they are not necessarily found everywhere.

The best criterion of the value of a set of population records is often the general one of the degree of interest shown at the time in population questions. The early missionaries in Mexico seem to have been interested in population, but Edward III's Poll-Tax of 1377 was solely to raise money and a count of people was only incidental, so that in the first instance one would expect more accuracy than in the second. Because there had not been a count of heads in England for a very long time, if ever, the 1377 enumeration must be liable to considerable human error also.

THE LIMITS OF INFERENCE

There are, obviously, limits to what can be done by way of inference from the known data. It is always impossible, for instance, to obtain greater accuracy than the size of a sample permits; this is equally true of a modern sample survey, but since there is no possibility of extending the coverage with historical data, the limitation of size has to be taken as absolute. Sampling errors are rarely the most serious source of error in a sample survey, however, and they are not likely to be the most serious shortcoming of historical data. Biases are very common in modern statistical practice, and ingenious experimental designs have been devised to eliminate bias and reduce random error as far as possible. The principle of replication, which amounts to taking comparable measurements on very similar material, is the statistician's means of effecting this end; but it is beyond the scope of an historical study, and although the researcher may suppose that hidden biases exist, he has no way of proving it or of eliminating them except his own judgment of what is or is not probable.

Intricate calculations often impress the outsider and persuade him that their results must somehow be more accurate than a simple average or percentage rate. But such complications are only statistically necessary when the data are of poor quality, and thus always produce poor results unless they were used upon good data merely for show. Of course it is necessary to make calculations when the data are poor, since any results are better than none. It is even more true, however, that the results depend heavily upon the quality of the data and that elaborate calculations are often necessary even to obtain an approximate result. If a calculation depends upon more than one set of figures (e.g. a rate of births divided by population), moreover, it is quite possible that the intrinsic biases in the two sets were different, and so did not cancel out when the calculation was made.

An ingenious system of working has been devised to calculate the main rates in parish register work without avoidable bias; but if the reconstitutable families are a demographically distinct subgroup of the population and are liable to random errors of omission through temporary absence, indifference to baptism as a rite, or carelessness of the registering priest, the demographic results which were so difficult to obtain will still be misleading.

The main point to remember is, therefore, not to squeeze the data too hard. Someone may already have obtained all that really can be obtained from a given set of data; and, if so, historical demography has here reached its natural limit. Interrelationships between different demographic statistics give a check upon each other, but this is no more than a check, it is not a proof of their validity. Arguing by analogy with some known population (e.g. as in a model life-table) may help, assuming that the analogy is sociologically fair, but the society in question may be unique in history, and consequently not susceptible to such an analogy.

Prior knowledge rules out certain impossibilities, of course, in the sense that certain combinations of levels and trends cannot occur. Conversely, it shows the implications of a given set of results in the sense that certain other results would be expected as concomitants. It is best to examine all such implications and to see if they are all reasonable before accepting the apparent results of a set of calculations. There are often not really enough data, however, for there to be any demographic implications worth considering, and all that can be done in such instances is to define the limits within which the true rates presumably lie, which then act as ranges of confidence around the rates actually calculated.

Because population is the best universal yardstick of economic progress, so much will be deduced from the apparent population trends that we must try to assess not just the trends but just how sure we are of their reality. It is all too easy to produce a picture such as Bennett's,[1] in which, with a few exceptions, population always grows; to build a general set of ideas upon it; and then for someone else to turn to the question of population armed with

[1] M. K. Bennett, 'Population, Food and Economic Progress', *Rice Institute Pamphlets*, XXXIX, 2 (July 1952), and reprinted as the first three chapters of his book, *The World's Food*, New York, 1954. His figures for the population of the world by nine major regions for each fiftieth year since A.D. 1000 have often been quoted, because they are unique. However, he does not give the basis of the estimates, and his idea of Indian population (almost constant, 1000–1500, at about 50 million; rising at an increasing rate to 130 million 1500–1750; increasing to 157 million in 1800 and 190 million in 1850) can best be ignored. Similarly, he makes no reduction in the Chinese population after the Mongol conquest, and seems in general a firm believer in the principle that no population can ever have declined unless the evidence for decline is overwhelming.

these very expectations. He is able, only too readily, to reproduce the original curve. This is scarcely confirmation of the first findings so much as copying them by a devious route.

CROSS-CHECKING

Results should always be checked, not merely arithmetically but in terms of historical sense. Indeed, historical interpretation itself can be looked upon as a form of verification of the demographic results, since if no likely explanation can be given for an apparent demographic change, we must begin to doubt whether any such change occurred, and look more closely for flaws in the reasoning or the data that might account for it. The converse, however, is unfortunately untrue; plausible explanations can be readily found for demographic events that later research may show never took place.

There are many ways in which the checking can be done, depending on the circumstances, and all we can do here is to give a number of examples in the hope that the general idea will be grasped. The most all-embracing checks are those using price changes, crop yields, and climatic changes, since these should have long-term and widespread effects if they have any effects at all. They only come in at this stage, and should not be used in the first instance, however, because it is impossible to be precisely quantitative about the effect of such general indicators of change.

Utterström, for instance, has studied the climatic evidence for Europe[1] over the centuries. The temperature has been generally falling since A.D. 600, and it appears that climate in the north of Europe was at its most favourable to population about 1100–1270. The Mediterranean countries, however, enjoyed their best spell rather later, about 1450–1600. While we cannot explain all the changes in population that we know occurred over this long period in terms of climate, or even explain the principal ones in

---

[1] G. Utterström, 'Climatic Fluctuations and Population Problems in Early Modern History', *Scandinavian Economic History Review*, **3**, 1 (1955), pp. 3–47.

such a way, the faster recovery from the Black Death in Italy than in England or Norway, at least, might well have been helped by a better climate.

An illustration of blending diverse historical sources together to make up a demographic picture is provided by Gomme's study[1] of the population of Athens in the fifth and fourth centuries B.C. Gomme not only shows how valuable it can be to cross-check the results from the different sources, but how difficult it is to study historical demography in general terms when even a single city can elicit a monograph that only covers two centuries of its history. Our remarks in Chapter 7 about Marco Polo's evidence on Sung Hangchow and on Moreland's study of Indian population in 1605 are further examples. The latter was partly based on the various writings of European travellers in India in the sixteenth century and on Indian archives for northern India as well as on military data, and is an excellent example of making calculations from the most flimsy data; it is not surprising that his estimate has been widely quoted. Yet he seems to have been chiefly concerned with showing that the population must have been at least as high as a hundred million and not in making a best guess at the true figure. Most critics of Moreland have accordingly increased his estimate by various amounts, although Datta concluded[2] that Moreland's estimate was about right, with a slight allowance for lands in Bengal not assessed by the land-revenue.

Hansen's very thorough study[3] of settlement in northern Jutland up to 1750, using all the available evidence, from Bronze Age mounds to place-name endings, is a similar example that extends much longer in time. He could deduce the changes in the areas of

---

[1] A. W. Gomme, *The Population of Athens in the Fifth and Fourth Centuries B.C.*, Oxford, 1933.

[2] J. M. Datta, 'A Re-examination of Moreland's Estimate of Population in India at the Death of Akbar', *Population Bulletin of India*, **1** (1960), pp. 165–82.

[3] V. O. Hansen, *Landskab og bebyggelse i Vendsyssel: studier over landbebyggelsens udvikling indtil slutningen af 1600-tallet*, Copenhagen, 1964. It includes an English summary, pp. 210–22.

principal settlement at different times, and among his sources were local records from the sixteenth and seventeenth centuries and the evidence of lost villages.

Finally, we give an extended illustration, attempting to estimate the population curve for Egypt ever since the Saïte period, which will lead us to an important general idea about population decline in the past. Eutychius asserts[1] that there were 6 million Egyptians liable to the Poll-Tax at the time of the Arab conquest. Of course, he was writing 200 years after the event, but let us accept his figure. Since this includes only men of fighting age, and a certain number must surely have been exempt from the tax, 25 million people is the most probable corollary as the total population of Egypt in the years following the disastrous plagues between 541 and 600, which means that in 541 Egypt's population would probably have been nearer 30 million. When we recall that in the early-nineteenth century Egypt had fewer than 3 million inhabitants and only 11 million by 1907, 30 million for A.D. 541 may appear unlikely, but that number was reached in 1966 without any very marked industrialization of the country or extension of the cultivable area by extraordinary irrigation works although fertilizers may have improved in 1400 years.

Wałeck-Czernecki used the same general argument,[2] namely that Egypt has changed little in its technology for millennia, and concluded that there might have been 20 to 25 million Egyptians at the time of the Persian conquest in 525 B.C., subject, of course, to a wide margin of error. A period of decline then probably followed if we believe Wałeck-Czernecki's earlier data,[3] leading to 12 or 13 million in about 50 B.C. and only $7\frac{1}{2}$ million in about A.D. 75. He himself, however, had preferred (in 1937) a rising

[1] Eutychius of Egypt, *Annales* (edited by E. Pocock), Oxford, 1658, Vol. II, p. 311. Dr. J. N. Mattock has kindly checked that Pocock's Latin is an accurate translation of the Arabic. See also Charanis (below, p. 391), p. 454.

[2] T. Wałeck-Czernecki, 'La population de l'Égypte à l'époque saite', *Bulletin de l'Institut d'Égypte*, **23**, 1 (1940-1), pp. 37-62.

[3] In his 'La population de l'Égypte ancienne', in *Congrès international de la population, Paris, 1937: Démographie historique*, Vol. II, pp. 7-13.

population for early Roman Egypt, from 8 to 8½ million in 31 B.C. and 8½ to 9 million in the first century A.D., but he wrote this before he realized the case for a high figure at the time of the Persian conquest. We can now sketch out Egyptian population history as follows, some of the figures being, of course, guesses:

	Millions	
664 B.C.	2½	Wałeck-Czernecki (1940–41)
525	20–25	
50	12–13	Wałeck-Czernecki (1937)
75 A.D.	7½	
541	30	
641	25	Eutychius
1798	2½	
1907	11	
1966	30	

Hamdan[1] presumably used surface areas and some multiplier for his statements about the population of medieval Arab cities, among which he says that Alexandria declined from 600,000 at the conquest of 641 to only 100,000 by the year 860. The loss of metropolitan status accounts for Alexandria's decline, no doubt, but its loss of area and presumed loss of population are so large that the population of Egypt must also be regarded as probably declining. We should then find that the Persian, Roman, and Arab conquests all had disastrous effects upon the size of the population of Egypt, just as the Spanish conquest had for Mexico and the Mongol conquest for China. The same thing did not happen after every conquest in history, but it might be worth while to look for examples (The Norman conquest of England probably produced a similar effect.) Animals in captivity often fail to breed; perhaps humans under foreign rule are somewhat the same, until the foreigners are assimilated. Syria, too, appears

[1] G. Hamdan, 'The Pattern of Medieval Urbanism in the Arab World', *Geography*, 47 (1962), pp. 121–34.

to have lost half its population between the second and eighth centuries A.D.[1]

The plagues that Egypt underwent in the nineteenth century are comparatively well known,[2] but the eighteenth century seems to have been no better. Indeed, severe epidemics (especially in Cairo), generally on a scale that surpasses all but the most extreme accounts in Europe, are continually reported in Egypt[3] at all times since 541 except between 719 and 1010. Well before the Black Death, heavy losses occurred in 1053–60 (10,000 deaths a day are claimed for Cairo), 1201 (two-thirds of the whole population died within a few months), and 1296. Cannibalism was reported in the first two of these outbreaks. Twenty thousand deaths a day were occurring in Cairo in November or December 1348, and Gibb and Bowen[4] guess that in the fourteenth century the population of Egypt might have been no more than about 4 million. As well as lesser subsequent plagues, 1437, 1459, 1619, 1643 and 1735 are said to have been especially disastrous years. Thus a possible cause of a great decline in population between 641 and 1800 does exist: epidemics that apparently were more virulent, or at least more fatal, than Europe had at the same period.[5] Unless crop yields were low in the past, a great decline seems irrefutable.

---

[1] See P. K. Hitti, *History of Syria, including Lebanon and Palestine*, London, 1951. In the second century (p. 292), Greater Syria had seven million inhabitants; in the first century after the Moslem conquest (p. 484), only three and a half million.

[2] See A. W. Wakil, *The Third Pandemic of Plague in Egypt. Historical, Statistical and Epidemiological Remarks on the first Thirty-Two Years of its Prevalence*, Cairo, 1932.

[3] *Ibid.*, p. 8.

[4] H. A. R. Gibb and H. Bowen, *Islamic Society and the West: a study of the impact of Western civilisation on Moslem culture in the Near East*, London, 1950, Vol. I, p. 209. They do not give any evidence for their guess, which we believe was rather low, nor do they say whether they mean the beginning or the end of the fourteenth century. See Figure 5.

[5] The extremely low level of nutrition in medieval Egypt has been demonstrated by E. Ashtor, in his 'Essai sur l'alimentation des diverses classes sociales dans l'Orient médiéval', *Annales (E.S.C.)*, **23**, 5 (September–October 1968),

If we take all the evidence on trust, we can now trace the demographic history of Egypt over the past 2,630 years. The Macedonian conquest and the return of the plague in 1010 have been allowed plausible effects, and the result is far from the nearly constant level often advocated (see figure 5). The rates of increase and decrease seem high in figure 5, but are not so in reality. The steepest are, in fact, only equivalent to about $1\frac{1}{2}$ per cent per annum.

The analogy of Greece also suggests that Egypt might well have been underpopulated in 1800; for, after a long period of Turkish rule, the population of Greece in 1829 was less than a million, which must be well below the level in classical times. Population growth in Serbia between 1834 and the present has been similarly rapid to the growth in Egypt and Greece, as though the whole western part of the Ottoman Empire had been restrained in some way.

Nevertheless, the curve of figure 5 is tentative. It is what the evidence suggests, taken at its face value; if we prefer to believe that few changes can possibly have taken place, it will not be difficult to disbelieve any inconvenient data. Although the notion that population tends to decline for a century or more after a foreign conquest cannot be proved from figure 5, it is a basis for further work on the possible validity of that notion. It is often wise to sketch such a population curve for a long period and to check it against every piece of information we have, since it is then much easier to see which pieces fit the assumed pattern and which do not.

EXISTENCE OF INFORMATION

We should distinguish in our minds between what records must have existed and what records probably were never kept, for if

---

pp. 1017–53. In the eleventh century, a humble working Egyptian could buy only food to the value of 1,087 calories per day, Ashtor estimates. Even by the fifteenth century, when this figure was 1,930 calories, it cannot have given much resistance to disease to the lowest class of Egyptians.

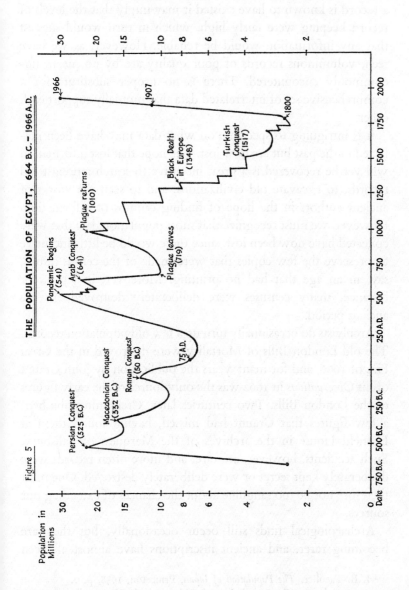

Figure 5

THE POPULATION OF EGYPT, 664 B.C. – 1966 A.D.

Population in Millions

1966
1907
1800

Turkish Conquest (1517)

Black Death in Europe (1348)

Plague returns (1010)

Plague leaves (719)

Pandemic begins (541)

Arab Conquest (641)

Persian Conquest (525 B.C.)

Macedonian Conquest (332 B.C.)

Roman Conquest (50 B.C.)

75 A.D.

Date 750 B.C. 500 B.C. 250 B.C. 1 250 A.D. 500 750 1000 1250 1500 1750 2000

311

a record is known to have existed it may imply that the levels of record keeping were fairly high, which in turn would suggest that any information would be reliable. However, as we have seen, voluminous records of poor quality are by no means uncommonly encountered. There is no proper substitute for a comprehensive set of interrelated data that mutually support each other.

It is intriguing to speculate on what data may have been collected in the past but are now lost. The hope that lost information will yet be recovered is a great incentive to search amongst old records, to excavate old civilizations, and to scan the works of ancient authors in the hope of finding crumbs of information. However, we must recognize that most population data that were collected have now been lost, since there would be little incentive to preserve the few copies that were made of the census results, say, in an age that had no printing. Moreover, in Japan, for instance, many censuses were deliberately destroyed[1] in the ancient period.

Archivists do occasionally turn up a few old population records. The old London Bills of Mortality were destroyed in the Great Fire of 1666, and for many years the publication by John Graunt of his *Observations* in 1662 was the only source of the early figures of the London Bills. Two centuries later, Creighton published[2] a few figures that Graunt had missed, having found them at Hatfield House in the archives of the Marquess of Salisbury. Such accidents, however, are rare, and more often records were deliberately kept secret or were deliberately destroyed. One must therefore not be too sanguine about the chances of extending our sources.

Archaeological finds still occur occasionally, but they are becoming rarer, and ancient inscriptions have almost all been

---

[1] I. B. Taeuber, *The Population of Japan*, Princeton, 1958, p. 9.

[2] C. Creighton, 'The Population of Old London', *Blackwood's Magazine*, 149 (April 1891), pp. 477–96. They refer to the years 1578 to 1583 and also appear in Creighton's book, *A History of Epidemics in Britain*.

read and translated except those of Central America. There is thus not much hope of further discoveries leading to any great changes in our ideas of ancient populations. Finds are rather more frequent for very early periods, but the difficulties of interpreting the ages of skeletons when found, or in establishing the area and density of population in some excavated city, are too great to hold out much promise.

Archaeology is nevertheless our main guide to population trends before the advent of written records. Ice Age remains are still occasionally found, but they really give us no clues to the size or movement of the populations except that we assume, on general grounds and because of the human bones found in a few places, that such populations must have been small and have lived relatively short lives. In Africa, evidence of ancient settlements is still being discovered under the jungle by archaeologists and there is thus some possibility that our ignorance of African populations, past and present, will yet be slightly alleviated. In America, we know that the pre-Columbian civilizations were highly centralized and interested in population numbers, but it has not proved possible to make more than rough guesses at their total size.

Many cities have been unearthed within the last hundred years, and much speculation as to their population has arisen. While these discussions will clearly continue, in the absence of clear knowledge of social conditions at the time it is scarcely possible to narrow the wide limits of our guesses at such ancient population levels. For example, we need to know not merely the area of land cultivated, but the principal crops and the method of cultivation as well, before we can judge how much food would have been produced by a community, and hence reach an upper limit for its population. The ancient Minoan and Etruscan scripts that have not been deciphered may yield us a few clues on the population of their times; and similarly, the Incas of Peru are known to have kept population records on their quippus by means of tying knots in pieces of cord. However, since these people had no written language, although we have many of these quippus we have not the slightest idea what populations they refer to or how large the numbers recorded are. It seems very unlikely that this information will ever be recovered.

Although valuable work may still be done in finding new information, therefore, and although new analysis can still be done, a more immediate task must be to digest the results that are now being produced so rapidly all over Europe. There has, for example, been no satisfactory theory yet explaining why France generally began to have lower levels of fertility during the eighteenth century when the rest of Europe did not. The rise of the medieval towns is not yet explained, except in a general way, and it should be possible to show why some cities grew rapidly while others did not grow at all. A reassessment of the role of plague is now due, and in particular of the mortality caused by the Black Death; the study of Appendix 2 is only meant as a tentative beginning. The social life of seventeenth- and eighteenth-century Europe was manifested in a relatively late age at marriage, and its origin also has received little attention apart from Hajnal's study.[1] Finally, the economic historian's problem of the cause of the first Industrial Revolution in eighteenth-century England has received little attention from demographers (although a good deal from historians), and even the facts on population trends have not been firmly established.

More subtle work on parish registers has a high potential value, although the registers can sometimes be misleading. We may hope to discover the local population trends, and often even their social, medical, economic, and political causes. The precise methods by which numbers were kept down (there is almost always some limitation of families) will be fundamental to our understanding of the society. Late marriages, longer intervals between births, prohibition of marriage for certain classes, infanticide, emigration, euthanasia for the old, various taboos on sexual

[1] J. Hajnal, 'European Marriage Patterns in Perspective', in *Population in History* (edited by Glass and D. E. C. Eversley), London, 1965, pp. 101–43.

intercourse, coitus interruptus, contraception itself—the list is almost endless, and any combination of them in any degree may have occurred. The reason for a change in the methods of restriction would be especially fascinating, but the data scarcely ever permit us to go so far. It can hardly be done for contemporary groups, so that one must not expect the impossible from the very scrappy existing data. Indeed, suggesting how far conclusions can justifiably be pushed is one purpose of this book.

Because it is very tedious to study large numbers of original records, small localities are often the subject of works of historical demography, but they cannot play much part in demographic history until very many such studies are collated. The same applies to short-period studies, where checks are hardly possible on the rates calculated. We cannot say from a short-period study whether the birth-rate, for instance, was evidently at some observed level for a long time, which could then imply an unlikely population at some other time. This would either throw doubt on the accuracy of the figures, or suggest that a change in the birth-rate really occurred, for which an explanation must be sought in turn.

POSSIBILITIES OF NEW HISTORICAL RESEARCH

A great deal of new analytical work is still waiting to be done in Europe, especially on parish registers. This gap has arisen mainly because searching through parish registers is extremely tedious and therefore costly, at least in terms of time. In England, a concerted effort has recently been made to collect and collate the information from most of the existing parish registers, organized by the Cambridge Group for the Historical Study of Population and Social Structure. Such organized co-ordination of results is very important, since as well as a check on the value of existing registers as a sample of the whole country, it may be possible to raise the rate of reconstitution of families and to measure local migration by relating the data from neighbouring parishes. It is an attractive field of study to many people, since it requires little previous training and yet yields important results. Voluntary work can therefore often help, but volunteers should know that a full investigation really takes a lifetime. One or two parishes studied for themselves can be completed in a year or two; but there is little value in such small-scale studies unless they can be related to many others.

The main unfulfilled need in English historical demography is for a careful re-working of data that have been available for a long time, such as the ecclesiastical censuses, in order to link Russell's medieval study with Krause's beginning on the turn of the eighteenth–nineteenth centuries.[1] It should be possible, in time, to assess: (1) the date at which the marriage-pattern changed to the modern one (perhaps in the sixteenth century); (2) the birth-rate in seventeenth- and eighteenth-century England; (3) the normal extent of under-registration of baptisms as compared with births, and of burials as compared with deaths, before 1780; (4) the height of the various mortality peaks after 1375, which Russell ignored (e.g. 1390–1, 1420, 1439, 1464–5, 1503–5, 1557–9, 1623, 1657–8, and 1728–9, all of which are indicated, by chroniclers, counts of wills, or Short's parish register analyses, as years of high mortality); and, of course, (5) the population itself, year by year, from 1377 or earlier to 1801. The results could not be final, but would at least serve as a guide to the Cambridge Group's studies, and their findings could later be used to modify the results.

Corresponding studies have been begun in most of the countries of Europe, and latterly in the north-eastern United States.

[1] It is surprising that Russell and Krause should both be Americans, but we English historians and demographers have mostly either used wrong methods or spent our efforts on particular studies at the expense of the general. Local history, fascinating as it may be, tells us little of interest about the progress of the nation. A tentative beginning has been made by G. S. L. Tucker, 'English Pre-Industrial Population Trends', *Economic History Review*, 2nd Series, XVI, 2 (1963), pp. 205–18, but he is surely mistaken in his view that the Dalrymple list might omit many Nonconformists.

Clearly, it would be valuable to relate the work of different national groups together, but owing to the purely local and voluntary interest that often underlies the fundamental work, publications are usually in rather obscure journals and almost invariably in the local language. To study current European work in the field of parish register research with thoroughness requires a fair knowledge of at least eight languages, as well as access to a wide range of journals. All that can be said is that the method of compilation of the data and of reconstituting families is always now done by the French method first published in 1956, and although this method might be varied or possibly improved upon to suit local conditions, for the sake of comparability one must hope that standardization will prevail.

Apart from parish register work, there is no particular boom in historical demography at present. Tax lists for medieval Turkey[1] apparently exist in immense numbers, unpublished and largely unread, in the archives at Istanbul. An opportunity clearly exists here for someone who knows the Turkish language. The taxation returns for sixteenth-century Mexico languished in Seville for many years, but in the last quarter of a century they have been studied extensively and some surprising conclusions have been drawn from them. Probably many other old sets of tax records exist; but in Europe, at least, most must have been studied by now except in what was once the Turkish Balkans. Wills, on the other hand, may yet yield a good deal of indirect data about mortality trends, especially in the fifteenth and sixteenth centuries, and the English ecclesiastical censuses of 1563, 1603, 1676 and 1688 deserve much more attention from demographers than they have received.

The Indian census of 1961 undertook to study population estimates of India before the first Indian census of 1872. These will be little more than compilations of the estimates made by foreign observers, chiefly agents of the East India Company, of population in areas of various size at various dates. However, the census authorities are attempting to delineate the areas in question and

[1] See pp. 132–3.

to ascertain the basis, if any, of each estimate. One volume has been published to date, dealing with estimates made in the decade 1820 to 1830, but eight other volumes, dealing with periods before and after, are planned.

Our information on India before the seventeenth century is at present extremely sketchy compared with that on China. Earlier than Moreland's estimate for 1605 and particularly before 1500, we really have no idea of the population of India at all, except for various attempts (see pp. 228–9) to estimate it in the fourth and third centuries B.C. Since the total population was then apparently not widely different from what it was nearly 2,000 years later, some people have argued that the population probably remained the same throughout the period, apart from minor fluctuations. Yet this clearly need not have been the case, and the population of medieval India, say from 1100 to 1500, is particularly worthy of attention for this is the India to which Columbus wished to find a new sailing route. Its wealth and power had captured the imagination of Europeans in a way that the China that Marco Polo had visited had not, and India may very well have been even more populous than China at that period and even more wealthy.

Information is usually scanty outside Europe except in places under direct European influence. The main exception is China, where voluminous records of population, taxation, army size, and famine relief exist, as well as historical fragments and genealogies, but few of them have been studied by Western scholars, and their reliability must be highly variable. A hundred and thirty years ago, Western knowledge of ancient and medieval Chinese population was little worse than it is today, although not because of any lack of basic material for further research. Printing was widespread in China at least 800 years earlier than in Europe, and so far fewer records were lost; further work will depend in the first instance, therefore, upon recovering these printed results. The population lists of medieval Japan have been more thoroughly studied, although with very conflicting results. It is possible that the population of Japan fluctuated between wide limits before 1600, but without thorough study of Japanese history it would be unwise to conclude either this or that the population was sensibly constant.

The eventual goal must be to determine as far as possible the complete history of the numbers of population in the world. Such a history will always be susceptible of improvement, and merely to attempt to write it is to see the shortcomings of our present knowledge.

CHAPTER 10

Implications

INTRODUCTION

History is really about people, and the statistical approach of demography is repugnant to many historians, although they recognize the value of demographic results; statisticians, on the other hand, are rarely much interested in history. An intermediate position, however, in which statistical data from too few places, for too short a time, and with too few cases, are analysed in detail as though they could tell us very much, is just as inadequate. The natural interest of individual lives and specific events is then sacrificed without any real gain in knowledge of general conditions.

The trend of population in history is no more than a convenient method of summarizing the experience of a society in time, although it should also be recognized that population is worthy of historical study in its own right. However, a thorough study of population requires a study of other conditions, especially social conditions. We cannot suppose that the age at which the king marries has much effect on his subjects, or that a long-lived prime minister is very relevant to longevity in the population at large, but the average man of the statistician is both more and less of a man than any real, representative man. He is more typical, but less probable; closer to the norm, farther from humanity. It is he that the demographer studies, not the rich variety of humankind. The demographer is the accountant of history, not the general manager.

Explaining the facts found by the demographer is all too easy; once the facts are known, possible explanations spring readily to mind. But since we cannot explain many contemporary demographic trends properly—the rise in the English birth-rate between

1955 and 1964, for instance, has not been explained satisfactorily—
it is presumptuous to suppose that we can really explain many past
trends in population. Historical demographers who have worked
for long at a series of data become very wary; and the author has
more than once discarded a piece of draft explanation for a result
that later turned out to have been caused by an arithmetical
mistake. The task of doing all one's own calculations has its
advantages.

Both more and less is, in fact, known about population in the
past than is often assumed. That is to say, partial censuses, parish
registers, nominative lists for certain places, and archaeological
findings, can give us more information than historians have
usually recognized; on the other hand, we really know little
about medieval population and less about such hoary problems as
the decline of the Roman Empire from the demographic point
of view. Our knowledge of non-European populations in history,
moreover, is extremely poor.

If population evidence is to be the yard-stick by which we
measure societies, many interesting discoveries may be made.
For example, armies became much larger during the Chou
dynasty in China from the time when the number of warring
states had been reduced to seven, which happened about half-way
through the dynasty. This suggests that population may have
increased, since the total number of men in China who might be
soldiers at one time was undoubtedly much larger when there
were only seven armies for a soldier to join than when there had
been hundreds. This in turn suggests that the political simplification had caused economic progress.

In contrast, the evidence on baptisms in England between 1780
and 1840, although much more detailed than the old Chinese
records, and probably quite complete as records of actual Anglican
baptisms, must first be made to tell us a good deal about religious
observance if we are ever to gain much from it about population.
Thanks to the accident that censuses were taken from 1801 onwards, we can see that the figures were well below the numbers

of births, and in fact represent a smaller fraction of the births after 1780 than they did earlier in the eighteenth century. An example in which the data become less accurate as time goes on is particularly valuable, since it probably happened often, but it is difficult to prove and offends our notions of progress.

Population is probably the fundamental reason why seventeenth-century Holland and Turkey and eighteenth-century France were powerful states, and why Russia was relatively weak until the middle of the nineteenth century. In these cases we can see that the size and trend of population was the dominating political factor of the day; but this is so only because we have independent information on political history.

The long-term trends in population are even more important than the immediate demographic causes of particular events if we are trying to study history from demography, but we may also study demography from history. When we consider the age of marriage in Roman times, the population of Renaissance city-states in Italy, or national populations before the Black Death, history in its normal meaning must be used to guide our thinking. Clues to the possible trends can be obtained from historical knowledge that will prevent at least the grosser mistakes of historical demography.

It is useful also to know the causes of demographic change whenever we can. Three examples where there is little doubt of the causes are given below:

1. The brown rat replaced the black rat in Europe during the first half of the eighteenth century, and one indirect result was that plague virtually disappeared from Europe after having been endemic for some 350 years.

2. The decline in the birth-rate in late-nineteenth-century Europe was chiefly socially determined. In an industrializing society, many children in the family were something of a liability during their upbringing, and not much insurance against their parents' old age. In agricultural communities, with the family as the unit of the work force, the opposite is true: the children

contribute to the family's wealth at an early age and because they do not often leave the family circle when adults, the old people are supported. Economic considerations, however, can also affect the birth-rate under either social system, and no doubt genetic and psychological factors are also important.

3. The great increase in Chinese population during the eighteenth century was mainly owing to migration into the thinly-settled south of China and the introduction on a wide scale of a new staple crop, maize—discovered, of course, in America by Europeans and previously cultivated there for millennia.

SOCIAL IMPLICATIONS OF DEMOGRAPHIC CHANGES

It may be unnecessary by now to remark that population has great implications for society at large. The most obvious implication is that man needs space and every society has always been limited in space. The history of how men have met, dodged, or ignored the problem of limited space and pressure of numbers has lessons for the present and future. It is not an encouraging story. The great migrations from Asia into Europe between the third and sixth centuries and between the twelfth and fifteenth centuries were almost certainly caused more by population pressure than by the ambition of conquerors.

War, it seems, is less often caused by individual men than by social causes, mainly demographic, going back for a long time before the event, and is then set off by the individuals of the day. Similarly, overcrowding in cities is caused less by the rapacity of property owners than by population pressure, the growth of trade, and the absence of mechanized transport. It may be too late to avert trouble by the time its threat is manifest.

There is still much debate about the typical European size of household before the Industrial Revolution, but it was certainly quite small, similar in fact to today and not normally in double figures; although in some towns there might be a large number living in a single house because several families shared it. The most frequent estimates of the average size of a household are 4 or 5 persons, with $3\frac{1}{2}$ and 6 maintained by a few scholars. This pattern was disturbed by the social changes, brought about by the economic changes, caused by the technical changes that we know collectively as the Industrial Revolution, which in turn was made possible by financial and political conditions—which in turn depended, of course, on social conditions. The unravelling of this complex of cause and effect is obviously a difficult task. In the age of rapid industrial growth we find, simultaneously, rising prosperity, booming towns, large families, and a great increase in migration.

It might be thought that, before the age of general use of contraceptives, fertility was always high and always about the same, at a level close to the maximum physically possible. This is much too naïve a view. It seems probable that births have been controlled in practice by one means or another since the dawn of civilization, and there is an unanswered question of how it was done, and how much, in every historical society and at every period.[1] The social consequences of small families and late marriage, both of which are more characteristic of northern and western Europe than elsewhere, provide another example. They might, indeed, be causes of the distinctive European attitude towards life. Of course, it is an open question whether the attitude caused the demographic trends or was caused by them; it is impossible to reach an ultimate cause, and a measured demographic trend is just as artificial a concept as a social attitude. However, much further work could be done in this field.

With a better knowledge of population movements, a good deal of history can be seen as drifting down a stream, most of the leading events fitting into the demographically determined pattern, and a few, interestingly, resisting it. For example, the Hundred Years War is made much more intelligible if we know

[1] For a general discussion of this subject, with ample documentation, see N. E. Himes, *Medical History of Contraception*, Baltimore, 1936, and (reprinted) New York, 1963.

that France had a population at least four times as large as England's instead of their being about the same, as they have been in the last thirty or forty years. The population of Japan before and after the Meiji restoration shows that what had happened was a great expansion following a period of stability, the explanation of which lies in the social changes that took place. The collapse of the social system of Mexico in the sixteenth century is reflected in the tremendous fall in population—the largest authenticated decline anywhere, although parts of China must have had a similar loss at the time of the Taiping rebellion. Germany in 1648, after the Thirty Years War, was depopulated about as much as Europe was in 1351, immediately after the Black Death, but this is a smaller scale of decline.

It might be thought dangerous to concentrate on numbers at the expense of quality, yet quality usually presupposes numbers. Where it does not, there is likely to be a sharp discontinuity in population trends, as when the Conquistadores invaded America, reflecting the sharp disparity between the Spanish and the American culture before Columbus. One may expect, therefore, to find signs that will warn against undue reliance upon mere numbers.

In a sense, population can thus be used to explain history, and memorizing the population curves becomes a simple way of memorizing history, as worthy of effort as memorizing dates of kings or of battles. The facts of increase or decrease, of course, are all-important, the explanations secondary. One may, indeed, trace trends in the very civilization and culture of mankind from the population figures, and conversely one may try to build up a population history from knowledge of the conditions of society. The whole sweep of man's existence is then reduced to a curve, the curve of population against time, and demography gives us an epitome of history; a useful device, similar to the economist's device of reducing a national economy to a single figure for national income. Such simplification requires skill from the simplifier but is easy to understand.

If the total numbers at only one date are well known, it may still be difficult to assess the trend of population. For instance, it would be relatively little use to know that India had around a hundred million inhabitants in the twelfth century (if indeed that is the case, for the period has received no study), since we have no idea of the expansion or contraction of the population at that time. If, however, the trend can be estimated, even roughly, we are in a strong position. For, *a priori* at least, we correlate increase with progress. The population data for Augsburg[1] from 1501 onwards, for example, are a sufficient guide to the state of the town for most purposes. Plagues struck Augsburg often during the sixteenth century but numbers were almost maintained. In the seventeenth century more deadly epidemics struck, and not until the nineteenth century were numbers regained. Clearly, the Thirty Years War was largely to blame, but the demographer can deduce that there was a calamity from the figures alone, and he knows in advance that it had a more serious effect than the earlier plagues.

DEMOGRAPHIC PATTERNS IN HISTORY

It needs to be recognized that population has not always and everywhere increased throughout the ages. A simple calculation shows that over a very long period the net rate of growth must have been extremely low—less, for instance, than the rate of

---

[1] See W. Maitland, 'Remarks upon the aforesaid Bills of Mortality for the Cities of Dresden and Augsburg', *Philosophical Transactions of the Royal Society*, 38, 428 (April–May–June 1733), p. 98; and A. Schreiber, 'Die Entwicklung der Augsburger Bevölkerung vom Ende des 14. Jahrhunderts bis zum Beginn des 19. Jahrhunderts', *Archiv für Hygiene und Bakteriologie*, CXXIII (March 1940), pp. 90–177. They both try to calculate the progress of the population from the Bills alone, although Schreiber also has data on the numbers of houses in the city. However, the population of over 50,000 in the first decade of the sixteenth century seems to have lived at an occupancy rate of about 18 to a house, which is so high that even a small variation in the rate would render calculations based on the number of occupied houses highly misleading.

growth found in England in any single year whatever for 200 years past. A constancy of this order is hardly credible, and quite large fluctuations are generally allowed to have occurred. But though these fluctuations are undoubted over short periods—five or ten years, say—they quite probably occurred sometimes over a century or more, and although they can be found for small communities, they can equally be postulated (by extrapolation) for whole nations and even continents or subcontinents. Whatever the cause of decline—bad harvests, civil strife, disease, repressive taxation, or the spread of ignorance of hygiene—it is more likely to apply to a large area than just to one village, even though it is only the village's records that we happen to find.

It is easy, too, to imagine that population cannot decrease unless an obvious reduction is set in train, by birth control or epidemics, for instance. Yet the Castilian re-conquest of Spain almost certainly resulted in a reduction of the total Iberian population, for the Moorish system of irrigation in Spain was highly elaborate and based upon extensive experience of countries where water is scarce. The Castilians, on the other hand, had little knowledge of such countries, apart from their own. They may not have appreciated sufficiently the overriding need to conserve water resources, and allowed the system to become inefficient. Water conservation requires, perhaps, more social control than a national liberation movement can command.[1] Had the Spaniards realized what the consequences of their inaction would be, no doubt they would have acted differently; but they could only be wise after the event.

A similar experience befell Mexico after the Spanish conquest, when the total population shrank rapidly at a time when the Spanish missionaries were most keen to save the souls of the natives. Although there was no policy of extermination, and not even the hostility towards the Indians that the English

---

[1] This is a main thesis of K. A. Wittfogel's book *Oriental Despotism. A Comparative Study of Total Power*, London, 1957. It has, however, met with strong criticism.

settlers in America had, the population fell until it was perhaps no more than 10 per cent of its pre-Columbian figure. The main cause seems to have been that the Spaniards over-taxed and over-worked the Indians, while new diseases ran riot amongst them. Without an explicit policy of conserving the Indian population, such a result was inevitable.

While the political and economic lessons to be drawn from these considerations may not be obvious, at least the historian's duty is clear. He must remember that population must have gone down as often (or very nearly as often), and as much, as it went up; and he should not expect all populations that he studies to be either steady or else increasing. It may be that he is more interested in the expanding than in the contracting phases of a society, but from the general point of view declines must be expected, and expected often.

This is not the place to analyse all the causes of population changes, nor to formulate a grand theory of population in relation to social change. The value to the historian of a wider knowledge of events than the contemporary scene and his own speciality is that it enables him to appreciate what are the connected signs to look for appropriate to a particular pattern of population evolution. Knowing the demography, he can consider what to look for in the history.

If, for example, a population appears to have a very high birth-rate, he will know that this does not relate to a rapid rate of increase unless the death-rate is fairly low; but it does imply that a large proportion of the population would have been young, and it is likely that marriage would have been early, and probably nearly universal. If some of these phenomena do not appear, it is likely that the premiss was wrong, and that the birth-rate was not especially high. Perhaps it is known, in another instance, that the death-rate was very high; his conclusion will then be that the population must have been declining, since the birth-rate cannot exceed a certain level. These are only examples, but they illustrate the kind of reasoning that is possible.

COMPARISONS OF TRENDS

Without formulating a cyclical theory of population change, it is often tempting to assert in social history that 'it's all happened before'. Apart from the sheer total size of modern world population, which is unprecedented, there must be few demographic problems, indeed, that have not been faced before. Even the high densities of modern cities could have been surpassed in ancient times. Periods of rapid growth must have occurred whenever a higher civilization overwhelmed a lower one, seized all the territory, and for a few generations had no problems of resources. There are many examples of this, from North America to Java, in the past 200 or 300 years, but it will also have happened earlier. Large-scale migrations have occurred before, as waves of conquerors, as slowly-moving herdsmen, or even as artisans and merchants gradually permeating an alien society.

Natural disasters have been the lot of man throughout history. He has been kept to a trivial rate of population growth at all periods save a few, but the last two or three centuries show rapid increase almost everywhere. This will not continue for more than one more century at the most without some disaster catching up with the human race. We stand wide open to new diseases, as mortal as the Black Death, or famines, or wars. In one view of history, national rivalry can be seen as a struggle between nations for population. In the summer, all can make hay; in the winter, starvation and death attack all but a few. The present summer has extended longer than most, but will not last for ever. The only alternative is almost universal birth control, yet our understanding of the social motivation that leads to any kind of restriction on fertility is still very imperfect. Such thoughts, however, are gloomy as well as speculative; one could equally recall that the human race has survived all calamities, and expect that demographic changes will appear within the next few decades that will make the present birth control efforts seem as odd as the populationist schemes of many countries thirty years ago now seem.

It is of considerable interest to consider demographic history in the broadest sense, as for example the question, raised in the eighteenth century by Montesquieu,[1] Hume,[2] and Wallace,[3] as to the relative size of the population of Europe (including South-West Asia and North Africa) in the age of classical Greece and Rome and in the eighteenth century. Hume, in particular, believed that ancient nations were not populous compared with his own day, while Montesquieu and Wallace advocated the contrary. Montesquieu, in fact, went so far as to claim that population had declined to one-tenth of what it was in the days of the Roman Empire.

This is, clearly, a most important matter. On the one hand, Montesquieu was arguing that Regency France was in a degenerate state, in numbers at least, compared with Trajan's day. It is easy to hang from his idea the implication that we should revere the ancients, study their works (both artefacts and literature), and strive to emulate that Golden Age. Our inferiority seems almost absolute, progress almost impossible; the best hope is to achieve anew what had been done long ago. Hume's view was totally different, and let us consider it first without regard to which of the two philosophers was nearer the truth. For Hume, George II's time represented the highest state of civilization yet achieved. Progress and prosperity were everywhere, and the ancients largely irrelevant. Some decline in population following the barbarian invasions may be allowed, but since the Renaissance the old level of population had once more been achieved, and 200 years of steady increase had raised numbers well above anything the Romans ever knew. Consequently, we should be confident, trust ourselves, pay little attention to any history except the

[1] Montesquieu, *Lettres Persanes*, Letters CXII to CXXII.

[2] D. Hume, 'Of the Populousness of Antient Nations', in *Political Discourses*, Edinburgh, 1752, pp. 155–261.

[3] R. Wallace, *A dissertation on the numbers of mankind in ancient and modern times; in which the superior populousness of antiquity is maintained. With an appendix, containing additional observations . . . and some remarks on Mr Hume's political discourse, of the populousness of antient nations*, Edinburgh, 1753.

immediate past, and expect even better things in the future. The Augustan Age is now.

It is a fact of the history of thought that Hume's view prevailed over Montesquieu's. On the whole, his idea that ancient nations could not be regarded as populous by modern (that is, eighteenth century) standards was accepted. The other implications were accepted also with, of course, very important results; it is, however, possible to overdo the belittling of population in the past.

One does not know to what extent Hume's arguments about population helped the various liberal movements of the eighteenth and nineteenth centuries. The possibility that his results may be used for a quasi-political purpose should, however, encourage every historical demographer to be as unambiguous and precise as he can.

CONCLUSIONS

Populations ebb and flow, and the current flow in almost all parts of the world must not blind us to the fact. Many historical populations might be regarded as stationary over a very long period, yet considerable increases or decreases could still have taken place within a part of that period, lasting perhaps a century or so. It may happen that the period of most historical interest coincides with only one phase in a longer cycle. Such spectacular changes in population are the clearest reminder that man is not in full control of nature, although he influences it to an incalculable extent. The full effect of human actions may follow the cause by a century or more, by which time the original intentions have been forgotten and the original protagonist is dead. The matter therefore arouses little political interest, but should concern those who are interested in human affairs at large.

The immediate future of mankind is not our concern in this book. It is impossible even to tell which would be better against the wintry blasts to come: plenty of people, or fewer but stronger people. It is next to impossible to achieve any particular goal of this nature by deliberate government action, even if there were agreement on what was desirable. It is difficult to argue that the continued survival of any one nation at the collective expense of all the others would be better or worse than its gradual extinction, and impossible to agree on international population growth quotas for the various countries. In the study of the past, everything is simpler.

The only further point that may be forgotten is that the inevitable declines in population often meant no records. The winners not merely write history; they handle the chronicles as well. The losers, exterminated or nearly so, are allowed to become as if they had never been. So is historical evidence on population: the absent evidence is mainly of tottering empires, crumbling cities, decadent peoples. Their numbers dwindled, and few or no records remain to tell us the fact, let alone its explanation.

Appendices

Appendices

APPENDIX 1

Stable Populations

INTRODUCTION

New techniques of demographic analysis, centring round the idea of a stable population, have been developed in recent years. The same techniques have wide applications in historical work, but their original purpose was to make estimates of the birth- and death-rates of present-day populations in the many parts of the world where registration of births and deaths is incomplete or non-existent. Historians may be able to benefit, therefore, from the great efforts that the United Nations and other bodies have been making to get fairly reliable modern demographic data from these countries. The high birth- and death-rates normally expected in both historical and developing countries' populations suggest that there is some comparison between them and hence that the same methods may elucidate the figures for both.

DEVELOPMENT OF THE IDEA OF A STABLE POPULATION

All the early authors on population recognized that mortality varied with age, and over the years a method of measuring mortality was developed that is widely used for life insurance calculations. This method depends upon two important ideas, a *stationary population* and a *life-table*. The research techniques that concern the historian depend upon extensions of these two ideas to those of a *stable population* and a *model life-table*.

Edmund Halley is usually credited with having invented[1] the life-table in 1693, but his life-table for the mortality of the city of Breslau between 1687 and 1691 was, as he realized, based on the assumption

---

[1] E. Halley, 'An Estimate of the Degrees of the Mortality of Mankind, drawn from curious Tables of the Births and Funerals at the City of Breslaw; with an Attempt to ascertain the Price of Annuities upon Lives', *Philosophical Transactions of the Royal Society*, **17**, 196 (January 1692/3), pp. 596–610, and 198 (March 1693), pp. 654–6.

that the population was stationary, for which he had no warrant. It was not until the nineteenth century that correctly calculated life-tables became commonplace and the theory of their construction was no longer a matter for debate. The principles are: first, calculate the death-rates by age that apply to the population in question, using registrations of deaths by age and census data for the numbers at risk at each age (in practice, the sexes are generally taken separately and the ages taken in 5-year groups); second, convert these death-rates by age into probabilities of dying between two particular moments of life (in practice, one takes birthdays, normally at five-year intervals, and so calculates the probability of dying between 20 and 25, between 25 and 30, and so on); third, suppose that a *constant* number of births will occur every year for ever, to which the probabilities of death just calculated perpetually apply.

It is then only a matter of arithmetic (with some special extra care about the first years of life) to calculate how many people survive at each stage of life. Since the annual number of births is constant and all the mortality rates never change, the population not only remains the same size for ever, but its age-distribution also does not change. Such a population is therefore aptly called *stationary*. The *life-table* associated with a stationary population comprises its age-distribution, its age-specific mortality rates, and the expectation of (future) life at each age, which is easily calculable from the table of survivors.

A stationary population, although interesting, hardly corresponds to reality, for populations do not remain unchanging in every respect for long periods of time. As an advance upon the idea of a stationary population, we relax the condition that the number of births remains invariable, and allow them to increase (or decrease) in a regular way by an arbitrary proportion each year. Applying the same age-specific mortality rates will now result in a population that increases (or decreases) indefinitely at a constant rate, but its age-structure, the relative numbers at each age, remains the same throughout—although the proportions of the population in the different age-groups do not stay the same as they were for the stationary population. Such a population, although continually changing (indeed, continuously changing, since it is purely theoretical), has therefore an important degree of stability, and is termed a *stable population*. We can see at once that a stationary population is merely a special case of a stable population, in which the arbitrary rate of change in the annual number of births is allowed to be nil.

This element of arbitrariness about a stable population is important. We can soon see, if we make the calculations, that the age-distribution that arises for a given set of mortality rates is highly dependent upon the birth-rate selected. If, however, we were to try rather different sets of mortality rates, and choose the arbitrary birth-rate to be the same each time, the age-distribution would be scarcely affected.[1] Because of this fact, knowledge of the age-distribution of a population (as at a census) gives us a good indication of fertility.[2] It is natural to want standard tables of reference for estimating birth-rates from the age-structure, and for this purpose *model life-tables* have been constructed for stable populations.

We have, however, anticipated the development of model life-tables, which must now be explained. It had long been obvious that mortality rates by age (which are the basis of any life-table) form a pattern with a peak immediately after birth, falling steeply in childhood, and afterwards rising steadily throughout adulthood. Various attempts have been made to fit mathematical expressions to the empirical data, and in 1955 the United Nations published its *Model Life Tables*,[3] intended for under-developed countries, and constructed by epitomizing statistically the experience of 158 life-tables in a single set of figures. These could be regarded as standard mortality patterns, and the idea was that if mortality could be accurately measured in some country only between two ages (as, for example, between 40 and 60), the mortality at all other ages could be read off from the tables, as well as the expectation of life at any age and (assuming the population was stationary) the death-rate.

Ledermann and Breas presently showed[4] that the U.N. Tables were

---

[1] See A. J. Coale, 'The Effects of Changes in Mortality and Fertility on Age Composition', *Milbank Memorial Fund Quarterly*, XXXIV, 1 (January 1956), pp. 79–114.

[2] Much of the early work on stable populations was done for Egypt. See M. A. El-Badry, 'Some Demographic Measurements for Egypt Based on the Stability of Census Age Distributions', *ibid.*, XXXIII, 3 (July 1955), pp. 268–305; and S. H. Abdel-Aty, 'Life-Table Functions for Egypt Based on Model Life-Tables and Quasi-Stable Population Theory', *ibid.*, XXXIX, 2 (April 1961), pp. 350–77.

[3] United Nations, Department of Social Affairs, Population Branch, *Age and Sex Patterns of Mortality. Model Life Tables for Under-developed Countries*, New York, 1955.

[4] S. Ledermann and J. Breas, 'Les dimensions de la mortalité', *Population*, 14, 4 (1959), pp. 637–82. See also Ledermann, 'Différence de Mortalité des

inadequate, however, in that mortality rates do not seem to depend upon a single parameter. Knowing the rate of mortality at one age does not, in fact, let us predict it with great accuracy at any other ages, except those that are close.

Coale and Demeny, after studying 326 life-tables for each sex, came to the conclusion that four regional patterns of mortality could be discerned,[1] corresponding roughly to Central Europe, Scandinavia, Southern Europe, and the rest of the world, calling them East, North, South, and West respectively. Several life-tables were rejected before making the calculations as being erroneous or inconsistent, and very few came before 1870. However, of those that were left, 31 life-tables were used to calculate the parameters of the 'East' model, 9 for 'North', 22 for 'South' and 130 for 'West'. The different patterns found are thus more exactly reflected than in a single set of tables, and it is interesting that as well as 77 tables for parts of Europe (20 of them from the U.K.), 53 more for other parts of the world conform to the 'West' pattern, which thus assumes the stature of normalcy, with the other three regional patterns as deviants from it.[2]

The major achievement of Coale and Demeny and their helpers at Princeton, however, is the construction of sets of tables[3] showing the age-distribution, age at death, birth-rate, death-rate, gross reproduction rate, dependency ratio, and several other demographic parameters that can be found, for stable populations for each sex, at each of 24 general levels of mortality, and for each of the four regional mortality patterns. In 864 pages of actual tables, a really comprehensive basis is thus laid for demographic calculations on stable populations.

Of course, questions may be raised about this procedure. The Tables are in fact based upon populations where the expectation of life at birth

Adultes selon le Sexe et les Causes de la Nosologie: Recherche Typologique', *International Population Conference* (New York), 1961, I, pp. 702–12. The latest French work on model life-tables is described in H. Le Bras, 'Nouvelles tables-types de mortalité. Presentation d'un cahier de l'I.N.E.D.', *Population*, **23**, 4 (July–August 1968), pp. 739–44.

[1] Coale and P. Demeny, *Regional model life tables and stable populations*, Princeton, 1966.

[2] See also R. S. Kurup, 'A revision of Model Life Tables', *World Population Conference* (Belgrade), 1965, Session B.7, paper 314.

[3] *Op. cit.*

was between 35 and 70, and so the mortality schedules calculated for expectations of life at birth of 20 to 35, which are important for historical demography in Western Europe because they are what is usually found before 1800, are really only extrapolations of observation. The mortality schedules that arise in pre-industrial populations in Europe may, moreover, either conform to a fifth pattern, or be caused by errors and omissions in the data.

The best data from before 1700, in the sense of being least liable to omission through migration or arbitrary methods of registration, are those for the ruling families of Europe, given by Peller.[1] If one attempts to fit a model life table for the age-specific mortality rates, an odd pattern emerges; the sovereign princes born between 1500 and 1700 seem quite different from those born after 1700. It makes little difference whether the U.N. Tables or the Princeton Tables are preferred, but in fact we choose the U.N. Tables in what follows because the ruling families were spread across Europe, and we shall express the best fit to the mortality rates by age in terms of the corresponding expectation of life. Between 15 and 49, female mortality alone is used, because males in this stratum of society were unusually liable to die violent deaths in the sixteenth and seventeenth centuries; the effect is a slight favourable bias in the estimated conditions.

The infant mortality of the ruling families then implies about 35 years of expectation of life; mortality between 1 and 4, 41 years; and between 5 and 14, 43 years. Mortality at ages 15 to 24 suggests a lower level, about 36 years' expectation of life at birth; ages 25 to 39 suggest an expectation of only 30; and ages 40 to 49, about 27. The expectation of life at 50, age-specific mortality rates no longer being available, was less than 15 years, suggesting that at birth it would only have been about 24.

From the age of 5 onwards, therefore, the observed mortality increases much faster than the mortality in a model life-table, and the overall level of mortality that seems appropriate falls steadily from an expectation of life at birth of 43 to one of 24. The mortality levels before 15 seem odd, however, since between the ages of 1 and 15, the princes and princesses of the sixteenth century (without the seventeenth)

---

[1] S. Peller, 'Births and Deaths among Europe's Ruling Families since 1500', in *Population in History* (edited by D. V. Glass and D. E. C. Eversley), London, 1965, pp. 87–100.

apparently enjoyed lower mortality rates than those of any subsequent period until the second half of the nineteenth century. The sixteenth-century child mortality might therefore be understated. However, after the age of 15 there is no scope for corrections on a wide enough scale to make the data conform to any existing model life-table, although it might be instructive to assess the extent of violent death amongst the princes of the sixteenth century.[1]

If the ruling families are in any way representative of mortality conditions before the modern era, model life-tables will have much less value in historical demography than has been hoped. Conceivably, plague might explain the great change in the mortality pattern. The mortality of the British nobility,[2] unfortunately, is not easy to check accurately against model life-tables, since before about 1750 the incidence of poorly known ages at death is rather high. The bunching at certain ages is an artefact of the method of analysis used, however, and further analysis of the data may yet help to decide the important question of whether or not a special mortality pattern is required. Under the age of 15, almost nothing can be said, because the corrections to the births and the conventional ages given to those dying 'young' or 'in infancy' create a large part of the apparent mortality before 1700 or 1750. The Colyton data[3] also suggest that mortality was relatively light for the generation born in the sixteenth century in infancy and childhood as compared with adult life. There are so many qualifications to make to this result, however, that it cannot be regarded as proved.

[1] Compare T. H. Hollingsworth, 'A Demographic Study of the British Ducal Families', originally in *Population Studies*, XI, 1 (July 1957), and reprinted with revision in *Population in History* (edited by Glass and Eversley), London, 1965, pp. 354–78. About 19 per cent of all males who died over 15 suffered violent deaths in the period in question (p. 359).

Another possible source of fairly good mortality data before 1700 is the Genevan registration records, which give deaths by single years of age and seem to be quite complete. See E. Mallet, 'Recherches historiques et statistiques sur la population de Genève, son mouvement annuel et sa longévité, depuis le XVIe siècle jusqua'à nos jours (1549–1833)', *Annales d'hygiène publique et de médecine légale*, XVII, 1 (January 1837), pp. 5–172.

[2] See Hollingsworth, *The Demography of the British Peerage*, supplement to *Population Studies*, XVIII, 2 (November 1964), pp. 52–70.

[3] Wrigley's analysis is discussed above on pp. 168, 185–95.

Stable Populations

Stable populations may not, of course, be found very often in the real world, even where mortality conditions can fairly be estimated from model life-tables. In any small area, migration will usually play a very important part in population change over a long period of time, so that a city population, for example, can scarcely ever be stable. Nevertheless, it is often possible to treat national populations as stable, and Coale and Demeny show,[1] as an illustration of the use of model life-tables, how, knowing the age-distribution and the life-table for England and Wales in 1881, the birth-rate can be estimated from their Princeton Tables. Livi Bacci used a variant of this method to estimate the birth-rate in Spain in the second half of the eighteenth century from a set of censuses giving the age and sex distribution of the population.[2] Although the life-table for the Spanish population of that time was not known, the rate of population growth could be assessed from the censuses over a long period, and this was equally sufficient to calculate the birth-rate from the model life-tables.

As a more complete illustration of the technique of stable population analysis, let us now apply Livi Bacci's method for Spain to England and Wales, using the 1821 census for the age-distribution. This is an earlier date than the illustrative study that Coale and Demeny gave, and there is no reason to expect the conditions to be the same as they were 60 years later. The stability of the population is not established, but we can note that emigration was generally not high before 1821, and that population had certainly been growing fast since about 1780. If we take Brownlee's estimates[3] of population for 1780 and 1790 and the census figures for 1801, 1811, and 1821, we have annual rates of growth as follows:

[1] Op. cit.

[2] M. Livi Bacci, 'Fertility and Nuptiality Changes in Spain from the late 18th to the early 20th Century, Part I', Population Studies, XXII, 1 (March 1968), pp. 83–102.

[3] Taken in fact here from Glass, 'Population and Population Movements in England and Wales, 1700 to 1850', in Population in History (edited by Glass and Eversley), London, 1965, pp. 221–46 (p. 240).

	Per thousand
1780–1790	9·12
1790–1801	9·55
1801–1811	13·07
1811–1821	15·33

Although the rate of growth seems, therefore, to have accelerated in the forty years before the 1821 census, to a first approximation we might regard the rate as steady at 11·77 per thousand per year. There is no point in striving for great accuracy at this stage, because Brownlee's estimates cannot be regarded as sacrosanct but are merely a rough guide to our ideas of the course of numbers a little before the first census.

The 1821 census gave an age-distribution for only about 88 per cent of the population, but almost all the omitted people were in particular administrative areas and therefore not in particular age-groups. Manchester and Salford (133,788 people) and Newcastle upon Tyne (35,181) were wholly omitted from the age returns, as were more than 80 per cent of the people of Birmingham, Bristol and Nottingham. The large towns, in fact, fared badly in general, but the ages in Liverpool, Plymouth and Portsmouth were, amongst others, completely returned. The London ages were about 75 per cent complete. The towns showed, on average, smaller proportions of people under 15 than the population at large, but the national figure should only be corrected by about 0·6 per cent for this, from 39·1 per cent under 15 to 38·5 per cent. Making full corrections is therefore scarcely worth while, and the national age-distribution is used as it stands.

Having settled the rate of growth and the age-distribution, the Princeton 'West' tables, which fit the 1881 age-distribution quite well, should clearly be used. For each sex, we take the proportions of the population under successive ages as given in the 1821 census. We can then interpolate the appropriate birth-rate from the table on the opposite page.

The male birth-rate is normally higher than the female, but the first four rows seem to give unusually large differences, with a sudden drop at age 30. The losses of men in the Napoleonic Wars could very well account for this. The female rates vary very little, which suggests that the population was indeed close to stability over the forty years prior to 1821, although the birth-rate might possibly have been a little lower (or

ESTIMATES OF THE BIRTH-RATES FROM THE AGE-
DISTRIBUTION OF THE 1821 CENSUS OF ENGLAND AND WALES
(STABLE GROWTH RATE, 11·77 PER 1,000 PER YEAR)

	Males		Females	
Age	Cumulative proportion of the population	Estimated birth-rate	Cumulative proportion of the population	Estimated birth-rate
5	15·38%	47·23	14·40%	40·32
10	28·86%	51·58	27·09%	42·85
15	40·58%	52·17	37·67%	41·44
20	50·47%	50·12	47·63%	41·55
30	65·14%	42·29	64·38%	41·54
40	76·67%	37·84	76·45%	39·25

the death-rate higher) before 1791 than after. (If growth was slower before 1801 than after, the population was, strictly speaking, only quasi-stable.) The simple average of all twelve estimates (Coale and Demeny prefer medians) gives us a mean birth-rate for 1781–1821 of 44·02 per thousand, and the expectation of life at birth was evidently about 31·5 years, the large sex difference (males 29·5, females 33·4) again being ascribable to the Napoleonic Wars. Although we might have corrected the 1821 census for omitted age returns, adjusted the growth rates from 1801 to 1821 to allow for armed forces abroad and net migration, taken other figures for 1780–1801, and allowed for the uneven sex-ratio at birth, these cannot make great differences to the results.

This is no idle example, for it provides almost the only evidence for a remarkable change in the English population between 1821 and 1841. Stability occurred again for about forty years after 1841, but at quite different fertility and mortality levels. Since the mean birth-rate was 44·02 before 1821 and we know that 11·77 was the mean rate of increase, the mean death-rate must have been 32·25; but after 1841, we know from registration data (when corrected for under-enumeration) that the birth-rate was about 35 per thousand and the death-rate about 22. The rate of growth was not much affected by the change, but both fertility and mortality evidently fell quite sharply. The expectation of life rose by about 30 per cent, from 31·5 (at birth) to more than 40 years, while the birth-rate fell about 20 per cent. The beginning of the decline in English fertility must therefore be placed about sixty years earlier than has been thought, not in 1880 but in 1820.

The fall in mortality is especially important, for it must have reduced substantially the losses of men and women during the most active years of life, while the fall in fertility lowered the proportion of dependent children. The expectation of life rose about 50 per cent, altogether, during the nineteenth century; but about half of this gain seems to have occurred within the two decades 1821-41. Possibly, indeed, this drop in mortality should be regarded as the most important historical event of the period, rather than such familiar affairs as the invention of steam locomotives or the passing of the Reform Bill.[1] However, it is conceivable that mortality fell almost continuously throughout the whole of the nineteenth century, with some check to its decline in the 1840's and 1850's.

We can sum up by saying that, around 1800, England's birth-rate was close to that of Spain or Prussia; her mortality level was close to that of France, although much above what obtained in Sweden. Both rates were approximately the same as in Bohemia[2] between 1785 and 1799, so that several other parts of Europe, even amongst those few for which there are any figures, were faring the same as England and Wales.

These conclusions differ greatly from what is often assumed about mortality conditions[3] between 1780 and 1870, which are often thought to have changed little. Krause, however, drew attention[4] to the strong argument that the age-distribution of the 1821 census provides for

[1] Controversy still exists about the standard of living in England at this period. For a pessimistic view, see J. T. Krause, 'Some Neglected Factors in the English Industrial Revolution', *Journal of Economic History*, XIX, 4 (December 1959), pp. 528-40, which argues for a steep rise in fertility between 1750 and 1810, a view which we of course are here rejecting. More recently, we have some support from R. M. Hartwell, 'The Rising Standard of Living in England, 1800-1850', *Economic History Review*, 2nd Series, XIII, 3 (1961), pp. 397-416.

[2] P. Horska, 'L'état actuel des recherches sur l'évolution de la population dans les pays tchèques aux XVIIIe et XIXe siècles', *Annales de Démographie Historique* (1967), pp. 173-95.

[3] For instance by W. A. Armstrong, 'La population de l'Angleterre et du Pays de Galles (1789-1815)', *ibid.* (1965), pp. 135-89.

[4] J. T. Krause, 'Changes in English Fertility and Mortality, 1781-1850', *Economic History Review*, 2nd Series, II, 1 (1958), pp. 52-70.

assuming a relatively high birth-rate during 1801–21 at least; and, if this be allowed, the rate of inter-censal increase at that time forces us to accept a high rate of mortality also. The population 'retrojection' that Armstrong,[1] following Farr and Brownlee,[2] relied upon is therefore useless.

The root cause of misunderstandings of the historical demography of England between 1700 and 1850 seems to be the very collection and publication of the copious parish register abstracts by Rickman in the early censuses.[3] If we ignored the baptism and burial data completely in the first instance, we should make fewer mistakes; and we could turn to them at the second stage of our investigations to measure the strength of religious adherence at different times, to study short-run changes of any magnitude (such as epidemics), and to interpolate the population curve. Even in the eighteenth century, 20 per cent of the vital events would seem to have gone unregistered, and between 1780 and 1830 the registers were still less complete. The high baptism figure for 1837, caused by apprehension over the new Civil Registration system which was just coming into operation, suggests that clerical slackness, rather than nonconformity, lay behind the poor level of recorded baptisms at that time.

If we try the same stable population technique on the age-distribution of the 1841 census, there is no sign of stability in the calculated birth-rates, which rise higher the higher the age we take up to age 35. The birth-rate in 1836–41 might have been as low as 33 per thousand, which would then be the lowest level of the first three-quarters of the century, but it was obviously a good deal higher before 1836, and indeed could well have been 44 per thousand early in the nineteenth century, just as the previous calculation has shown. There is thus a fair degree of corroboration in the 1841 census to the results based on 1821, and we might now place the major fall in fertility between 1818 (allowing for a probable high post-war birth-rate) and 1836.

[1] *Loc. cit.*

[2] W. Farr, Census of England and Wales 1871, *General Report*, pp. xiii–xiv and 54–6. The *Eighth Annual Report, 1848* of the Registrar-General, also contains (p. xxvi) retrospective population estimates, presumably by Farr, as does the *General Report* on the 1861 census, p. 22. J. R. Brownlee, 'The History of the Birth- and Death-Rates in England and Wales taken as a Whole, from 1570 to the Present Time', *Public Health*, 29 (June 1916), pp. 211–22, and (July 1916), pp. 228–38.

[3] These have already been discussed on pp. 152–5.

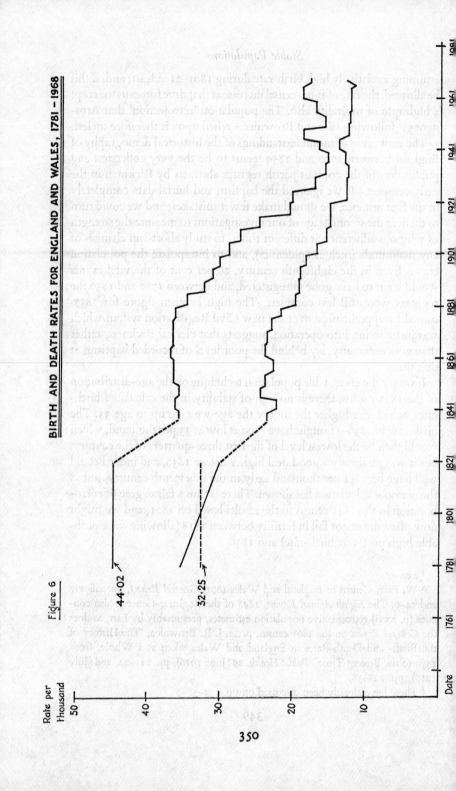

BIRTH AND DEATH RATES FOR ENGLAND AND WALES, 1781 – 1968

Figure 6

Figure 6 shows the whole pattern of the birth- and death-rates since 1781, using Glass's corrected estimates[1] for 1841–70 and quinquennial figures for 1841–1965. The probable effect of falling mortality in 1781–1821 is simply indicated by a straight line, but in fact the question really merits more detailed treatment than can be given here. Nevertheless, it provides strong evidence for the view that the great population increase in England after 1780 was caused primarily by a fall in mortality rather than by any rise in fertility.

A further interesting point is that Brownlee's estimate for 1780, 7,531,000, taken together with the King–Glass estimate of 4,838,100 for 1695 (as on page 86) yields an increase in 85 years of 55·7 per cent, or 5·2 per thousand per year between 1695 and 1780. The death-rate in 1781 was probably somewhat above 32·25 per thousand, and in fact it has been placed at 35 in figure 6. Unless mortality mysteriously increased during the eighteenth century—for which no reason seems convincing—we are inexorably led to a mean birth-rate of 37·5 at the very lowest; 40·2 would be rather more probable, and 44·0 would agree very nicely with the idea that the fall in mortality began before 1781. Moreover, Gregory King's age-distribution for England and Wales in 1695, oddly derived though it may be, also agrees with a birth-rate of about 44 per thousand ever since 1635. The most likely reconstruction of the main trends of English demographic history, therefore, is: (1) a constant birth-rate (apart, perhaps, from a few 'crisis' years) of 44 from about 1635 to 1820, followed by a fall for more than a century, merely interrupted between 1840 and 1880; and (2) a mean death-rate of about 41 during the seventeenth century, easing to 39 in the eighteenth, but falling steadily after about 1770, again except for the middle years of the nineteenth century. The two accidents that civil registration began at the beginning of the one anomalous period and that the parish register data for before 1800 were printed as part of the 1801 census report have led to grave misconceptions; about 30 per cent of some 225,000 births in 1700, for instance, were probably not recorded as baptized. Before 1635, a higher birth-rate than 44 per thousand is quite probable, but it will not be easy to prove. The Swedish birth-rate in the eighteenth century, similar to the English level in the mid-nineteenth, has also contributed to our confusion. Just as in England, registration may have begun not long after a decline in the birth-rate; in

---

[1] Glass, 'A Note on Under-Registration of Births in Britain in the Nineteenth Century', *Population Studies*, V, 1 (July 1951), pp. 70–88.

Sweden this could well have occurred between 1696 and 1721.[1]

There are, of course, numerous other examples of the use of stable populations in historical work. Morita, for example, has computed birth- and death-rates for Japan[2] between 1872 and 1915, which are substantially higher than the figures from registrations at the same period.[3] It was always thought that the registrations were in some way deficient, but Morita was able to show by how much. Coale[4] has given a general discussion of stable populations in theory and practice.

LIMITATIONS AND FURTHER DEVELOPMENTS

Difficulties arise, however, when a population is definitely not stable. Nevertheless, since one particular case of this, constant fertility and steadily falling mortality, is of great importance in the modern world, such populations have been widely studied.[5] Detailed quasi-stable population theory requires more intricate work, but Demeny has made[6] a start towards understanding the exact development of a quasi-stable population.

[1] Compare N. Friberg, 'The Growth of Population and its Economic-Geographical Background in a Mining District in Central Sweden 1650–1750. A methodological study', *Geografiska Annaler*, **38** (1956), pp. 395–440. The rapid growth of 1660–96, in this region at least, depended on a birth-rate of over 40 per thousand.

[2] Y. Morita, 'An Estimation on the Actual Birth and Death Rates in the Early Meiji period of Japan', *Population Studies*, XVII, 1 (July 1963), pp. 33–56.

[3] See I. B. Taeuber, *The Population of Japan*, Princeton, 1958, p. 41.

[4] Coale, 'Estimates of Various Demographic Measures through the Quasi-stable Age Distribution', in *Emerging Techniques in Population Research* (Milbank Memorial Fund), 1963, pp. 175–93.

[5] See: G. J. Stolnitz, 'Mortality Declines and Age Distributions, *Milbank Memorial Fund Quarterly*, XXXIV, 2 (April 1956), pp. 178–215; Coale, 'How the Age Distribution of a Human Population is Determined', *Cold Spring Harbor Symposia on Quantitative Biology*, XXII (1957), pp. 83–9; and United Nations, Manuals on methods of estimating population, Manual IV, *Methods of Estimating Basic Demographic Measures from Incomplete Data*, 1967, (ST/SOA/Series A/42).

[6] Demeny, 'Estimation of Vital Rates for Populations in the Process of Destabilization', *Demography*, **2** (1965), pp. 516–30.

One can extend the whole notion to fertility[1] also, but as yet there has been relatively little effort to do so. Nuptiality tables, for marriage, have also been constructed, but the problems connected with them are considerable.[2] Yet the value of the work described in this chapter will be very great to the historian, and would repay his extensive study.

[1] See H. V. Muhsam, 'Moderator's Introductory Statement on Vital Statistics from Limited Data', *International Population Conference* (Ottawa), 1963, pp. 25–46, and S. Mitra, 'Model fertility tables', *Sankhya*, Series B, **27**, 1–2 (September 1965), pp. 193–200.

[2] L. Henry, 'Approximations et erreurs dans les tables de nuptialité de générations', *Population*, **18**, 4 (October–December 1963), pp. 737–76.

The Demography of Plague— an Approach

THE NATURE OF PLAGUE

The Bills of Mortality, in London at least, were instituted as a check on the progress of the plague, and the demographic problems posed by plague statistics are worthy of special attention, for as well as being historically important plague often caused such a large mortality that some rough measurement of it is usually possible even from the poor data that exist. It may even be possible, as we shall see later, to assess the total size of a city's population from data on the progess of a plague epidemic, week by week. The assessment of plague mortality is therefore an important part of historical demography. Accounts exist of many plagues, and although it is scarcely possible to study changes in fertility in the more distant past because imperfections in the records could obscure any small real changes that may have occurred, mortality changes were larger and hence are easier to study. There is relatively little point in discussing the precise trend of fertility, for example, in seventeenth-century England, interesting though it would be. Improved registration of births, changes in age-structure and marriage pattern, and changes in population structure owing to migration, make the reality of any changes apparently occurring doubtful and their analysis hazardous.

When there are large changes in population, however, we can be on safer ground. Except for very obvious cases of massive migration, which are rare and ought always to be noticed by the chroniclers of the day, all very large population changes in a short time must be caused by heavy mortality. Indeed, we can go further, for war and famine can be practically ruled out as immediate causes of any very heavy mortality; they sometimes provided the conditions for a great increase in deaths, but an epidemic disease (or diseases) will always have been the immediate cause. This is true, for instance, of the Thirty Years War in

Germany[1] when the population fell by about a half. The prime causes were not battles nor devastation of crops, but typhus fever and (even more) plague.

It seems probable that on only three occasions in history a plague epidemic of world-wide proportions, or pandemic, has broken out, and that all the other notable epidemics in history have been other diseases than plague.[2] The first, of which a few slight indications exist, would begin about the third century B.C., but its identification with plague is not certain;[3] the second pandemic reached Europe in A.D. 542, and disappeared early in the tenth century; and the third came from Asia at the end of 1347 and left Western Europe in 1722. In the two last pandemics at least, the rate of mortality for the first sixty years or so was evidently greater than during any other historical period of that length, and it affected every part of the known world as well as Europe. The last of the three pandemics is generally known nowadays as the Black Death,[4] although the term is also used for its first wave, which devastated Europe between 1347 and 1352. Another pandemic threatened to spread from Canton in 1894, but although it reached India it was definitely checked by 1920 and has now been virtually eliminated.

The medical causes of plague are known, although until 1894 there were many theories to account for it, some of which now seem very odd. It is caused by a bacillus that attacks a certain species of flea, parasitic on the black rat, and occurs in two main forms: pneumonic and

[1] See F. Prinzing, *Epidemics Resulting from Wars*, Oxford, 1916, pp. 25–78, and G. Franz, *Der Dreissigjährige Krieg und das deutsche Volk. Untersuchungen zur Bevölkerungs- und Agrargeschichte*, Stuttgart, 1961.

[2] J. F. D. Shrewsbury, *The Plague of the Philistines, and other medical-historical essays*, London, 1964. He argues that smallpox, dysentery, and such other diseases must have caused most of the notable epidemics, partly on the grounds of their recorded symptoms, and partly on the linguistic evidence that no word for 'rat' appears in such languages as classical Greek.

[3] The plague at Athens during the Peloponesian War that Thucydides describes was probably not bubonic plague. See, as well as Shrewsbury, *op. cit.*, F. von Bormann, 'Attische Seuche 430–426 v. Zw.', *Zeitschrift für Hygiene und Infektionskrankheiten*, CXXXVI, 1 (December 1952), pp. 67–84.

[4] The name dates from the sixteenth century at the earliest. See Sir W. P. MacArthur, 'Old-Time Plague in Britain', *Transactions of the Royal Society of Tropical Medicine and Hygiene*, **19**, 7 (January 1926), pp. 355–71, and 'Out of Oldë Bokës', *Lancet*, **235** (22 October 1938), pp. 967–9. In the latter, MacArthur derives 'Black' from a translation of the Latin 'ater', terrible.

bubonic (a third form, septicaemic, is relatively rare and demographically rather like the pneumonic form). Bubonic plague is the most common form: the sufferers are afflicted by buboes on various parts of the body which, as well as being extremely unsightly, result in death within a week for about half the cases. It very rarely spreads from man to man, and normally requires flea-bites for each case. Certain varieties of bubonic plague have been distinguished, with morbidity rates varying between about 30 per cent and 70 per cent. The size of the black rat population, which is semi-parasitic upon the human population, is also a strong influence upon the spread of bubonic plague. Outbreaks are, in fact, epizootics amongst rats rather than epidemics (in the true sense) amongst human beings. We shall ignore this factor in the discussion that follows later, in order to simplify the problems of plague demography.

The pneumonic form of plague is very deadly indeed, recovery being rare. Pneumonic plague is, in fact, about the most fatal infectious disease that is known. It can readily be spread from one person to another by the breath as well as by bites from rat-fleas. Death normally occurs within three or four days (septicaemic plague kills even more quickly, but not quite so surely). It is not even necessary to have actual physical contact with afflicted persons, or to have worn their clothes; it may be sufficient to be near an afflicted person in order to contract the disease. Since on the first day or two no very marked physical signs appear, in a city afflicted with pneumonic plague it is not surprising that everyone stays indoors and is terrified of meeting strangers. Procopius describes this in Constantinople[1] in the spring of 542.

---

[1] Procopius, *Persian Wars*, Book II, Chaps. 22–3. For a general treatise on plague, see W. J. Simpson, *A Treatise on Plague dealing with the Historical, Epidemiological, Clinical, Therapeutic and Preventive aspects of the Disease*, Cambridge, 1905. Some of the medieval medical documents on the plague are reprinted in D. W. Singer, 'Some Plague Tractates', *Proceedings of the Royal Society of Medicine*, **9**, 2 (1916), pp. 159–212. *The Journal of Hygiene* devoted a whole issue to plague investigations in India in Vol. **7** (December 1907) of its publication, and for more modern sources we might cite L. F. Hirst, *The Conquest of Plague: a study of the evolution of epidemiology*, Oxford, 1953, and C. F. Mullett, *The Bubonic Plague and England. An essay in the history of preventive medicine*, Lexington, Kentucky, 1956. There are, however, far too many works, even among the few the author has spent a little time examining, to list them all.

HISTORY OF PLAGUE

The Black Death originated in China about the year 1333 and spread slowly westwards, wreaking havoc in its path, until it had affected the besiegers of the Genoese colony of Caffa in the Crimea. This was possible because the Tartar conquests of the previous century had made regular intercourse between East and West much more frequent than before. The siege was eventually raised in 1347, and the Genoese merchants who sailed home left plague in Constantinople and Messina as well as in Genoa itself. During the next three or four years every country of Europe was attacked in turn; the plague reached southern England in 1348. Carpentier has drawn maps[1] showing the 'front' of the plague at half-yearly intervals which give a most striking impression of its steady progress. The mortality was described as immense by all the chroniclers of the day, but naturally it is difficult to determine which estimates were correct and which were fanciful, and to attach a meaning to vague expressions such as 'dreadful mortality'.

This may not have been an entirely new plague so much as a more violent form of an old one, for ever since the early eleventh century 'plague' had been present in the Near East, as we saw in the discussion on Egyptian population on pp. 307–11. Just as in the sixth century, there were sporadic outbreaks of great virulence for many years after the first onslaught. In England, the years 1361, 1369, 1375, 1390–1, 1405–7, 1439, 1478–9, 1499–1500, 1513, 1531–2, 1563, 1603, 1625 and 1665 were particularly noted for high mortality, although latterly it was mainly confined to London.[2] There were many other years as well in which the plague was plainly very strong in many parts of Europe, but the original levels of mortality were never, apparently, approached again after it had reached the end of its first course, in 1352.[3] After 1679, when Rotherhithe[4] had the last plague death, England was completely free

---

[1] E. Carpentier, 'Autour de la peste noire: famines et épidémies dans l'histoire du XIVe siècle', *Annales (E.S.C.)*, **17**, 6 (November–December 1962), pp. 1062–92.

[2] C. Creighton, *A History of Epidemics in Britain*, Cambridge, 1891–4 (and 1965 reprint), Vol. I.

[3] The basis of most of the histories that have been written of the Black Death in Europe is J. F. K. Hecker's work, published (London, 1833) in an English translation by B. G. Babington under the title *The black death in the fourteenth century, from the German*.

[4] W. G. Bell, *The great plague in London in 1665*, London, 1951, p. 329.

of plague; plague remained in the Baltic countries (Copenhagen[1] lost over 40 per cent of its population in 1711), but for fifty years before the Marseilles outbreak of 1720 Western Europe had very little plague indeed. After 1722, all of Northern and Western Europe were plague free, but Central Europe still suffered from plague up to 1740,[2] and Moscow had an outbreak as late as 1771. After that, plague in Europe was confined to the Balkans, emanating from Turkey from time to time. By 1850, plague had left Europe completely.

It has long been realized that the economic consequences of the Black Death in Europe must have been far-reaching.[3] The mortality was large enough to have caused a very serious shortage of labour, and real wages were generally much higher[4] in 1448 than in 1348. Many government edicts attempted to control wages and prices, but without success. There must, presumably, have been economic advantages for the survivors of the Black Death, in so far as there were more material goods available per head and more land that could be cultivated per family.

The social changes of the Middle Ages[5] that are associated with the

---

[1] J. Chamberlayne, 'Remarks upon the plague at Copenhagen in 1711', *Philosophical Transactions of the Royal Society*, **28** (1713), pp. 279–81.

[2] The details of the 1739–40 outbreak at Debrecen are given by R. Horvath, 'La statistique de la peste de Debrecen (1739–40) et du choléra de Pest (1831) en Hongrie et leurs conséquences sociales', *Acta Universitatis Szegediensis: Acta Juridica et Politica*, IX, 4 (1962), pp. 3–20. This paper had evidently previously been given at the meeting of L'Institut International de Statistique in Paris in 1961.

[3] See H. P. Potter, 'The Oriental Plague in its Social, Economical, Political, and International Relations, special reference being made to the labours of John Howard on the subject', *Journal of the Statistical Society*, **43** (December 1880), pp. 605–42. A more recent essay in the same vein is J. M. W. Bean, 'Plague, Population and Economic Decline in England in the Later Middle Ages', *Economic History Review*, 2nd Series, XV, 3 (1963), pp. 423–37. An interesting and more specific study is H. R. Schubert, 'The Black Death of 1348–9 and its Effect upon the Iron Industry', *Journal of the Iron and Steel Institute*, **157** (1947), pp. 525–6.

[4] B. H. Slicher van Bath, *The Agrarian History of Western Europe, A.D. 500–1850* (translated by O. Ordish), London, 1963, p. 327.

[5] See: A. E. Levett, *The Black Death on the estates of the see of Winchester*, Oxford, 1916; E. A. Power, 'The Effects of the Black Death on Rural Organisation in England', *History*, **3**, 2 (July 1918), pp. 109–16; Y. Renouard, 'Conséquences et intérêt démographiques de la Peste noire de 1348', *Population*,

end of feudalism and the beginning of banking and the mercantile system of trade were at least helped by the aftermath of the Black Death, and according to some were actually caused by it. Social bonds seemed insecure in the years following the epidemic, and while there was a trend towards fanaticism in religion, there was also a tendency to disregard the established moral code and to experiment in such matters as literature and dress in a way that was unprecedented in Europe. In a world in which a man might have seen his family, in a broad sense, reduced from twelve persons to two within a few months, it is hardly surprising that a search for new meanings in life should have been initiated.[1]

DATA ON MORTALITY OF PLAGUES

Contemporary witnesses of the Black Death yield extremely diverse figures for the mortality, and many modern articles[2] describe it in

3, 3 (1948), pp. 459–66; J. Nohl, *The Black Death. A Chronicle of the Plague compiled from Contemporary Sources* (translated by C. H. Clarke and abridged), London, 1961 (first published 1926); and S. L. Thrupp, 'Plague Effects in Medieval Europe', *Comparative Studies in Society and History*, **8**, 4 (July 1966), pp. 474–83. As so often, there are many more studies of interpretation than there are establishing what facts have to be interpreted.

[1] Historians of the plague, as well as those already mentioned in slightly different connections, include: E. Bascombe, *A History of Epidemic Pestilences from the earliest ages, 1495 Years before the Birth of our Saviour to 1848: with Researches into their Nature, Causes, and Prophylaxis*, London, 1851; F. A. Gasquet, *The Black Death of 1348 and 1349*, London, 1893, 2nd edn 1908 (this deals solely with the first wave of plague, as the title implies, and is largely confined to a detailed study of its progress in England); G. Sticker, *Abhandlungen aus der Seuchengeschichte und Seuchenlehre, Vol. I: Die Pest; Fase 1: Die Geschichte der Pest*, Giessen, 1908 (although not very critical, Sticker does aim at a universal coverage and has a large bibliography); and H. Zinsser, *Rats, Lice and History, Being a study in biography, which after 12 preliminary chapters . . . deals with the life history of typhus fever*, London, 1935.

[2] See H. van Werveke, 'De Zwarte Dood in de Zuidlijke Nederlanden 1349–1351', *Mededelingen van de Koninklijke Vlaamse Akademie voor Weten-schappen*, klasse der letteren, 12 aflevering, 3 (1950); the excise returns show that Flanders and Brabant almost escaped the Black Death altogether. A detailed local study is E. Carpentier, *Une ville devant la peste. Orvieto et la peste noire de 1348*, Paris, 1962; and Orvieto seems to have been badly hit,

special localities. In Italy, it has been said that only 8 out of every 100 persons survived; and Boccaccio, in a moving account of the Black Death in Florence,[1] asserts that 100,000 people died there between March and July 1348, although on the basis of bread consumption the population only a decade earlier is estimated[2] at only 90,000. Fifty thousand people are similarly said to have been buried in one graveyard alone in London, and over 57,000 people are stated to have died of the plague in Norwich.[3] On the other hand, some chroniclers put the mortality figure as low as 10 per cent, and a rough consensus of estimates would be between 30 per cent and 40 per cent. However, there is no particular reason to suppose that the average of the chroniclers' statements represents the best guide to the truth. In order to reach fair conclusions, we must consider all the evidence we can. Hecker, for instance, gave a figure[4] of 124,434 Franciscan friars as dying in Germany alone, but Bigelmair[5] reduced this to 24,434 on the grounds that there could not have been more than 45,000 Franciscans at risk. The earliest authority for the larger figure actually wrote more than 200 years after the event.

The chief source that has been used in England to provide estimates of the mortality caused by the Black Death is the records of institutions to benefices in many dioceses, using methods described on pp. 232–5, but Russell developed another method of mortality estimation, using the

although she cannot be certain of the mortality from the scanty returns. Bohemia, however, escaped lightly; see F. Graus, 'Autour de la peste noire au XIVe siècle en Bohême', *Annales (E.S.C.)*, **18**, 4 (July–August 1963), pp. 720–4. The second wave of plague, in 1359–61, struck Bohemia much harder, and the same happened in Milan. Italian cities in general, however, were unquestionably more affected by the initial outbreak than any later one; see W. M. Bowsky, 'The impact of the Black Death upon Sienese government and society', *Speculum*, **39**, 1 (January 1964), pp. 1–34, for example. A chronicle of Siena put the mortality there at 75 per cent, and although this cannot be verified, Bowsky is sure it was over 50 per cent.

[1] G. Boccaccio, *Decameron*, in the prologue, before the first story.
[2] G. Villani, *Cronica*, Book XI, Chapter 94.
[3] See below for a discussion of the London and Norwich figures.
[4] *Op. cit.*, above on p. 358 (footnote 3). About p. 60.
[5] A. Bigelmair, 'Zur Statistik der grossen Pestepidemie des 14. Jahrhunderts: Die Zahl der Opfer im Franziskanerorden', *Archiv für Hygiene und Bakteriologie*, CXXX (August 1943), pp. 196–204.

records of *post mortem* inquisitions. He most ingeniously estimated the rate of mortality by age, but he had too few data to be able to distinguish properly between the Black Death and the general mortality of the period.[1] The main criticism of both these methods of approach is that the population in question need not be representative of England as a whole.

Taxation returns are usually the only source of direct information on population in the Middle Ages. They are particularly good in Italy, yet Herlihy has recently studied Pistoia[2] over the period 1201 to 1430 and shown that the system of taxation was steadily deteriorating and became useless as a guide to population. There were plenty of figures, but the figures were unreliable. The population was in fact in decline before the Black Death reached Italy, that of Herlihy's area of study declining to only one-third of its former level over some 180 years. Fiumi has shown[3] a similar remarkable phenomenon in San Gimignano, where the thirteenth- or early-fourteenth-century peak of population has scarcely been surpassed even today. If the tax returns are thus unreliable, it will not be sufficient to rely even upon such English returns as the Poll Tax of 1377. It was a single tax, taken once for all, although there were many other attempts to tax the entire population. It is chiefly because the 1377 figures far exceed all others that they have been assumed practically complete; it would have been a remarkable achievement administratively if they had been.

NORWICH AND LONDON, 1349

The number of persons who died in Norwich in the Black Death in 1349, which was recorded in the city archives as 57,343, might seem

---

[1] See G. Ohlin, 'No Safety in Numbers: Some Pitfalls of Historical Statistics', in *Industrialization in Two Systems: Essays in Honor of Alexander Gerschenkron* (edited by H. Rosovsky), New York, 1966, pp. 68–90.

[2] D. Herlihy, 'Population, Plague and Social Change in Rural Pistoia, 1201–1430', *Economic History Review*, 2nd Series, **18**, 2 (August 1965), pp. 225–44; *idem, Medieval and Renaissance Pistoia, The Social History of an Italian Town, 1200–1400*, New Haven and London, 1967. See also our reference to this work on p. 118.

[3] E. Fiumi, *Storia economica e sociale di San Gimignano*, Florence, 1961, especially p. 174.

completely authoritative.[1] It is, however, difficult to accept such a high figure even for the total population of Norwich at the time, and various ingenious ways of explaining it have been suggested. If once we start rejecting figures that seem inconvenient it is hard to say when to stop, however; since we cannot tell whether any other figures, based upon other sources, might not themselves be in error. A possible explanation of the discrepancy, admittedly somewhat far-fetched, is offered below.

There were 57,343 deaths, in fact, attributed variously to both London and Norwich; and also 57,104 to Norwich and 'over 50,000' to London.[2] The Norwich plague in 1349 seems to have lasted no more than the six months 1 January to 1 July, which (as we shall see later) suggests a high mortality; and yet, after the Black Death, 100 men-at-arms were required from London, 60 from Norwich, and 20 or fewer from every other town.[3] Let us suppose that a city official in London, bred to business (and ordinarily using Arabic numerals), had in front of him the true figures (as far as they were known) for the recent plague deaths (or total deaths, which would be nearly the same), one day about August or September 1349. Let us assume these were: London, 17,343; Norwich, 17,104. Obliged to write in Latin, and in the Roman figures that (as we suppose) were not his habitual method of writing, he wrote 'in London there were ivijMiijCxliij deaths, and in Norwich only xxClix fewer'. He would have made only one mistake, the putting of 'i' instead of 'x' at the beginning of his number. Roman figures in tens of thousands are rarely needed, and easy to get wrong.

Years later, a Norwich clerk of a literal cast of mind may have come across the report. He would see the impossible number, and could well believe that it must have been meant for 57,343, reading 'l' for the 'i' that should have been an 'x'. Interested in Norwich rather than London, he might misread the figure as being Norwich's deaths. Knowing that Norwich had declined very much in population since 1348, 57,343 would seem to him a likely enough number of deaths. This error would

---

[1] The figure seems first to have appeared in Blomefield's *History of Norfolk*, Vol. III, p. 93. See J. Marshall, *Mortality of the Metropolis*, London, 1832, p. ix and p. xiii, and Creighton, *op. cit.* above on p. 358 (footnote 2), Vol. I, p. 129.

[2] Marshall, *loc. cit.*

[3] T. Rymer, *Fœdera, conventiones, litterae, et cujuscunque generis Acta Publica, inter Reges Angliæ et alios quosvis Imperatores, Reges, Pontifices, Principes vel Communitates*, London, 1825, Vol. III, Part I, pp. 193–4. The order is dated 20 March 1349/50.

have been spotted, but 57,104 for Norwich was so like the first figure, which would have achieved widespread notice by then, that little interest would be taken in the slight mistake. Interest would then be revived in London, and result in extravagant claims of 'up to 100,000' deaths, since Norwich had no right to challenge the capital so closely.

If this be accepted, the reconstruction of London's Black Death mortality made on p. 369 will be vindicated, with some deaths outside the new burial ground. Moreover, if the mortality was just over 30 per cent as suggested, the initial population in 1348 would come to 57,351. The population in the summer of 1349 (just after the Black Death) would then be 40,008. Now the armed men required in 1350 must have been based upon post-plague population—it is not possible that Edward III would have chosen to ignore the plague figures, if there ever were any, and he would have had them before 1350.[1] If Norwich then had 60 per cent of the people of London, its population immediately after the Black Death was about 24,005. We presume that 17,104 had died in the plague, which gives 41,109 in Norwich at the beginning of 1349, and a mortality rate of 41·6 per cent—about right for a plague that did not last more than six months altogether.[2]

Russell estimated the 1311 population of Norwich[3] at 13,000, but it would seem that 4,800 households on the leet roll (and not 3,680) follow from his data. As a rapidly growing borough, Norwich's hearth multiplier should be high—5 at least. With clergy, the population in 1311 would be about 25,000, which would have to grow by a further 64 per cent in the next 37 years to reach 41,109 in 1348, a high but entirely possible growth rate.

[1] However, it must be admitted that armed men are not a very firm basis for making any assumptions about population. On 5 March 1346 (*ibid.*, p. 71), as well as some men at arms from London, the figures were, for the army that was to fight at Crecy: London, 500 armed men; Norwich, 120; Bristol, 60; Coventry, 40; and other towns 30 or fewer. The two series, for 1346 and for 1350, would imply that London suffered worse than the provincial towns, and Bristol worse than Norwich.

[2] Creighton, *op. cit.* above on p. 358 (footnote 2), Vol. I, p. 130, argued for 17,000 rather than 57,000, as does M. R. Taylor, 'Great Epidemics of the Middle Ages, with special reference to Norwich and Norfolk', *Journal of State Medicine*, **43** (1935), pp. 361–9, who apparently, however, merely follows Creighton.

[3] J. C. Russell, *British Mediaeval Population*, Albuquerque, 1948, pp. 292–3.

The Demography of Plague—An Approach

A THEORETICAL APPROACH TO PLAGUE MORTALITY

Since medieval demography is so uncertain, we must try every method we can that may be of use. Modern epidemiological theory may add a little to our knowledge of plague mortality, at least providing a check on the data of the past. Bailey has written a book[1] on the mathematical theory of epidemics in which he describes how, on a deterministic model, an epidemic will grow and die away again in time.[2] It works quite well on modern data for measles or influenza; here we shall apply it to the two main forms of plague.[3]

We need to know two things about each form of plague: the infective period and the proportion that die once they have caught it (the morbidity rate). Without making any deep study, let us take the following figures for granted:

	Infective	Morbidity
Pneumonic Plague	2 days	96%
Bubonic Plague	3 days	50%

Epidemiologists will, no doubt, cavil at this simplification of a complex disease. However, the figures must be approximately right as averages, and all we shall show in what follows is how the death-rates will then behave in an epidemic. The morbidity rate serves to measure the rate of infection, and the two types of plague are each fitted to Bailey's table[4] A overleaf.

A remarkable feature is that the less time the plague lasted, the higher the total proportion that died. Knowing how many died per day at the height of the plague, the total deaths will give us the population. (Table B overleaf).

The 'effective duration' columns have been calculated on the assumption that the distribution of deaths over time would be triangular, so that there would be a uniform climb to the peak and a uniform fall after it; in fact, symmetry before and after the maximum mortality.

[1] N. T. J. Bailey, *The Mathematical Theory of Epidemics*, London, 1959.
[2] *Ibid.*, pp. 22–9.
[3] In an entirely different way, some mathematical analysis of plague death curves is found in J. Brownlee, 'Certain Aspects of the Theory of Epidemiology with special relation to the Plague', *Proceedings of the Royal Society of Medicine*, **11**, 1–2 (Section on Epidemiology and Statistical Medicine) (1918), pp. 85–127.
[4] *Op. cit.*, p. 28.

Historical Demography

Almost all the deaths actually would occur during this period. We can estimate the ratio between the total duration of a plague and the period during which more deaths were caused by plague than by all

TABLE A: 1,000 A DAY DYING OF PLAGUE AT THE PEAK

Intensity (%)	Pneumonic Population	Total deaths	Bubonic Population	Total deaths
10	1,600,000	154,000	4,620,000	231,000
20	371,000	71,300	1,070,000	107,000
30	156,000	45,000	451,000	67,700
40	81,600	31,300	235,000	47,000
50	48,400	23,200	140,000	35,000
60	30,600	17,600	88,100	26,400
70	20,100	13,500	58,100	20,300

TABLE B: TOTAL DEATHS 10,000

Intensity (%)	Pneumonic Population	Daily deaths at the peak	Effective duration (weeks)	Bubonic Population	Daily deaths at the peak	Effective duration (weeks)
10	104,000	65	44	200,000	43	67
20	52,000	140	20	100,000	93	31
30	34,700	222	13	66,700	148	19
40	26,000	318	9	50,000	213	13
50	20,800	429	7	40,000	287	10
60	17,300	565	5	33,300	377	8
70	14,900	737	4	28,600	492	6

other causes combined, if we examine actual experience. In London in 1625,[1] the plague might be said to have lasted 42 weeks altogether (11 March to 29 December); in 19 of these (10 June to 26 October) it would have been causing more than half the deaths, if we allow for some extra deaths from plague returned as from other causes. Out of about 42,800

[1] Creighton, *op. cit.* above on p. 358 (footnote 2) (1965), Vol. I, pp. 508–9.

deaths from plague in the 42 weeks, 41,300 would have occurred during the central 19 weeks, and only 1,500 in the peripheral 23 weeks. The 'effective' duration is even shorter. About 16 August, a peak of around 730 plague deaths a day must have occurred, sufficient to produce, by uniform changes in mortality, all the deaths in just 17 weeks.

Example (1) Constantinople, 542

Now let us consider a few applications. We have to treat solely of cities, since there is nothing approaching adequate information for any rural areas. Procopius tells[1] us that the plague in Constantinople in 542 lasted four months, although it was at its greatest virulence only three months. The incubation period was two days, and it seems apparent also from the symptoms and case-history he describes that the plague was pneumonic rather than bubonic. Procopius also says that the daily total of deaths rose to 5,000, to 10,000, and even higher than that before it subsided. Procopius' four months must be the total period that plague was present in the city; in only seven weeks (corresponding, by simple proportion, to the seventeen in the London of 1625) all the mortality would therefore have been achieved if there had been no tails to the curve of deaths. This means that it was a plague of 50 per cent intensity, from Table B. We can take the peak mortality as 10,500 deaths a day, since if it had reached 11,000 Procopius might have said so. Hence, multiplying the first table by 10·5, the population was 508,000 and the deaths numbered 244,000.[2]

(2) London, 1348–9

A second example is London in 1348–9. The plague apparently began on 29 September 1348 and lasted until 31 May 1349, or 35 weeks.[3] It, too, was evidently pneumonic. The period of effective duration, corresponding to 17 weeks in 1625, was therefore only about 14 weeks in 1349, and so the intensity of the Black Death in London was evidently

---

[1] *Loc. cit.* above on p. 357 (footnote 1).

[2] According to Bartsocas, Byzantium lost 300,000 from plague in 716–17, mentioning Marianus Scotus as his source. See C. S. Bartsocas, 'Two Fourteenth Century Greek Descriptions of the Black Death', *Journal of the History of Medicine and Allied Sciences*, XXI, 4 (October 1966), pp. 394–400.

[3] Creighton, *op. cit.* above on p. 358 (footnote 2) (1965), Vol. I, p. 126. There is some ambiguity, in fact, about the date at which the plague began. See below.

about 27 per cent. Now we are told that between Candlemas and Easter (2 February and 12 April, 69 days) almost 200 people a day were buried in the new cemetery given by Sir William Manny to the city (this seems the clearest meaning of the text),[1] and so about 13,500 people were buried in a period amounting to about two-thirds of the effective duration of the plague. We must ask ourselves, therefore, what proportion of the 1625 plague deaths occurred within about 80 days at the height of that epidemic, and calculate for 1348–9 in proportion. Between, say 7 July and 24 September 1625, about 36,800 plague deaths must have occurred,[2] leaving 6,000 outside that time. *Pro rata*, in 1348–9, the total plague mortality in London (assuming the 69 days 2 February to 12 April were the worst) would have been 15,710. The population would then have to be 60,050, a likely enough figure. The mortality, a mere 26 per cent, seems rather light.

However, an alternative, and probably better, procedure is as follows. Two different dates are given in the chronicles for the start of the plague: 29 September and 1 November 1348. It may be argued that the most likely explanation of *two* dates for such an event is that there was a minor outbreak of plague—or some similar disease—that began on 29 September. The Black Death was awaited with dread, and many people, in panic, assumed that it had come. But there was then a lull, and the true epidemic struck on 1 November. Otherwise, it is a little hard to understand how there could be any confusion about such a matter.

Let us therefore take only 7 months, or 211 days, as the extreme length of the epidemic. The 'effective' length of the plague is now only 85 days, and its intensity about 31·5 per cent (see Table B.) Still by analogy with the 1625 bubonic plague, the highest mortality would come *after* the mid-point in time (which was on 15 February 1349) and occur around 23 February 1349, a date similarly placed in relation to the time-scale of the epidemic to 16 August in the 1625 plague of London. (It is in fact almost invariably the case that after an epidemic reaches its height it dies down somewhat faster than it built up, and Bailey's theory also predicts this.) The Court of Hustings data (see pp. 237–40) also suggest that March and April were the worst months for the upper classes of London in 1349.

---

[1] *Ibid.*, p. 127.
[2] By calculation from *ibid.*, pp. 508–9.

The period 2 February to 12 April 1349, for which alone we have any estimate of the number of deaths, does not therefore quite correspond to the height of the Black Death in London. Since the 1625 plague lasted longer than the 1348–9 outbreak, we need a rather longer period in 1625 for comparison. The appropriate period comes to 96 days instead of 69, and runs from 18 July to 21 October 1625. In that time, 39,500 deaths from all causes (more or less) must be reckoned. About 30 a day would be from ordinary causes (or less, if many had fled London after March 1625), so that 36,600 are left as plague deaths. The point that concerns us at present is that 6,200 other plague deaths occurred in the 1625 epidemic, outside these 96 days, from which we can infer that the 13,500 plague deaths between 2 February and 12 April 1349 need to be augmented by 2,270 to get an estimate of the whole of the Black Death mortality in London.

On this new calculation, although we have made only two quite small changes, the total plague deaths now come to 15,770 (versus 15,710), the mortality to just over 30 per cent (versus 26 per cent) and the population of London at the beginning of the epidemic to 52,150 (versus 60,050). The whole method is, in fact, highly sensitive to our assumptions and estimates. It must also be remembered that the whole basis of these two estimates was the burials in one cemetery. They must, therefore, be minimum figures of population. If our explanation of the mortality data for the Black Death in Norwich and London, given above,[1] be accepted, the initial population of London was 57,351 and the mortality 17,343. This would then allow for some burials outside Manny's cemetery in the 10 weeks before Easter.

(3) London, 1625

The 1625 plague of London was bubonic. Since we have been using the weekly mortality figures for it already, we can easily calculate the population of London in that year from the data given above. The 17 weeks that were the 'effective' duration suggest an intensity of $31 \cdot 8$ per cent and the 42,800 deaths then imply 269,000 inhabitants. This is in general agreement with other opinions.

(4) London, 1665–6

The 1665–6 plague of London also caused more deaths than the Bills of Mortality[2] show. Between 21 December 1664 and 6 June 1665 there

[1] pp. 362–4. [2] Creighton, p. 662.

were 9,194 non-plague deaths in the 24 weeks, an average of 383 a week. The non-plague deaths were then above this figure for the next 20 weeks (until 24 October), by a total of 9,650; following Graunt's opinion,[1] we shall count them as plague deaths not reported as such. There were 68,592 plague deaths recorded in the Bills of Mortality from 3 May to 19 December, giving 78,242 deaths from plague altogether. In addition, 1,998 more deaths occurred[2] during 1666, and even though a few of these should probably be treated as a different, much weaker, epidemic, we shall count them as well. The total mortality from the Great Plague of 1665–6 will therefore be taken as 78,242 + 1,998 = 80,240. About 15 September, approximately 1,420 people must have been dying daily, making an 'effective' duration of 113 days for the epidemic. It was, like the 1625 outbreak, a bubonic plague, and of slightly stronger intensity (according to the table) at 32·3 per cent. The population of London would be 497,000 if the assumptions hold. Emigration from London, of course, might spoil this calculation, but it is not likely that the poor could leave the metropolis. A figure of rather under half a million is usually estimated for London at this time.

(5) *Prague, 1680*

Kryl has published the weekly plague deaths in Prague[3] between 25 May 1680 and 22 February 1681, although they only begin when the plague was already raging through the city. Bailey's theory does not assume symmetry, but suggests that 48 per cent or 49 per cent of the deaths would occur before the peak in an epidemic of the strength we may expect to find. From Kryl's data, we can guess a peak mortality around 24 June 1680 at about 95 deaths a day. After it, there would be about 3,460 more deaths before 20 December 1680. In the week preceding that date, only 3 plague deaths occurred, and the epidemic must be regarded as over—even though another began at once. If 48½ per cent of the plague deaths were before the peak, 3,257 occurred before 24 June; so that we must assume that 1,312 plague deaths occurred in this epidemic before 25 May 1680, when Kryl's table actually begins. They mostly would have taken place after February 1680. The total

[1] J. Graunt, *Natural and political observations upon the bills of mortality, etc.*, first published in 1662; see above, p. 40.

[2] Creighton, p. 679.

[3] R. Kryl, 'Mor v Praze v roce 1680–1681', *Demografie*, 4, 1 (1962), p. 91.

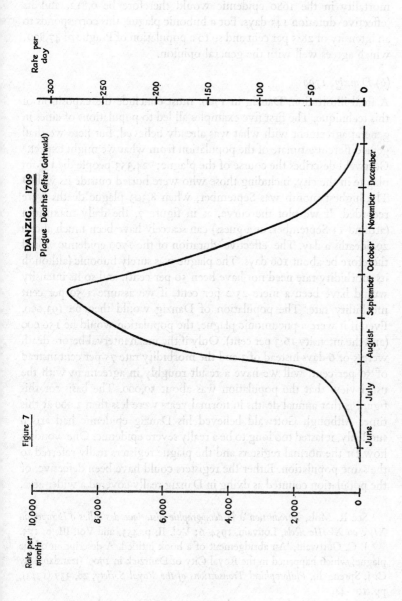

Figure 7

DANZIG, 1709
Plague Deaths (after Gottwald)

mortality in the 1680 epidemic would therefore be 6,812, and its 'effective' duration 143 days. For a bubonic plague, this corresponds to an intensity of 28·5 per cent and so to a population of Prague of 47,800, which agrees well with the general opinion.

(6) Danzig, 1709

A final illustration, Danzig in 1709, must conclude the exposition of this technique. The first five examples all led to populations of cities in general agreement with what was already believed, but here we shall get a different estimate of the population from what we might expect.[1] Gottwald describes the course of the plague;[2] 24,353 people died from plague in the city, including those who were buried outside its walls.[3] The highest month was September, when 8,303 plague deaths were recorded. If we plot the curve, as in figure 7, the daily maximum (around 13 September, at a guess) can scarcely have been much above 294 deaths a day. The 'effective' duration of the 1709 epidemic would therefore be about 166 days. The plague was surely bubonic (although its morbidity rate need not have been 50 per cent), and so its intensity would have been a mere 25·2 per cent, if we assume a 50 per cent morbidity rate. The population of Danzig would then be 193,000. Even if it were a pneumonic plague, the population would be 156,000 (and the intensity 16·3 per cent). Only if the mean interval before death were 5 or 6 days instead of 3 and the morbidity rate 75 per cent instead of 50 per cent, will we have a result roughly in agreement with the usual view that the population was about 50,000. The basis for this figure is that annual deaths in normal years were less than 2,000 at this time. Although Gottwald believed his Danzig epidemic had arisen suddenly, it lasted too long to be a really severe epidemic. One wonders how far the normal registers and the plague registers really referred to the same population. Either the registers could have been defective, or the population counted as dying in Danzig really covered a wider area,

[1] See R. Mols, *Introduction à la démographie historique des villes d'Europe, du XIVe au XVIIIe siècle*, Louvain, 1954–6; Vol. II, p. 453, and Vol. III, p. 175.

[2] J. C. Gottwald, 'An abridgement of a book intitled, A description of the plague, which happened in the Royal City of Dantzick in 1709' (translated by C. J. Sprengell), *Philosophical Transactions of the Royal Society*, **28**, 337 (1713), pp. 101–44.

[3] However, Prinzing, *op. cit.* above on p. 356 (footnote 1), p. 85, says that 32,599 people died in this plague.

or perhaps the Danzig plague was of a medically different type from others we have considered.

LIMITATIONS OF THE THEORY

Other manipulations of plague figures are clearly possible. The two interesting points are that the shorter the duration of the plague, the greater the proportion that die, and that of two plagues, both destroying the same fraction of the population, a bubonic plague will have a *higher* peak death-rate and a *shorter* duration than a pneumonic plague, although the latter has the higher rate of morbidity. The reason is that a bubonic plague has to infect at a higher rate in order to achieve the same mortality; this can only happen if it is actually more intense, and therefore if it does not last so long.

The outbreak at Varna, in Bulgaria, in 1829 is an example of a really rapid and intense plague.[1] The first cases occurred in May, the climax was reached in the latter part of June and the end came soon after 26 August. About 115 days were sufficient, it would seem, for the entire epidemic; the 'effective' duration would have been only about 47 days. The intensity, according to Table B, works out at about 64 per cent, and so the mortality would have been 32 per cent. However, the morbidity rate was probably higher in this outbreak than the 50 per cent we have uniformly allowed for all cases of bubonic plague.

The siege of Antioch in 1097–8 might be another example. One hundred thousand people are said[2] to have died between September and 24 November, a period of 85 days at most. This suggests an intensity of 60 to 80 per cent (Table B) with a mortality between 40 and 60 per cent, the exact level depending upon the form of plague, pneumonic or some kind of bubonic. In Perpignan, Emery has similarly found[3] a mortality above 50 per cent and an effective duration of about two months.

The epidemics of plague in India (especially Bombay) early in the twentieth century are of a different type, as are the chronic plagues of London in the 1630's. They were not truly epidemic (or epizootic, to be correct), but endemic. The mortality level never fell to zero, but no more than 1 or 2 per cent of the population died in a year. Changes of

[1] *Ibid.*, pp. 167–8. [2] *Ibid.*, p. 13.
[3] R. W. Emery, 'The Black Death of 1348 in Perpignan', *Speculum*, **42**, 4 (October 1967), pp. 611–23.

climate with the seasons were enough to cause local flare-ups of plague in certain sectors of a city, but the truly epidemic stage was never remotely approached.

It will be clear that the method of estimating population size outlined in this section can only work: (1) within a city; (2) when the epidemic is not confused with other diseases; (3) when there is no question of an endemic plague; and (4) when there is a fairly high level of mortality. Under these conditions, however, it can act as a rough guide to the size of the population and a check on other estimates.

There is, of course, an immense literature on plague, especially from the medical point of view, and the cursory treatment we have given above ignores several of the complications in describing the disease accurately. Demographically, accounts of plague are also numerous but are less complex. One might cite Bell[1] on the London plague of 1665, and Biraben[2] on the late plague outbreak in southern France in 1720–2, during which the value of quarantine and a *cordon sanitaire* were amply demonstrated. Keyser gives[3] a review of some of the earlier post-war German articles on plague, while among many local studies Pickard's of Exeter[4] is one of the most thorough, and Rees found[5] some unpublished data suggesting the level of Welsh population in 1349, as well as the mortality rates. Presumably, many local records await analysis; one of the purposes of this book is to suggest what can be done.

[1] *Op. cit.* above on p. 358 (footnote 4).

[2] J.-N. Biraben, 'Certain Demographic Characteristics of the Plague Epidemic in France, 1720–22', *Daedalus* (Spring 1968), pp. 536–45.

[3] E. Keyser, 'Neue deutsche Forschungen über die Geschichte der Pest', *Vierteljahrschrift für Sozial- und Wirtschaftsgeschichte*, XLIV, 3 (1957), pp. 243–53.

[4] R. Pickard, *The population and epidemics of Exeter in pre-census times*, Exeter 1947.

[5] W. Rees, 'The Black Death in England and Wales as exhibited in Manorial Documents', *Proceedings of the Royal Society of Medicine*, **16** (Section of the History of Medicine) (21 February 1923), pp. 27–45.

Replacement Rates in Medieval England

METHOD AND RESULTS

We here do nothing except calculate the generation replacement rates that Russell came very near to finding in his study of twenty years ago, and then make a few deductions from the results.

Russell's raw material[1] was taken from the *inquisitiones post mortem*, and consisted of the nature of the succession to a man who had died, the men being divided into quinquennia by date of death, from 'To 1255' (presumably roughly 1250-5) to 1501-5, using 7,931 such men in all. There were three categories of succession: (1) no direct heirs, (2) sons or their heirs, and (3) daughters as heirs. If there was at least one son, we were not told how many sons there were; but if there were a number of daughters and no sons, the number of these heiresses was given. This fact is extremely important, and Russell, with great ingenuity, almost managed to use the data on daughters to calculate the probable number of sons. If he had done so, he would have had a measure of the rate of replacement from generation to generation. All we do here is complete what Russell began.

It might appear that the rate at which sons tended to survive their fathers is all that these data can yield; but because the persons included are only those who ever held property, if a son did not live on to be as old as his father had been, the fact will appear as a son who is less likely to have had sons of his own. There is, of course, an uncertainty as to the period to which the replacement can be said to refer. If a group of men died in 1400, leaving 10 per cent more sons than they numbered themselves, we can say that the generation replacement rate was 1·1, but at moment of time? During the past generation, some of the men have begotten these sons, and some of the sons have died; other men have

---

[1] J. C. Russell, *British Mediaeval Population*, Albuquerque, 1948, pp. 92–117.

had no sons and have lived on. The best moment to allot to the replacement rate as calculated would seem to be half a generation before 1400, i.e. about 1382 or 1385. The length of a generation is important, but will be assumed (when we have to make such an assumption) to be 32 years. This is slightly short compared with modern experience, but under conditions of high mortality, the generation would be shortened somewhat, since it is the average age of men at the birth of their sons.

Russell's method began by assuming, provisionally, that there were equal numbers born of each sex. In the group of fathers dying in 1300 and earlier, for example,[1] there were 133 families consisting solely of daughters; these co-heiresses can be arranged in a frequency table, viz:

No. of daughters	1	2	3	4	5	6	7	Total
Frequency	57	35	19	16	4	1	1	133

Now to produce 57 families, each of 1 surviving daughter, 114 families (Russell argued) would have been necessary, the other 57 each consisting of 1 son. Another 140 families would have comprised 35 with 2 daughters, 70 with 1 son and 1 daughter, and 35 with 2 sons. Proceeding along the frequency table, 152 3-child families are required to produce 19 consisting of 3 girls, all the other 133 having at least 1 son. Eventually, 128 7-child families must be hypothesized to produce the 1 7-daughter family. Russell calculated that 982 families in all would have been required for the group in question, 133 of them having daughters only and 849 having one or more sons. These 982 hypothetical families comprise 3,794 hypothetical children, an average of 3·86 per family. Exactly half the children are, of course, sons and half are daughters.

The actual observed number of son-families corresponding to the daughter-families, however, is not 849, as on the theory of equal numbers of each sex, but 952, a surplus of 103 son-families. As Russell remarked, there seems to have been a real heavier mortality for daughters that accounts for the excess of sons, as well as fewer girls born. It is an interesting result, although not the point of the study. It certainly does not conflict with other knowledge of societies in which mortality is heavy (e.g. India ever since census statistics began in 1872, the ancient data of burial grounds, and the British aristocracy before 1750). Non-inclusion of heiresses in the inquisitions if they had entered a

[1] *Ibid.*, p. 244.

nunnery also possibly reduced their numbers,[1] as well as excess mortality.

It was in attempting to allot children to his surplus son-families (103 in this instance) that Russell's ingenuity failed him. Perhaps his interest flagged, since he dropped the problem soon after. Noticing that he knew of 1,085 actual families, Russell calculated a coefficient (1,085 + 103) ÷ 1,085; squared it; and multiplied the result by the surplus families (103) times the average number (1·93) of sons in the theoretical population. The result is, accidentally, about right in this example; but there is no theoretical justification for it, and one could construct examples in which the number of sons so calculated would be negative.

A better way of proceeding is to calculate the ratio of hypothetical sons to hypothetical son-families. In the example we have used, this ratio is 1,897 to 849. Multiply it by 103, the number of surplus son-families; and we then have a number of supplementary sons to add to the 1,897 already assumed to exist. We have, in fact, 230 + 1,897 = 2,127 sons. Their fathers number 1,317 (including 233 fathers who had no direct heir, as well as 133 with daughters but no sons) and the ratio 2,127 ÷ 1,317 is the male generation replacement rate, showing a rise of about 60 per cent from one generation to the next in the thirteenth century—a much higher rate of increase, incidentally, than Thrupp envisages.[2]

This method works, not just for the broad periods of half a century or so, but for the quinquennial data also. Occasionally a negative surplus appears, and then some sons have to be subtracted from the first estimate of the total number of sons. The replacement rates themselves, however, are never biologically or logically impossible when calculated in this way, and the variation they show over the years gives a better guide to population trends than the aggregated figures over longer periods that Russell attempted to find. We give the results below, together with the calculated rate of increase on the assumption that each generation lasts 32 years. (Anyone wishing to check the calculations is warned of at least 5 errors in Russell's figures[3] for 'equivalent cases with sons expected'. His one 10-daughter family, in 1501–5, is treated as such—possibly it should have been taken in 1496–1500 instead—and

[1] See S. L. Thrupp, 'Plague Effects in Medieval Europe', *Comparative Studies in Society and History*, **8**, 4 (July 1966), pp. 474–83.

[2] *Idem*, 'The Problem of Replacement-Rates in Late Medieval English Population', *Economic History Review*, 2nd Series, **18**, 1 (August 1965), pp. 101–19.

[3] Russell, *op. cit.*, pp. 240–2.

is chiefly responsible for the very high rate of growth found in that last quinquennium.)

Period	Deaths	Sons calculated	Replacement rate	Period	Annual population growth per 1,000
Up to 1255	170	327	1·924	1234 (say)–1239	20·66
1256–60	86	118	1·372	1240–4	9·93
1261–5	91	123	1·352	1245–9	9·47
1266–70	68	83	1·221	1250–4	6·26
1271–5	130	185	1·423	1255–9	11·08
1276–80	117	160	1·368	1260–4	9·84
1281–5	131	153	1·168	1265–9	4·86
1286–90	122	136½	1·119	1270–4	3·52
1291–5	204	290	1·422	1275–9	11·06
1296–1300	198	370	1·869	1280–4	19·74
1301–5	233	247	1·060	1285–9	1·82
1306–10	217	216	0·995	1290–4	− 0·15
1311–15	191	212	1·110	1295–9	3·27
1316–20	191	346	1·812	1300–4	18·75
1321–5	244	360	1·475	1305–9	12·22
1326–30	243	296	1·218	1310–4	6·18
1331–5	237	293	1·236	1315–9	6·64
1336–40	178	240	1·348	1320–4	9·38
1341–5	186	202	1·086	1325–9	2·58
1346–8 (Aug.)	95	95	1·000	1330–2 (Aug.)	0
1348–50 (Sept.)	408	470	1·152	1332–4 (Sept.)	4·43
1351–5	149	143	0·960	1335–9	− 1·27
1356–60	150	110	0·733	1340–4	− 9·66
1361–5	358	312	0·872	1345–9	− 4·27
1366–70	203	164	0·808	1350–4	− 6·64
1371–5	157	114	0·725	1355–9	− 10·00
1376–80	115	81	0·704	1360–4	− 10·91

Period	Deaths	Sons calculated	Replacement rate	Period	Annual population growth per 1,000
1381–5	146	100	0·685	1365–9	− 11·75
1386–90	140	160	1·143	1370–4	4·18
1391–5	117	87	0·744	1375–9	− 9·19
1396–1400	172	129	0·750	1380–4	− 8·95
1401–5	142	126	0·887	1385–9	− 3·74
1406–10	137	119	0·869	1390–4	− 4·38
1411–15	128	97	0·758	1395–9	− 8·62
1416–20	226	182	0·805	1400–4	− 6·76
1421–5	132	90	0·697	1405–9	− 11·22
1426–30	154	126	0·818	1410–4	− 6·26
1431–5	113	94	0·832	1415–9	− 5·73
1436–40	144	136	0·944	1420–4	− 1·80
1441–5	139	137	0·986	1425–9	− 0·44
1446–50	112	140	1·250	1430–4	7·00
1451–5	116	145	1·250	1435–9	7·00
1456–60	129	122	0·946	1440–4	− 1·73
1461–5	135	151	1·118	1445–9	3·49
1466–70	141	200	1·418	1450–4	10·97
1471–5	167	160	0·958	1455–9	− 1·34
1476–80	230	315	1·370	1460–4	9·89
1481–5	132	137	1·038	1465–9	1·17
1486–90	217	264	1·217	1470–4	6·16
1491–5	214	343	1·603	1475–9	14·84
1496–1500	248	351	1·423	1480–4	11·08
1501–5	211	665	3·152	1485–9	36·53

Given a single point of time at which the population is known, a curve of English population from 1234 to 1489 can be drawn from the rates of growth calculated. If we take Russell's estimate for 1377, it is possible, taking this as the population on 1 January 1377, or 1376/7 for short, to produce an annual series of figures for the population of England from 1233/4 to 1489/90. See figure 8. We do not give the detailed figures here, however, because the fertility of the land-holding class was probably a little higher than the national average, making the true curve slightly different, and we hope to produce adjusted figures eventually. Vielrose, however, goes too far when he calls them the aristocratic families.[1]

INTERPRETATION

The figures for population growth do suggest, however, that the population was tending to grow fast between 1234 and 1304, but in only three quinquennia (1234–9, 1280–4, and 1300–4) was the full potential of almost 2 per cent per annum achieved. Allowing for some spread of the effect of disasters such as famines or epidemics, we should look next at evidence of disasters to the population in quinquennia non-adjacent to these three 'good' ones—i.e. in the years 1245–74, 1290–4, and 1310 and after. Creighton[2]—tells of five major disasters between 1235 and 1348, as well as another in 1322 that may be important:

1. 1247: Pestilence in autumn; dearth and famine.
2. 1257–9: Bad harvests; famine and fever.
3. 1271: Great famine and pestilence.
4. 1294: Great scarcity; epidemics of flux.
5. 1315–16: General famine; great mortality from fever, flux, etc.

All the disasters occur in periods when we expected them, and the first three of these were so close together that a good quinquennium could never emerge. England up to 1304 was thus a country where the natural increase was normally high—the average for the three good quinquennia is 18·72 per thousand per year. This suggests (say) a birth-rate of 53 and a death-rate of 34 under good conditions, although the death-rate must have averaged about 40 over these years if Ohlin's

[1] E. Vielrose, *Die Bevölkerung Polens vom X bis XVIII Jahrhundert*, Marburg, 1958, p. 11. This is a translation by E. Meyer of his paper 'Ludność Polski od X do XVIII wieku', *Kwartalnik historii kultury materjalnej*, V, 1 (1957), pp. 3–49.
[2] C. Creighton, *A History of Epidemics in Britain*, *A.D. 664–1866*, Cambridge 1891–4, and reprinted 1965. Vol. I, p. 17.

Figure 8

THE POPULATION OF ENGLAND, 1254 - 1489 (i)

Based on inquest generation survival rates

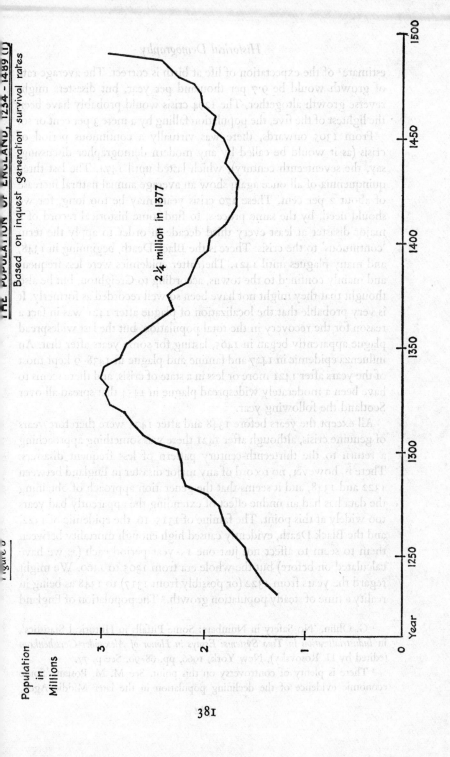

2¼ million in 1377

Population
in
Millions

Year

estimate[1] of the expectation of life at birth is correct. The average rate of growth would be 9·7 per thousand per year, but disasters might reverse growth altogether. The 1294 crisis would probably have been the lightest of the five, the population falling by a mere 3 per cent or so.

From 1305 onwards, there was virtually a continuous period of crisis (as it would be called by any modern demographer discussing, say, the seventeenth century), which lasted until 1474. The last three quinquennia of all once again show an average annual natural increase of about 2 per cent. These 170 crisis years may be too long, for we should need, by the same process, to find some historical record of a major disaster at least every third decade in order to apply the term 'continuous' to the crisis. There is the Black Death, beginning in 1348, and many plagues until 1421. Thereafter epidemics were less frequent and mainly confined to the towns, according to Creighton, but he also thought that they might not have been so well recorded as formerly. It is very probable that the localization of plague after 1421 was in fact a reason for the recovery in the total population, but the last widespread plague apparently began in 1465, lasting for some years after that. An influenza epidemic in 1427 and famine and plague in 1438–9 kept most of the years after 1421 more or less in a state of crisis, and there seems to have been a moderately widespread plague in 1454 that spread all over Scotland the following year.

All except the years before 1348 and after 1474 were therefore years of genuine crisis, although after 1421 there was something approaching a return to the thirteenth-century pattern of less frequent disasters. There is, however, no record of any major disaster in England between 1322 and 1348, and it seems that the generation approach of obtaining the data has had an undue effect of extending the apparently bad years too widely at this point. The famine of 1315–16, the epidemic of 1322, and the Black Death, evidently caused high enough mortality between them to seem to affect not just one 15–year period each (as we have calculated on before) but the whole era from 1305 to 1360. We might regard the years from 1322 (or possibly from 1317) to 1348 as being in reality a time of steady population growth.[2] The population of England

[1] G. Ohlin, 'No Safety in Numbers: Some Pitfalls in Historical Statistics', in *Industrialization in Two Systems: Essays in Honor of Alexander Gerschenkron* (edited by H. Rosovsky), New York, 1966, pp. 68–90. See p. 77.

[2] There is plenty of controversy on this point. See M. M. Postan, 'Some economic evidence of the declining population in the later Middle Ages',

on the eve of the Black Death would be, on this basis, in excess of $3\frac{1}{4}$ million (see figure 9), although direct calculation back from a 1376/7 estimate of $2\frac{1}{4}$ million (figure 8) never shows it as exceeding 3 million.

Russell did not analyse plague mortality in detail after 1377, and his evidence for the population trend between 1377 and 1430 seems to depend heavily upon the extents. Since these are really numbers of landowners, changes in the number of separate holdings owing to changes in social structure are quite possible. Saltmarsh believed there was a steady decline in general prosperity from about 1350 to about 1460,[1] and not one sudden drop in 1349 and then a recovery, as Rogers had once argued.[2] The results found here agree with Saltmarsh's view.

It is also of some interest that on these assumptions (birth-rate 53 per thousand, normal death-rate 34), there would have to be both early and practically universal marriage, as Hajnal, considering Russell's Poll-Tax data for 1377, has suggested,[3] since the birth-rate could not otherwise be maintained at such a high level. England, together with other nations, probably adopted the familiar pattern of marriage being rare under 20 and commonly around 25, with about 10 per cent never marrying at all, before 1650; but the change might have occurred at almost any time

---

Economic History Review, 2nd Series, **2**, 3 (1950), pp. 221–46. This article has proved valuable for spreading the view that the recovery from the decline began later than 1400, but economic evidence for population change, as we hinted on pp. 254–5, is never very good because of the uncertainty of how economic change affects population. See also: W. C. Robinson, 'Money, Population and Economic Change in Late Medieval Europe', *ibid.*, **12**, 1 (1959), pp. 63–76, and Postan's reply following it; and B. F. Harvey, 'The Population Trend in England between 1300 and 1348', *Transactions of the Royal Historical Society*, 5th Series, XVI (1966), pp. 23–42. Russell himself has returned to the matter in his 'The Preplague Population of England', *Journal of British Studies*, V, 2 (May 1966), pp. 1–21; see also D. G. Watts, 'A Model for the Early Fourteenth Century', *Economic History Review*, 2nd Series, **20**, 3 (December 1967), pp. 543–7.

---

[1] J. Saltmarsh, 'Plague and economic decline in England in the later Middle Ages', *Cambridge Historical Journal*, **7**, 1 (1941), pp. 23–41.

[2] J. E. T. Rogers, *Six Centuries of Work and Wages. The History of English Labour*, London, 1884, pp. 215–42.

[3] J. Hajnal, 'European Marriage Patterns in Perspective', in *Population in History* (edited by D. V. Glass and D. E. C. Eversley), London, 1965, pp. 101–43.

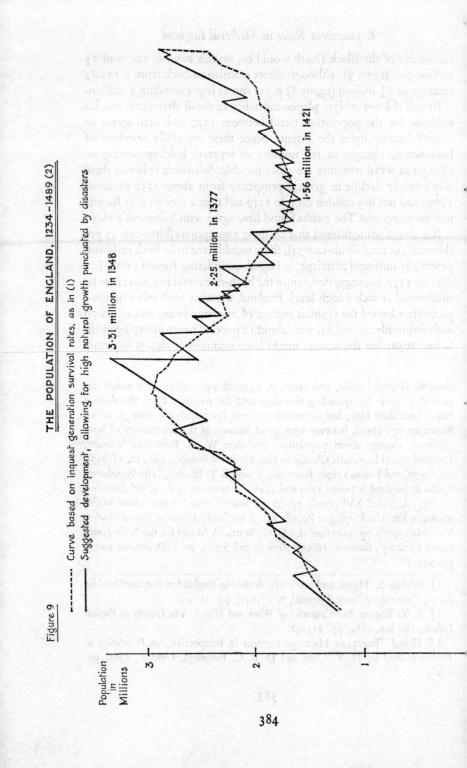

Figure 9

THE POPULATION OF ENGLAND, 1234–1489 (2)

- - - - - Curve based on inquest generation survival rates, as in (1)

———— Suggested development, allowing for high natural growth punctuated by disasters

3·31 million in 1348

2·25 million in 1377

1·56 million in 1421

Population in Millions

after 1400. Under such conditions, the birth-rate can scarcely exceed about 45 per thousand. It is evident that, up to 1304 at least and probably up to 1489, England must have had a non-European marriage pattern. Russell's estimate of $2\frac{1}{4}$ million for 1377, in which one-third of the population were children under 14, agrees with this if we assume that the population was declining fast owing to the plague.

ADJUSTMENT TO THE NATIONAL POPULATION

If we extrapolate the curve of figure 9, taking note of epidemics, we are sure to get much too small a population for 1086 compared with any estimate based on the Domesday Book; and we also get much too large a population for 1603 compared with the number of communicants in England for that year (perhaps 2,091,554). Without doing the calculations in detail, which we hope to do at some later date, we can say that over the whole 517 years 1086–1603, the average rate of increase implied by figure 9 is roughly 5 per thousand too high, or slightly more. Accordingly, if we reduce all annual rates of change by 5 per thousand we shall get a more likely set of figures for 1234–1489 (see figure 10). Again, we prefer to keep the figures themselves away from misguided people who would read into them more than is justified, although the maxima and minima are shown. On the eve of the Black Death, England *and* Wales would be about 4 million.

The difference between the general population and the population to which the *inquisitiones* refer can be attributed either to higher fertility or to lower mortality (or, of course, a combination of them), but there is no obvious way of distinguishing one from the other.

The low point of English population must have come about 1444, but for most of the early- and mid-fifteenth century the population seems to have hovered over the nadir, which agrees remakably well with current ideas of economic historians. The number of people alive in 1444 would have been much the same as in 1086. The high point, just before the Black Death in 1348, was three times as high as this, and would not have been regained until about 1600.

The guesses we have finally made of the losses in the more severe epidemics are as follows: 1348–50, 39 per cent; 1360–1, 24 per cent; 1369–9, 18 per cent; 1375, 19 per cent; 1390–1, 34 per cent; 1405–7, 31 per cent; 1420–1, 22 per cent; 1438–9, 22 per cent; and 1465–7, 19 per cent. These are, however, guesses, and there is evidence from counts

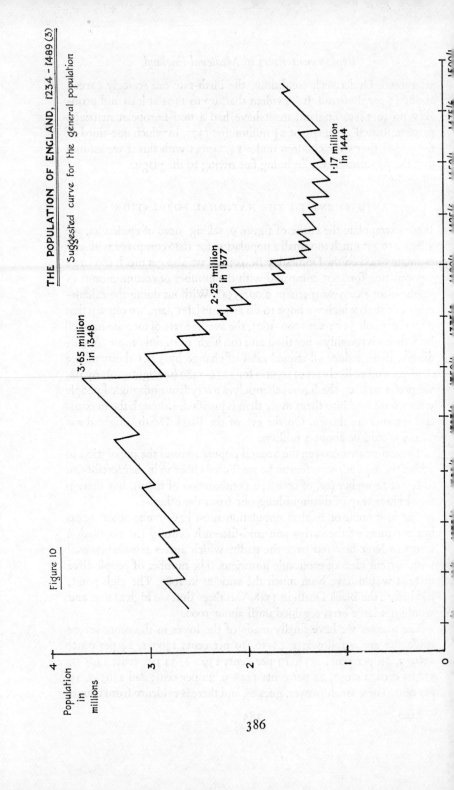

THE POPULATION OF ENGLAND, 1234-1489 (3)

Suggested curve for the general population

3·65 million in 1348

2·25 million in 1377

1·17 million in 1444

Population in millions

4

3

2

1

0

1250 1275 1300 1325 1350 1375 1400 1425 1450 1475 1500

Figure 10

of wills that leads to quite different figures, particularly for the later mortalities.

Sampling error must cause some mistakes in the shape of the curves of figures 8, 9 and 10, since the number of deaths and heirs in one quinquennium only averages about 160. The coefficient of variation of each generation replacement rate is presumably about 8 per cent, although the devious method of calculation of the number of sons really means that it must be rather higher. However, the quinquennia are statistically independent, so that 125 years away from 1377 (25 quinquennia) the range of sampling error in the population estimates, as calculated, will only be $\pm 3 \cdot 2$ per cent with 95 per cent confidence. Clearly, other kinds of error, such as false assumptions, are here much more important than sampling error.

FURTHER ANALYSIS

It will be apparent from what we have said that we could produce a complete population curve for England from 1086 to 1603, and hence indeed (using the ideas developed in Appendix 1) by working backwards from the age-distribution at the 1821 census a population curve for the past 900 years. This ambitious project must await detailed calculation, but for the present let us suggest the following tentative additional points, which have emerged from our preliminary work:

(1) The evidence of epidemics in medieval England suggests that the main period of population growth was from 1143 to 1175, rather than in the thirteenth century.

(2) The main recovery in population from the Black Death apparently occurred between 1475 and 1556, including a setback between 1500 and 1510.

(3) Renewed growth between 1560 and 1587 may have been retarded by later marriages, which became a permanent feature of English demography by the seventeenth century.

(4) The seventeenth century was not an age of great increase, especially between 1653 and 1684, although after 1688 a substantial advance in population is probable until 1719.

(5) A near-constant plateau of population, corresponding roughly to full agricultural exploitation of the land for the first time, might be suggested for the period from 1720 to 1742, followed by a slow increase.

Historical Demography

(6) The absence of serious epidemics after 1759 and better nutrition and the spread of cleanliness and ventilation after about 1770 presently produced a steady fall in the rate of mortality.

(7) Fertility only responded to this decline in mortality after a delay of some fifty years, the population having doubled meanwhile.

(8) As soon as mortality stopped falling, in the 1840's, fertility stopped falling also.

Perhaps we have now gone too far, for the demographic history of England was never envisaged as part of this book. A close and systematic study of all the available sources, however, showed that several advances could be made which seemed both simple and incontrovertible. It seemed advisable to sketch the population trend for England at the same time. While the subject is not, of course, closed, we hope that the reasons why we have reached our main conclusions are clear, and that we shall one day also be able to explain in more detail the basis for each of our subsidiary points, or such of them as then still seem valid.

Notes on the Bibliography

The works are listed in 20 unequal sections, according to their main tendency. No work is listed more than once. It is, necessarily, a highly selective list although a long one; for, as we saw in Chapter 2, in only four years the *Annales de Démographie Historique* have already filled more space with bibliography than this entire book. More than half the 400-odd titles first appeared in 1959 or later. Many works referred to in the footnotes are omitted, and a number of extra works are cited. The aim is to give a comprehensive (although not exhaustive) reading list, and I have included a number of interesting titles, mostly less than two years old, that I have not yet been able to obtain.

Many readers will know a good deal about some part of the subject already. They will no doubt wish first to see if I have unearthed some masterpiece that will solve all their problems, and next to see what gems I have unwittingly omitted. It is to be hoped that their interest will go further, however, and lead them to works beyond their immediate needs. If service in the Hampshire militia helped the historian of the Roman Empire, a knowledge of Ming census practice might aid the student of the Industrial Revolution, and the fifteenth-century population trend in England might give a hint to anyone interested in eighth- or ninth-century Egypt.

Bibliography

SECTION I. SOURCES IN GENERAL

P. Charanis, 'Observations on the Demography of the Byzanti Empire', *Proceedings of the XIIIth International Congress of Byzantine Studies* (Oxford, 1966), pp. 445–64.

Comitato Italiano per lo Studio dei Problemi della Popolazione— Commissione di Demografica Storica, *Fonti archivistiche per lo studio dei problemi della popolazione fino al 1848. Presentate al Congresso Internazionale per gli Studi sulla Popolazione, Roma 7–10 settembre 1931–ix*, Rome, 1933.

Idem, Fonti archivistiche per lo studio dei problemi della popolazione fino al 1848, Rome, 1940, Serie II.

Zoltán Dávid,* 'A történeti demográfiai források értékelésének kérdései', *Demográfia*, **6**, 4 (1963), pp. 515–25, with a summary in English, p. 525.

Jozsef Kovacsics (editor), *A Történeti Statisztika Forrásai*, Budapest (Central Hungarian Office of Statistics), 1957.

C. Legeard, *Guide de recherches documentaires en démographie (Documentation et Information)*, Paris (Gauthier-Villars), 1966.

Lionel Munby, *Hertfordshire Population Statistics, 1563–1801*, Hitchin (Hertfordshire Local History Council), 1964.

Stefan Pascu, 'Les sources et les recherches démographiques en Roumanie (Période prestatistique)', *Actes du Colloque international de Démographie Historique* (edited by Paul Harsin and Etienne Hélin) (Liège, 1963), pp. 283–303.

Bernard H. Slicher van Bath, *Voorlopige systematische bibliografie van de Nederlandse demografische geschiedenis*, Wageningen, 1962.

Joan Thirsk, 'Sources of Information of population, 1500–1760', *Amateur Historian*, **4**, 4 (Summer, 1959), pp. 129–33, and 5 (Autumn, 1959), pp. 182–5.

* Hungarian and other names are given with surname last, to comply with the English practice.

Karl Theodor von Inama Sternegg, 'Die Quellen der historischen Bevölkerungsstatistik', *Statistische Monatschrift*, **12**, (1886), pp. 387–408.

SECTION 2. CENSUS DATA

Keith John Allison, 'An Elizabethan village "census",' *Bulletin of the Institute of Historical Research*, **36**, 94 (May 1963), pp. 91–103.

S. A. Aluko, 'How many Nigerians? An analysis of Nigeria's census problems, 1901–63', *Journal of Modern African Studies*, **3**, 3 (October 1965), pp. 371–92.

Bernard Benjamin, 'Quality of Response in Census Taking', *Population Studies*, VIII, 3 (March 1955), pp. 288–93.

Henry Beverley, 'The Census of Bengal', *Journal of the Statistical Society*, **37**, 1 (March 1874), pp. 69–107.

Idem, 'Census of Bengal, 1881', *ibid.*, **46**, 4 (December 1883), pp. 680–9.

Hans Bielenstein, 'The Census of China during the Period 2–742 A.D.', *Bulletin of the Museum of Far Eastern Antiquities*, **19** (1947), pp. 125–63.

Edouard Biot, 'Sur la population de la Chine et ses variations, depuis l'an 2400 avant J. C. jusqu'au XIIIe siècle de nôtre ère', *Journal Asiatique*, Ser. 3, I (April 1836), pp. 369–94 and (May 1836) pp. 448–74.

Idem, 'Addition au Mémoire sur la population de la Chine et ses variations', *ibid.*, II, (July 1836), pp. 74–8.

Idem, 'Mémoire sur les recensements des terres consignés dans l'histoire chinoise et l'usage qu'on en peut faire pour évaluer la population totale de la Chine', *ibid.*, V (April 1838), pp. 305–31.

C. W. Chalkin, 'The Compton census of 1676: the dioceses of Canterbury and Rochester', *Kent Records* (Kent Archaeological Society), **17**, A Seventeenth-Century Miscellany (1960), pp. 153–83.

Hubert Charbonneau and Jacques Légaré, 'La population du Canada aux recensements de 1666 et 1667', *Population*, **22**, 6 (November–December 1967), pp. 1031–54.

Julian E. Cornwall, 'An Elizabethan Census', *Records of Buckinghamshire*, **16**, 4 (1959), pp. 258–73.

Sir John Dalrymple, Bt., 'The Number of Freeholders in England,' in *Memoirs of Great Britain and Ireland. From the dissolution of the last Parliament of Charles II until the sea-battle off La Hogue*, Edinburgh and London, 1771-3. (Volume II, appendix, pp. 11-5.)

Dezsö Danyi, 'Az 1777. Évi Lelkek Összeirása', *Történeti statisztikai évkönyv*, 1960, pp. 167-77.

John D. Durand, 'The Population Statistics of China, A.D. 2-1953', *Population Studies*, XIII, 3 (March 1960), pp. 209-56.

I. I. U. Eke, 'Population of Nigeria: 1952-1965', *Nigerian Journal of Economic and Social Studies*, 8, 2 (July 1966), pp. 289-309.

Tenney Frank, 'Roman Census Statistics from 225 to 28 B.C.', *Classical Philology*, 19, (1924), pp. 329-41.

Nils Friberg and Inga Friberg, 'Folkräkningar från 1600-talets Östergötland', *Statistisk Tidskrift*, 3 Ser., 2, 1 (1964), pp. 5-28; and English summary, pp. 75-7.

Peter Froggatt, 'The census in Ireland of 1813-15', *Irish Historical Studies*, 14, 55 (March 1965), pp. 227-35.

František Gabriel, 'Lidnatost čech na počátku 18. století', *Demografie*, 9, 3 (1967), pp. 241-9 and 4, pp. 343-9.

David V. Glass, 'Two Papers on Gregory King', in *Population in History* (edited by Glass and David E. C. Eversley), London (Arnold), 1965, pp. 159-220.

Tomas Gonzalez, *Censo de población de las provincias y partidos de la corona de Castilla en el siglo XVI*, Madrid, 1829.

E. L. Guilford, 'Nottinghamshire in 1676', *Transactions of the Thoroton Society*, 28 (1924), pp. 106-13.

H. E. Hallam, 'Some thirteenth century censuses', *Economic History Review*, 2nd Series, X, 3 (1958), pp. 340-61.

Harleian MSS, British Museum, MS 280 includes data from the 1603 count of communicants.

Ibid., MS 594 comprises data from the 1563 diocesan counts of families and the 1603 count of communicants.

Ibid., MS 595 is similar to MS 594.

Ibid., MS 618 consists of the 1563 diocesan count of families for the diocese of Lincoln.

Ping-ti Ho, *Studies on the Population of China, 1368-1953*, Cambridge, Mass. (Harvard University Press), 1959.

Marcel Hombert and Claire Préaux, *Recherches sur le recensement dans l'Egypte romaine*, Leyden (Papyrologica Lugduno-Batava, Vol. V) (Brill), 1952.

Gregory King, 'Natural and political observations and conclusions upon the state and condition of England 1696', in George Chalmers,

An estimate of the comparative strength of Great Britain and of the losses of her trade from every war since the revolution, London, 1802.

Idem, Papers in Harleian MS 6832, British Museum, including the age-census of Buckfastleigh, Devon, 1698, pp. 107–18.

Peter Laslett and John Harrison, 'Clayworth and Cogenhoe', in *Historical Essays,* 1600–1750, *presented to David Ogg* (edited by H. F. Bell and R. L. Ollard), London, 1962.

D. K. Lieu, 'The 1912 census of China', *Bulletin de l'Institut International de Statistique,* **26**, 2 (Madrid) (1931), pp. 85–109.

Sigismund Peller, 'Zur Kenntnis der städtischen Mortalität im 18. Jahrhundert mit besonderer Berücksichtigung der Säuglings- und Tuberkulosesterblichkeit', *Zeitschrift für Hygiene und Infektionskrankheiten,* **90** (1920), pp. 227–62.

Earl H. Pritchard, 'Thoughts on the historical development of the population of China', *Journal of Asian Studies,* **23**, 1 (November 1963), pp. 3–20.

Joseph Ruwet, 'La population de Saint-Trond en 1635', *Bulletin de la Société d'Art et d'Histoire du Diocèse de Liège,* **40** (1957), pp. 151–93.

Robert C. Schmitt, 'Population estimates and censuses of Hawaii, 1778–1850', *Hawaii Historical Review,* **1**, 8 (July 1964), pp. 143–55.

Idem, 'Population characteristics of Hawaii, 1778–1850', *ibid.,* 11 (April 1965), pp. 199–211.

Idem, 'The missionary "census" of Tahiti, 1797–1830', *Journal of the Polynesian Society,* **76**, 1 (1966), pp. 27–34.

C. T. Smith, 'Population', in *Victoria County History of Leicestershire,* Vol. III, London (Institute of Historical Research), 1955, pp. 129–75.

Ta Chen, *Population in Modern China,* distributed with *American Journal of Sociology,* LII, 1 (July 1946).

József Tamaśy, 'Az 1784–1787, évi elsö magyarországi népszámlálás család- és háztartásstatisztikai vonatkozásai', *Demográfia,* **6**, 4 (1963), pp. 526–37, with an English summary, p. 538.

A. J. Tawney and R. H. Tawney, 'An occupational Census of the Seventeenth century', *Economic History Review,* **5** (1934–5), pp. 25–64.

H. Waterfield, 'Census of British India of 1871–72', *Journal of the Statistical Society,* **39** (June 1876), pp. 411–16.

A. B. Wolfe, 'Population Censuses Before 1790', *Journal of the American Statistical Association,* **27**, 180 (December 1932), pp. 357–70.

SECTION 3. VITAL REGISTRATION DATA AND ITS ANALYSIS IN
THE AGGREGATE

Homer Aschmann, *The Central Desert of Baja California: Demography and Ecology*, Berkeley and Los Angeles (University of California Press) (Ibero-Americana 42), 1959.

Athos Belletini, 'Le naciste a Bologna del secolo XV al 1860', *Statistica*, **21**, 2 (1961), pp. 294–349.

Idem, *La popolazione di Bologna dal secolo XV all'unificazione italiana*, Bologna (Fonti e ricerche per la storia di Bologna) (Zanichelli), 1961.

Daniele Beltrami, *Storia della popolazione di Venezia dalla fine del secolo XVI alla caduta della repubblica*, Padova (Cedam), 1954.

John R. Brownlee, 'The History of the Birth- and Death-Rates in England and Wales taken as a Whole, from 1570 to the Present Time', *Public Health*, **29** (June 1916), pp. 211–22 and (July 1916), pp. 228–38.

Jonathan D. Chambers, 'The Vale of Trent, 1670–1800. A Regional Study of Economic Change', *Economic History Review Supplement* **3** (1957).

Idem, 'Population Change in a Provincial Town, Nottingham 1700–1800', in *Studies in the Industrial Revolution, Essays presented to T. S. Ashton* (edited by L. S. Presnell), London, 1960.

John Charles Cox, *The parish registers of England*, London, 1910.

John Crawford, 'Vital Statistics of a District in Java; with preliminary remarks upon the Dutch Possessions in the East, by Colonel Sykes', *Journal of the Statistical Society*, **12** (1849), pp. 60–71.

Michael Drake, 'An Elementary Exercise in Parish Register Demography', *Economic History Review*, 2nd Series, XIV, 3 (1962), pp. 427–45.

Idem, 'The growth of population in Norway, 1735–1855', *Scandinavian Economic History Review*, XIII, 2 (1965), pp. 97–142.

David E. C. Eversley, 'A survey of population in an area of Worcestershire, 1660–1850', *Population Studies*, X (1957), pp. 253–79.

Nils Friberg, 'Dalarnas befolkning på 1600-talet. Geografiska studier på grundval av kyrkböckerna med särskild hänsyn till folkmängdsföhållandena', *Geografiska Annaler*, **35** (1953), pp. 145–414. English summary, pp. 390–400.

Idem, 'The Growth of Population and its Economic-Geographical

Background in a Mining District in Central Sweden 1650-1750. A methodological study', *ibid.*, **38** (1956), pp. 395-440.

David V. Glass, 'A Note on the Under-Registration of Births in Britain in the Nineteenth Century', *Population Studies*, V (1951), pp. 70-88.

Pierre Goubert, 'Registres paroissiaux et démographie dans la France du XVIe siècle', *Annales de Démographie Historique*, 1965, pp. 43-8.

L. O. Henderson, 'Parish Registers', *Amateur Historian*, **4**, 6 (Winter, 1959-60), pp. 232-4.

William Johns, 'Reports upon the working of the Registration and Marriage Acts during 1837-8 and 1838-9, in the Registration District of Manchester', *Journal of the Statistical Society*, **3**, 2 (July 1840), pp. 191-204.

John T. Krause, 'Changes in English Fertility and Mortality, 1781-1850', *Economic History Review*, 2nd Series, XI, 1 (1958), pp. 52-70.

Idem, 'English Population Movements between 1700 and 1850 (I)', *International Population Conference* (New York), 1961, I, pp. 583-9.

Idem, 'The Changing Adequacy of English Registration, 1690-1837', in *Population in History* (edited by Glass and Eversley), London, 1965, pp. 379-93.

Idem, 'Some Aspects of Population Change, 1690-1790', in *Land, Labour and Population in the Industrial Revolution, Essays presented to J. D. Chambers* (edited by E. L. Jones and G. E. Mingay), London (Arnold), 1967, pp. 187-205.

Kenneth A. Lockridge, 'The Population of Dedham, Massachusetts, 1636-1736', *Economic History Review*, 2nd Series, XIX, 2 (August 1966), pp. 318-44.

Elio Lodolini, 'Los libros parroquiales y de estado civil en América Latina', *Archivum*, VIII (1958), pp. 95-113.

David J. Loschky, 'The Usefulness of England's Parish Registers', *Review of Economics and Statistics*, XLIX, 4 (November 1967), pp. 471-9.

Édouard Mallet, 'Recherches historiques et statistiques sur la population de Genève, son mouvement annuel et sa longévité, depuis le XVIe siècle jusqu'à nos jours (1549-1833)', *Annales d'hygiène publique et de médecine légale*, XVII, 1 (January 1837), pp. 5-172.

Clifford H. Mardon, 'A History of the Registration of Births, Deaths, and Marriages in England and Wales, *Population Registration*, **5**, 3 (September 1967), pp. 3-22.

G. J. Mentink and A. M. van der Woude, *De demografische ontwikkeling te*

Rotterdam en Cool in de 17e en 18e eeuw, Rotterdam (Town Archives), 1965.

George W. Roberts, 'A Life Table for a West Indian Slave Population', *Population Studies*, V, 3 (1952), pp. 238–43.

Nicholás Sánchez-Albornoz,'Les registres paroissiaux en amérique latine. Quelques considérations sur leur exploitations pour la démographie historique', *Revue suisse d'histoire*, **17**, 1 (1967), pp. 60–71.

George Seton, *Sketch of the history and imperfect condition of the Parochial Records of Births, Deaths and Marriages in Scotland, in illustration of the important advantages which would be derived from the introduction of a system of compulsory registration*, Edinburgh (Constable), 1854.

Thomas Short, *New observations natural, moral, civil, political and medical, on city, town and country bills of mortality. To which are added, Large and Clear Abstracts of the best Authors who have wrote on that subject. With an Appendix on the Weather and Meteors*, London, 1750.

D. J. Steel, *Sources of Births, Marriages and Deaths before 1837 (I)*, London (National Index of Parish Registers Vol. I), 1968.

Swedish Central Bureau of Statistics, *Historical Statistics of Sweden. I: Population, 1720–1950*, Stockholm, 1955.

Peter Walne, 'Parish registers and the registration of births, marriages and deaths in England and Wales',*Archivum*, VIII (1958), pp. 79–87.

SECTION 4. TAXATION SOURCES AND STUDIES FROM THEM

Maurice A. Arnould, *Les dénombrements de foyers dans le comté de Hainaut (XIVe–XVIe siècles)*, Brussels (Palais des Académies), 1956.

Édouard Baratier, *La démographie provençale du XIIIe au XVIe siècle, avec chiffres de comparaison pour le XVIIIe siècle*, Paris (S.E.V.P.E.N.) (École pratique des Hautes Études, Coll. Démographie et sociétés no. V), 1961.

Ömer Lufti Barkan, 'Essai sur les données statistiques des registres de recensement dans l'Empire Ottoman aux XVe et XVIe siècles', *Journal of the Economic and Social History of the Orient*, **1** (1957–8), pp. 9–36.

Robert Bautier, 'Feux, population et structure sociale au milieu du XVe siècle. L'exemple de Carpentras', *Annales (E.S.C.)*, **14** (1959), pp. 255–8.

Maurice W. Beresford. *Lay subsidies and poll taxes*, Canterbury (Phillimore), 1964.

Louis Binz, 'La population du diocèse de Genève à la fin du Moyen

Age', in *Mélanges d'histoire économique et sociale en hommage au professeur Antony Babel*, Geneva, 1963, Vol. I, pp. 145–96.

Jean-Noël Biraben, 'La population de Toulouse au XIVe et au XVe siècles', *Journal des Savants* (October–December 1964), pp. 284–300.

Woodrow Borah and Sherburne F. Cook, 'The Rate of Population Change in Central Mexico, 1550–1570', *Hispanic American Historical Review*, **37**, 4 (1957), pp. 463–70.

Idem, The population of Central Mexico in 1548, Berkeley (University of California Press) (Ibero-Americana 43), 1960.

Idem, The Aboriginal Population of Central Mexico on the Eve of the Spanish Conquest, Berkeley and Los Angeles (University of California Press) (Ibero-Americana 45), 1963.

Julian E. Cornwall, 'The people of Rutland in 1522', *Transactions of the Leicestershire Historical Society*, **37** (1961–2), pp. 7–28.

Idem, 'English Country Towns in the Fifteen Twenties', *Economic History Review*, 2nd Series, XV, 1 (1962), pp. 54–69.

Václav Davídek, 'Statistické příspěvky o osídlení a zalidnění České země v 16. a 17. století', *Demografie*, **7**, 2 (1965), pp. 128–44.

Idem, 'Statistické příspěvky o demografii České země v 18. století a do poloviny 19. století', *Demografie*, **9**, 2 and 3 (1967), pp. 142–54 and 250–260.

Ph. Dollinger, 'Le chiffre de population de Paris au XIVe siècle: 210.000 ou 80.000 habitants?', *Revue historique*, **216** (July–September 1956), pp. 35–44.

Jacques Dupâquier, 'Des rôles et tailles à la démographie historique. L'exemple du vexin français', *Annales de Démographie Historique*, 1965, pp. 31–42.

Idem, 'Démographie et sources fiscales', *ibid.*, 1966, pp. 233–40.

Giuseppe Felloni, 'Per la storia della popolazione di Genova nel secoli XVI e XVII', *Archivio Storico Italiano*, **110** (1952), pp. 236–53.

Idem, 'Popolazione e case a Genova nel 1531–35', *Atti della società ligure di storia patria*, N.S. IV (78), Fasc. 2 (1964), pp. 305–23.

Enrico Fiumi, *Storia economica e sociale di San Gimignano*, Florence, 1961.

Idem, 'La popolazione del Territorio Volterrano Sangemignanese ed il problema demografico dell'età communale', in *Studi in onore di A. Fanfani*, Vol. I (1962), pp. 251–90.

Idem, 'Stato di popolazione e distribuzione della ricchezza in Prato secondo il catasto del 1428–29', *Archivio Storico Italiano*, **123**, III (No. 447) (1965), pp. 277–303.

Bibliography

Guy Fourquin, 'La population de la région parisienne aux environs de 1328', *Le Moyen Age*, LXII (1956), pp. 63–91.

Bertrand Gille, *Les sources statistiques de l'histoire de France. Des enquêtes du XVIIIe siècle à 1870*, Geneva (Droz) and Paris (Minard), 1964.

J. Krause, 'The Medieval Household: Large or Small?', *Economic History Review*, 2nd Series, IX, 3 (1957), pp. 420–32.

Aksel Lassen, 'The Population of Denmark in 1660', *Scandinavian Economic History Review*, XIII, 1 (1965), pp. 1–30.

J. Longdon, 'Statistical Notes on Winchester Heriots', *Economic History Review*, 2nd Series, XI, 3 (1959), pp. 412–17.

Ferdinand Lot, 'L'état des paroisses et des feux de 1328', *Bibliothèque de l'École des Chartres*, **90**, (1929), pp. 51–107 and 256–315.

Lydia Marshall, 'The Levying of the Hearth Tax, 1662–88', *English Historical Review*, **51**, 204 (October 1936), pp. 628–46

C. A. F. Meekings (editor), *Surrey Hearth Tax, 1664*, London (Surrey Record Society, XVII, 41 and 42), 1940.

J. Nadal and E. Giralt, *La population catalane de 1553 á 1717. L'immigration française et les autres facteurs de son développement*, Paris (S.E.V.P. E.N.) (Coll. École pratique des Hautes Études, VIe section, Centre de recherches historiques. Démographie et société, III), 1960.

M. M. Postan and J. Titow, 'Heriots and Prices on Winchester Manors', *Economic History Review*, 2nd Series, XI, 3 (1959), pp. 392–411.

Josiah Cox Russell, 'The Medieval Monedatage of Aragon and Valencia', *Proceedings of the American Philosophical Society*, **106** (1962), pp. 483–504.

Sir John Sinclair, Bt, *The History of the Public Revenue of the British Empire*, London, 1790. See Part III, pp. 9–11 for the Marriage Duty of 1695–1706 or 1695–1700, as the case may be.

Robert S. Smith, 'Fourteenth-Century Population Records of Catalonia', *Speculum*, **19** (October 1944), pp. 494–501.

H. J. van Xanten and A. M. van der Woude, 'Het hoofdgeld en de bevolking van de Meierij van 's-Hertogenbosch omstreeks 1700', *Afdeling Agrarische Geschiedenis Bijdragen*, **13** (1965), pp. 3–96, including an English summary of the text, pp. 41–3.

SECTION 5. GENEALOGIES

Arthur H. Bailey and Archibald Day, 'On the Rate of Mortality prevailing amongst the Families of the Peerage during the 19th

Century', *Journal of the Institute of Actuaries*, IX (1861), pp. 305–26.

L. Diepgen, 'Statistisches über Fürstenehen 1500–1900', *Archiv für Hygiene und Bakteriologie*, CXX (1938), pp. 192–4.

P. E. Fahlbeck, *Der Adel Schwedens (und Finnlands). Eine demographische Studie*, Jena, 1903.

Erik Fügedi, 'A 15. századi magyar arisztokrácia demográfiai viszonyai', *Történeti statisztikai évkönyv*, 1963–4, pp. 35–72. English summary, pp. 298–9.

T. Furtak, 'Kilka zagadnień z demografii historycznej szlachty polskiej', *Rocznik dziejów spotecznych i gospodarczych*, **6** (1937), pp. 31–58.

Jacques Henripin, *La Population Canadienne au Début du XVIIIe Siècle*, Paris (I.N.E.D.), 1954.

Louis Henry, *Anciennes familles genevoises—Étude démographique: XVIe-XXe siècle*, Paris (Travaux et Documents de l'I.N.E.D., Cahier No. 26,) 1956.

Idem, 'Démographie de la noblesse britannique', *Population*, **20**, 4 (July–August 1965), pp. 692–704.

Idem and Claude Lévy, 'Ducs et pairs sous l'ancien régime', *ibid.*, **15**, 5 (1960), pp. 807–30.

Thomas H. Hollingsworth, 'A Demographic Study of the British Ducal Families', *Population Studies*, XI, 1 (July 1957), pp. 4–26.

Idem, The Demography of the British Peerage, supplement to *Population Studies*, XVIII, 2 (November 1964).

M. Kemmerich, 'Die Todesursachen innerhalb der deutschen Kaiser- und Königsfamilien', *Saluti senectutis* (Leipzig) (1909), pp. 105–94.

Sigismund Peller, 'Births and Deaths among Europe's Ruling Families since 1500', in *Population in History* (edited by Glass and Eversley), London, 1965, pp. 87–100.

Ernst Rodenwaldt, 'Untersuchungen über die Biologie des venezianischen Adels', *Homo*, **8**, 1 (1957), pp. 1–26.

SECTION 6. NOMINATIVE STUDIES FROM PARISH REGISTERS, ETC.

Yves Blayo and Louis Henry, 'Données démographiques sur la Bretagne et l'Anjou de 1740 à 1829', *Annales de Démographie Historique*, 1967, pp. 91–171.

Karl Bücher, *Die Bevölkerung von Frankfurt am Main im XIV und XV Jahrhundert, t. 1er*, Tübingen (Sozialstatistische Studien, 1), 1886.

E. J. Buckatzsch, 'Places of Origin of a group of immigrants into Sheffield, 1624–1799', *Economic History Review*, 2nd Series, II (1950), pp. 303–6.

Raymond Deniel and Louis Henry, 'La population d'un village du Nord de la France, Sainghin-en-Mélantois, de 1665 à 1851', *Population*, 20, 4 (July–August 1965), pp. 563–602.

Michel Fleury and Louis Henry, *Des registres paroissiaux à l'histoire de la population: manuel de dépouillement et d'exploitation de l'état civil ancien*, Paris (I.N.E.D.), 1956.

Idem, Nouveau manuel de dépouillement et d'exploitation de l'état civil ancien, Paris (I.N.E.D.), 1965.

Paul Galliano, 'La mortalité infantile (indigènes et nourrissons) dans la banlieue Sud de Paris à la fin du XVIIIe siècle (1774–1794)', *Annales de Démographie Historique*, 1966, pp. 139–77.

Etienne Gautier and Louis Henry, *La population de Crulai, paroisse normande. Étude historique*, Paris (I.N.E.D.), 1958.

Pierre Girard, 'Aperçus de la démographie de Sotteville-lès-Rouen vers la fin du XVIIIe siècle', *Population*, 14, 3 (1959), pp. 485–508.

David V. Glass, 'Notes on the Demography of London at the End of the Seventeenth Century', *Daedalus* (Spring 1968), pp. 581–92.

Pierre Goubert, *Beauvais et le Beauvaisis de 1600 à 1730, contribution à l'histoire sociale de la France du XVIIe siècle*, Paris (S.E.V.P.E.N.) (Coll. Ecole pratique des hautes études. VIe section, Centre de recherches historiques. Démographie et sociétés. IVe), 1960.

Idem, 'Legitimate Fecundity and Infant Mortality in France During the Eighteenth Century: A Comparison', *Daedalus* (Spring 1968), pp. 593–603.

P. E. H. Hair, 'Bridal Pregnancy in Rural England in Earlier Centuries', *Population Studies*, XX, 2 (November 1966), pp. 233–43.

G. Heckh, 'Unterschiedliche Fortpflanzung ländischer Sozialgruppen aus Südwestdeutschland seit dem 17. Jahrhundert', *Homo*, 3, 4 (1952), pp. 169–75.

Hannes Hyrenius, 'Fertility and Reproduction in a Swedish Population Group without Family Limitation', *Population Studies*, XII, 2 (1958), pp. 121–30.

Jaroslava Kalserová, 'Populační vývoj jihočeské vesnice v 17. st. av první polovině 18 st.', *Historická Demografie*, I (1967), pp. 28–34 and French summary pp. 43–5.

J. Lestocquoy, 'Tonlieu et peuplement urbain à Arras aux XIIe et

XIIIe siècles', *Annales (E.S.C.)*, **10**, 3 (July–September 1955), pp. 391–5.

Denise Leymond, 'La communauté de Duravel au XVIIIe siècle (Démographie-Économie)', *Annales du Midi*, **79**, 4 (October 1967), pp. 363–85.

C. Conyers Morrell, 'Tudor Marriages and Infantile Mortality', *Journal of State Medicine*, **43** (1935), pp. 173–81.

Jean-Pierre Poussou, 'Expérience aquitaine et méthodologie des contrats de mariage au XVIIIe siècle', *Annales du Midi*, N.S. **76**, 1 (1964), pp. 61–76.

Otto Konrad Roller, *Die Einwohnerschaft der Stadt Durlach im 18. Jahrhundert in ihren wirtschaftlichen und kulturgeschichtlichen Verhältnissen dargestellt aus ihren Stammtafeln*, Karlsruhe, 1907.

T. E. Smith, 'The Cocos-Keeling Islands: A Demographic Laboratory', *Population Studies*, XIV, 2 (November 1960), pp. 94–130.

E. Anthony Wrigley, 'Family Limitation in Pre-Industrial England', *Economic History Review*, 2nd Series, XIX, 1 (April 1966), pp. 82–109.

Idem, 'Mortality in Pre-Industrial England: The Example of Colyton, Devon, Over Three Centuries', *Daedalus* (Spring, 1968), pp. 546–80.

SECTION 7. PROFESSIONAL GROUPS

Casper, 'De la durée vitale probable chez les médecins', *Annales d'Hygiène Publique*, XI (1834), pp. 375–84.

Robert Christie, 'On the rate of mortality amongst officers retired from the Indian army', *Journal of the Statistical Society*, **1** (September 1838), pp. 279–83.

William A. Guy, 'On the Duration of Life as affected by the Pursuits of Literature, Science, and Art: with a Summary View of the Duration of Life among the Upper and Middle Classes of Society', *Journal of the Statistical Society*, **22** (1859), pp. 337–61.

SECTION 8. DISEASE MORTALITY: MEDICAL

Norman T. J. Bailey. *The Mathematical Theory of Epidemics*, London (Charles Griffin), 1959.

John R. Brownlee, 'Certain Aspects of the Theory of Epidemiology with special relation to the Plague', *Proceedings of the Royal Society of Medicine*, **11**, 1–2 (Sect. Epid. Stat. Med.) (1918), pp. 85–127.

Justus F. K. Hecker, *The black death in the fourteenth century, from the German* (translated by B. G. Babington), London, 1833.

Leonard Fabian Hirst, *The Conquest of Plague: a study of the evolution of epidemiology*, Oxford, 1953.

Karl Kisskalt, 'Epidemiologisch-statistische Untersuchungen über die Sterblichkeit von 1600–1800', *Archiv für Hygiene und Bakteriologie*, CXXXVII, 1 (March 1953), pp. 26–42.

Charles F. Mullett, *The Bubonic Plague and England. An essay in the history of preventive medicine*, Lexington, Kentucky (University of Kentucky Press), 1956.

Thomas McKeown and R. G. Brown, 'Medical Evidence Related to English Population Changes in the Eighteenth Century', *Population Studies*, IX, 2 (November 1955), pp. 119–41.

Thomas McKeown and R. G. Record, 'Reasons for the decline in mortality in England and Wales during the nineteenth century', *ibid.*, XVI, 2 (November 1962), pp. 94–122.

John F. D. Shrewsbury, *The Plague of the Philistines, and other medical-historical essays*, London, 1964.

W. J. Simpson, *A Treatise on Plague; dealing with the Historical, Epidemiological, Clinical, Therapeutic and Preventive aspects of the Disease*, Cambridge (Cambridge University Press), 1905.

Hans Zinsser, *Rats, Lice and History. Being a study in biography, which after 12 preliminary chapters . . . deals with the life history of typhus fever*, London, 1935.

SECTION 9. DISEASE MORTALITY: DEMOGRAPHIC

Edward G. Balfour, 'Statistical Data for forming Troops and maintaining them in Health in different Climates and Localities', *Journal o the Statistical Society*, **8**, 3 (September 1845), pp. 193–209.

J. M. W. Bean, 'Plague, Population and Economic Decline in England in the Later Middle Ages', *Economic History Review*, 2nd Series, XV, 3 (1963), pp. 423–37.

Jean-Noël Biraben, 'Certain Demographic Characteristics of the Plague Epidemic in France, 1720–1722', *Daedalus* (Spring, 1968), pp. 536–45.

James Bird, 'On the Vital and Sanitary Statistics of our European Army in India, compared with those of French troops under like Conditions of Climate and Locality', *Journal of the Statistical Society*, **26**, 4 (December 1863), pp. 384–405.

William M. Bowsky, 'The impact of the Black Death upon Sienese government and society', *Speculum*, **39**, 1 (January 1964), pp. 1–34.

Dino Camavitto, *La Decadenza delle popolazione messicane al tempo della Conquista*, Rome (Comitato italiano per lo Studio dei Problemi della Popolazione), 1935.

Élisabeth Carpentier, 'Autour de la peste noire: famines et épidémies dans l'histoire du XIVe siècle', *Annales (E.S.C.)*, **17**, 6 (November–December 1962), pp. 1062–92.

Charles Creighton, *A History of Epidemics in Britain, A.D. 664–1866*, Cambridge, 1891–4; reprinted 1965.

Arthur Dimock, 'The Great Pestilence: A Neglected Turning Point in English History', *Gentleman's Magazine*, **283** (1897), pp. 168–88.

Richard W. Emery, 'The Black Death of 1348 in Perpignan', *Speculum*, **42**, 4 (October 1967), pp. 611–23.

F. J. Fisher, 'Influenza and inflation in Tudor England', *Economic History Review*, 2nd Series, XVIII, 1 (August 1965), pp. 120–9.

Günther Franz, *Der Dreissigjährige Kreig und das deutsche Volk. Untersuchungen zur Bevölkerungs- und Agrargeschichte*, Stuttgart (Gustav Fischer), 1961.

David V. Glass, 'John Graunt and his Natural and political observations', *Proceedings of the Royal Society*, Series B, **159**, 974 (17th March 1964), pp. 1–32.

John Graunt, 'Natural and political observations mentioned in a following index, and made upon the bills of mortality. With reference to the government, religion, trade, growth, ayre, diseases, and the several changes of the said city [London]', *Journal of the Institute of Actuaries*, **90**, 384 (1964), pp. 4–61. (Originally published, 1662.)

Daniel Griffin, 'Inquiry into the Mortality occurring among the Poor of the City of Limerick', *Journal of the Statistical Society*, **3** (January 1841), pp. 305–30.

Eino K. I. Jutikkala, 'The Great Finnish Famine in 1696–97', *Scandinavian Economic History Review*, III, 1 (1955), pp. 48–63.

Erich Keyser, 'Neue deutsche Forschungen über die Geschichte der Pest', *Vierteljahrschrift für Sozial- und Wirtschaftsgeschichte*, XLIV, 3 (1957), pp. 243–53.

Karl Kisskalt, 'Die Sterblichkeit im 18. Jahrhundert', *Zeitschrift für Hygiene und Infektionskrankheiten*, **93** (1921), pp. 438–511.

Henry S. Lucas, 'The Great European Famine of 1315, 1316, and 1317', *Speculum*, **5** (1930), pp. 343–77.

Johannes Nohl, *The Black Death. A Chronicle of the Plague. Compiled from Contemporary Sources* (translated by C. H. Clarke and abridged), London, 1961.

William Ogle, 'An inquiry into the trustworthiness of the old Bills of Mortality', *Journal of the Royal Statistical Society*, **55**, 3 (September 1892), pp. 437–60.

Henry Percy Potter, 'The Oriental Plague in its Social, Economical, Political, and International Relations, special Reference being made to the Labours of John Howard on the subject', *Journal of the Statistical Society*, **43** (December 1880), pp. 605–42.

Friedrich Prinzing, *Epidemics Resulting from Wars*, Oxford (Clarendon) (Carnegie Endowment for International Peace, Division of Economics and History), 1916.

Josiah Cox Russell, 'That Earlier Plague', *Demography*, **5**, 1 (1968), pp. 174–84.

John Saltmarsh, 'Plague and economic decline in England in the later Middle Ages', *Cambridge Historical Journal*, **7**, 1 (1941), pp. 23–41.

Robert S. Smith, 'Barcelona "Bills of Mortality" and Population, 1457–1590', *Journal of Political Economy*, XLIV, 1 (February 1936), pp. 84–93.

Conrad Joachim Sprengell, 'Bills of Mortality of several considerable towns in Europe. Beginning with the Year 1717, i.e. from Christmas 1716, to Christmas 1717. Extracted from the Acta Breslaviensia', *Philosophical Transactions of the Royal Society*, **32**, 380 (November–December 1723), pp. 454–69.

Idem, 'The Bills of Mortality for the Town of Dresden, for a whole Century, viz. from the Year 1617 to 1717, containing the Numbers of Marriages, Births, Burials, and Communicants', *ibid.*, **38**, 428 (April–May–June 1733), pp. 89–93.

SECTION 10. CITY POPULATIONS AND ARCHAEOLOGY

Keith J. Allison, 'The Lost Villages of Norfolk,' *Norfolk Archaeology*, **31**, 1 (1955), pp. 116–62.

Idem et al., *The deserted villages of Oxfordshire*, Leicester (Leicester

University Press) (Department of English Local History, Occasional Papers, 17), 1965.

Keith J. Allison, Maurice W. Beresford, J. G. Hurst *et al.*, *The Deserted Villages of Northamptonshire*, Leicester (Leicester University Press), 1967.

Andreas Michael Andréadès, 'De la population de Constantinople sous les empereurs byzantins', *Metron*, **1**, 2 (December 1920), pp. 68–119.

Maurice W. Beresford, *The Lost Villages of England*, London, 1954.

Don Brothwell and Eric Higgs (editors), *Science in Archaeology. A Comprehensive Survey of Progress and Research*, London (Thames and Hudson), 1963, esp. pp. 325–64.

Colin Clark, 'Urban Population Densities', *Journal of the Royal Statistical Society*, Series A, **114**, 4 (1951), pp. 490–6.

Sherburne F. Cook, *The Historical Demography and Ecology of the Teotlalpan*, Berkeley and Los Angeles (University of California Press) (Ibero-Americana 33), 1949.

Charles Creighton, 'The Population of Old London', *Blackwood's Magazine*, **149** (April 1891), pp. 477–96.

R. P. Duncan-Jones, 'City Population in Roman Africa', *Journal of Roman Studies*, **53**, 1–2 (1963), pp. 85–90.

Robert F. Heizer and Sherburne F. Cook, *The Application of Quantitative Methods in Archaeology* (Viking Fund Publications in Anthropology, No. 28), 1960.

Étienne Hélin, *La démographie de Liège aux XVIIe et XVIIIe siècles*, Brussels (Royal Academy of Belgium. Classe des Lettres. Mémoires. Coll.-in-8⁰, 2e ser. Tome LVI fasc. 4), 1963.

David Herlihy, *Pisa in the Early Renaissance. A Study of Urban Growth*, New Haven (Yale University Press), 1958.

P. E. Jones and A. V. Judges, 'London Population in the late seventeenth century', *Economic History Review*, VI, 1 (October 1935), pp. 45–63.

Ferdinand Lot, 'Capitales antiques, capitales modernes. Rome et sa population à la fin du IIIe siècle de notre ère', *Annales d'histoire sociale*, VIII (1945), pp. 29–38.

Roger Mols, *Introduction à la démographie historique des villes d'Europe, du XIVe au XVIIIe siècle*, Louvain (Publications Universitaires), 1954–6.

Jean-Marie Pesez and Emmanuel Le Roy Ladurie, 'Les villages désertés

Bibliography

en France: vue d'ensemble', *Annales (E.S.C.)*, **20**, 2 (March–April 1965), pp. 257–90.

Kenneth E. Rosing, 'A rejection of the Zipf model (rank size rule) in relation to city size', *Professional Geographer*, **18**, 2 (March 1966), pp. 75–82.

Leopoldo Torres-Balbas, 'Extension y demografía de las ciudades hispanomusulmanes', *Studia Islamica*, **3** (1955), pp. 35–59.

SECTION 11. RURAL POPULATIONS AND ANTHROPOLOGY

M. K. Bennett, 'British wheat yield per acre for seven centuries', *Economic Journal*, Supplement *Economic History*, **3** (February 1935), pp. 12–29.

Robert L. Carneiro and Daisy F. Hilse, 'On determining the probable rate of population growth during the Neolithic', *American Anthropologist*, **68**, 1 (February 1966), pp. 177–81.

Sherburne F. Cook and Robert F. Heizer, *The quantitative approach to the relation between population and settlement size*, Berkeley (Reports of the University of California Archaeological Survey, 64), 1965.

Étienne Juillard, *La vie rurale dans la plaine de Basse-Alsace. Essai de Géographie Sociale*, Paris (Les Belles Lettres) (Publications of the Faculty of Letters, University of Strasbourg), 1953.

Ludwik Krzywicki, *Primitive Society and Its Vital Statistics*, London (Publications of the Polish Sociological Institute), 1934.

Li Chi, *The Formation of the Chinese People. An anthropological inquiry*, Cambridge, Mass. (Harvard University Press), 1928.

Kåre Lunden, 'Four Methods of Estimating the Population of a Norwegian District on the Eve of the Black Death (1349–1350)', *Scandinavian Economic History Review*, XVI, 1 (1968), pp. 1–18.

Angel Rosenblat, *La población de América en 1492: viejos y nuevos cálculos*, Mexico (College of Mexico. Publications of the Centre of Historical Studies, 1), 1967.

Bernard H. Slicher van Bath, *The Agrarian History of Western Europe*, A.D. *500–1850* (translated by Olive Ordish), London (Arnold), 1963.

SECTION 12. EYE-WITNESS DATA

D. Alden, 'The population of Brazil in the late eighteenth century: a preliminary study', *Hispanic American Historical Review*, **43**, 2 (May 1963), pp. 173–205.

Julian Bharier, 'A Note on the Population of Iran, 1900–1966', *Population Studies*, XXII, 2 (July 1968), pp. 273–9.

Durgaprasad Bhattacharya and Bibhavati Bhattacharya (editors), *Report on the Population Estimates of India Vol. IV (1820–1830)*, New Delhi (Census of India 1961, Office of the Registrar-General), 1964.

R. A. Butlin, 'The Population of Dublin in the Late Seventeenth Century', *Irish Geography*, 5, 2 (1965), pp. 51–66.

Enrico Fiumi, 'La demografia fiorentina nelle pagine di Giovanni Villani', *Archivio Storico Italiano*, CVIII (1950), pp. 78–158.

Arnold W. Gomme, *The Population of Athens in the Fifth and Fourth Centuries B.C.*, Oxford (Blackwell), 1933.

Robert Montgomery Martin, *The History, Antiquities, Topography, and Statistics of EASTERN INDIA; comprising the districts of Behar, Shahabad, Bhagulpoor, Goruckpoor, Dinajepoor, Puraniya, Rungpoor, & Assam, in relation to their geology, mineralogy, botany, agriculture, commerce, manufactures, fine arts, population, religion, education, statistics, etc. Surveyed under the orders of the supreme government, and collated from the original documents at the E.I. House, with the permission of the Honourable Court of Directors*, London (Allen and Co.), 1838.

Idem, *Statistics of the colonies of the British Empire ... With the charters and engraved seals. From the official records of the Colonial Office*, London, 1839.

Idem, *The British colonial library, comprising a popular and authentic description of all the colonies of the British Empire*, London, 1844.

Sir F. Maurice, 'The Size of the Army of Xerxes in the Invasion of Greece, 480 B.C.' *Journal of Hellenic Studies*, 50 (1930), pp. 210–35.

SECTION 13. TOMBSTONES AND OTHER INSCRIPTIONS

Andrew R. Burn, 'Hic Breve Vivitur: A Study of the Expectation of Life in the Roman Empire', *Past and Present*, 4 (1953), pp. 2–31.

Louis Henry, 'La mortalité d'après les inscriptions funéraires', *Population*, 12, 1 (1957), pp. 149–52.

Idem, 'L'âge au décès d'après les inscriptions funéraires', *ibid.*, 14, 2 (1959), pp. 327–9.

M. Keith Hopkins, 'The Age of Roman Girls at Marriage', *Population Studies*, XVIII, 3 (March 1965), pp. 309–27.

Bibliography

Idem, 'On the Probable Age Structure of the Roman Population', *ibid.*, XX, 2 (November 1966), pp. 245–64.

F. G. Meyer, 'Römische Bevölkerungsgeschichte und Inschriftenstatistik', *Historia*, **2**, 3 (1954), pp. 318–51.

SECTION 14. SKULLS AND SKELETONS

György Acsádi, 'A középkori magyar halandóságra vonatkozó paleodemográfiai kutatások eredményei', *Történeti statisztikai évkönyv*, 1963–4, pp. 3–34 and 295–7.

J. Lawrence Angel, 'The Length of Life in Ancient Greece', *Journal of Gerontology*, II, 1 (January 1947), pp. 18–24.

Idem, 'Human Biology, Health, and History in Greece from First Settlement until Now', *American Philosophical Society Yearbook*, 1954, pp. 168–72.

Sherburne F. Cook, 'Survivorship in Aboriginal Population', *Human Biology*, **19** (May 1947), pp. 83–9.

Jatindra Mohan Datta, 'Demography of Prehistoric Man', *Man in India*, **39**, 4 (October–December 1959), pp. 257–70.

William W. Howells, 'Estimating Population Numbers through Archaeological and Skeletal Remains', in Heizer and Cook's book (see page 406, above), pp. 158–76.

Henri V. Vallois, 'La durée de la vie chez l'homme fossile', *L'Anthropologie*, **47** (1937), pp. 499–532.

SECTION 15. DEMOGRAPHIC THEORY AND STABLE POPULATIONS

A. S. M. Mohiuddin Ahmed, 'Vital Rates of East Pakistan's Muslims: an Estimate from Stable Population Model', *International Population Conference* (Ottawa), 1963, pp. 47–63.

George W. Barclay, *Techniques of Population Analysis*, New York (Wiley), 1958.

John C. Caldwell and Chukuka Okonjo (editors), *The Population of Tropical Africa*, London (Longmans), 1968.

Remy Clairin, 'The assessment of infant and child mortality from the data available in Africa', in the above book, pp. 199–213.

Ansley J. Coale, 'Estimates of Various Demographic Measures through the Quasi-stable Age Distribution', in *Emerging Techniques in Population Research* (Milbank Memorial Fund), 1963, pp. 175–93.

Idem and Paul Demeny, *Regional model life tables and stable populations*, Princeton (Princeton University Press), 1966.

Paul Demeny, 'Estimation of Vital Rates for Populations in the Process of Destabilization,' *Demography*, **2** (1965), pp. 516–30.

Idem and Paul Gingrich, 'A Reconsideration of Negro-White Mortality Differences in the United States', *ibid.*, **4**, 2 (1967), pp. 820–37.

Reynolds Farley, 'The Demographic Rates and Social Institutions of the Nineteenth-Century Negro Population: A Stable Population Analysis', *ibid.*, **2** (1965), pp. 386–98.

John Hajnal, 'Age at marriage and proportions marrying', *Population Studies*, VII, 2 (November 1953), pp. 111–36.

Louis Henry, 'Un exemple de surestimation de la mortalité par la Méthode de Halley', *Population*, **12**, 1 (1957), pp. 141–2.

Idem, 'Réflexions sur l'observation en démographie', *ibid.*, **18**, 2 (April–June 1963), pp. 233–62.

Idem, 'Approximations et erreurs dans les tables de nuptialité de générations', *ibid.*, **18**, 4 (October–December 1963), pp. 737–76.

Nathan Keyfitz *et al.*, 'On the interpretation of age distributions', *Journal of the American Statistical Association*, **62**, 319 (September 1967), pp. 862–74.

Sully Ledermann and Jean Breas, 'Les dimensions de la mortalité', *Population*, **14**, 4 (1959), pp. 637–82.

Massimo Livi Bacci, 'Fertility and Nuptiality Changes in Spain from the late 18th to the early 20th Century', *Population Studies*, XXII, 1 (March 1968), pp. 83–102 and 2 (July 1968), pp. 211–34.

S. Mitra, 'Model fertility tables', *Sankhya* (Series B) **27**, 1–2 (September 1965), pp. 193–200.

Yuzo Morita, 'An Estimation on the Actual Birth and Death Rates in the Early Meiji period of Japan', *Population Studies*, XVII, 1 (July 1963), pp. 33–56.

Roland Pressat, *L'analyse démographique: méthodes, resultats, applications*, Paris (P.U.F.), 1961.

A. Romaniuk, 'Estimation of the Birth Rate for the Congo through Nonconventional Techniques', *Demography*, **4**, 2 (1967), pp. 688–709.

Ralph Thomlinson, *Population dynamics: causes and consequences of world demographic change*, New York (Random House), 1965.

United Nations, Department of Social Affairs, Population Division,

Bibliography

The Determinants and Consequences of Population Trends, New York (United Nations Population Studies No. 17), 1953.

Ibid., *Age and Sex Patterns of Mortality. Model Life Tables for Under-developed Countries*, New York (U.N. Population Studies, No. 22), 1955.

United Nations, Department of Economic and Social Affairs, *Methods of estimating basic demographic measures from incomplete data*, New York (Manuals on methods of estimating population, manual 4; U.N. Population Studies, No. 42), 1967. (Written by Coale and Demeny.)

V. G. Valaoras, 'A comparative study of actual versus stationary populations', *Bulletin de l'Institut International de Statistique*, **36**, 2 (Stockholm) (1958), pp. 198–217. See also 1, p. 138 for the discussion on this paper.

Dennis H. Wrong, *Population and Society*, New York (Random House), 1963.

M. Zelnik, 'Fertility of the American Negro in 1830 and 1850', *Population Studies*, XX, 1 (July 1966), pp. 77–83.

SECTION 16. METHODS OF HISTORICAL DEMOGRAPHY

Jean Bourdon, 'Les méthodes de la démographie historique', *Bulletin of the VIIth International Congress of Historical Sciences*, **5**, 3 (Warsaw) (1933), pp. 588–93.

Hubert Charbonneau, Jacques Légaré, René Durocher, Gilles Paquet, and Jean-Pierre Wallot, 'La démographie historique au Canada', *Recherches Sociographiques*, VIII, 2 (May–August 1967), pp. 1–4.

Carlo M. Cipolla, J. Dhondt, M. M. Postan, and Philippe Wolff, 'Rapport collectif: Moyen Age. Anthropologie et démographie', *IXth International Congress of Historical Sciences*, *I: Reports* (Paris) (1950), pp. 55–80.

Léopold Génicot, 'A propos des preuves d'une augmentation de la population en Europe occidentale du XIe au XIIIe siècles', *Cahiers d'Histoire Mondiale*, **1**, 2 (October 1953), pp. 446–62.

Pierre Goubert, 'Recent Theories and Research in French Population between 1500 and 1700', in *Population in History* (edited by David V. Glass and David E. C. Eversley), London (Arnold 1965), pp. 457–73.

Paul Harsin and Étienne Hélin (editors), *Problèmes de Mortalité. Méthodes, sources et bibliographie en démographie historique*, Liège

(University of Liège) (Report of a colloquium held at the University of Liège in April 1963), 1965.

Louis Henry, *Manuel de démographie historique*, Geneva and Paris (Librarie Droz) (Centre de recherches d'histoire et de philologie de la IVe Section de l'École pratique des Hautes Études. V, Hautes études médiévales et modernes, 3), 1967.

Idem, 'The Verification of Data in Historical Demography', *Population Studies*, XXII, 1 (March 1968), pp. 61–81.

Idem, 'Historical Demography', *Daedalus* (Spring 1968), pp. 385–96.

Thomas H. Hollingsworth, 'The Importance of the Quality of the Data in Historical Demography', *Daedalus* (Spring 1968), pp. 415–32.

Eino K. I. Jutikkala, 'Can the Population of Finland in the 17th Century be Calculated?', *Scandinavian Economic History Review*, V (1958), pp. 155–72.

Witold Kula, 'Stan i potrzeby badań nad demografją historyczną dawnej Polski (do początków XIX wieku)', *Roczniki dziejów spotecznych i gospodarczych*, **13** (1951), pp. 23–106 and summary in French pp. 107–9.

T. H. Marshall, 'The Population problem during the Industrial Revolution: A Note on the Present State of the Controversy', *Economic Journal*, Supplement, *Economic History* I, 4 (January 1929), pp. 429–56.

Michel Morineau, 'Démographie ancienne: monotonie ou variété des comportements?', *Annales (E.S.C.)*, **20**, 6 (November–December 1965), pp. 1185–97.

P. Göran Ohlin, 'No Safety in Numbers: Some Pitfalls of Historical Statistics', in *Industrialization in Two Systems: Essays in Honor of Alexander Gerschenkron* (edited by Henry Rosovsky), New York, 1966, pp. 68–90.

Pierre Riché, 'Problèmes de démographie historique du Haut Moyen Âge (Ve–VIIIe siècles)', *Annales de Démographie Historique*, 1966, pp. 37–55.

H. K. Roessingh, Jr. *Historisch-demografisch onderzoek*, 's Gravenhage (Vereniging voor demografie, Publ. No. 5), 1959.

Bernard H. Slicher van Bath, 'Report on the study of Historical Demography in the Netherlands', *Afdeling Agrarische Geschiedenis Bijdragen*, **11** (1964), pp. 182–90.

Idem, 'Voorbeeld van verschillende bronnen van belang voor de historische demografie', *ibid.*, pp. 191–209.

Bibliography

Ta Chen, 'The Need of Population Research in China', *Population Studies*, I, 4 (March 1948), pp. 342–52.

E. Anthony Wrigley (editor), *An Introduction to English Historical Demography. From the Sixteenth to the Nineteenth Century*, London (Weidenfeld and Nicolson), 1966.

SECTION 17. DEMOGRAPHIC HISTORY: INTERCONTINENTAL

Andreas Michael Andréadès, 'La population de l'Empire byzantine', *Actes du IVe Congrès des études byzantines* (Sofia) (1934), pp. 117–26.

K. Julius Beloch, *Die Bevölkerung der griechisch-römischen Welt*, Leipzig (Duncker and Humblot), 1886.

E. Kirsten, E. W. Buchholz and W. Kollmann, *Raum und Bevölkerung in der Weltgeschichte*, Würzburg (Ploetz), 1955–6.

P. Göran Ohlin, 'Historical Outline of World Population Growth', *World Population Conference* (Belgrade), (1965), Background paper: General, No. 486.

Marcel R. Reinhard, André Armengaud and Jacques Dupâquier, *Histoire générale de la population mondiale*, Paris (Montchrestien), 1968.

Josiah Cox Russell, *Late Ancient and Medieval Population*, comprising *Transactions of the American Philosophical Society*, New Series, 48, 3 (1958).

Boris Ts. Urlanis, Рост населения в Европе (Опыт исчисления), Moscow, 1941.

Abbott Payson Usher, 'The History of Population and Settlement in Eurasia', *Geographical Review*, 20, 1 (1930), pp. 110–32.

Walter F. Willcox, 'Increase in the population of the earth and of the continents since 1650', in *International Migrations, Vol. II* (edited by Willcox), New York (National Bureau of Economic Research), 1931, pp. 33–82.

SECTION 18. DEMOGRAPHIC HISTORY: NATIONAL OR REGIONAL

Saxe Bannister, 'Account of the Changes and present Condition of the Population of New Zealand', *Journal of the Statistical Society*, 1 (October 1838), pp. 362–76.

K. Julius Beloch, *Bevölkerungsgeschichte Italiens*, Berlin (de Gruyter), 1937–61.

413

L. G. Beskrovny, V. M. Kabuzan, and V. K. Yatsunsky, 'Bilan démographique de la Russie en 1789–1815', *Annales de Démographie Historique*, 1965, pp. 127–34.

Wilhelm Bickel, *Bevölkerungsgeschichte und Bevölkerungspolitik der Schweiz seit dem Ausgang des Mittelalters*, Zürich (Büchergilde Gutenberg), 1947.

Demétrius Bikélas, 'Statistics of the Kingdom of Greece', *Journal of the Statistical Society*, **31**, 3 (September 1868), pp. 265–98.

Jean-Noël Biraben, 'Le peuplement du Canada français', *Annales de Démographie Historique*, 1966, pp. 104–38.

P. Bonnoure and Jacques Dupâquier, 'Statistiques tchèques', *ibid.*, 1966, pp. 399–410.

J. C. Breman, 'Java: bevolkingsgroei en demografische structuur', *Tijdschrift van het Koninklijk Nederlandisch Aardrijksiedig Genootschap*, 2 Ser. **80** (July 1963), pp. 252–308.

Carlo M. Cipolla, 'Four Centuries of Italian Demographic Development', in *Population in History* (edited by David V. Glass and David E. C. Eversley), London (Arnold), 1965, pp. 570–87.

Colin Clark, 'L'accroissement de la population de la Chine', *Population*, **19** 3 (June–July 1964), pp. 559–68.

Idem, 'La population de la Chine depuis 1915', *ibid.*, **21**, 6 (November–December 1966), pp. 1191–9.

K. H. Connell, *The Population of Ireland, 1750–1845*, Oxford (Oxford University Press), 1950.

Sherburne F. Cook and Lesley Byrd Simpson, *The Population of Central Mexico in the Sixteenth Century*, Berkeley and Los Angeles (University of California Press) (Ibero-Americana: 31), 1948.

Ajit Das Gupta, Samuray Chotechanapibal, Thrip Chalothorn and Winit Siripak, 'Population Perspective of Thailand', *Sankhya* (Ser. B), **27**, 1–2 (September 1965), pp. 1–46.

Jatindra Mohan Datta, 'A Reexamination of Moreland's Estimate of Population in India at the Death of Akbar', *Population Bulletin of India*, **1** (1960), pp. 165–82.

Idem, 'Population of India about 320 B.C.', *Man in India*, **42**, 4 (October–December 1962), pp. 277–91.

Kingsley Davis, *The Population of India and Pakistan*, Princeton, 1951.

D. Demarco, 'Statistiques napolitaines', *Annales de Démographie Historique*, 1966, pp. 411–16.

Paul Deprez, 'The Demographic Development of Flanders in the

Eighteenth Century' (translated by Margaret Hilton), in *Population in History* (edited by Glass and Eversley), London, 1965, pp. 608–30.

Baron F. de Reiffenberg, 'Essai sur la statistique ancienne de la Belgique, jusque vers le XVIIe siècle', *Mémoires de l'Académie Royale Belge*, 4to serie, **7** (1832), No. 9 and **9** (1835), No. 5.

G. Diouritch, 'A Survey of the Development of the Serbian (Southern Slav) Nation. An Economic and Statistical Study', *Journal of the Royal Statistical Society*, **82**, 3 (May 1919), pp. 293–334.

P. Granville Edge, 'Pre-census Population Records of Spain', *Journal of the American Statistical Association*, **26** (1931), pp. 416–23.

Artur Eisenbach and Barbara Grochulska, 'La population de la Pologne aux confins du XVIIIe et du XIX siècle', *Annales de Démographie Historique*, 1965, pp. 105–25.

E. Esmonin, 'Statistiques du mouvement de la population en France de 1770 à 1789', *ibid.*, 1964, pp. 27–130.

Halvor Gille, 'Demographic history of the Northern European Countries in the XVIIIth Century', *Population Studies*, III, 1 (1949), pp. 3–65.

George Graham, 'On the Progress of the Population of Russia', *Journal of the Statistical Society*, **7** (September 1844), pp. 243–50. (Graham was Registrar-General of England and Wales.)

M. S. Hasan, 'Growth and Structure of Iraq's Population, 1867–1947', *Bulletin of the Oxford University Institute of Statistics*, XX (1958), pp. 339–52, and reprinted with omissions in *The Economic History of the Middle East, 1800–1914* (edited by Charles Issawi), Chicago and London, 1966, pp. 154–62.

Eijirō Honjō, *Nihon jinkō shi*, Tokyo, 1941.

Pavla Horska, 'L'état actuel des recherches sur l'évolution de la population dans les pays tchèques aux XVIIIe et XIXe siècles', *Annales de Démographie Historique*, 1967, pp. 173–95.

Eino K. I. Jutikkala, 'Finland's Population Movement in the Eighteenth Century', in *Population in History* (edited by Glass and Eversley), London, 1965, pp. 549–69.

Vladimir M. Kabuzan, Народонаселение России в XVIII первой половине XIX в. (по материалам ревизий), Moscow (Academy of Sciences of U.S.S.R.), 1963.

Ludmila Kárníková, *Vývoj obyvatelstva v českých zemích 1754–1914*, Prague (Československá Akademie Věd), 1965.

Erich Keyser, *Bevölkerungsgeschichte Deutschlands*, Leipzig, 2nd ed., 1941.

A. I. Kopanev, 'население Русского государства в XVI в'., *Исторические Записии*, **64** (1959), pp. 233–54.

József Kovacsics (editor), *Magyarország történeti demográfiája: Magyarország népessége a honfoglalástól 1949-ig*, Budapest (Közgazdasági és Jogi Könyvkiadó), 1963.

Aksel Lassen, 'The Population of Denmark', 1660–1960', *Scandinavian Economic History Review*, XIV, 2 (1966), pp. 134–57.

Frank Lorimer, *The Population of the Soviet Union: History and Prospects*, Geneva (League of Nations), 1946.

William Harrison Moreland, *India at the death of Akbar: an economic study*, London (Macmillan), 1920. Especially pp. 9–22.

Jorge Nadal, 'Sur la Population catalane au XVIIIème Siècle', *International Population Conference* (New York), 1961, I, pp. 591–600.

Idem, La población española: siglos XVI a XX, Barcelona (Ariel) (Coll. Economic Science, Economy and Society), 1966.

F. G. P. Neison, 'Analysis of the Census of New South Wales', *Journal of the Statistical Society*, **11**, 1 (March 1848), pp. 38–54.

Karl Obermann, 'Quelques données statistiques sur les États de la confédération germanique dans la première moitié du XIXe siècle', *Annales de Démographie Historique*, 1966, pp. 79–95.

Otto Placht, *Lidnatost a společenská skladba. Českého státu. v 16–18. století*, Prague (Czechoslovak Academy), 1957. There is a summary in German, pp. 326–9.

J. Potter, 'The Growth of Population in America, 1700–1860', in *Population in History* (edited by Glass and Eversley), London, 1965, pp. 631–88.

E. E. Rich, 'The Population of Elizabethan England', *Economic History Review*, 2nd Series, II, 3 (1950), pp. 247–65.

Javier Ruiz Almansa, *La población de Galicia, 1500–1945. Según los documentos estadísticos y descriptivos de cada época*, Madrid, 1948.

Josiah Cox Russell, *British Mediaeval Population*, Albuquerque, 1948.

Idem, 'The Preplague Population of England', *Journal of British Studies*, V, 2 (May 1966), pp. 1–21.

P. A. Schleisner, 'Vital Statistics of Iceland', *Journal of the Statistical Society*, **14** (March 1851), pp. 1–10.

Naotarō Sekiyama, *Nihon no jinkō*, Tokyo, 1959.

Bibliography

Conrad Taeuber and Irene B. Taeuber, *The Changing Population of the United States*, New York (Census Monograph Series), 1958.

Irene B. Taeuber, 'Ceylon as a demographic laboratory', *Population Index*, **15**, 4 (1949), pp. 293–304.

Idem, The Population of Japan, Princeton, 1958.

Sigurdur Thorarinsson, 'Population Changes in Iceland', *Geographical Review*, **51**, 4 (October 1961), pp. 519–33.

J.-C. Toutain, *La population de la France de 1700 à 1959*, Paris (Cahiers de l'Institut de Science Économique Appliquée, No. 133), 1963.

Gustaf O. Utterström, 'Two Essays on Population in Eighteenth-Century Scandinavia', in *Population in History* (Glass and Eversley), London, 1965, pp. 523–48.

J. A. Vandellós, 'La evolución demográfica de España', *Bulletin de l'Institut International de Statistique*, **27**, 2 (Mexico) (1933), pp. 180–90.

Egon Vielrose, 'Ludność Polski od X do XVIII wieku', *Kwartalnik Historii Kultury Materjalnej*, V, 1 (1957), pp. 3–49.

Idem, 'Historickà demografie Polska', *Demografie*, **2**, 2 (1960), pp. 124–33.

Paul E. Vincent, 'French Demography in the Eighteenth Century', *Population Studies*, I, 1 (1947), pp. 44–71.

SECTION 19. SOCIAL IMPLICATIONS

Ettore Cicotti, 'Motivi demografici e biologici nella rovina della civiltà antica', *Nuova Rivista Storica*, **14**, 1–2 (January–April 1930), pp. 29–62.

K. H. Connell, 'Peasant Marriage in Ireland: its Structure and Development since the Famine', *Economic History Review*, 2nd Series, XIV, 3 (1962), pp. 502–18.

Dezsö Danyi, 'A történeti demográfia tárgya és módszera', *Történeti statisztikai évkönyv*, 1961–2, pp. 5–21.

Jatindra Mohan Datta, 'Variation in Sex-Ratio in Bengal During 150 Years', *Man in India*, **37**, 3 (June 1957), pp. 133–48.

Václav Davídek, 'Počet obyvatelstva ve starověku', *Demografie*, **4**, 4 (1962), pp. 300–8.

Paul Demeny, 'Early Fertility Decline in Austria–Hungary: A Lesson in Demographic Transition', *Daedalus* (Spring 1968), pp. 502–22.

John Demos, 'Notes on Life in Plymouth Colony', *William and Mary Quarterly*, 3rd Series, **22** (April 1965), pp. 264-86.

Michael Drake, 'Marriage and Population Growth in Ireland, 1750–1845', *Economic History Review*, 2nd Series, XVI, 2 (1963), pp. 301–13.

H. Faes, 'Aspecten van het sociaal-economisch leven te Hoogstraten tijdens de eerste helft van de Tachtigjarige Oorlog (1568–1609)', *Koninklijke Hoogstratens Oudheidkundige Kring. Jaarboek H.O.K.*, 1966, pp. 1–90.

F. D. Fenton, 'Observations on the State of the Aboriginal Maori Inhabitants of New Zealand', *Journal of the Statistical Society*, **23** (December 1860), pp. 508–41.

Jean Fourastié, 'De la vie traditionelle à la vie "tertiaire"', *Population*, **14**, 3 (1959), pp. 417–32.

D. Friedlander and R. J. Roshier, 'A Study of Internal Migration in England and Wales, Part I: Geographical Patterns of Internal Migration 1851–1951', *Population Studies*, XIX, 3 (March 1966), pp. 239–78.

John Hajnal, 'European Marriage Patterns in Perspective', in *Population in History* (edited by David V. Glass and David E. C. Eversley), London (Arnold), 1965, pp. 101–43.

Karl F. Helleiner, 'The Vital Revolution Reconsidered', *Canadian Journal of Economics and Political Science*, XXIII, 1 (1957) pp. 1–9.

David Herlihy, *Medieval and Renaissance Pistoia. The Social History of an Italian Town, 1200–1430*, New Haven (Yale University Press), 1967.

Norman E. Himes, *Medical History of Contraception*, Baltimore (Williams and Wilkins), 1936. (Reprinted 1963.)

D. Jacoby, 'Phénomènes de démographie rurale à Byzance aux XIIIe, XIVe et XVe siècles', *Études Rurales*, **5–6** (April–September 1962), pp. 161–86.

John Knodel and Étienne van de Walle, 'Breast Feeding, Fertility and Infant Mortality. An analysis of some Early German Data', *Population Studies*, XXI, 2 (September 1967), pp. 109–31.

P. Göran Ohlin, *The positive and the preventive check, a study of the rate of growth of the preindustrial population*, Ph.D. thesis, Harvard University, 1955.

Theodore Papadopoullos, *Social and Historical Data on Population (1570–1881)*, Nicosia (Cyprus Research Center: Texts and Studies of the History of Cyprus No. 1), 1965.

Bibliography

Ernst Georg Ravenstein, 'The Laws of Migration', *Journal of the Royal Statistical Society*, **48**, 2 (June 1885), pp. 167–227 and **52** (June 1889), pp. 241–301.

Josiah Cox Russell, 'The Ecclesiastical Age: A Demographic Interpretation of the Period 200–900 A.D.', *Review of Religion*, **5**, 2 (1941), pp. 132–47.

G. S. L. Tucker, 'English Pre-Industrial Population Trends', *Economic History Review*, 2nd Series, XVI, 2 (December 1963), pp. 205–18.

Gustaf O. Utterström, 'Some population problems in preindustrial Sweden', *Scandinavian Economic History Review*, II, 2 (1954), pp. 103–65.

SECTION 20. ECONOMIC IMPLICATIONS

Daniele Beltrami, *La penetrazione economica dei Veneziani in terraferma. Forze di lavoro e proprietà fondiarie nelle campagne venete dei secoli XVII e XVIII*, Venice and Rome (Istituto per la collaborazione culturale), 1961.

George Douglas Campbell, 8th Duke of Argyll, 'On the Economic Condition of the Highlands of Scotland', *Journal of the Statistical Society*, **29**, 4 (December 1866), pp. 504–35.

Jonathan D. Chambers, 'Enclosure and Labour Supply in the Industrial Revolution', *Economic History Review*, 2nd Series, V, 3 (1953), pp. 319–43.

Georges Duby, first chapter (demographic) of *Villages désertés et histoires économiques, XIe–XVIIIe siècle*, Paris (S.E.V.P.E.N.) (Ecole pratique des Hautes Études, VIe Section, Centre de recherches d'histoire. Men and the land, No. XI), 1965, pp. 14–24.

J. A. Faber, H. K. Roessingh, B. H. Slicher van Bath, A. M. van der Woude, and H. J. van Xanten, 'Population changes and economic developments in the Netherlands: a historical survey', *Afdeling Agrarische Geschiedenis Bijdragen*, **12** (1965), pp. 47–113.

William Farr, 'The Influence of Scarcities and of the High Price of Wheat on the Mortality of the People of England', *Journal of the Statistical Society*, **9** (1846), pp. 158–74. (Farr was Compiler of Abstracts in the Registrar-General's office from 1838 to 1879.)

David V. Glass and Eugene Grebenik, 'World population, 1800–1950', in *Cambridge Economic History of Europe, Vol. VI* (edited by H. J. Habakkuk and M. M. Postan), London, 1965, pp. 56–138.

Susan B. Hanley, 'Population Trends and Economic Development in Tokugawa Japan: The Case of Bizen Province in Okayama', *Daedalus* (Spring, 1968), pp. 622–35.

Barbara F. Harvey, 'The Population Trend in England between 1300 and 1348', *Transactions of the Royal Historical Society*, 5th Series, XVI (1966), pp. 23–42.

Karl F. Helleiner, 'The Population of Europe from the Black Death to the Eve of the Vital Revolution', in *Cambridge Economic History of Europe*, Vol. IV (edited by E. E. Rich and C. H. Wilson), Cambridge, 1967, pp. 1–95. (This article was written nearly twelve years before it was published.)

Reginald H. Hooker, 'Correlation of the marriage rate with trade', *Journal of the Royal Statistical Society*, **64** (September 1901), pp. 485–92.

Ryoichi Ishii, *Population Pressure and Economic Life in Japan*, London (P. S. King and Son), 1937.

Lydia M. Marshall, *The Rural Population of Bedfordshire, 1671 to 1921*, Aspley Guise (Bedfordshire Historical Record Society, Vol. XVI), 1934.

Jean Meuvret, 'Les crises de subsistances et la démographie de la France d'ancien régime', *Population*, **1**, 4 (1946), pp. 643–50.

Pran Nath, *A study in the economic conditions of ancient India*, London (Royal Asiatic Society monographs, 22), 1929.

E. H. Phelps Brown and Sheila Hopkins, 'Wage-rates and Prices: Evidence for Population Pressure in the Sixteenth Century', *Economica*, New Series, **24**, 96 (1957), pp. 289–306.

Idem, 'Builders' Wage-rates, Prices and Population: Some Further Evidence', *ibid.*, **26**, 101 (February 1959), pp. 18–38.

M. M. Postan, 'Some economic evidence of the declining population in the later Middle Ages', *Economic History Review*, 2nd Series, II, 3 (1950), pp. 221–46.

W. C. Robinson, 'Money, Population and Economic Change in Late Medieval Europe', *Economic History Review*, 2nd Series, XII, 1 (1959), pp. 63–76.

James E. Thorold Rogers, 'On a Continuous Price of Wheat for One Hundred and Five Years, from 1380 to 1484', *Journal of the Statistical Society*, **27**, 1 (March 1864), pp. 70–81.

Vladimir G. Simkhovitch, 'Hay and history', *Political Science Quarterly*, **28**, 3 (September 1913), pp. 385–403.

Bibliography

Jacob van Klaveren, 'Die wirtschaftlichen Auswirkungen des Schwarzen Todes', *Vierteljahrschrift für Sozial- und Wirtschaftsgeschichte*, **54**, 2 (July 1967), pp. 187–202.

J. Verbeemen, 'De Werking van economische factoren op de stedelijke demografie der XVIIe en der XVIIIe eeuw in de Zuidelijke Nederlanden', *Revue Belge de Philologie et d'Histoire*, **34** (1956), pp. 680–700 and 1021–55.

D. G. Watts, 'A Model for the Early Fourteenth Century', *Economic History Review*, 2nd Series, XX, 3 (December 1967), pp. 543–47.

E. Anthony Wrigley, *Industrial Growth and Population Change*, Cambridge (C.U.P.), 1961.

Index

Berkshire 241
Berlin 251
Berne 175
Bernstein, M. E. 218
Besigheim 159
Beskrovny, L. G. 414
Beverley, H. 93, 392
Bharier, J. 244, 408
Bhattacharya, B. 91, 134, 408
Bhattacharya, D. 91, 134, 408
Bhutan 297
Bible 211
  see also Chronicles, Exodus, Jonah,
    Joshua, Judges, Numbers,
    Samuel
Bickel, W. 414
Bielenstein, H. 65, 392
Bigelmair, A. 361
Bikélas, D. 414
Bills of Mortality 23, 43, 45, 106,
    145–8, 150, 312, 355, 369–70,
    404–5
Binz, L. 398
biometric method of analysing infant
    mortality 183
Biot, E. 59–60, 65–6, 392
Biraben, J.-N. 71, 129, 161, 374, 398,
    403, 414
Bird, J. 403–4
Birdsell, J. B. 259–60
Birmingham 346
birth-intervals 22, 160, 165, 179, 208,
    212
  see also family limitation
birth-rates and age-distribution 98,
    340–1, 345–7
  assumed constant 148, 315
  deductions from 331, 385
  falling 100–2, 206, 325
  high 70, 75, 134, 180, 383
  in England 86, 122, 125, 155, 185,
    316, 323, 346–9, 380, 383
  low 120, 150, 172–3, 190, 247–8,
    252–3
  moderate 69, 116, 165, 171
  rising 166–7, 185, 323
  useless 33, 143
  variable 173, 176
  see also family size, fertility, etc.
Bisset-Smith, G. T. 143
Björnstjerna, Count 92
Black Death 314, 332, 360, 403–5

consequences of 38, 120, 124, 234,
    267, 359–60, 420–1
  in Bohemia 361
  in Cairo 309
  in Dublin 269
  in England 215, 222–3, 323–5, 382
  in Europe 328, 356, 358
  in Florence 46, 361
  in Genoa 242
  in London 237–40, 362–4, 367–9
  in Milan 361
  in Norwich 362–4, 369
  in Orvieto 360–1
  in Paris 235–6
  in Perpignan 373
  in Siena 361
  in South Netherlands 360
  in Wales 374
  in Yarmouth 252
  population of England before 222–3,
    263–5, 382–7, 416, 420
  population of Norway before 259,
    407
  rate of recovery from 306, 387
  see also disasters, plague, etc.
Black people 180, 410–11
  see also slaves
Blakely, E. T. 93
Bland, R. 219
Blandford Forum 150
Blayo, Y. 158, 161, 182, 400
Blench, B. J. R. 127
Bloch, M. 129
Blomefield, F. 363
Boccaccio, G. 46, 361
Bochum 202
Bohemia 72, 104, 114, 130, 348, 361,
    393, 398, 401, 415–16
Bologna 177, 395
Bolton 88
Bombay 78–9, 280, 373
Bombay Presidency 214
Bonnoure, P. 414
Borah, W. 135, 398
Boucher, C. E. 233
Boulay 162
bounty for mustering 231
Bourdon, J. 56, 411
Bourgeois-Pichat, J. 90, 183
Bowen. H. 309
Bowles, G. T. 218
Bowring, Sir John 95

Index